EL CELLER DE CAN ROCA

EL CELLER DE CAN ROCA

—JOAN, JOSEP AND JORDI ROCA

GRUB STREET • LONDON

INTERNAL MOTIVATION

III.
APPENDIX

JOAN

JOSEP

JORDI

ROCA

Books are always a way of processing knowledge; in the following pages, we try to show who we are and what we have learnt. The challenge of this endeavour has been to gather and order our thoughts conscientiously, to open the door to what we do and to how and why we do it, so that if you don't know very much about us, you can understand our personality and our background—Girona, an exceptional place. We wanted to reconstruct our sweetest, most fruitful and professional experiences. We who have benefited from different culinary sources, now wish to be a fountainhead. We want to be like three Rocks have been shaped by the passage of time; we want to show our three-party game, our brotherly connection, our professional polish... And to illustrate how we have given wings to the creative process: with six hands and three heads under a single hat.

The book *El Celler de Can Roca. Una sinfonía fantástica* (Jaume Coll, 2006) was a way of emphasizing our respect for gastronomic literature. Jaume Coll, doctor in philology, gave us an important piece of literature, reworking it into culinary language with his experience and talent. That book, which he left by the door of the new restaurant, honoured us in its last lines stating the author's wish to finish what he called "the fifth movement of a fantastic symphony", that is to say, to carry on the literary and gastronomic process undertaken with a second volume. This time, however, we felt the need to speak with a unique voice. Our own voice. A modest voice, but delivered in first person and with the aim to explain what we know best: our labour, our work focused on vanguard cuisine. As Dr. Jaume Coll would say: *Ars culinaria nova*. But we didn't want to do without the convergence between 'object cookery book' and the literary arts, which is why we entrusted a section of the book to the prestigious author Josep Maria Fonalleras. He approaches every chapter with linguistic precision, clarity and brilliance. Also, at the end of the book you will find fragments of an account written by him that is a record of a day spent at El Celler. A captivating text, rich in details, in which not a single word is out of place.

When the restaurant moved, on 15 November 2007, it marked a decisive point in our work. We improved our traceability for such ingredients as holm oak embers and had a complete set of equipment with a Rotaval. We reinforced our ability to seduce. The expectation of those who visit us grows and that stimulates us. We created unbeatable conditions to dig into the secret paths of cooking, we went on to have a factory of dreams, a utopia made reality, and many challenges for the future. That is where the desire was born to share our journey and show you the ways of the culinary process that have made it possible for what began as acoustic to become symphonic.

We want to underscore our creative vitality, share it and be loyal to a teaching tradition. To reflect a conceptual maturity. To assemble the groundwork of a cuisine that is created, lived and shared with the family (we can never thank enough Montse, Josep, Anna, Marc, Marina, Encarna, Martí, Maria, Ale, grandparents Payet, Paquita, Salvador, Encarna and Angeleta for past times...), and with a competent team that has changed through the years and is now spread out around many points of the planet.

To them all we also owe part of the merit of this work, to them and to the great number of collaborators and our chef and server friends who, in these first twenty-five years have made our history their own, working shoulder to shoulder with us. We are aware of the human and emotional richness that their support has meant during all the time we have been cooking. To them, who have felt close to Montse, to *el Jefe*, and to grandma Angeleta, the muse to whom Salvador Garcia-Arbós dedicated an emotional memoire, we would like to show our gratitude.

Special thanks and acknowledgment also to all those people who feel great fondness for our restaurant and who have even grown with us. The truth is that, if before we had customers, we now have friends and followers. This book is also for them. And we must not forget to express our gratitude to the essential and crucial role of food journalists; sharp and brilliant ambassadors with a special sensibility to communicate the vitality in gastronomy.

Lastly, we also want to mention that the book we now present to you wouldn't have been possible without the support of Cèlia Pujals, who together with the team at Bisdixit has maintained its thematic coherence, taking great care of its design and editing. Everything is easier if you have someone like her sorting out ideas. The photographs of the dishes, under the charge of Francesc Guillamet, have allowed us to show a rigorous, luminous and precise vision of our cooking, and the atmospheric work of David Ruano has provided us with a poetic patina and the desired tone to evoke the warmth and intimacy of a secret whispered in your ear.

As a final point, the book you have in your hands gathers the projects and memories of over twenty-five years, and at the end it includes as an evolutionary synthesis, a documentary catalogue of some of the most emblematic dishes of our restaurant, emerging from a history that began in August 1986. It's an attempt to gather the *joie de vivre*, gastronomy in capital letters and in the first person, to show a life persistent in its search of flavour and knowing how to feel, with constant learning, luck, joy, stubbornness, perseverance, divertimento, faith and passion. We want to leave a physical and lasting proof of all of it and also deliver an account of our groundbreaking cuisine of the end of the 20th century and the beginning of the 21st century, the best years of our lives.

EL CELLER DE CAN ROCA, (TECHNO) EMOTIONAL REVOLUTION

We relate to the idea of an emotional revolution, allied to technology, the product of our dialogue with science. We relate to the term "techno-emotional cuisine" coined by Pau Arenós (*La cocina de los valientes*, 2011). We have blind faith in the force of feelings, the ability to study the psychological impact produced by flavour, and the power to evoke memories, in those who visit us. We know the variety of taste in each that different ingredient can help to unlock a door into the emotions, the senses, into seduction itself and we want to convey this to the reader through our cuisine.

In this book we divide the creative process into sixteen chapters that will help you understand that, where there was discipline and rigidity, we try to add audacity and transgression. We try to exchange snobbish coldness for closeness and eclectic vision for sustainability, recapturing the often neglectful dialogue with the producer and the landscape. We want to substitute obsequiousness and sobriety in our offers with a sense of humour and fantasy; redundant maturity for innocence and imagination; classicism for courage; routine for reflection and the will to open many roads. And finally, we have brought the ever presence of wine into the kitchen and it is there to stay.

Advances in science, nourished with information technology and communication, have positioned us at the doors of the third millennium, in a new gastronomic world we continue to experience. In this new reality emerges a sort of triangle of knowledge formed by the fields of physics, biology and new technologies, with the creation of fascinating synergies between one and the other, which will offer us moments of great emotional well-being.

We try to stage the colours of emotions, both internal and external, through taste, smell and the sight. We want our cuisine to flirt with poetry. We want to awaken yearning, a wish, and to fill it with memories. Here is where techno-emotional cuisine takes over from *nouvelle cuisine* and we are convinced by it. To enjoy more and more the smell and taste and feel of our memories. To commit to suggestion and essence brings us closer to a more highly evocative sense, a sense that is most linked to emotions, images, memories and stories—smell. With our creative lines in cooking we hope to exhibit colour, transitoriness, awareness, science, boldness and social agriculture, in addition to showing a specific geo-climatic location, but also exuding the fusions that have come to us from past generations and faraway places. We get inspiration from the Mediterranean, its luminosity, spirit of freedom and ancestral cultural leadership, with flavour as the central theme. We take in a light that doesn't blind, a light that doesn't hide; a privileged light. In a society of global tendencies, we try to display our closer cultural habits with pride. We think universally but emphasise food's connection with local produce.

For us, the future of cuisine will oscillate between the importance placed on the product and the process at any one time, as has always been the case in the history of gastronomy. We are convinced that cannelloni, ham croquettes and gazpacho can live side by side with spherification and mimetic tricks.

The cuisine of El Celler de Can Roca wants to make a fresh and thoughtful offering that undresses and dresses (as if undressing and dressing were one thing) with techniques coming from the development of a concept, but always prioritizing flavour.

The creative process captured in the sixteen chapters of this book—Tradition, Memory, Academia, Product, Landscape, Wine, Chromatism, Sweetness, Transversal Creation, Perfume, Innovation, Poetry, Freedom, Boldness, Magic and Sense of Humour—is a life built from everything we have done in the last twenty-five years.

Even if the calling of the cook leads us through the paths of craftsmanship, the aim comes closer to goldsmithing, with an artistic and innovative attitude as a fundamental incentive. In our view, the cook is not exactly an artist, but certainly should act freely, vindicating creativity and constantly navigating in a fertile environment , where the simplicity of live performance has its place, as well as the symphonic option of a more complex construction. The culinary tendency we want to follow has four cardinal points: authenticity, boldness, generosity and hospitality. We rely on a simple and proactive attitude toward new culinary horizons of emotional revolution. We "cook to generate feelings".

This book hopes to be proof of our strong commitment and conviction that we must know how to live harmoniously and believe cuisine is a way to happiness, culture and connection to the land. Turn the pages and we will guide you through the secrets of the cuisine of El Celler through a wide open door.

I.

—THE PATH TO THE NEW CELLER

I.

—A SHORT ACCOUNT OF ITS BEGINNINGS

Cookery was written in the fate of the Roca brothers. Or perhaps they have written their fate in their own handwriting with the effort, patience and rigour that have characterized them over the last twenty-five years and that still defines them. Hard work has earned them recognition and a name, but their childhood upbringing was, without a doubt, a determining factor in their development.

Can Roca, the restaurant opened by their parents in 1967 in Taialà—an outlying district of Girona populated by immigrants from Andalusia—was the living room where the three brothers grew up, tossed coins, did homework and watched *Un, Dos, Tres*, a popular Spanish TV show back in the seventies. "Our table at the bar was next to a gas stove," recalls Joan. A crowded bar prevented their parents from dedicating more time exclusively to the boys. So the restaurant's kitchen and dining room became the perfect place for them to spend hours, first as spectators of the hustle and bustle and, soon after, as active participants. "Our grandparents and even the customers, who often times were also our friends, looked after us. It was a very fun place, we spent time with many people and many things happened," says Josep. Upstairs from the restaurant there were five or six rooms that were part of the inn to accommodate workers from Navarre, Andalusia, or Aragon working in Barcelona factories like the neighbouring Nestlé, or in the construction of the AP-7 motorway. "Suddenly our family was very big. We shared a roof and even, sometimes, a table with all these people who came to our house. We spent time with them and that, for us, was rewarding and enriching," explains Joan.

The elder brother looked after the two younger ones; he was the more responsible, diligent, and the one who established rigour and order. From an early age, the role of Joan Roca was to be the most mature of the three. Dedicated, hard-working, serious and passionate about the profession of his grandmother, Angeleta, and his mother, Montserrat, the

cook of Can Roca. As young as nine, his mother had a chef jacket tailor-made for him, which he still has and lets his son occasionally dress up in it. He spent his afternoons in the kitchen and, unknowingly, began to engineer his future. When the time came, he didn't hesitate to decide what he wanted to be when he grew up: "I saw that people were happy at my parents' restaurant." That was all he needed; he wanted to keep making people happy.

The smells of his childhood include the *escudella i carn d'olla*, stocks and, in the afternoon, vanilla for custards. Back then, there was a lot of work to do at Can Roca, there was never a break and, as soon as the three lunchtime shifts were over, it was time to prepare the dishes for the following day or the upcoming week. After school, Joan helped in any way he could: "Every Tuesday afternoon I made sausages with my father. We minced the meat, and then we seasoned and stuffed it. I practised so much with the hand mincer that I won every arm-wrestling competition in school! Grandma Angeleta, grandma Francisca and other elderly ladies, friends of the grandmothers, were always in the kitchen peeling garlic, onions or beans; and spent the afternoon chatting and solving the problems of the world. It was, after all, our home kitchen."

In spite of being well aware of his calling, Joan achieved good grades and, in those times, a studious boy had to go to university. Professional training was stigmatized, but fate lent him a hand and one of the only two culinary arts schools in the country opened in Girona, only a few kilometres from home. "Life is full of circumstances that make things go in a certain direction, and I'm sure the Culinary Arts School made it possible for me to study cooking at the time. If I hadn't done it at that moment, everything would have turned out different." The school didn't only determine Joan's future, but also that of his brothers, who followed in his footsteps a few years later.

No esperem el blat,

EXPECT NO WHEAT

sense haver sembrat,

WITHOUT SOWING,

no esperem que l'arbre

EXPECT NO TREE

doni fruits sense podar-lo;

BEARING FRUIT WITHOUT PRUNING;

l'hem de treballar,

THEY MUST BE WORKED ON,

l'hem d'anar a regar,

THEY MUST BE WATERED

encara que l'ossada ens faci mal.

EVEN IF OUR BONES HURT.

. . .

Cal anar endavant

WE MUST MOVE FORWARD

sense perdre el pas.

WITHOUT FALLING OUT OF STEP.

Cal regar la terra amb la suor

THE EARTH MUST BE WATERED WITH THE SWEAT

del dur treball.

OF HARD WORK.

Cal que neixin flors a cada instant.

FLOWERS MUST BE BORN EVERY MOMENT.

«CAL QUE NEIXIN FLORS A CADA INSTANT»,
(«FLOWERS MUST BE BORN EVERY MOMENT»), LLUÍS LLACH

Josep recalls perfectly the first time he served a bag of crisps to a customer and put the money in his pocket. His father reacted quickly and warned him that things at home didn't work that way. That is how he became aware that it was his home but also a restaurant where business took place.

Josep's eyes light up when he talks about how, as young as five, he was assigned the task of refilling with wine—of the Cariñena variety from the Empordà—the empty litre bottles used for serving. A nervous and mischievous kid, he was unable to sit around doing nothing while a bottle filled up: "I used to see how many bottles I could fill up at once and I would always spill the wine of one of them. To me, it was a wine-scented game." Josep played with wine, soaked in wine. It became clear it was a world that fascinated him and it slowly became more than a game. "When I was eight, I used to go fishing with my uncle and what thrilled me the most was breakfast, because I knew he would bring his wineskin and let me have a sip. Some went fishing to return with fish. My aim was different." Without realizing, he started collecting the flavours of those childhood sips, not only of wine, but also, when the time came, liquor: "The bar was like the UN, we had liquors from all over the world. I tried it all and still remember that my favourites were Quina San Clemente and Ponche Caballero. On the other hand, I didn't like Cynar, made with artichokes; it was very astringent."

Josep has a special sensibility for the earth. He is passionate about wine, but also about geology and botany, which he considered studying when the time came to decide his future. But this option required maths—which he deemed mostly a nuisance—and excluded philosophy and literature—two subjects he enjoyed greatly. "I was interested partly in the earth itself, but also the whole philosophical approach. It was all too pure and too extreme for me to opt for one thing or the other." And it was in that moment of doubt when the zeal of his brother Joan, two years the elder, gave him the answer: "Joan has always had a special ability to make any mad idea understandable and to get involved in scientific method. He was already rigorous, methodical and meticulous when he was a young boy. I, on the other hand, was just the opposite: clumsy, mischievous, rebellious, a hooligan... I made my dad, my mother, the customers angry... I had ants in my pants and

was insecure; I was left-handed and thought I wouldn't be able to serve with tongs, to debone a fish, or to peel an orange in front of a customer." But Joan's passion helped Josep decide to follow the road he's always known at home, gastronomy.

We have to jump ahead in time to speak of Jordi's childhood, fourteen and twelve years younger than Joan and Josep, respectively, an age gap that conditioned him from very early on. The youngest, he was spoiled and refused to study. He was the kid at home who adored prawns, cockles and ham from Jabugo, who was perfectly able to detect a common Serrano ham when someone was trying to con him. "By living in a bar, I had a lot more luxuries than my friends. There were always cockles, olives, ham... or suddenly popular packaged chocolate-filled sweets!" Times had changed and his parents allowed him to have things his brothers probably wouldn't have even dreamt of.

Jordi went from having to help his parents in their restaurant to having to help his brothers in theirs. At that time, they were to him the equivalent of two additional parents to whom he had to answer and show a certain degree of respect. But not only that. To him, Joan and Josep were role models, idols he looked up to: "I remember the first day an unknown man called the restaurant asking for Pitu (Josep). At that moment I realised there were people who did not belong to my family, who were not part of our surroundings, people from the industry who knew him. And that stayed with me."

His childhood was therefore spent among kitchens and customers, without a clear calling for gastronomy, but with the hope—perhaps hidden in his subconscious—of being able to do something that would make his family proud, especially his older brothers. And at fourteen, without having fully sorted out his ideas, he enrolled in the Culinary Arts School of Girona. Back then, Joan and Josep still couldn't have imagined the little brat at home would become a key figure in the future of El Celler.

Joan, Josep and Jordi grew up between the classrooms of the Culinary Arts School of Girona and the cooker of Can Roca. Laughing ironically, Josep recalls the day trips organised by their parents, who were unaccustomed to thinking about leisure time. On Saturday afternoons, their only time off as a family, they went out to explore the world: "Our great celebration was visiting sanctuaries. Hilarious! They took us to Sant Miquel del Faig, to Salut, to the Àngels sanctuary... Very cheerful day trips! People asked: 'Don't you go out?' And I replied: 'No, we're very monastic people'."

"It was unthinkable to close our doors on Sunday, the busiest day of the week, because that was when the neighbourhood people had family meals. After much struggle, Montserrat talked *el Jefe* into allowing the family a few hours of privacy on Saturdays without customers or menus, first only afternoons but, later, the whole day. But the head of the family broke their pact and started letting regular customers in for breakfast, somewhat in secret... through the back door! For the first time Can Roca was closed, but the restaurant was still crowded, just like before. It was a combination of generosity, caring, and also the fear of losing those customers, because you would be subject to punishment if you made them drink their coffee at a competing restaurant for a day. It was a feeling of hesitation, odd, hard for everyone to swallow; for my father, but especially for us, because we didn't understand a thing," recalls Josep. When the last customers, the tramps fond of anisette and coffee, had left the restaurant, the most highly awaited moment arrived: the family snack that has had such an impact on the culinary memories of the three brothers: "It was like a sacred fizzy drink, we were finally completely alone, and that moment was transformed into a celebration with cockles and squids."

Joan lived his childhood and teenage years at Can Roca and learnt to cook from his mother and grandmother, but it was at the Culinary Arts School where he discovered that behind the lentils, escudella, macaroni, or potato salad they served at home, there were the ravigotes, meunières, veloutés or parmentières he read about in classical French cuisine manuals. These terms, unknown at home, started to make sense and manifest themselves in his gastronomic imagination during his years of academic instruction. *Le Guide Culinaire* by Auguste Escoffier, *Modern Culinary Art* by Henri Paul Pellaprat, and some works by Catalan gourmet Ignasi Domènech, were reference books in his classes. Baroque presentations, heavy sauces and opulence defined the French cuisine he learnt about: lobster à la parisienne, sole à la meunière or Thermidor lobster are some examples. Joan recalls his teachers back then, chefs who inspired respect: "Mr. Barberà really commanded respect, he came from prestigious restaurants in Barcelona; Mr. Andreu was a maître d', an admirable person; and then came professors Romero and Ruiz from Granada, who are still teaching and have done a great educational job."

Because only Girona and Madrid had culinary arts schools in the whole country, their educational institution became a welcoming site for people from Murcia, Valencia, Aragon and all over Catalonia. On the top floor of the building, constructed by the old Spanish Trade Union Organisation, were dormitory rooms for first-year students. Then, as they familiarised themselves with the city and the dynamics of their classes, the students moved into shared flats. Joan joined the 'group of Lleida': "Those from Lleida lived in a flat near our house and I joined the group along with Salvador Brugués. We went to all the parties and gatherings of the time in Girona. It was a lot of fun." And it was with those friends that Joan began to discover good food and enjoy life outside the kitchen.

To turn eighteen meant going to military service. Joan was sent to Alicante, but he was transferred to Valencia and appointed as cook to the captain general: "I remember the first day I was very scared. When a recruit is told he has to cook for the captain general, he panics. We got off on the right foot right away, and the captain's wife was very affectionate and treated us like her sons." At the Valencian barracks he found a much better equipped kitchen than that of the restaurant at home, but it was of no use: the captain's wife ate light, almost religiously, and accepted little more than boiled vegetables, omelettes and grilled meat. He abided this simplicity, but his trips to the Russafa market and frequent days of leave to visit his family facilitated his adaptation into a new military life. Upon his return to Girona, he had a chance to get back to real cookery, doing both the usual and what he learnt at the Culinary Arts School.

Josep was a vigorous boy who spent his day thinking about the football match of that afternoon or over the weekend, and made use of the few minutes he had between serving tables to kick the ball around a bit. "I was somewhat of a hooligan and sporty on the street. I would talk my friends into playing football using the kitchen door as a goal. We would play 'shoot

to score' and I was the keeper. The goal was easy to spot: if the kitchen's metallic door was hit and the loud noise was followed by my mum's screams, it was considered a goal."

He helped out in the kitchen but was always after additional entertainment, making his co-workers or customers laugh, finding a joke or a comical situation to play down the hard work required in a restaurant. "When you peel onions, a lot of onions, and just think I was peeling two sacks every Tuesday and Thursday, you want to wipe your tears with your sleeve. Big mistake. As you bring your hand closer to your eyes, you feel an unbearable burning that makes you cry. Tired of crying for no reason and with my typical playfulness, I made the decision to stop the tears. The first few minutes you would be fine, but when the sulphur goes up your nostrils, your tear ducts get irritated. The solution was to wear diving goggles: eyes and nose covered, breathing through the tube, avoiding the spattering from the damned onions."

The potato and onion sacks drove him mad. Soon it became clear that he was made for the dining room. At fifteen or sixteen, he challenged himself to balance as many plates on his arms as he could: he did balancing acts and played at arranging the chicken thighs and pork loins and macaroni and soups as if they were a puzzle. He was left-handed and very clumsy, but that lack of skill never manifested itself in the dining room, because the plates and trays became natural extensions of his hands that danced to his own tune. The first day at the Culinary Arts School he noticed that, while his fellow students had to work hard to keep a tray in balance, he could do pirouettes, and while the others barely began to practise coffee-making techniques, he already had internalised the movements of his coffee-making arm. And that was how the feeling of insecurity that had triggered comparisons with Joan's culinary abilities disappeared. He mastered the more mechanical aspects of the dining room, but realized there was a world of knowledge ahead of him: "The career of a waiter is fascinating because it includes everything. Everything related to cooking and everything representing the polyhedral nature of gastronomy, including the world of wines, breads, oils, products, psychology, chemistry, physics, and geology." And so, this complexity furthered even more his passion for the trade he was meant to join. By the same token, with time his admiration for the world of wine grew and, unaware of it, Josep brought his friends into his circle and established a meeting point in a bar in Girona called *El Museu del Vi*: "I took charge and forced them to drink a sacramental wine before going out to party. One or two or three or four wines."

And Josep not only urged his friends to drink sacramental wine. He spent years doing trial-and-error, experimenting and discovering the world of cocktails. "The office in the dining room upstairs from my parents' bar was reserved for my friends and I. Defiant, I showed off my acrobatic talents and they got drunk on sugary alcohol. I used up the Bacardí bottles. When we emptied them, I refilled them by making a hole on the dripping cap; then I would cover it with Sellotape to imitate the same dripping produced when the bottle is new and full. That way I could practise many times and counted the seconds it took to pour the centilitres needed for a third, two quarters, three halves... for me it was a game, but a nightmare for the parents of my friends."

Jordi finished his primary education and had no plans to continue in school. He didn't like studying and studying didn't suit him: "I did everything out of duty; I did not care, it was everything I had learnt at home. My brothers wanted it, they earned it. But I didn't have my own plan. I was in the middle, between my parents and my brothers. I felt responsible because I had to prove something." There came even more pressure, because at the Culinary Arts School, where he started at fourteen, his brother was already a role model, a good student and good teacher. "Having my brother as a teacher was uncomfortable for both of us. Joan didn't want

anyone thinking he favoured me, and so he put me down me in front of people, even if he thought differently. He gave me lower grades than I deserved." In class, both brothers hardly spoke to each other; they kept their distance and had a somewhat odd relationship.

Jordi remembers a trimester in particular in which he failed every class except sports. But he studied hard and was so driven to pass that in a matter of months he made up for lost ground—proof that if he didn't get better grades in school it was not out of a lack of ability, but of a lack of interest. The anger at home was tremendous, but it helped him realize he was wasting his time at the school.

In those years, Jordi was the 'errand boy' at Can Roca, lending a hand where needed. "On weekends there were four waiters, all family members. I was a child and was always mixed up in something. I didn't even think of being in the kitchen. It seemed like such a complicated world, forbidden... It was a different world." Then the moment came to help his brothers and, for a summer, he worked in the dining room at El Celler. "I was eighteen and finished work at three in the morning. But I wanted to party... I realized cooks finished at midnight and decided I liked the kitchen better. That's why I moved to the kitchen!" Jordi continued without a definite path, and took any given road according to external circumstances, without conviction, unable to find his place. To help him find his way, Joan thought the best option was for the youngest sibling to leave home and work in a different environment. He sent him to the Aiguablava Hotel, in Begur (Costa Brava). "I worked an entire summer without one single day off, working from eight in the morning to two at night. And that first work experience outside familiar surroundings had an impact on me, because it was then that I realized how good I had it at home." So, he returned home, where soon after Damian Allsop showed up and became a crucial figure in the formation of the Roca triangle.

Joan was twenty-two and had recently returned from doing military service. He had had to cook so many omelettes for the captain general of Valencia that it became clearer than ever that what he wanted to do was to cook. Josep, who was then twenty years old, was told there was no space for him to do his compulsory military service and that therefore he wouldn't have to wear the uniform. It was the perfect moment. Both were at home, both had finished their catering studies, and both were toying with the idea of opening a gastronomic restaurant, without really knowing what it entailed.

"For us, it was simply about doing something more fun than our parents did back then, which is the same menu they do today: Monday, rice with fried eggs and tomato sauce; Tuesday, macaroni..." states Joan.

"At school we learnt about the demi-glace, hollandaise sauce, tartar sauce... everything represented by the cuisine of Escoffier, and the most powerful cuisine of the 19th and early 20th centuries. We began with the desire to show people everything we had learnt. It's a big change to go from making a green or a Catalan salad, to a shrimp salad with raspberry vinaigrette. It is extraordinary, one has nothing to do with the other," adds Josep.

What the two brothers wanted more than anything was for people to enjoy the experience of eating at El Celler: "We observed that people at our restaurant enjoyed themselves. Even when eating a six euro menu they were happy. And we wanted the same: for people to eat well and to have a good time. And we built it little by little."

Their parents had bought a house right next to Can Roca for the boys to live in when they got married, and instead they asked for permission to start their own project there.. Indeed, later on Joan and Josep married, but the first marriage those walls witnessed was that of the two older brothers with cuisine. "I never thought of opening a restaurant there. It was never part of my plans. But my sons knocked down my plans and also the walls," admits their mother Montserrat, laughing.

Opening a haute cuisine restaurant in the mid-1980s in a working-class neighbourhood in the outskirts of Girona seemed like an insane idea. A row of provisional barracks, built to accommodate immigrants arriving from southern Spain, separates the neighbourhood of Taialà from the wealthy neighbourhoods in Girona. "For people, it was a difficult border to cross. Our neighbourhood, all in all, was no more than a land that received people and immigration. We were located between Sant Gregori, originally a farming town, and the Girona of the most private and introverted bourgeoisie. People had to take make a great effort to come and see us," says Josep.

Their mother tried to understand and encourage them: "Effort, sacrifice and, especially, bravery, are values we learnt from our mother. She encouraged us to keep going; she understands the concept of 'audacity' and our father doesn't. Back then, he was taken aback: they had a restaurant that did well serving three daily meals. It was absurd to him to do anything different," recalls Joan. 'The boss'—Josep Roca senior—has always been a pragmatic man. He was a bus driver, and his idea was to open Can Roca right across from one of the bus stops he drove by every day, because he saw the flow of people as a good opportunity to do business. And now that the restaurant operated perfectly well and was crowded every day the kids, who went to school to continue in the business, wanted to open another establishment next door. He had no other choice but to wonder if they have gone mad.

In spite of doubts, the reluctance amongst the family and the limited initial logic of the whole idea, Joan and Josep got started. On their own and looking forward to seeing what was brewing, they began remodelling the house: "We knocked down the four partitions that divided the rooms and left a mark on the floor where the walls used to be, which we covered with cement; the construction job was completely botched!" With a half-smile, Joan recalls that dear botched job for the first Celler, also decorated by them with hanging plants around the dining room and lamps with tassels they dug out of a chest.

Then, one day in August 1986, their dream took the first step to becoming a reality: El Celler de Can Roca opened its doors. "We don't remember the date we opened. It was probably the day we had installed a neon sign that read 'El Celler de Can Roca.' And nobody came in." It is significant that, as Joan says, they don't remember the date, because it speaks of the innocence, modesty and humility with which they started their first restaurant, not suspecting it would grow and without any pretentions. "We didn't think the date was important, we didn't want to have an opening ceremony, we didn't want to tell people. We thought we had to have an opening our way and then the customers would come. We knew if it didn't go well, we could return to our parents' restaurant," explains Josep who, on the other hand, recalls perfectly who was the first person to enter the new establishment: "It was the then mayor of Girona, Quim Nadal, who was probably on his way to Can Roca and saw what the kids had done and went in to take a look."

El Celler back then was very different from that which now occupies one of the first places in the world in restaurant rankings; it was a Celler that set out with a very precarious infrastructure, with some machines kept at the kitchen of Can Roca and the rest in theirs. According to Joan, "We built a griddle out of hard chrome. We approached the blacksmith and they installed a sheet of chrome over one of steel, then we placed some flan tins under it to create an incline for the fat from the griddle to slide into a kitchen sink... It was a true botched job!"

At the beginning, the roles of each of them were still not well defined, they had to roll up their sleeves and help out wherever it was required. Josep was not only in charge of the dining room, but also placed orders, and served tables whenever necessary, always with mischief in mind: "I went into the kitchen to help out wherever it was needed. I tried to combine peeling potatoes with the potato peeling machine and playing football in the kitchen, because I knew each potato took a certain number of minutes.

At the beginning, the idea was to help out, get hands from anywhere." The truth is that he dared to do much more than peeling potatoes. When Joan began teaching at the Culinary Arts School of Girona, it was he who organized the *mise en place*, always under the culinary eye of his older brother.

The first dish of El Celler was HAKE IN GARLIC AND ROSEMARY VINAIGRETTE, inspired by a trip Joan took to the Basque Country a few weeks before opening the restaurant. The first menus clearly showed the influence of this traditional cuisine, but also of classical French dishes—a lot more baroque and learnt from books, like the SEA BASS FILLED WITH SHELLFISH: "Poor sea bass... we treated it so poorly! I remember we used to remove the bones, fill it with a shellfish paste, wrap it in bacon and, as if that was not enough, slice it and reheat it, then top it with a white wine sauce. People were fascinated. It was a new and very elaborate dish, not common at all." At the time, people were used to eating and cooking stuffed squid, but never a sea bass like the one the Roca brothers were offering. It was haute cuisine at a time when Girona still didn't have a gastronomic culture.

The community of Girona who tried the first El Celler de Can Roca were also marvelled by the CHICKEN WITH PRAWNS or the FIDEUEJAT WITH CLAMS, a version of the fideuà they learnt at home but that was yet not common in restaurants. Other highlights of those first years of experimentation are also the LOBSTER PARMENTIER (1988) or the PIG TROTTER CARPACCIO (1989). Later on appeared the APPLE AND FOIE GRAS TIMBALE WITH VANILLA OIL (1996), one of the most outstanding and elaborate creations of the restaurant's history.

The grand finale of the meals of the time was the dessert cart, a luxury offered in the past by other renowned establishments like El Bulli or Hotel Empordà. Cakes, mousses, flans, creams and fruits were brought to the guest like a show of freshness and sweetness with a special garnish. Jordi was still a child when the two brothers prepared these delicacies, but he already felt the attraction: after school, the first thing he did at home was stop by the kitchen of El Celler and have a small afternoon snack of cake left over from lunch. He still couldn't imagine he would someday revolutionise this part of the restaurant's cooking.

El Celler also impressed its customers from the start by incorporating French service rituals, such as peeling an orange with a fork and knife before the guest, a surprise for the senses back in the eighties. It was a time when they drew with creams and coulis on desserts prepared in front of the guest, garnishes prepared by Encarna, Josep's wife, who joined the restaurant in 1987.

In the summer of 1989, Joan spent a month and a half in the cold section of El Bulli and became aware of what was starting to happen in Cala Montjoi. They were years of great restlessness, travelling, practising, experimenting, getting to know other people in the business and forming the basis of what would be the future of haute cuisine in Catalonia and the world. But they were also years of uncertainty, because while the traditional restaurant of their parents was always crowded at every meal, not a soul came into their new restaurant. Josep, who could see the positive side of everything, made use of the slow hours to play table football on a table they installed in an isolated area of the dining room: "It was a gift for Jordi and we kept it for ourselves. We put it in the back dining room, which normally wasn't full so we transformed it into a playing area. It even bothered us when people came in when the match was getting exciting!"

By the mid to late 80s news began to arrive in Catalonia about a new Basque cuisine and the consolidation of the French Nouvelle Cuisine. In 1991, both brothers took a revealing tour to the best kitchens in the neighbouring country. "When we went to Pic de Valence or Troisgros de Roanne, the great three-star restaurants in France, we began to have a dream, we were reinvigorated. That was when I thought this is what I wanted to be, that I wanted to be a chef, that those people had a great time!" explains Joan with conviction. The Roca brothers studied the great French cuisine but had never experienced it up close. And their first experience fascinated, captivated and left them flabbergasted. These are restaurants with large infrastructures, well-organized areas, an elevated concept of what it means to cook and what it means to eat. "We also realized that the customers at these restaurants were much happier, and probably the chefs too, because they had a lot more means and resources, the ideal structure, and worked with the best products. When you visualize the dream, you go after it," exclaims an enthusiastic Joan.

And Josep agrees, particularly fascinated with the images of their visit to the restaurant of old Pic (André Pic, a three-star Michelin restaurant since 1934): "Seeing old Pic was like meeting the Pope. I don't know what very devout Catholics feel when they see the Holy Father, but I had the sensation of meeting someone very important. If I try to recall role models I've met face-to-face, I would say Dalí in the first place, followed by Monsieur Pic."

Of that day, what Josep remembers best are the ice creams he discovered: "They were not balls, or set on a cone, or a bar. They were rectangular frozen parfaits, but not crystallised. That, back in the eighties, to me seemed something

mind-boggling, a cold ice cream, with the texture of a cream…"
But he was not only captivated by that ice cream, but by
the great difference he saw up close in the level of French
gastronomy. "Parameters of flavour, interpretations, product
quality, texture in the sauces, aesthetics, exaggeration in the
assortment of breads, cheeses, three sommeliers at our disposal,
a garnish for each dish, a change of cutlery for desserts, golden
cutlery… It was excellence in catering. It awakened our senses;
it was a world we wanted to make our own."

When they visualized the dream, they did, in fact, go after
it. It was a world they wanted to adopt. All of a sudden, it
was clear which road to take, all obstacles disappeared. They
shared this desire and dived in with both feet.

And slowly but surely, either by mistake or out of curiosity,
guests started to walk in. The restaurant began to consolidate
and the tables filled with customers. The city of Girona
began to appreciate what the two brothers had created and
the rumour of a possible Michelin award began to spread.
In 1991, for the first time, an inspector from the prestigious
French guide tried to visit El Celler de Can Roca. He tried
and failed because, perhaps, fate decided it was not yet time
for a first star: the critic entered their parents restaurant by
mistake instead of visiting the creation of their sons.

The following year, nevertheless, he returned and this
time found the right door. Josep, who didn't then know he
was talking to Victoriano Porto Canosa, one of the most
important bosses of the Michelin guide, served him a baby
squid stew with lentils and a sirloin with foie: "I served
the sirloin on a marble plate, those pretty ones we had in
the past, cold. When he finished, I asked if he had liked
it. He said: 'I'm a bit finicky and found the sirloin cold in
the middle. But take into account I'm very particular…' he
added." After that encounter, Josep and Mr. Porto Canosa
began a cordial relationship.

Also in 1992, Rafael García Santos visited the restaurant for
the first time, and had a meal Josep remembers perfectly.
"After six years, for the first time somebody came to eat and
described my brother the same way I saw him. It was the first
time I came across a coherent, sensible and talented critic
with a depth in tasting I had never seen before. I discovered
true gastronomic criticism. He was probably the most
visionary character in gastronomy back then."

From then on, they began to appreciate the feeling of
recognition and admiration for their pure concept of
gastronomy. They didn't have a desperate need to earn
Michelin stars because they were savouring what was

happening in Catalan cuisine. In 1995, Joan's sous-vide
cuisine—using the Roner he designed together with Narcís
Caner and Salvador Brugués, which allows cooking at low
temperatures—appears on the restaurant's menu with a dish
that became famous: COD WITH SPINACH, CREAM OF IDIAZABAL
CHEESE, PINE KERNELS AND PEDRO XIMÉNEZ REDUCTION. The
new technique was a true revolution in cooking methods and
opened many doors for the future of the restaurant and haute
cuisine.

The first Michelin star finally arrived in 1995 and it found
them fully prepared. "That was truly wonderful. It was a
historic milestone. The first star places you on the map
in culinary terms and we got it under very precarious
conditions," explains Joan. Josep, on the other hand, is
convinced that the first star was not as important for the
people of Girona as the participation of El Celler in preparing
the menu for the wedding of Infanta Elena in Seville. "In
Girona, nobody knew what a Michelin star was. But people—
republicans, independents, conservatives and socialists—were
happy because it was the wedding of the first Infanta and the
Roca brothers were cooking in Seville. This wedding put us
in the spotlight. Today we are used to it, but back then, for a
cook to appear on TV was something very exceptional."

But what is most important for the Roca brothers is the trust
they earned from their customers. "The summit for a chef is
when the customer trusts him and comes to the restaurant
to be happy. That is everything, because it gives you a margin
for creativity and also for experimenting and establishing the
dialogue and commitment that give significance to your work
and that we like so much," explains Joan.

With this great leap ahead arose the increasingly urgent need
to have a larger kitchen and a better infrastructure. And the
second El Celler de Can Roca began to take shape.

Eleven years had passed since Joan and Josep opened the first restaurant. The little house next to Can Roca not only helped them to get their project going, but also to position themselves in the world of gastronomy and get a Michelin star, in spite of having the odds stacked against them. This time, however, it was becoming increasingly difficult to keep growing: they ran into every obstacle in that small, thirty square-metre kitchen, where before there were two people working, now there were seven or eight. It wasn't just that they couldn't do their job, but they practically couldn't move. They depended on their parents' kitchen to get by: their mother rolled cannelloni surrounded by waiters coming and going, and cooks on the other side removed the rice from the heat because they needed the burners to make an olive oil caramel sweet. The Riedel glasses were washed in the sink at the bar and, invariably, an inadvertent nudge by a customer having *barreja* and coffee with liquor, ended up breaking one.

"We have always determined our needs and growth. We have sought improvements according to our own demands," states Joan. Recognition from the restaurant guides and the arrival of criticism were not the only factors that determined the widening of the space; they wanted to continue evolving and began to study the best options to do so.

In 1993, the brothers bought the Torre de Can Sunyer hoping to move there one day. In the midst of the financial crisis of the 90s, with interest rates as high as 16%, they were forced to find ways to pay their debt to the bank, as Joan explains: "We thought of offering receptions at this property to pay the credit off and that's what we did for sixteen years. We worked seven days a week: from Monday to Friday at the restaurant and then organising weddings and communions at the weekends. We decided to save to avoid financial burdens in the future and we spent ten years without rest, some very tough years."

In fact, the initial idea when they bought the Torre was not only to organise events, but to combine them with the daily activities of the restaurant. But the date when they realised how unfeasible that was became engrained in Josep's mind: "On February 12, 1995, with our first event, we realised what we wanted was impossible. The space was not enough; the intimacy of a wedding was counterproductive to the meaning of an à la carte menu. And it was a moment of disappointment, a failed dream."

After this moment of frustration, the key to get ahead and not get discouraged was patience, one of the most important virtues of the Roca brothers throughout their career. Going slowly, breathing deeply, step by step, that's what helped them evaluate what the best answer to their deficiencies was at that time. They were aware they still didn't have enough of their own resources to make a definite move, and after the debt they had incurred with the purchase of the Torre, they didn't want to play around too much with banks. The issue was not losing the freedom to cook, that is, not having to make concessions with more commercial concepts in cuisine, which would probably bring them further financial gains but not the personal and professional satisfaction they were after.

This is how the idea of reinvesting their savings in restructuring and expanding El Celler was born. Joan reveals that this decision, at least for him, was not the end of the road, but simply another step before reaching the summit: "It was still not time for the dream to come true. We made a concession on time; we were prudent and decided to start the remodelling. It was an important turning point, a change of structure... But the truth was that we already sensed we would encounter other limitations. We knew we would have to take another step later on." But in spite of this sideways glance into the future, they wanted the new site to seem permanent, that the public as well as the industry would see it as a mature change, the result of much thought. Idealism and wisdom were again the basis of evolution for the three brothers.

The remodelling project was tackled by an interior designer from Girona, Joan Bosch, who understood the needs of the restaurant from the beginning. For the three months when bricklayers, carpenters and electricians flooded the building, their activity moved to the Torre de Can Sunyer, in a sort of premonitory rehearsal. Joan admits the improvement was substantial: "We made the space more intimate, comfortable, warm, not lavish, but austere and elegant at the same time, and we made it integrate well. One of the advantages of that space was that everything was very compact: the kitchen, the dining room and the small cellar for daily use were together."

The second El Celler de Can Roca meant significant changes in their work organisation, starting with the hiring of more personnel, which finally allowed them to organise the kitchen into sections, as it is done in all large culinary establishments. "In the first Celler we had one person preparing hot dishes and another doing cold dishes! But now meats, fish, starters and desserts had their own sections. In other words is, we began to create a kitchen with a more conventional crew. We began to look more like a restaurant," explains Joan as he compares the before and after.

Moreover, in 1997 Jordi joined the team permanently, taking charge together with pastry chef Damian Allsop of developing their sweet cuisine. "It was an important move and the point at which we incorporated a more carefree and daring aspect into the kitchen we were slowly building," says Joan. With this breath of fresh, young air, the Roca triangle began to take shape: savoury, sweets and wines—three worlds perfectly represented by the three brothers.

Another key factor should be mentioned: the expansion of the space allowed for the installation of all the necessary machinery to bring the cook's ideas to fruition and thus contributed to the foundation of a period of complete creative activity. To get an idea of the transformation it is important to consider that, until that moment, pastries at El Celler were baked in a normal gas oven, without temperature control. They acquired a new professional convection oven when they made the structural changes of 1997.

Two years earlier, sous-vide cooking had first appeared on the restaurant's menu (with the WARM COD AND SPINACH, IDIAZABAL CREAM, PINE KERNELS AND PEDRO XIMÉNEZ REDUCTION). But it was not until the end of the 90s when the space permitted the installation of a Roner in the kitchen of El Celler. "By having the Roner in the kitchen we were able to introduce the use of modern technology to our processes and work more precisely. That is, we began to use technology in a closer, more practical way."

At this stage, other innovative concepts also evolved, such as distillation or perfume-cooking—preparing products, basically crustaceans, to which they incorporated the aroma of some spice or liquor. Joan's prominent creations developing from this idea were the SAFFRON LOBSTER (2004) or SCAMPI PERFUMED WITH CARDAMOM AND CITRUS FRUITS (2005).

"We were, creatively speaking, at the most explosive moment in the history of the restaurant", says Joan: "It was a very productive time in terms of techniques, ideas, creativity... It offered us many joys and very good times. The culminating point in our work takes place when we discover something new, because that's what boosts up our energy and makes us feel good. This gets harder and harder, because we're becoming more demanding, but when it happens it's fantastic. And back then it happened a lot. We were all in very high spirits."

The emotional and professional environment of El Celler de Can Roca had been propelling them towards their second Michelin star, which caught them, just like the first, with all their homework done. When this second acknowledgement finally came in 2002, Joan, Josep and Jordi achieved the credibility they deserved from the world of gastronomy, and the necessary peace to work free of pressure. The second star is the fondest to their mother: all three of her sons were at home when they heard the news, and Can Roca as well as El Celler came together in a general hug, a sea of laughter and congratulations: "Now we have lots of good news, but back then there wasn't much, and we felt it very intensely. That day we released a lot of tension, a lot of emotions and a whole lot of joy."

Joy and success at El Celler are celebrated with the extended Roca family, which includes not only the parents of the three brothers, but also their lifelong customers at the restaurant. The Roca universe has two sides: the more rigorous and elevated—the luxury of a gourmet restaurant—and the more relaxed and informal—the abandon of a roadside establishment. According to Joan, they are two worlds in one, separated only by a wall: "The proximity of Can Roca was not only physical, but also one of coexistence. The backstage of El Celler was the bar at our parents' restaurant: our servers went there for coffee and the bar's waiter washed the Riedel glasses for El Celler." For lifelong customers, it was fun to see the show unfold: they saw the work being done offstage in a world-renowned establishment. The personnel in a suit and tie of the upscale restaurant mingled with the parents' clientele, and they all had breakfast, coffee, lunch, or dinner and even watched Barça matches together. "That was also our space," concludes Joan. This may have been the reason why it was so hard to cut the cord that tied them to their parents' house and make the definitive move that would be the third and permanent El Celler de Can Roca.

The triangle of El Celler de Can Roca was complete when Jordi formed the third vertex, that of sweet cuisine. In 1997, the youngest of the three brothers joined the restaurant for good, led still—and once again—by inertia. At the time, their desserts consisted of the typical dessert cart, a display of sweetness that never really suited the restaurant's discourse. It was a time when cakes were garnished with filigrees made of some sweet sauce such as custard or berry coulis. Joan was not satisfied with this part of the restaurant's offerings, he was uncomfortable: "Cooking is anarchy and pastry making is precision. And it was very noticeable we were making pastries like cooks. For us back then, desserts were a necessary evil we had to endure." He needed another person to improve this section. And then someone showed up who would be a deciding factor in the history of El Celler: the Welshman, Damian Allsop.

Allsop was one of the best dessert chefs in Europe at the time. He had passed through the kitchens of Alain Ducasse, Joël Robuchon, and Gordon Ramsay, and knew traditional pâtisserie techniques by heart. He arrived in Girona for personal reasons and began to work at La Magrana, befriending the Roca brothers and getting on well with them. "We went there for lunch and found these incredible desserts...," recalls Joan.

When Allsop decided to return to his homeland, Joan offered him the opportunity to stay and work with them, and he accepted. That day represented a turning point. Jordi, who had been through different sections, immediately offered his assistance; he was drawn to this particular character, who showed him a world unknown. "The first time I saw him in action I thought he was singular, different. Everything he wanted to do I regarded as very technical and complicated, but at the same time fun and powerful. I remember that, when he was working, his hands moved swiftly, going over every

plate, placing every ingredient correctly and, finally, presenting desserts with a gesture of perfection, of finality," remembers Jordi.

With passion and perseverance, Damian conveyed the basics of sweet cuisine: millefeuilles, soufflés, creams, sablées... And El Celler went from offering classical desserts such as FIG TATIN, or HONEY AND MATÓ CHEESE CAKE, to adding to the menu—after eradicating the cart—innovative dishes such as APPLE, WITHIN AN APPLE, WITHIN AN APPLE.

"The year Damian was here, our desserts acquired a new identity, a greater importance, and we realised it was in fact another type of cuisine, a different story," admits Joan, grateful. The Welsh pastry chef brought rigour and method to the sweet side of El Celler, introducing techniques like blown sugar, which until then they had only seen in references in some old book. He taught them that a Royal Gala was completely unrelated to a Golden apple when it came to certain dishes; he was as precise with the technique as he was with the product.

For Jordi, the time spent with Damian was like an intensive master's degree not only in terms of cooking, but also of humbleness: to get a good soufflé he had to prepare it over and over, and he realised the difficulty of pastry techniques, the importance of mastering the basics in order to create new things: "We made an incredible soufflé, technically perfect. But I wanted to make it airier, my own way, so I made an adaptation. Clearly, I killed it." One, two, three, four mistakes... each a test, an exercise in patience, obedience to the masters, and humility. And slowly, Jordi learnt. But it wasn't until two years later that his creations would revolutionise this section of the cuisine of El Celler.

One day in early 1998, Allsop had an accident and was hospitalised. Jordi had to face—for the first time—a great

"If I had been subjected to the teachings at home, I would have made it to second maître, or sous-chef, always with a complex. I would have stayed in the role of a child who doesn't know what to do. But I was lucky that a very interesting person from outside came to El Celler. The fact that he taught me things neither Joan nor Josep knew, gave me my own knowledge. I finally had an added value, a space in my own house, a voice."

JORDI ROCA

test at his brothers' restaurant. And it was then that he decided to take the bull by the horns, prove what he had learnt and take the opportunity to demonstrate that he also had a lot to contribute to El Celler.

In the first stage of heading the dessert section, he reproduced the creations of his teacher, Allsop, but shyly began to introduce new items. His first desserts were CHOCOLATE MOUSSE WITH BERRIES, and MOJITO, both from the year 2000. For the first time, Jordi saw clearly that this was what he wanted to do, that he liked it and it motivated him, and that he had a talent for it. His older brothers realised the young one in the house was no longer so young and that his theoretical knowledge and acquired practice in dessert making were very superior to their own. "Jordi discovered a world neither Josep nor I mastered. And because of it he earned his own place in this triangle. A space that gave him confidence and also, in time, prominence and importance," says Joan.

Jordi experienced it the same way, feeling fortunate: "If I had been subjected to the teachings at home, I would have made it to second maître, or sous-chef, always with a complex. I would have stayed in the role of a child who doesn't know what to do. But I was lucky that a very interesting person from outside came to El Celler. The fact that he taught me things neither Joan nor Josep knew, gave me my own knowledge. I finally had an added value, a space in my own house, a voice."

It wasn't easy to join the duo formed by his two older brothers, when they were already exemplary in their work. The age difference also created an emotional distance difficult to overcome, but that disappeared in time and as each of them shaped their own personality thanks to their individual experiences.

Jordi immediately understood his mission was to give to sweet cuisine the same seal Joan had imprinted in the savoury cuisine of the restaurant: "My obsession was to bring the cuisine of El Celler closer to desserts, and that's what I've been doing: creating my own voice, a complement to the roles of Joan and Josep, but with my own character." Maybe it was harder for him, but like his brothers, as soon as he visualised the dream, he went after it.

A year after daring to make his first creations, he entered the world of ice creams with the help of Angelo Corvitto, a Sicilian living in Torroella de Montgrí. From him, he learnt about the need for purity of air when making ice cream and it was from this that the opposing thought came to Jordi's mind: to 'contaminate' the air and achieve, for example, smoke ice cream. With the help of Josep — they shared an ability and

love for inventions—Jordi created a pump to smoke a cigar without actually having to do it, and transfer the smoke into a container. And so, he came up with one of his star creations: ICE CREAM PARTAGÁS CIGAR which, together with MOJITO, formed the TRIP TO HAVANA, a Cuban dessert duo that started to offer a hint of the new sweet style of El Celler.

At the age of twenty-three, Jordi spent a summer at the dessert section of El Bulli, an experience that proved revealing, similar to that of the two older brothers in their first trips to the great French restaurants: "I was still a kid and that summer really moved me... I was in a restaurant with an incredible influence. It was still not known around the world, but people in gastronomy were already talking proudly about working at the best restaurant in the world. That team spirit and symbolism was already perceived. The way it feels with Barça today!" Next to Rubén García (Albert Adrià was then working at the El Bulli workshop, its centre for creativity and innovation), Jordi submerged himself into the sweet section of Cala Montjoi.

That same year, Jordi embarked on a creative line that marked his career: perfume versions. A friend who sells fruits and plants sent some boxes of bergamot to the restaurant, a little-known citrus fruit at the time that awakened the sense of smell of the three brothers. Josep was convinced the aroma of this fruit was present in Eternity by Calvin Klein and, after researching its composition, they confirmed it to be the case. An idea arose then: to put together in one dish all the ingredients perceived in this fragrance so that it cannot only be smelled, but eaten. Vanilla cream, orange blossom water jelly, basil sauce, maple syrup jelly, tangerine slush and bergamot ice cream... were the ingredients that made up the new ETERNITY by El Celler—not to be smelled, but eaten. "I arrived at the idea that it was a good way to create new dishes, from a reference that had nothing to do with cooking.

I learnt to identify aromas and connect them to edible things. The fruitier perfumes were the clearest candidates," recalls Jordi, who in order to experiment had to make several trips to the perfumery and leave loaded down with fragrances. "The employees asked whether I wanted all those women's perfumes gift-wrapped and I would say no. Naturally, they looked at me as if I was a weirdo," he says laughing. And so other desserts are born out of sniffing perfumes, deconstructing their ingredients and reproducing their edible aspects, among them MIRACLE, or TRÉSOR BY LANCÔME, POLO SPORT BY RALPH LAUREN, or ANGEL BY THIERRY MUGLER, to name a few. Jordi was doing with perfumes what Joan did with wines: transfering their essence to the plate, after Josep deciphered them.

Shortly after starting his research of perfumes, in 2003 Jordi was considered the Best Pâtissier of the Year and creator of the Best Desserts according to the guide *Lo Mejor de la Gastronomía*, acknowledgements that consolidated him as a worldwide reference in pâtisserie. Joan and Josep then began to take their younger brother more seriously, and the three of them became closer. And this was how the brotherly relationship that has shaped one of the best restaurants in the world was consolidated.

Savoury cuisine, sweet cuisine, and wines. The meeting of the three vertices made it possible for El Celler de Can Roca to create dishes from three sides. Now, each brother had a different role to play, but all three have the same weight. Josep provides a few tasting notes from a wine and the machinery is set in motion: the other two, in the kitchen, figure out ways to introduce them into a new preparation, with the most suitable textures, fitting cooking techniques, and correct proportions.

The perfect example of a three-sided creation is the CHABLIS OYSTER, a dish that brings together Brittany oysters and Chablis wine. Josep explains that, in this geographical area, the land is made up precisely of small broken oyster shells… and to depict them, Jordi makes candies in the shape of stones from acacia honey brandy. Josep points out that it must include a velvety sauce, in which the oyster seems plant-like while communicating the warmth of a bountiful year… and immediately, Joan creates an oyster and fennel soup. Josep adds that Chablis has subtle mushroom nuances… and Joan creates mushroom air. Josep speaks of the notes of green apple with a malic acidity highly present in wine… and Joan reproduces a green apple purée. Josep describes mineral essences in wine… and Joan makes a soil distillate — something of an interpretation of soil in its purest state. "All of this constitutes a dish in which aromatic nuances, together with sweet and savoury cooking techniques, come together and form a single concept. The creative triangle, of course," concludes Josep. So, the limits between savoury and sweet cuisine vanish. Desserts are no longer essential to introduce sweet flavours. Or perhaps desserts mix with savoury dishes. Or maybe it is neither because everything is one thing.

BROTHERS AND COWORKERS

Many people wonder how it is possible for three brothers to work so many hours together, day after day, and have such an excellent relationship. Joan's answer is short and simple: "We don't know how to do it differently. We've always worked together." And adds, thoughtfully: "Maybe we don't consider it, we don't think too much about it. It probably has to do with the fact that we understand one another, we like what we do, the type of restaurant we have is the one we want, with its virtues and complexities. We have been lucky in that respect. We have no strategy or are smarter than the rest, but favourable circumstances have been linking us over time." Favourable circumstances have made the three pieces of the puzzle that is El Celler fit to perfection. When one of them is having a bad day, the other two compensate. When the three of them are very serious at work, one of them jumps in and makes a joke that dissolves any tension.

"It's both fun and odd, because I'm lucky enough to be near two brothers I trust completely and who are the best." Jordi has always admired his brothers and they continue to fascinate him now that he shares their recognition and prestige. The devotion that in adolescence was burdensome is now one more reason to value his work and appreciate the opportunity of constant learning they offer him: "Their knowledge was acquired with time, thanks to their interaction with people. They know a lot of everything. It is more important to learn from the knowledge and experience of Pitu and Joan than from combinations of products or techniques."

Now, in the Roca triangle, Jordi's youth and freshness have also been crucial. "If I weren't here everything would be more boring at El Celler. They have a blast with me, I tell them what is going on with me, I joke around… Also, when you grow older you lose perspective of what happens in the next generation and, since cooks at the restaurant are my age, I connect with them. For Joan and Pitu I'm their link to the younger staff," he explains.

Three-sided battles, in general in life, are won two against one, but that's not what happens at El Celler. Any quarrels at Can Roca are won by the minority. When one of them doesn't agree with his brothers, he always ends up persuading the other two. It's a very democratic brotherly relationship, according to Jordi, who's convinced of this theory: "The individual wishes and dreams of each one of us happen, they come true."

Josep, who thanks to that democracy ruled by the minority has been able to have his sanctuary of wines, defines the triangle they have formed with these words: "If El Celler de Can Roca was a wine, it would be Cava. A sparkling wine made locally, under the Mediterranean sun and of the three local varieties, of old root and new sap.

"From a simple free run wine of a humble base (our parents' restaurant, Can Roca, an excellent popular establishment) we took refuge in a second opportunity, a change of cycle. The breeding ground that was our family and training (at our dear Culinary Arts School of Girona) and a second project of slow aging that acquired its best qualities with maturity. There isn't a sensation of haste, but a bright serenity and a small, quality bubble. Long aging that is also expressed in the chromatic scope and boosts flavours.

"Purity, identity, varieties and the strong links of the three: structure, longevity and tannins are the Xarel·lo—Joan; perfume, fruit, the pursuit of changes and the most aniseed-flavoured aromas of prosperity are provided by the Macabeu—Josep; and the freshest, liveliest and brightest, and ever moving side is the Parellada—Jordi."[1]

Joan, playing the same game, ponders: "If El Celler was a dish, it could be a recent creation, like the LAMB WITH PA AMB TOMÀQUET. Because it's new but it's inspired by memories from childhood. It combines reflection (taking, for example, the knowledge of Eastern processes, such as Beijing-style

lacquered duck, where the most important part is the skin)
but also takes the element of personal experience (the aroma
of cumin experienced during his travels through Northern
Africa). It begins with the research of an interesting product
(using Ripollesa, an example of the limited old lineage
lamb breeding still carried out in our country). It combines
traditional know-how and the experimental introduction of
the latest technical resources, controlled temperature cooking
(in which El Celler is influential because for years it has been
conducting research, developing technology and working with
scientists). But there is also the playfulness (like an inverted
sandwich, with the bread in the middle and the lamb on the
outside), the more imaginative and fun aspect."[2]

The youngest brother, Jordi, had to think which of his
desserts could define El Celler: "Perhaps ANARCHY (a very
complex and elaborate dessert, a disorderly palette with
dozens of different preparations combined as the guest and
chance dictate, a chaos that generates new personalised
organoleptic experiences). For me, this dish means anything
is possible, that—at least in principle—anything can work. It
means not having to set limits to sweet, savoury and liquid. It
also shows freedom, which is what El Celler looks like from
my point of view. Perhaps due to the fact that in the world
of restaurant pâtisserie there are fewer role models—and
what doesn't exist is that which can become something—it
shows that harmony often comes from cultural or hereditary
sources. The dish was born on a day in which the three of
us were analysing how to make a St. George's mushroom
consommé with avocado and obsessively trying to figure
out the reason for everything, for every ingredient, every
technique. That's when I thought: Why does there have to
be a reason? Let's avoid overthinking. That's what started the
fire. Yes, freedom. Asking: 'why not?'"[3]

1. MASSANÉS, T. «El Celler de Can
Roca; un restaurant que enlluerna».
Què fem? Barcelona: La Vanguardia,
28 November 2008.

2. *Ibíd.*

3. *Ibíd.*

—2007:
THE THIRD
CELLER

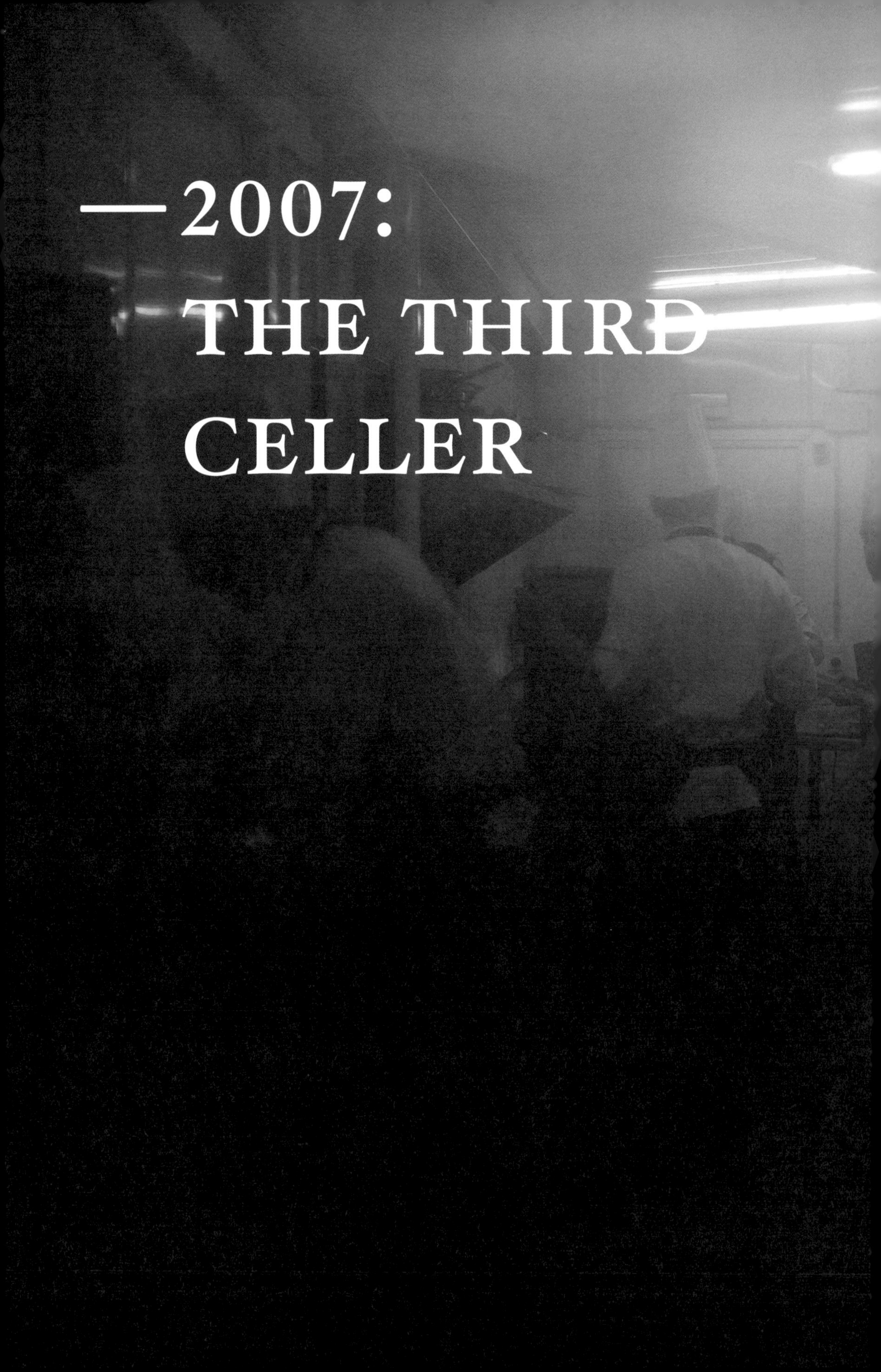

Just like in 1997, when there was a need to abandon the first kitchen and make an important restructuring of the space, ten years later the remodelling performed was insufficient and scarcity was once again hindering. Jordi was in charge of a staff of five in the dessert section, but had only enough space for three: the other two chefs had to work from the kitchen at Can Roca. They only had a one-and-a-half-metre-long table with a refrigerator underneath and an oven on the wall. To heat ingredients in the microwave or whip cream, they had to go to their parents' kitchen. Something as necessary—and delicate—in pâtisserie as tempering chocolate, became an odyssey: they had to do it in the morning, in the dining room, with the air conditioner at the coolest temperature. "There were days when I would wake up feeling optimistic and wanted to believe that, with that infrastructural distribution and machinery, it was like having a fifty-square-metre bakery just for me. But then reality struck and I realised it was not the case. I managed, I did what I could, and I learned the rigour of order," remembers Jordi. He had a space designed for a dessert cart like they had at the beginning, with a very limited surface area and lots of heat.

Josep's wine stock kept growing with time and, due to the lack of space, his exemplary collection was scattered through garages and premises around El Celler, leased for that purpose. Thanks to his proverbial memory, Josep was the only one able to remember that the Burgundy was two streets up and the Rieslings were stored in the back parking lot. His cellar became, then, an interesting puzzle, but not a very practical one.

Several options were contemplated in order to continue growing and the idea of moving the restaurant for good to the Torre de Can Sunyer was again taken into consideration. Now, that meant finding a new site for events, so they began to study alternatives in nearby plots of land. Finding a perfect solution wasn't easy, remembers Jordi: "Five years went by from the time we began to talk about moving until we took the first step to start remodelling.. We designed several projects for El Celler and each of us visualised their own space, not knowing where it would end up located. After

closing we spent hours talking and drawing, sometimes up to four or five in the morning... we really thought about how everything would be. We would come to a decision and go to bed, and the next morning we had changed our minds. It became an obsession."

But racking their brains during sleepless nights ended up bearing fruit. They made the decision to begin the total remodelling of the Torre and the time came to get to work on the project. Joan, Josep and Jordi were convinced that construction had to be paid for without resorting to the bank or asking for credits. Having learnt the lesson of the financial burden suffered years before with the purchase of the building, this time they wanted to take this new step using the savings they amassed during many years of intense work. "The new restaurant wasn't a rational decision. We knew it was like buying a yacht or a Ferrari. You really don't need it, because you can drive a different type of vehicle. It was like a gift to ourselves, we had to earn it and we didn't want our customers paying for it." It was an idea based on ethics and good sense, two values underestimated by society in general when the outlook is good, but that are always present and work well at El Celler. Paradoxically, during the years of harsh economic crisis they had enjoyed the best international renown, acknowledged in the country and abroad, and obtaining the greatest personal satisfactions.

According to these principles, the initial premise of a change of venue was not to have more space and accommodate more guests, therefore increasing profits, but the opposite: to give more satisfaction and comfort not only to their customers, but also the staff. "We wanted to stay true to what we do. We wanted to expand, not to make more money, but to work better. And people have understood this well," explains Joan. Changes in size often affect quality and customer service; but at El Celler, the move satisfied everybody, because every aspect of the transition was positive.

For years, the kitchen staff had to work in close physical proximity and do their best in a reduced space. That is why,

"This is how the circle closes;
we completed the dream
that began to brew
twenty-five years ago"

JOAN ROCA

"This new restaurant
was, for many years,
only uncertainty"

JOSEP ROCA

"The new Celler became
an obsession"

JORDI ROCA

when the moment came to finally make the dream come true, it became clear that the change had to be made without restrictions, obstacles, buts or half-measures. They had to go for gold. Josep knew from the start that the kitchen was to be the most important part of the new establishment: "People come here for the food and it is the people in the kitchen who have the priority to work comfortably; that is why they had to be the first to choose the space they wanted. And the space they didn't want, whatever was left unused, that would be my cellar."

The metamorphosis of the Torre was entrusted to the interior design team of Sandra Tarruella and Isabel López. Although a relationship of absolute trust was established with the professional team, the three brothers specified some fundamental requirements for the new restaurant from the beginning, just as they envisioned it. "We wanted the restaurant to have light, organic materials, wood; we wanted to see time go by, to have small private areas, that these separate areas were designed with functional furniture for serving, and to have completely separate areas for waiters and guests," explains Josep in detail and totally logically. And they not only thought of the physical space, but also about other sensory or atmospheric concepts that were very important to them: "We were obsessed by acoustics and the privacy of conversations; that is, we wanted to have the ideal acoustics to allow people to talk freely without other guests eavesdropping."

Once the letter to the North Pole was written, they only had to wait to get what they asked for, and for the final result to match the image they saw for years in their dream.

The Torre de Can Sunyer is a special, intimate and welcoming space. The triangle that defines the history of El Celler with the convergence of the three brothers was the point of reference when designing the architectural project: this is why the triangular floor plan of the dining area (redesigned in 1994) was emphasised and three different gardens were created.

From the beginning, the interior design team was asked to structure an area for a specific number of diners, exactly the same amount that fit in the old Celler. That was proof that the basis of the whole project was to continue being true to the discourse and philosophy that has always distinguished them. "We radically avoided adding more tables by emptying a triangle in the centre of the dining room and placing a garden in it," explains Joan. Therefore, by having a central garden the available space is at once reduced in a structural sense, as well as organised. That is one of the contributions made by the designers that most amazed them: now they had a small forest in the dining area, through which they could observe the day go by and the changing seasons... in other words, time. "We never imagined the richness in atmosphere they have created, that during the day is a source of peace and a Zen space, and at night seclusion and a play of mirrors, with a very intimate light," states Josep.

The dining area became a triangular cloister that received natural light from the interior forest and facilitated the structuring of the flow of waiters, creating a more reduced space and a warmer atmosphere. They only had to place the tables in twos and isolate them with some auxiliary furniture that demarcated the spaces, offering privacy to each group of customers and their conversation. On each table, three white stones that symbolised, once again, the triangle.

The kitchen of the new Celler quadrupled in size that of the old restaurant. "I spent many afternoons with the draughtsman of the project designing the kitchen, trying to place everything, distributing spaces. We drew everything up to thirty-two times!" explains Joan. If for two decades nearly twenty people worked huddled in under fifty square metres, now the kitchen boasted two-hundred metres for the cooking staff to organise the different sections, and even included a fireplace for cooking over embers, smoke or open flame.

To the right of the entry hallway that leads to the kitchen, Joan set up a small office with everything he needed to perform his daily tasks as practically and comfortably as possible: he had shelves with his collection of reference books, a desk with a computer and, by just turning his head, a full view of the kitchen.

Josep's new wine cellar deserves special attention. If the new Celler was a dream come true for the three brothers, for him, this change entailed exceptional, emotional connotations. He didn't let interior design define his space because his plan was to create a new dimension to convey his passion for wines: "I wanted it to be my private interpretation of wine. I wanted to free the channels of seduction from a subjective view. I wanted to try to say something about me, provide energy, open up, fill with intangible values an approach that has always been seen as tangible: the bottle, the label..." Josep refuses to see wine as a symbol of luxury, exclusiveness and ostentation, and brings to the table a new understanding of this world, through the senses.

He collected different wooden boxes to make the packaging of what would be five chapels or receptacles dedicated to his five essential types: Burgundy, Riesling, Priorat, Sherry and Champagne: "Five wines, five chapels, five senses to explain everything in an approach that arose from personal

growth through wine." In each chapel, a plasma screen displays images of the original region of each vineyard, accompanied by carefully chosen musical pieces to fit each atmosphere. Josep has managed to interpret each grape variety in a multisensory way, so he also incorporates touch. Steel balls embody the effervescence of the bubbles and cold temperature of Champagne. Green silk, suggesting subtlety, defines the German Rieslings. Small bags made of red velvet symbolize the elegance of the Burgundy. A piece of slate over an olive wood receptacle represents the roughness of the wild vineyards of the Priorat region. A temperature of fourteen degrees, over two-thousand-five-hundred wines, about thirty-thousand bottles and twenty-five years of lees transform this space into a wine paradise.

Before moving to the new restaurant, between the years 2003 and 2006, Josep endeavoured to create a digital menu that would offer the customer the opportunity to know the origin of each bottle, see pictures of its surrounding landscape and obtain information about each harvest... "It was an ambitious project that included over five-thousand-five-hundred photographs I already had. But when I came in here and showed our customers the cellar in this manner, I understood that it no longer made sense and I no longer had the strength to demand more attention from the customer." But all this material wasn't assembled in vain: a smartphone app was created with some of this content—Josep's favourite wines (*The Top 153 Wines of 2010*).

Before relocating, Josep, who always has a poetic view of life, wanted his friends to help transport the bottles from the old warehouses and garages to the new site under a full moon, and end the night with a breakfast, at dawn, to celebrate making the dream come true. "I was so naïve! I realised, right as we were about to move, that transporting the wine would take us months and months." And so, the move was inevitably gradual.

The move and inauguration of the new site, like everything that happens at El Celler, was done without much ceremony, there was no great party or opening: lunch was served at the old restaurant and they moved to the Torre in the afternoon to prepare dinner, using the new pots without previous rehearsal. Jordi, who had internalised rigour and order deep in his methodology, didn't feel comfortable. He got lost in the huge, new space dedicated exclusively to his section: "When we came here, it was absolute chaos. We didn't rehearse how the kitchen would work, and my section—in proportion—was the biggest of all. I don't remember ever getting the runs like that day. It took me a month to adapt to the new space. I missed my chaos, I misplaced everything!"

It took a while for Jordi, who was probably the more insistent in moving, to make the kitchen his own. But he already knew how easy it was to get used to improvements. In a matter of weeks, all three had adapted to the Torre de Can Sunyer and came to realise what this step meant: they felt the satisfaction of a dream fulfilled.

DESCRIPTIVE REPORT OF THE PROJECT
OF INTERIOR DESIGN FOR EL CELLER DE CAN ROCA

SANDRA TARRUELLA AND ISABEL LÓPEZ
2007

The new location for El Celler de Can Roca is at the old Torre de Can Sunyer and its surrounding buildings, where until now big events and celebrations took place. This Torre, dating to 1911, underwent two expansions: one large, open triangular dining area overlooking the street, built in 1994, and a curved porch in the back garden, in 1999. Both spaces, joined to the original Torre via the old porch, provided the establishment with a larger space for events, although they operated separately.

The commission, to host a limited number of people in the new restaurant, due to the elaborate and exquisite nature of the cookery and the aim to produce a relaxed and intimate atmosphere, collided head-on with the characteristics of the existing space.

The success of El Celler de Can Roca throughout the years has been based on the contribution of the three Roca brothers, a three-party game that has achieved perfect harmony between fine food and wine, in addition to excellent service.

This three-party game has been the starting point to develop the new architectural project, therefore the aim was to maximise the triangular floor plan of the existing dining area and work on the idea of three gardens of a completely distinct, but complementary nature.

The intent of this architectural intervention was to connect the different spaces visually and open the building up to the immediate surrounding gardens —the first, an access garden, and the second hidden behind the Torre where the vegetable garden is located— in order to take full advantage of them while creating new ones to organise the interior room.

The project is based around a large void that penetrates the fabric of the existing construction of the main area. This intervention, together with the opening of large windows and the help of the reflection of mirrored surfaces, has created new relationships inexistent until now; all the spaces come together as a whole and face and communicate with every single part of it. These arrangements connect the immediate exterior with the interior, expanding the borders of the rooms and helping establish the hierarchical structure, while organising the uses of the different spaces.

In the triangular floor plan of the existing dining area, the design pierces the central body with a triangular glass box that provides light and openness to the interior. This void in the middle, this new exterior element inside, reorganises the flow of people and the diners around it. Additionally, it strengthens and illuminates the dining room, and balances the remaining surface area in relation to the intimate space required by this type of cuisine. This intervention creates space suitable for contemplation, or an intimate introspection, which can be seen from every corner but not in its entirety thanks to the reflection of the glass and the new vegetation that shoots up into the sky. This is how the third garden is born.

From the street, a new wood-panelled facade conceals the door that leads to the access garden. The dramatic entrance to the first of the gardens is emphasised by a ramp that is deliberately narrow, dark and heavily vegetated, and then reveals the opposite effect: an open and bright space.

The access garden is a reinterpretation of the existing courtyard, where the flooring is composed of pieces of prefabricated concrete, conferring energy against the stern facade of the Torre and leading the visitor to the main access. This is a welcome point where a dialogue is established between the existing greenery and the flooring; as well as the existing facade of the Torre and the new wall surfaces and openings.

The Torre's facade has been left intact, but the annexed porch leading inside has been closed entirely with panels of recycled teakwood; also, the construction next to the main area has been opened up thanks to a large glass box that brings transparency into the cigar room and contributes to the visual communication down to the interior dining area.

The reception, located in the old porch of the Torre, shows no traces of its original appearance except for the

Catalan vault. Upon crossing the solid access door, the visitor encounters two white-lacquered surfaces on both sides, two walls framing the way and clearly accentuating the accesses to the adjacent rooms, as well as highlighting the interstitial paths that lead to them. It is a place that contrasts the roughness of the original ceiling with the new lacquered surfaces, the initial stillness with the activity of the wait staff and diners, the opacity of the door with the brightness from the reflection of the garden at the end. This is where the customer begins to discover the crossing glances among the spaces, the reflections on the mirrors.

The cigar cellar area opens up to the right of the entrance. It is a rectangular room that contains the cigar cellar and liquor room, and the transparency of the dining room and garden on each of the side walls. It is a showcase, a white box where only the counterpoint of wine-coloured furniture breaks the serenity. This space of rest and contemplation, exceptionally located, creates the play of crossed glances between the people arriving or leaving, and the people enjoying the dining room.

Access to the dining room is through the white reception area via two long and narrow ramps leading to the vast room presided by the triangular central courtyard. The first tangential view of the courtyard facilitates the pathways around it, allowing tables only on two of its sides, pushed toward the perimeter of the room; the hustle and bustle of the wait staff, therefore, takes place around this light box. Just like the foliage of the planted birch trees in the new garden, the dining area plays with this duality of shades; the slightly inclined oak wood wall-panelling creates a contrast of white and oak, depending on the direction of the walk. This combination of brilliant white and oak wood is present in the whole dining area: roof, floor and furniture.

Again, at the end of the hall emerges the image of the third garden. The first is a welcome garden, the second for contemplation and introspection, and the last for testing and creating. There, behind the kitchen, are the vegetable garden and aromatic herbs, accomplices to culinary experimentation and essences. At the beginning of the old curved porch, a superposition and succession of inclined mirror planes hide the toilets and offices that can be seen in the reflection of the back garden of the Torre. And as you move toward them, they bring the new wine cellar into view.

Five large wooden boxes arranged in a disorderly way around the back garden penetrate the enclosure of the old curved porch, imitating the dance of wine boxes waiting to be opened to let us savour their content. Behind the exterior panelling made of old recycled wine boxes, these crates hide wines from different very special regions, and invite all the senses to participate in their tasting. The rest of the wine cellar, protected by the old porch, is distributed in the shape of a fan, according to the organisation of the wine shelves.

And lastly, the most important element: the kitchen. In the heart of the old Torre, this is the core for culinary creation around which the whole project revolves. The kitchen, seen from the main door of the Torre, welcomes the visitor directly but gently, and its lengthwise design outlines the connection between the access garden and the back garden.

Contrast and surprise are present all throughout the restaurant. The duality of opposing concepts such as the opacity of the main access and the transparency of the cigar room, the luminosity of the access garden and the secluded semidarkness of the reception hall, its warm, matt and natural materials against the cold, white and bright materials of the dining room, is repeated in every space to maintain the dialogue and element of surprise sought.

All of this creates a metaphor about the architecture involved in gastronomy, not only on the surface, but exploring the same feeling of initial surprise that, in the end, will take in and make the visitor comfortable. A sweet balance of sensations.

Thus, we may say El Celler de Can Roca features a new space meant to maintain and reinforce expectation, surprise, contrast and the quality that has always defined the spirit of the restaurant.

The third Celler is the biggest, most complete, studied, equipped and spectacular restaurant of the three that have shaped the history of the house. "Coming here means having no limitations," according to Joan. The new site meant having the necessary square metres, tools and equipment at hand to achieve excellence; in other words, to be surrounded by everything they needed to continue building their dream.

However, the most difficult aspect about leaving Can Roca, their home restaurant, was that for years it was their living room, dressing room and racetrack. The separation—even of only a few metres—was the emotional price they had pay to move forward, according to Joan: "The change made us grow professionally because it made everything more rigorous. Before, we always had a mischievous side, but here everything took a more serious tone." However, those short two-hundred metres that separate both worlds allow them to maintain the connection with the mother house and, every day around noon, a legion of cooks and waiters from El Celler parades dressed in uniform on the road of Taialà to eat the lentils, macaroni, or rice with eggs and tomato sauce made by Montserrat every day, dishes Joan usually eats standing in the kitchen, next to his mother. To share meals, coffees or football matches with the extended family of the restaurant helps them keep their feet on the ground and remember their origins.

"We have built a world where we feel comfortable and where everything makes sense. Life means building your own world and this is definitely ours," says Joan. He has made his home at the Torre de Can Sunyer, separated by only a set of stairs from the new restaurant. He has developed his own living, working and thinking space, an atmosphere suitable for creativity, but also for conciliating the tough days at work and time with the family. When the kids come home from school, before they go to do their homework, they can stop by the kitchen of El Celler and say hello to their father.

At the Torre, the Roca brothers have found a perfect space to work intensely and relax when necessary. The building has been transformed into their own small but complex universe, and perhaps that is the reason why they can work fifteen hours a day and wake up the next morning with the same passion for their job as the day they started. "We have a great ability to regenerate," says Joan, "You go to bed late, exhausted, and the following day you have forgotten all about it. The day starts over, you welcome your guests again..." Without a doubt, their surroundings play an important role; nevertheless, contact with different people from many different fields of knowledge also produces interesting moments every day. Their interpretation of the relocation couldn't be more positive: "We arrived four years ago and we're really happy. Every morning when I arrive at the restaurant I thank, from the distance, the city and its people." Joan, as do Josep and Jordi, thanks the people of Girona for always standing by their side. El Celler de Can Roca may be the restaurant of haute cuisine most deeply rooted in the area. It became clear the day they received, from their neighbours and friends, the biggest reward.

The restaurant was full to capacity on a daily basis, but the Roca brothers felt for their community, who demanded another Michelin star; their third. Inspectors—as usual—play hard to get, but two years after their permanent move into the Torre, in 2009, that star arrived. The day after the news became public, the three brothers were at the restaurant, freshly arrived from Madrid and managing everything the new milestone entailed, when they heard a rumour outside. At the door they were greeted by dozens of people clapping passionately in their honour. Their neighbours in Girona were happy, they felt they had taken part in the success and had organised via mobile phone messages to gather at eight that evening in front of the door of El Celler. "It was the most beautiful acknowledgement we have ever received, because it means they all feel they

own this project. The people of Girona really value the fact
that we settled in this working-class neighbourhood when
it may have seemed like the least suitable place. And all of
this is work, commitment, self-improvement. Our story is
very emotional, but at the same time very understandable."
When they walk around the city people stop them to thank
them and they, humble by nature, cannot help but be moved,
because those are the gestures that give a sense of purpose
to their work. Even their professional colleagues—other
restaurateurs in the city—express their gratitude for being
such good ambassadors of the local cuisine: now visitors
come to this land convinced they will eat well.

The third Michelin star didn't alter whatsoever the essence
of El Celler de Can Roca, but it increased the impact of
their work, as Joan says: "Clearly, (the third star) changes
some things, because we enter a select club of restaurants
that maintain a high level of excellence accepted by many
gourmets everywhere. The world is large and, for those who
don't know you, the stars are a sort of a pre-established ISO."
Suddenly, their work acquired international magnitude and
people from all over the world began to arrive in Girona.
Whenever they travel abroad to attend congresses, they
sense a total consensus with regard to their cuisine. With the
perspective of time, they have come to realise that the new
space helped transform the perception of the people and
critics: "We enjoyed great professional recognition in the
sector, but we had to take this step to persuade international
guides and voters in the big lists of restaurants."

In the spring of 2011 El Celler de Can Roca was elected the
second best restaurant in the world by the British *Restaurant
Magazine*, one of the most prestigious publications read by
the gourmet public—and this outstanding acknowledgment
reoccurred in 2012.

More awards, more creations, more conferences, more
prominent positions in other rankings... Before they realised
they had turned twenty-five. But, as usual, they didn't
celebrate: "We don't know how to organise parties," they say.
They don't pay any special attention to events or remember
exact dates. They know they opened in August 1986 and,
therefore, it's August 2011 when they have to commemorate
their silver anniversary. There are no celebrations, but they
feel the personal satisfaction of the great successes they've
cooked over very low heat for twenty-five years.

"A restaurant must be built over time, it's a long road. It's
a way of life, a path. And you must try to be happy in that
path, because goals go by very quickly. You are awarded a
star and the following day you must get back to work. You
get the second, and the exact same thing happens, you get
the third and it's exactly the same. Life goes on and you must
be happy with the daily routines, which is what endures,"
concludes Joan.

—CREATIVE LINES AND BASES

—EXTERNAL INSPIRATION

—INTERNAL MOTIVATION

II.

—EXTERNAL
INSPIRATION

A

—TRADITION

RED MULLET STUFFED
WITH ITS LIVER, SUQUET
AND FENNEL, ORANGE
AND SAFFRON GNOCCHI

84

COD BRANDADA

88

NECK OF LAMB
FILLED WITH
SWEETBREADS
AND PEAS

90

SQUAB LIVER
WITH ONION

92

FIGS WITH FOIE

94

VEAL TENDONS
WITH MUSHROOMS
AND HAZELNUTS

95

BABY SQUIDS
WITH ONION ROCK

96

To lay the foundations of a culture, we need to have acquired the knowledge of what has been bequeathed to us in order to be capable of passing on a new, different baton that incorporates the body of tradition with a new vision. This knowledge may be obtained via the intellect, or in a way we could deem epidermal. That is, through the books we have read, the experiences we have had, or the osmosis created between two solutions of different concentrations.

The Roca brothers have soaked up tradition in order to move forward. Eugeni d'Ors wrote that, "What is not tradition is plagiarism". And he said it to emphasise the fact that these footprints are fundamental if one wishes to avoid the absurdity of pretending there is nothing in the past; that we are the ones who have created a new world. We do not create it, but recreate it, that is, we give birth to it a second time starting from what we know.

It is also about proximity, about what has reached us across the centuries, what we have eaten in a country that has been shaped by making the most of the products at hand. A cuisine, that of El Celler, enriched by many sources and defined by its optimum use of the product, celebration, and richness of flavours. A solid gastronomy to the extent that it takes root in a region, in a type of culinary literature—read, learnt, internalised—in a daily routine that has been consolidated with the slow passage of time.

According to the Roca brothers

We do not want to renounce the ancestral depth of our deep-rooted cuisine. Our cuisine is a piece of the local world in which we live, bound up with land and landscape, culture and people who inspire and inform us. It is part of our footprint. Made up, perhaps. Made ours...

Every generation will lose one value, but may gain another. One must experiment in order to preserve and know how to separate the wheat from the chaff: What do we rescue from the past that we want to preserve, and what can we get rid of? That is the fundamental choice.

We dislike the word 'tradition' because it may carry the connotation of motionlessness. But we uphold our cultural heritage—the ways of living, working, cooking, eating and thinking that determine who we are. The memories of home and the examples from the *Corpus Culinari de Catalunya*, promoted by The Culinary Institute of Catalonia, are essential tools in the kitchen we always bear in mind when projecting into the future.

We keep in mind the products entrenched for many years and the collection of recipes we have amassed, and they are retrospectively useful. Like the brandada we had for the first time at the Bahía de Tossa restaurant in the early 80s that enlightened us about the modern treatment of cod. Or the pig's trotter terrine with caramelised cabbage from Motel Empordà that revealed how the cuisine stemming from slaughter can be clever and local.

And so many other dishes whose flavours always re-emerge, here and there, from the corners of our memory:

The sautéed peas our mother dreams about, accompanied by the Easter lamb of the holidays in the post-war days of scarcity.

The fried calamari and onions, a sugary bond between lightly fried and ink-stained sofritos, are now set in a soft and macerated rock, a fusion consisting of equal parts onion and salt-roasted baby squids.

The liver and onions of the fiestas of Sant Esteve de Llémena; or its fork breakfasts with botifarra, crowned with a Farias cigar and coffee with a dash of brandy that expanded the lungs and narrowed the eyes.

The takeaway Christmas seafood casserole ordered at Can Roca, our parents' restaurant, a symbol of days of special meals, and the secret mince recipe...

Duck and fig. Endemic relationship. Inside the foie and outside the meat—inside out like a wrapping. And royal goose meat, and its liver, with the fig as its loyal servant. The duck liver ruined from eating figs, and the good health of he who eats foie and fig...

And dishes like the veal tendon stew.

And the cartilage, conveying the texture of the tendon and intensifying the memory of a part we used to avoid and we now praise. Tendons which we now prepare outstretched in a precise cooking time that softens them to the limit...

In short, the present and the evolution of what we stand for today will be the pantry for our children's tradition. In evolution. In a mutating transition... Just like the recipes of our childhood have nourished our bodies, our lives, and therefore, our cuisine.

In the dining room...

In the dining room of El Celler de Can Roca, the elements that seek to come closer to tradition are the three rocks: three rocks that represent matter, memory, perseverance, fortitude, clearness...

They signify the awareness of wanting to carry out a flowing review of nuances that can be rebuilt and shaped, but that maintain their coherence in form.

The aim is also to contribute a sense of the local, of proximity, because these are stones from the bank of the Ter River, that came from afar, that have rolled, that have arrived and their function is to show three elements of different personalities, different personal structures, but that play the lead in an enriching three-party game.

You may find them at your table, chairing your meal. It's our way of keeping you company. Discreetly, but always present.

RED MULLET
STUFFED WITH
ITS LIVER, SUQUET
AND FENNEL,
ORANGE AND
SAFFRON GNOCCHI

SERVES 8 PEOPLE

COMPOSITION

Red mullet
Red mullet liver pâté
Fennel gnocchi
Orange gnocchi
Saffron gnocchi
Red mullet suquet

—RED MULLET
YIELDS 8 RED MULLETS WEIGHING 40 G EACH

8 red mullets (about 80 g each)
Brine for fish (basic recipes, p.429)

Clean and scale the red mullets; reserve the livers to make the pâté.

Fillet without removing the tail and separate the bones to make the stock. Submerge in brine for 4 minutes, then remove and dry excess moisture. Reserve.

—RED MULLET LIVER PÂTÉ
YIELDS 180 G

110 g red mullet liver
10 g extra virgin olive oil
110 g butter
Salt

Leave livers in iced water for 12 hours to soak. Next, remove bled livers from the water and dry well. Heat the olive oil in a frying pan and sauté the livers leaving the centre undercooked. Blend the livers with the butter and adjust salt, run through a fine sieve, cool and reserve in piping bags.

—FENNEL WATER
YIELDS 70 G

50 g fennel leaves
25 g blanching water, cold
25 g water

In a casserole, bring water to a boil. Blanch the fennel leaves for about 20 seconds and remove. Cool in iced water.

Mix the blanched fennel leaves with the water used for blanching when it's cold, and the water previously indicated, and blend to a thin, smooth liquid. Run through a fine chinois, pressing to obtain as much fennel water as possible.

—FENNEL GNOCCHI
YIELDS 22 GNOCCHI

60 g fennel water (previously prepared)
15 g kuzu
200 g potato purée (basic recipes, p.428)
5 g fresh fennel leaves

Dissolve the kuzu in cold fennel water, then mix with potato purée and transfer the mixture into a casserole. Bring to a boil and stir until it turns into dense dough. Let cool, add chopped fennel leaves and blend. Leave to stand in a piping bag for 12 hours, refrigerated.

Next, make cylinders 1.2 cm in diameter on a tray, and cut them into 1.5-cm-thick slices. Reserve.

—ORANGE GNOCCHI
YIELDS 22 GNOCCHI

1 orange
15 g kuzu
20 g water
40 g orange reduction (basic recipes, p.427)
200 g potato purée (basic recipes, p.428)

Grate orange zest with a Microplane grater and reserve.

Dissolve the kuzu in cold water together with the orange reduction. Then, mix with the potato purée and transfer the mixture into a casserole. Bring to a boil and stir until it turns into dense dough. Leave to cool, add orange zest and blend. Leave to stand in a piping bag for 12 hours, refrigerated.

Next, make cylinders 1.2 cm in diameter on a tray, and cut them into 1.5-cm-thick slices. Reserve.

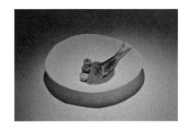

—SAFFRON INFUSION
YIELDS 250 G

250 g water
2.5 g saffron

Wrap the saffron in kitchen foil and heat lightly over a griddle pan. Heat the water and add saffron. Cover and infuse for 15 minutes. Reserve.

—SAFFRON GNOCCHI
YIELDS 22 GNOCCHI

60 g saffron infusion (previously prepared)
15 g kuzu
200 g potato purée (basic recipes, p.428)

Dissolve the kuzu in cold saffron water, then mix with potato purée and transfer the mixture into a casserole. Bring to a boil and stir until it turns into thick dough. Leave to stand in a piping bag for 12 hours, refrigerated.

Next, make cylinders 1.2 cm in diameter on a tray, and cut them into 1.5-cm-thick slices. Reserve.

—RED MULLET STOCK
YIELDS 2 KG

2 kg red mullet bones and heads
365 g mirepoix (basic recipes, p.427)
3 kg water
15 g lard

Submerge the bones and heads in iced water to soak. Strain, place in a baking tray in the oven and brown at 180°C/356°F for 30 minutes.

Put the oven-browned red mullet bones and heads in a stockpot along with the mirepoix and cold water. Bring to a boil, skim. Add the lard and cook on low heat. Strain and reduce to 2 litres of stock.

—ALIOLI
YIELDS 145 G

3 garlic cloves
40 g red mullet stock (previously prepared)
110 g garlic oil (basic recipes, p.427)
Extra virgin olive oil
Salt

Blanch the garlic cloves three times starting with cold water, then transfer into a baking tray with a dash of olive oil and bake at 160°C/320°F for approximately 12 minutes.

Purée the roasted garlic with the red mullet stock and emulsify with garlic oil to make alioli. Adjust salt and reserve.

—RED MULLET SUQUET
YIELDS 1.2 KG

2 kg red mullet stock (previously prepared)
145 g alioli (previously prepared)
1.5 g xanthan gum
Salt

Run the red mullet stock and xanthan gum through a hand blender. When the mixture is smooth, emulsify with alioli and adjust salt.

GARNISHING AND PLATING

8 fennel leaves
8 saffron strands
Orange zest
Guindilla pepper oil (basic recipes, p.427)

Before plating, stuff the red mullets with red mullet liver pâté, seal in a vacuum pack bag at 100% and cook in the Roner at 55°C/131°F for 4 minutes.

Regenerate the gnocchi on the salamander. Place one gnocchi of each flavour on one side of the plate and garnish with a saffron strand, a fennel leaf, or some orange zest slightly dehydrated in the salamander.

Serve a base of suquet on the plate and set the red mullet on top. Garnish the red mullet with 3 drops of guindilla pepper oil.

COD BRANDADA

SERVES 8 PEOPLE

COMPOSITION

Cod foam
Cod stock
Cod brandada
Lemon peel
Cod tripe
Lemon purée
Pak choi stalks
Honeyed shallots

—COD FOAM
YIELDS APPROXIMATELY 1.2 KG

4 garlic cloves
750 g desalted centre cut cod fillet
400 g cream
80 g egg whites
30 g extra virgin olive oil
100 g potato purée (basic recipes, p.428)
3 g xanthan gum
Salt

Slice the garlic cloves thinly and cook on low heat until soft, without browning, with a dash of olive oil. Add the desalted cod, cut into regular cubes, and cook for a few more minutes. Add the cream and cook for 10 minutes over medium heat. Remove from heat, blend in the Thermomix and run the mixture through a fine chinois. Add the egg whites, olive oil, potato purée and xanthan gum, then mix with a hand blender. Taste, adjust salt, and place the mixture in a one-litre whipped cream dispenser with 3 chargers.

—COD STOCK
YIELDS APPROXIMATELY 650 G

2 leeks
1 garlic clove
500 g cod bones
2 potatoes
1 kg water
200 g extra virgin olive oil

Clean, peel and cut up the leeks and garlic. Toss with a dash of oil in a medium casserole; add the cod bones, potatoes—peeled and chopped—and water. Boil for 30 minutes.

Discard the cod bones, blend the mixture (stock, potatoes, garlic, leeks) and emulsify with olive oil. Reserve hot.

—COD BRANDADA
YIELDS 400 G

200 g desalted cod
1 garlic clove
180 g extra virgin olive oil
50 g cod stock (previously prepared)

Slice garlic thinly and toss it in olive oil, add the cod, crumbled, and cook slowly over very low heat. Mix with a hand blender, while slowly pouring in the oil used to cook the garlic, until a thick emulsion is obtained. Add the cod stock to thin down and reserve.

—COD TRIPE
YIELDS APPROXIMATELY 150 G

100 g cod tripe (soaked for 12 hours)
1 garlic clove
30 g extra virgin olive oil
5 g ñora pepper pulp
25 g cod stock (previously prepared)

Remove the outer skin of the cod tripe and cut into 0.5 cm cubes. Reserve.

Slice the garlic thinly and cook slowly in oil over low heat to flavour. Remove the garlic slices and add chopped tripe and ñora pepper pulp, cook for 10 minutes and add cod stock. Pour olive oil in slowly, while stirring until the liquid emulsifies.

—LEMON PEEL
YIELDS 500 G

500 g water
100 g sugar
500 g lemon peel

In a casserole, place 500 g water with 100 g sugar and the lemon peel. Bring to a boil and then cool. Repeat 4 times and, finally, reserve the peel completely dry.

—RESTING THE LEMON PEEL
YIELDS 500 G

500 g sugar syrup (basic recipes, p.428)
500 g lemon peel (previously prepared)

Mix the syrup and peel, blanched, and leave
to stand for 24 hours.

—LEMON PURÉE
YIELDS 750 G

500 g lemon peel (previously prepared)
100 g lemon juice
70 g cream
25 g butter

Remove the peel from the syrup, blend in the
Thermomix for 10 minutes at 65°C/149°F and
incorporate the lemon juice, cream and butter
into the mixture.

If necessary, thin down some of the syrup used
for settling peel to obtain a creamy texture.
Reserve refrigerated in piping bags.

—PAK CHOI STALKS
YIELDS 72 TRIANGLES

12 pak choi (celery cabbage,
    Brassica pekinensis) leaves
Extra virgin olive oil
Salt

Separate the pak choi leaves, which will be
used in other recipes, and reserve the stalks.
Wash them well and cut into small triangles,
no bigger than 3 mm. Brown lightly with olive
oil on the griddle pan, and adjust salt. Reserve.

—HONEYED SHALLOTS
YIELDS 24 UNITS

200 g shallots (12 units)
Extra virgin olive oil
20 g honey
Guindilla pepper oil (basic recipes, p.427)
Thyme blossoms

Cook shallots without removing the skin,
starting with cold water and bringing to a boil.
When cooked, peel and remove the core; slice
cores in half.

In a frying pan with a dash of oil, brown the
shallot cores along the cut side and, when
lightly brown, add the honey. Cook until
caramelised.

Separate 8 halves caramelised with honey; mix
8 halves with guindilla pepper oil; and 8 more
with the thyme blossoms. Reserve.

GARNISHING AND PLATING

Carrot leaves
Purple basil
Thyme
Baby mustard

Arrange the cod brandada on a plate with
some of the braised tripe on top, and three
dots of lemon purée around it.

Stick 3 pak choi stalks into each lemon drop;
arrange one shallot half between each dot and
the next, alternating thyme flowers, guindilla
pepper oil, and caramelised shallots.

Finish with the cod foam and a few leaves of
carrot, purple basil, thyme and baby mustard.

NECK OF LAMB FILLED WITH SWEETBREADS AND PEAS

SERVES 6 PEOPLE

COMPOSITION

Neck of lamb terrine
Lamb gravy
Lamb bacon
Pea purée
Serrat sheep cheese Parmentier
Mint gel

—NECK OF LAMB TERRINE
YIELDS 6 PORTIONS

1 (1kg) neck of lamb
Brine for meat (basic recipes, p.429)
Extra virgin olive oil
50 g lamb sweetbreads

Soak the neck of lamb for 3 hours in iced water. Next, strain and leave in brine for 2 hours. Strain again, seal in a vacuum pack bag with oil and cook in the Roner for 24 hours at 68°C/154°F. When ready and while still hot, bone it, leaving the shape of the neck.

Blanch the sweetbreads, starting with cold water, with a pinch of salt. Cool down and remove their connective tissue.

Fill the neck with the sweetbreads, form a 3.5-cm-thick cylinder by rolling it in cling film, press well, and seal in a vacuum pack bag again. Cook again at 68°C/154°F for 1 hour. Blast chill and keep refrigerated. Cut 3-cm-wide slices and pack to regenerate at 68°C/154°F before plating.

—LAMB GRAVY
YIELDS 250 G

2 kg lamb bones and trimmings
220 g mirepoix (basic recipes, p.427)
2.5 kg water
40 g kuzu thickening agent (basic recipes, p.427)

Set the bones and trimmings on a baking tray and brown on high temperature.

When brown, remove excess fat and transfer into a stockpot together with the mirepoix. Deglaze the baking tray with cold water and add the juice to the stockpot. Cover with cold water and cook for 3 hours. Next, strain and reduce to 250 g. Bring to a boil and add the kuzu mixture while stirring constantly. Strain and reserve.

—LAMB BACON
YIELDS 7 SQUARES 3X3 CM EACH

1 suckling lamb rack
Extra virgin olive oil
Brine for meat (basic recipes, p.429)

Submerge the rack in brine for 1 hour.

Seal the rack in a vacuum pack bag with oil and cook in the Roner at 72°C/162°F for 12 hours. Bone while hot and remove the outer fat and meat.

Sear the rack skin on the griddle pan with some weight on top to keep it flat and crisp. Reserve.

—PEA PURÉE
YIELDS 250 G

250 g fresh green peas
75 g butter
Salt

Blanch the peas and cool in iced water.

Strain and purée with the butter until obtaining a smooth paste. Run through a fine chinois to discard any remaining skins and adjust salt. Reserve.

—SERRAT SHEEP CHEESE PARMENTIER
YIELDS 400 G

200 g potatoes
60 g Serrat sheep cheese
100 g milk
60 g cream
4 g egg white powder

Wash potatoes, unpeeled, wrap in kitchen foil and roast in the oven at 160°C/320°F for 45 minutes.

In a saucepan, heat the milk, cream and cheese. Leave to infuse and let the cheese melt. Mix with a hand blender until smooth and, lastly, run through a fine strainer and reserve.

Peel the potatoes while hot and run them through a purée sieve. Stir with the cheese infusion and use the hand blender to obtain a smooth cream. Add egg white powder, introduce in a ½ litre whipped cream dispenser with 2 chargers, and keep in a hot bain-marie.

—MINT GEL
YIELDS 250 G

300 g mint leaves
75 g blanching water
75 g water
0.5 g xanthan gum
Salt

In a casserole, bring water to a boil. Blanch the mint leaves for about 20 seconds and remove. Cool in iced water.

Place the blanched mint leaves with 75 g of the blanching water, cold, and an additional 75 g of water in the Thermomix and blend until obtaining a fine, smooth liquid. Run through a fine chinois, pressing to obtain as much mint water as possible. Blend the liquid obtained with xanthan gum, adjust salt and reserve.

GARNISHING AND PLATING

Tear peas
Pea sprouts
Pea blossoms
Cumin powder
Mint sprouts

At the centre of a rectangular plate, set a portion of neck of lamb terrine regenerated at 68°C/154°F. On top, arrange the tear peas —blanched right before serving—add lamb gravy and crisp lamb rack skin. Next to it, serve the pea purée, one pea sprout and one pea flower. On the other side, serve the Serrat sheep cheese Parmentier. Garnish with a few drops of mint gel, a pinch of cumin powder and a mini mint leaf.

SQUAB LIVER
WITH ONION

SERVES 8 PEOPLE

SERVES 8 PEOPLE

COMPOSITION
Squab parfait
Breast of squab
Caramelised walnut
Onion gel
Onion sponge cake
Onions

—SQUAB PARFAIT
YIELDS 300 G

300 g squab livers
10 g extra virgin olive oil
10 g butter
150 g butter
60 g chicken stock
1.25 g iota
Salt

Soak the squab livers with abundant iced water for 12 hours, changing the water every 3 hours. Wash well and strain.

In a frying pan with the 10 g olive oil and 10 g butter, brown the livers on both sides for 5 minutes. Place the livers into a Thermomix bowl with the remaining butter at 70°C/158°F for 5 minutes. Run through a fine sieve and adjust salt. Blend the resulting mixture with the chicken stock and iota. Bring to a boil and serve 20 g servings on the plates while hot. Reserve refrigerated.

—BREAST OF SQUAB
YIELDS 8 AIGUILLETTES

8 squab breasts

Seal the breasts of squab in a vacuum pack bag and cook in the Roner at 63°C/145°F for 22 minutes. Blast chill and remove the aiguillette from the squab breasts. Reserve the breasts for a different recipe.

—CARAMELISED WALNUT
YIELDS 110 G

100 g water
60 g sugar
100 g walnuts
40 g icing sugar
Sunflower oil

Place water with sugar in a casserole and bring to a boil. Add walnuts and cook over low heat until very soft, almost translucent. Strain and leave to dry on a silicone mat. Cut each walnut in four and dust with icing sugar. Fry in sunflower oil at 180°C/356°F until brown and crisp. Remove from oil and place on kitchen towels. Reserve.

—ONION GEL
YIELDS 250 G

1 kg onions
500 g water
2 g xanthan gum
Salt

Julienne the onion and cook in oil until it turns golden brown (about 250 g will remain). Add the water, boil over low heat and reduce to half. Strain, add xanthan gum, purée and adjust salt. Reserve.

—ONION SPONGE CAKE
YIELDS 400 G

120 g sweated onion (basic recipes, p.428)
125 g egg whites
80 g egg yolks
80 g isomalt
Salt
20 g plain flour
2 g baking powder

Mix all the ingredients with a hand blender and run through a fine chinois. Introduce the mixture into a ½ litre whipped cream dispenser and add 3 chargers, shaking continuously. Refrigerate the whipped cream dispenser for 12 hours. Transfer the mixture into microwave safe plastic moulds and cook on the highest setting for 1 minute. Leave to stand and remove from the moulds.

Store in an airtight container until garnishing and plating.

—ONIONS

4 shallots
1 Figueres onion
4 spring onions
Salt

Cook the shallots unpeeled, starting with cold water, and bring to a boil. Cook for 5 minutes and cool in a cold bain-marie. Peel the shallots, cut them in half with a paring knife and reserve half a shallot for each plate.

Blanch the Figueres onion 5 times, starting with cold water, and cook in a pressure cooker with abundant water for 5 minutes, adding salt to taste. Remove from the cooker and cool in a cold bain-marie. Peel and cut onions into 0.3x1-cm-long strips. Reserve 3 strips for each plate.

Only the white part of the spring onions will be used. Cut onions 1.5 cm long and blanch in boiling water, adding salt to taste. Cool the onions in a cold bain-marie, cut in half to use one half for each plate, and reserve.

GARNISHING AND PLATING

Orange peel confit cubes (basic recipes,
    p.427)
Juniper powder
Curled chives
Rosemary flowers

Heat the plate with the set squab parfait and
cover it with the poached onion jelly. On top of
the jelly, set half a shallot, half a spring onion,
2 strips of Figueres onion and the onion
sponge cake, then crown with the squab
aiguillette, preheated on the salamander for
a few seconds. Around the parfait, arrange
2 dots of onion jelly, 3 pieces of caramelised
walnut and 1 cube of orange peel confit, and
dust with juniper powder. Garnish with curled
chives and rosemary flowers.

FIGS WITH FOIE

COMPOSITION
Cooked foie
Fig purée
Foie soup
PX veil
Stuffed figs

—COOKED FOIE
YIELDS 300 G

300 g foie gras
22.5 g Pedro Ximénez
1 g Sichuan pepper
Salt

Seal foie gras in a vacuum pack bag with the Pedro Ximénez, salt, and Sichuan pepper. Cook in the Roner for 30 minutes at 65°C/149°F. Next, remove from the bag and set on a baking sheet to remove the veins. Adjust salt. Cool the foie down slightly and blend to a smooth purée in the Thermomix. Reserve in a piping bag.

—FIG PURÉE
YIELDS 350 G

500 g fresh figs

Peel the figs to obtain the pulp. Mash to a smooth purée and reserve.

—FOIE SOUP
YIELDS 350 G

250 g foie gras
75 g chicken stock (basic recipes)
50 g cream
25 g Pedro Ximénez
Sichuan pepper
Salt

Sear the foie on both sides without overbrowning, add chicken stock, cream, PX, and salt and pepper to taste. Boil and blend. Run the mixture through a fine chinois, cool and reserve.

—PX VEIL
YIELDS 35 UNITS

200 g Pedro Ximénez
1 g agar-agar
½ gelatine sheet
Glycerine

Grease a 30x40 cm tray with a few drops of glycerine and reserve.

Mix the PX with the agar-agar and bring to a boil; remove from heat, cool down and, when the temperature reaches 35°C/95°F, add the gelatine sheet, previously hydrated. Pour the mixture into the glycerine-coated tray and leave to set. When the PX solidifies, use a pastry cutter about 5 cm in diameter to cut the veil and reserve on the same tray.

—STUFFED FIGS
YIELDS 2 STUFFED FIGS

2 fresh figs
Cooked foie (previously prepared)
PX veil (previously prepared)

Peel the figs and, with a very sharp knife, cut into 4 horizontal layers. Using a piping bag, cover each fig sheet with an approximately 0.5-cm-thick layer of cooked foie, then reconstruct the fig by joining the different layers, and wrap it in film, pressing lightly to compact. Leave to stand refrigerated until the foie has cooled down.

Carefully cut the reconstructed fig in four and cover each quarter with a disc of PX veil. Reserve refrigerated.

GARNISHING AND PLATING

24 truffle sheets
Purple basil flowers

Draw a tear shape on the base of the plate with the fig purée; arrange a quarter of a stuffed fig and 3 sheets of truffle on the side. Garnish with a few drops of foie soup and purple basil flowers.

VEAL TENDONS WITH MUSHROOMS AND HAZELNUTS

COMPOSITION

Veal tendons and gravy

Texturised stock made with golden enoki stems

Hazelnuts

Curled chives

—VEAL TENDONS AND GRAVY

8 veal tendons (approximately 10 cm long)
6 g salt
3 kg water
100 g beeg gravy (basic recipes, p.428)

Clean veal tendons and eliminate the fat and any lean parts they may have. Leave in a container with iced water for 24 hours to soak, changing the water every 6 hours.

Blanch the tendons 3 times starting with cold water. Reserve.

Fill a stockpot with 3 litres of water, and add the salt and tendons; bring to a boil, skim to remove any impurities that may float to the surface and cook for 4 hours over medium-low heat until soft. Remove the tendons from the water, drain well, place them in a baking tray lined with greaseproof paper, without touching each other, and cool quickly.

Using a paring knife, round the ends of the tendons to 1 cm in diameter, then divide them into 1.5-cm-thick slices. Seal the tendons into a vacuum pack bag, without overlapping, and add the reduced veal gravy. Cook in the Roner at 90°C/194°F for 1 hour. Next, remove the vacuum pack bags from the thermal bath and blast chill. Reserve.

—TEXTURISED STOCK MADE WITH GOLDEN ENOKI STEMS
YIELDS 180 G

400 g enoki golden mushrooms
200 g water
0.3 g xanthan gum
Salt

Remove the caps from the enoki mushrooms and reserve for garnishing.

Boil the water in a casserole and add golden enoki stems, cover and infuse for 15 minutes. Run through a sieve, add xanthan gum to the resulting stock and blend with a hand blender. Adjust salt and reserve.

—HAZELNUTS
YIELDS 16 QUARTERS

4 hazelnuts

Roast the hazelnuts in the oven at 170°C/338°F for 8 minutes. With a dry, clean cloth, rub them together to easily remove the skin. Quarter the hazelnuts and reserve.

—CURLED CHIVES

4 chive stems
500 g water

Divide chive stems lengthwise into 2 to 3 sections, submerge in an iced water bath for a few minutes until they curl. Remove from the water, and they are ready to use.

GARNISHING AND PLATING

Chervil leaves
Baby mustard leaves
Basil blossoms
Hazelnut oil
Golden enoki caps

Heat the texturised stock made with golden enoki stems. Regenerate the vacuum packed tendons in the Roner at 63°C/145°F until they are very hot.

Add the enoki caps previously reserved to the golden enoki stems stock.

Remove the tendons from the vacuum pack bags, strain excess stock and set 3 pieces of tendons in a soup dish; then add golden enoki stems stock with the caps facing down so they look like lentils. Add 4 quarters of roasted hazelnuts and 4 drops of hazelnut oil. Garnish with the curled chives, a few leaves of chervil, basil blossoms and baby mustard.

BABY SQUIDS
WITH ONION ROCK

SERVES 8 PEOPLE

COMPOSITION

Baby squids
Onion and ink rock
Potato and ink purée
Baby squid sauce

—BABY SQUIDS
YIELDS 3 BABY SQUIDS PER PLATE

24 baby squids
Brine for fish (basic recipes, p.429)

Clean baby squids, submerge them in brine for 1 minute, and strain. Seal in a vacuum pack bag. Before serving, cook in the Roner at 55°C/131°F for 5 minutes. Remove from the bag and serve.

—ONION AND INK ROCK
YIELDS 215 G

60 g onion confit
60 g egg whites
40 g egg yolks
40 g isomalt
10 g plain flour
1 g baking powder
1 g salt
Squid ink

Mix all the ingredients with a hand blender and run through a fine chinois. Introduce the mixture in a ½ litre whipped cream dispenser with 2 chargers and leave to stand refrigerated.

Transfer the mixture into microwave safe plastic moulds and cook on the highest setting for 1 minute. Leave to stand, remove from the moulds and reserve.

—POTATO AND INK PURÉE
YIELDS 990 G

600 g potatoes
125 g milk
2.5 g ink
250 g butter
10 g salt

Roast and peel potatoes, then run them through a fine sieve to obtain a lump-free purée.

Place the potato purée in a bowl with warm milk and squid ink, and mix well, then add the butter slowly. Adjust salt and reserve.

—BABY SQUID SAUCE
YIELDS 150 G

350 g tentacles and fins from a medium-sized squid
50 g extra virgin olive oil
100 kg mirepoix (basic recipes, p.427)
400 g water
50 g butter
Salt

In a frying pan, heat the olive oil and brown the fins and tentacles, chopped irregularly, on both sides; deglaze with a dash of water and strain. Repeat this process twice more with the same squid. Place the resulting liquid and browned squid in a casserole together with the mirepoix, add the remaining water and cook for 1 hour, skimming when necessary. Reduce to half, strain and reserve. Before serving, adjust salt and blend together with the butter, trying to form some air. Keep very hot.

GARNISHING AND PLATING

Matcha green tea powder
Pistillata seaweed

Arrange the purée as a base for the plate, and place the onion and ink rock on top. Sprinkle green tea on the rock and stick pistillata seaweed sprigs in it. Spread the baby squids around the rock, foam the sauce, and serve on top of the baby squids.

litera-
ture

**The influence
of classic and modern
culinary literature in
the dishes of El Celler**

Reading the classics opens the door to making revisions and facilitates the emergence of new ideas. Let's imagine pigeon with bay leaves and acorns; partridge with chestnuts; robin with snails, or grapes and olives, and with its fat, elder and juniper; woodcock with fig tree leaves; song thrush marinated with bay leaf, roasted with vine leaves; mallard with seaweed; rooster with sloe sauce... All of them dishes inspired by the cookery book, *Teatro venatorio y coquinario gallego* by Castroviejo, Cunqueiro and Álvarez Montenegro. Likewise, when reading *L'art du bien manger* by Edmond Richardin, wild quail with orange, wheat and barley comes to mind. Culinary literature has always been a source of inspiration in our cuisine. Not only as an academic and cultural contribution, but also in practical terms. This is why we want to pay homage to some of the fundamental, classic, modern and contemporary international manuals that have influenced us and enrich our kitchen.

JOAN, JOSEP AND JORDI ROCA

MEDIEVAL EUROPEAN CULINARY LITERATURE

In order to approach a reflection on culinary literature, we must look for the origins of the genre in two essential works: *De re coquinaria* by Coelius Apicius and *Naturalis Historia* by Pliny the Elder (the latter for the gastronomic references it contains).

Next, however, we jump ahead in time to medieval Europe in search of the reference books that laid the foundations for cooking in the Old Continent at the time.

France has yielded some cookery books like the collection of *Le viander Sion,* (written in the late 13th century, it is one of its oldest manuscripts), *Le petit traité* (trade manuscript from the 14th century), *Livre fort excellent de cuisine* (edited later as *Le grand cuisinier*) or *Le ménagier de Paris* (from the late 14th century). **Italy**, not counting some fragments, has three: *Anonimo toscano* (manuscript from the 15th century), *Anonimo veneziano* (from the late 15th century) and *Libro de arte coquinaria* by Master Martino da Como (15th century).

As for contemporary books about medieval times, some of the highlights are: *La gastronomie au Moyen Age* by Odile Redon, Françoise Sabban and Silvano Serventi, which gathers 150 recipes from France and Italy. Also the book *A tavola nel Rinascimento,* by the same gastronomic historians, Sabban and Serventi. Let's also remember *L'arte della cucina in Italia,* the anthology of Italian gastronomic literature from the Middle Ages to this day and age that inspired our insolence in reinterpreting charcoal-grilled oysters. "Oysters taste better if dressed with a dash of oil and are heated over charcoal in half of their shell. Rich and lustful people who eat them raw don't know this," writes Leonardo da Vinci during the Renaissance. In our restaurant, we cook them on the grill with ginger and also a dash of oil and orange segments. Lastly, *La scienza in cucina e l'arte di mangiar bene,* by Pellegrino Artusi, is an Italian cookery book from a later time (1891) but important because of its culinary history.

There are no known cookery books in the Spanish or Occitan languages prior to the 16th century.

From **Germany** we know *Daz Buch von guter Spise* (manuscript from the second half of the 15th century). **England** is the country with the greatest collection of medieval cooking manuscripts. The most important: *The Form of Cury* (from the late 14th century), *Ancient Cookery* (from 1381), *Harleian ms.279* (from around 1435).

With regard to the type of cuisine these cookery books represent, in general, the bases are similar to those of our medieval gastronomy. That is, cooking takes place in a home kitchen with similar techniques and analogue basic dishes (roast – pot – pie). These books reflect the taste of the privileged class. There are some courtly dishes common throughout Christian Europe; of course, ingredients vary depending on geography, adapting them to the region.

HARE: *FAISANDAGE OUI, FAISANDAGE NON...*

Dishes like hare have made us look back at the masters and analyse the academic techniques of the *faisandage,* considered unwise in the following examples:

> —*"Le lièvre peut être mangé frais, au boit du fusil ou si on l'a laissé refroidir, après deux ou trois jours de mortification, selon la saison; il ne doit jamais être faisandé. On ne fait pas faisander le lièvre, qui s'altère, au bout de quarante-huit heures"* (*Larousse gastronomique,* 1938, 1967-1984,1996)

> —*"Surtout ne jamais faisander le lièvre, qui doit être mangé frais"* (A. Guillot, 1976)

> —*"Ce gibier doit être mangé frais, car il a tendance à se corrompre facilement"* (P. Bocuse, 1973)

All of them and many others support a single idea: one should never *faisander* —that is, hang—the hare. We agree, but we also like to think of Josep Pla dedicating it a few lines in *El que hem menjat,* concerned by the sarcolactic acid secreted by the animal when it is killed while performing muscular exercises and the unwillingness of the people of this country to eat meat somewhat rotten: "The only way to eliminate the effects of said acid is to *faisander* the hare, that is: to transform them into a light microbial infection that substitutes the stiffening of the animal for a softness in its meat—that distends and un-stretches it, put in plain words. There is no other way to achieve these results but to hang the animal on the nail of the pantry door for a certain amount of time—never in the refrigerator—like they do in France, where they have a certain understanding of this [...]. That is, once it's properly *faisandée,* the slightly rotten animal must be transferred into a stock pot—I use this word now because it's the one people are most bothered with [...]. If a certain amount of people don't appreciate game meat cooking, they are better off eating confits."

We haven't always listened to the content of the delicious prose of the brilliant writer from Palafrugell. Pla's opinion, as scholar Jaume Coll would say, is obviously out of date, stale, and more attuned to the tastes of a different time. The only objection is that one cannot generalise. Each game animal, furred or feathered, needs a different waiting time before cooking. Hare and quail, the sooner the better; where as woodcock, within one to three weeks. Curnosky (Maurice Edmond Sailland) in *Souvenirs littéraires et gastronomiques* (1958) explains that during his adolescence (by the end of the 19th c.) there were many people expressing vehement passion for game in advanced state of decomposition. Tastes evolve, without a doubt. Or at least change. And to a great extent in this field.

We, at El Celler, apply long cooking times to hare and let the meat soften and hydrate slowly with all of its flavour. Nothing is lost, everything is gained. But we preserve the aiguillette to charcoal-grill with holm oak and love.

WOODCOCK

We cook the long-beaked queen of the forest, the woodcock, after ten days of *faisandage,* previously roasted to let the nuances of the Maillard reaction settle in. The breast tissue softens slowly and it keeps the unique and delicate texture of the brain. We can exhibit the excellence of the aiguillette, the inner part of the breast of birds: a sort of well-formed fillet between the carcase and the coarser and rougher part of the breast. We truly value this part that hides under the breast and, as soon as we have a chance, we love to show it on top of a brioche with its entrails. We also like to work the entrails with current academic formalism, because tastes evolve. The parfait, the pâté, the entrail purée... are always present in the cuisine of El Celler. That original SQUAB PARFAIT WITH JUNIPER AND CORIANDER has been surpassed in technical, craftsmanship and nuance complexity by the squab parfaits, the squab brioche, the turtledove, the woodpidgeon, or the thrush pâté. Our attempt is to preserve the syntactic power of the animal.

Once in a while we cook a *rara avis,* such as a wild quail, and we dream of one day seeing again in our pot a flycatcher or the ortolan served on a cold and metallic January day in the no longer existent restaurant Drolma, with Fermí Puig and Jaume Coll, that will always stay in our memory. We accompany it with a restorative 1942 Laverdolive armagnac. *Pas mal!*

It was precisely Jaume Coll who crafted and narrated *El crepúsculo de la becada* (2004), an account for a symposium at Ca l'Enric, a restaurant specialising in game, that is part of our life like an unforgettable and enriching, as well as educated, anthropological, loving dialogue. An after-dinner conversation where an ornithologist, some hunters, cooks, sommeliers and writers expressed their opinions and unknowingly intertwined the prelude to an essay that overflows with sensitivity, tradition, wisdom and rapture about the beauty of the mysterious woodcock. The art of conversation, a space of friendly respite and cultural activity with a common thread: the woodcock.

THE ROYALES

Cooking 'à la royale' is to us a sort of pinnacle in educated (classic) culinary art in the West.

We start with two classic versions of different geographic backgrounds, from the French school: Périgord (*La bonne cuisine du Périgord,* 1929) and Poitou (*Les soupes de la cour,* 1755). The first is shaped as a Swiss roll with foie and truffle. The image of a hare à la royale served with a Château Beaucastel 1985 at the former Lucas Carton restaurant (now Senderens, in Paris), leaves an indelible mark and represents a moment of beauty in academic cuisine. It enacts the grandeur of an indestructible cuisine. The second recipe, that of Poitou, part of great simplicity and modesty: instead of foie and truffle, garlic, wine and shallots. And it is precisely that austerity, the appearance of a humble dish, what makes it fascinating. It is the hare for itself, without embellishments.

The dish (*Lièvre à la royale*) was documented for the first time in 1886 in *L'Art culinaire,* a prestigious Parisian magazine. We owe Poitou's version to Aristide Couteaux, a senator from Poitiers who wrote it in the newspaper *Le Temps* in 1898. Both Bocuse (1973) and Robuchon (1986) make a definitive and brilliant contribution. The *Larousse gastronomique* encyclopedia, in its three editions of sixty years (1938, 1967, 1996), takes on the important mission of leaving proof of the recipe and its history.

The approach of El Celler is a complex and integrating dish that derives from both schools, not wanting to relinquish anything and hoping to project its academic magnitude and complexity in a single dish. Declination. Craftsmanship. The HARE A LA ROYALE is served over a bed made of this type of hare pie, with a quenelle of hare in the style of Poitou with beetroot, female hare thighs cooked over low heat with cinnamon, and the thermal effect of ginger and a hare loin seared on the charcoal grill, accompanied with a charcoal-grilled raspberry coulis. The garnish is an essential foam made from the poetic SOIL DISTILLATE and the crown jewel of the forest, truffle. Airs of grandeur, academic culture and an obstinate claim to the earth and its taste, its richness. Yes, Mr. Pla, a landscape dish on the casserole. The SOIL DISTILLATE takes us to the forest, next, we can go looking for the hare...

THE INFLUENCE OF HISPANIC-ARABIC CUISINE AND CULINARY LITERATURE
IN THE SPANISH LANGUAGE

The cuisine of **Muslim Spain** is one of the ways in which Roman and Visigoth cuisine evolved, and shares some similarities with Catalan cuisine due to their common roots rather than mutual influence.

The study of this Hispanic-Arabic cuisine comes to us from two extensive cookery books: one anonymous and incomplete, published and translated into Spanish by Huici Miranda, and the other by Ibn Razin, titled *Fadalat Al-jiwan*. The first was written by an Andalusian in the first third of the 13th century; the second by an author from Murcia around 1230. Their characteristics show a preference for sweets and spices. Products such as ñora peppers and paprika give way to colourful dishes and sauces, such as *romesco*, *xató*, *salvitxada*, *allipebre*, *salmorreta*, among others. According to linguist Joan Coromines, the terms *xató* and *romesco* come from Arabic-Catalan.

From our time spent at the Culinary Arts School we highlight the books by Ignasi Domènech, *La nueva cocina elegante española*, from 1915, a practical manual that was our bible for many years; *Arte de cocina*, by Álvaro Cunqueiro Mora, and *Arte de la caza*, by José María Castroviejo Blanco Cicerón, show us how one person can capture the attention of the highest experts with beautiful, orderly writing and popular gastronomic wisdom.

The more professional books, such as the "Pellaprats" (works by Henry-Paul Pellaprat, author of the famous *Modern French Culinary Art*) and the *Prácticos* (several editions of a work by Ramon Rabasó originally written in the first quarter of the 20th century), are extremely useful because they are not recipe collections, but mainly deal with analysis of combinations. They explore the period of the great cuisine of Auguste Escoffier, which tried to homogenise concepts on an

international scale, so that the same dish could be found at the Ritz in Paris, the Ritz in London, or even the Savoy or the Palace. Chefs follow a single pattern, reproduced identically in these books. With these manuals we learn the basic sauces, stocks, bases and garnishes that have names and surnames and that are still current: the Parmentier comes from this time and we still use it.

We very often use this academic cuisine because we've had to work with it extensively, we've had to explain it, and it is very much present in our culinary ideas. But as time goes by we tend to speak of a chickpea purée instead of a garbure, as we used to call it; that has always been our way of seeing things. Now, for example, in order to make a chickpea stock we reduce more than half of the water used to boil the chickpeas and keep the essence of the chickpeas—their stock. That is how we try to extol the spirit of the books we carry in our baggage.

CATALAN MEDIEVAL CUISINE AND THE *LLIBRE DE SENT SOVÍ*

Medieval Catalan cuisine was very influential in Europe, proof of which is its footprint in Italy, in the Languedoc and Provence regions.

The *Llibre de Sent Soví* is one of our most widely read classics. We keep the edition by Rudolf Grewe —dedicated to Joan by his friend (and the author's niece) Rosa Maria Esteva from Grupo Tragaluz: "So you can see how my fondness comes from afar"—like a treasure. Noticeably, since the publication in 1979 of the critical edition of *Llibre de Sent Soví*, by Grewe (1924-1994), studies on medieval cuisine in the old Crown of Aragon have gathered momentum. It represents the first all-encompassing view of Catalan cuisine in the 14th and 15th centuries, an image that is in many ways still valid today. The publication two years prior of the *Llibre del Coch: Tractat de cuina medieval*, by master Ruperto de Nola, was influential in enriching our knowledge of medieval gastronomy. It was the year of 1977, we were starting to become interested in cooking and began, intuitively and with great curiosity, a process of acknowledgement of the footprint of culture. The base of which was knowledge within our reach.

The *Llibre de Sent Soví*, by an unknown author, is a delicious example of the exquisite use of the language, without a single foreign word, loyal to Catalan literature of the time, and decidedly interesting in linguistic terms. The ingredients available then are still current in contemporary cuisine. It doesn't include sous-vide cooking, but we have kept some culinary techniques such as *perbullir* (submerging something in boiling water for a short period of time, or sprinkling it with boiling water; similar to blanching) or *sosengar* (frying a product with a dash of oil or fat on low heat, which became the sofrito with the arrival of tomato and peppers, one of the bases of cooking today).

We know Catalan cuisine is of great importance in the 14th and 15th centuries. The numerous dishes in the Catalan style that appear in foreign cookery books attest to this. As an example, Renaissance Italian gourmet Bartolomeo Platina (1475) said: "Catalan *mig-raust*. Catalans, who are very distinguished and brilliant people, are not very different in mental and physical abilities to Italians, they have a dish called *mig-raust* [...]. I don't remember having eaten anything so

tasty with my friend Vallischara." Francesc Eiximenis expresses the opinion that "the Catalan nation was an example for all Christian peoples in their honest food and moderate drinking; and evidently, it is all true: Catalans are the most tempered men in their way of living in the world" (Eix., Ch. 29).

The factors that contributed to shaping this cuisine were the political strength of Catalan countries in those centuries, their economic prosperity, extensive financial trading in the Mediterranean, the excellence of their agricultural and stockbreeding products, as well as the inventiveness and refinement of Catalan men.

In an attempt to better define the Catalan cuisine that is the bedrock of our cookery at El Celler, we can describe it as part of Western Christian cuisine —with a fireplace, roasts and pots, and old Roman ovens. At the same time, it is enriched by Arabic contributions and Mediterranean products, which it incorporates with much refinement. It's a cuisine that makes generous use of almonds and onion, mild elements that round off stews and sauces; that savours the sweet-and-sour and light and fiery spices like ginger; and that sprinkles roasts and stews with drops of bitter orange or rose water.

The best of Catalan cuisine are, undoubtedly, its stews and sauces, characterised by their diversity and excellence and because, fortunately, they have preserved the *Sent Soví* for us. But it also has an excellent repertoire of desserts, creams, turron, marzipans and sweetened fruits.

JEWISH HERITAGE: GIRONA

If Catalans, together with the rest of the Latin people, eat cod—a remote, Nordic product—it is due to an old religious principle: Lent. Then, in order to get to know our own roots, we must approach the Jewish legacy; Sephardic cuisine helps us understand better the culinary habits of the Jewish people. For some time, we prepared some special menus of Sephardic cuisine to participate in the promotion of the Jewish quarter of Girona. We have good memories of that experience, which expanded our culinary vision of some products, like aubergine.

MODERN CULINARY LITERATURE IN CATALAN LANGUAGE

La cuynera catalana from 1850 contains, paradoxically, combinations that would seem modern today and

were daring in the past, such as mixing orange and cloves. It is a sort of compilation of gastronomic transversal creations in a period when Catalan cuisine was merging with French and Italian. It was the cuisine being prepared in the large bourgeois establishments of Barcelona, influenced by large restaurants in the making and great hotels from the early 1900s, such as the Ritz. Although the book was published previously, it was all gestating already, and it was precisely the beginning of Modernism. The book contains surprising and everyday things, recent and contemporary, but that have been around for many years, like preparations with butter, beurre noisette... It's laudable that all of this could come together in a domestic book: it means that there was a high level of cuisine in Catalonia. So, what do we gather from the book? Well, combinations we never imagined before: red mullets with an orange reduction, reduced fruit sauces, caper purées... The lesson is that we can be inspired by old things that can also be current.

GASTRONOMY IN OUR MOST IMPORTANT PIECES OF LITERATURE

The marvellous prose of Josep Maria de Sagarra, the self-controlled and exquisite poetry of Josep Carner, or Josep Pla disguised as a shrewd peasant. They all have written about cooking: as art, as the essence of the Catalan character, as a *bon vivant* attitude... *Noucentisme*, the Catalan cultural movement of the beginning of the 20th century, should consist of exactly that.

El que hem menjat is a book we like to read because we like how Pla writes, and we are glad to mention that, as an example, we began to prepare the charcoal-grilled prawns we offer today because, according to him, that is the best way to cook them. Never before had we tasted charcoal-grilled prawns! They were always grilled, or fried on a frying pan... But when we tried them his way we realised Pla was right. He assumes his highly dogmatic point of view is shared by everybody, and us chefs don't listen to him, or at least not until we tested his opinion and realised it was correct. We don't agree with many of his statements because of his excessive dogmatism. I'm sure Pla today would not accept techno-emotional cuisine and would call us a lot of loonies. Or maybe not, but in any case, he had a very traditionalist view of cooking.

CONTEMPORARY WRITINGS

From the latest, more recent writings, we can't fail to mention:

· *El libro de la cocina española: gastronomía e historia,* by Néstor Luján (1977)

· *La cocina catalana: el arte de comer en Cataluña,* by Manuel Vázquez Montalbán (Península, 1979)

· *La cuina gironina,* by Jaume Fàbrega (Graffiti Ed., 1985)

· *La cuisine sous vide,* by Georges Pralus (1985)

· *El Bulli: el sabor del Mediterráneo,* by Ferran Adrià and Juli Soler (Empúries, 1993)

· *Les secrets de la casserole,* by Hervé This (Éditions Belin, 1993)

· *Les receptes del Motel Empordà,* by Jaume Subirós (La Magrana, 1994)

· *La cuina catalana,* by Jaume Fàbrega (La Magrana, 1995)

· *La cuina de l'Empordà i la Costa Brava,* by Jaume Fàbrega (La Magrana, 1995)

· *Révélations gastronomiques,* by Hervé This (Éditions Belin, 1995)

· *Fórmules magistrals,* by Narcís Comadira (Empúries, 1997)

· *Los genios del fuego,* by Pau Arenós (Península, 1999)

· *La cocina de Santi Santamaria: la ética del gusto,* by Santi Santamaria (Everest, 2000)

· *Sous-Vide Cuisine,* by Joan Roca and Salvador Brugués (Montagud Editores, 2003)

· *El crepúsculo de la becada,* by Jaume Coll (Montagud Editores, 2004)

· *On Food and Cooking. The Science and Lore of the Kitchen,* by Harold McGee (Scribner, 2004)

· *La cocina catalana de toda la vida,* by Joan Roca (Viena, 2005)

· *Léxico científico gastronómico,* by Alícia Foundation and El Bulli Taller (Planeta, 2005)

· *Viaje a Francia: rutas literarias y gastronómicas de un viajero singular,* by Néstor Luján (Tusquets Editores, 2005)

· *Corpus culinari de Catalunya,* by The Culinary Institute of Catalonia (Columna, 2006)

· *La cocina de los valientes,* by Pau Arenós (Ediciones B, 2011)

· *Modernist Cuisine: The Art and Science of Cooking,* by Nathan Myhrvold, Chris Young, Maxime Bilet (Taschen Benedikt, 2011)

In the same way kitchens, burners, fires and food are part of our day-to-day, books have nourished, are nourishing and will continue to nourish our work. We do not eat them, yet..., but they enrich every single one of our dishes. In the same manner, we hope this book you now have in your hands nurtures your inventiveness and gastronomic culture. We offer our contribution humbly, but with the spirit of academic formalism we have always hoped to respect. Black over white. At your service.

La Cuisine chez Régis Marcon

ALAIN CHAPEL
LA CUISINE
des recettes

GRANDES CHEFS, PEQUEÑOS COCINEROS

bacalao

THE HEALING CUISINE of CHINA

5500 RECETAS

B

—MEMORY

RUSSIAN SALAD

112

FRIED CALAMARI

113

GREAT CHOCOLATE
BONBON

116

LAMB AND
PA AMB TOMÀQUET

118

ANCHOVY
ESCALIVADA

120

GRAPEFRUIT AND
CAMPARI BONBON

122

ROTISSERIE
CHICKEN TUILE

123

STRAWBERRIES
AND CREAM

124

CARAMEL APPLE

126

We live in evanescence, we are that which vanishes. That which has nothing to cling on to beyond subtle, elusive, fleeting echoes. We are what springs to mind, without evocation, without intention. Unexpectedly, the memory of who we were comes to us through what we ate, the flavours that surface and break through, like a battalion marching into the fog. Coming from a shapeless cloud and disappearing into a different nebula.

Capturing that instant, the flash of a scene from the past, solidifying it. That is one of the cornerstones of El Celler. To open the door and let in anyone who is willing to take this journey. Childhood is paradise only to the extent we can recapture it with an adult view. Everything that shaped (smell and texture) the years when we started tasting, recognizing and capturing combinations, now returns because it has been modified by eyes that are no longer the same. We keep a naïve outlook, modulated by the filter of knowledge, by the force of an emotional rather than melancholic process that distorts in order to reawaken those fleeting instants.

It astonishes us, because the explosion of those hours returns and settles with the fascination of he who evokes, of he who wants to leave proof, who wants to treasure (not to hide, but to establish, to keep) the passage of time. To nurture it, which means to make it tangible, accessible. It means not to recall that which has faded, but to revitalise it.

According to the Roca brothers

When Proust goes 'in search of lost time', he relives the days of happiness and memory through taste. It is the madeleine dipped in lime blossom tea that transports him into the past. Taste awakens our sensations and triggers our memory. And sensations become a promise of pleasure...

In gastronomy, olfactory memory, before taste, is key to arousing emotions. Memories, like little closed drawers full of tiny bits of our history, open in the form of a sensory flash, reactivating all we had stored away but not forgotten, latent but discreetly isolated, asleep... Smell and taste, at specific moments, stimulate the neural networks that transport us to pleasure, to the desire or even the need to bring back a feeling.

So, when we cook we like to bring back our personal memories and past experiences to serve in a dish. And we use our memories as a starting point for some recipes. We come from Can Roca, a restaurant where we practically lived our entire childhood. Our parents maintained a frenzied rhythm at a time in which holidays were frowned upon, and therefore the three of us grew up in the family business. For us, the bar is the memory of the times we shared with our parents, drinking a fizzy drink and eating cockles. This memory lives in our mind as a positive influence. And from here, from this corner of our emotional memory, came the dish CLAMS WITH RED GRAPEFRUIT SORBET AND CAMPARI, and its update in 2007, CLAMS WITH RED GRAPEFRUIT AND CAMPARI. There is no better chef than memory. There is no tastier ingredient than nostalgia...

So, cooking creates a link with the emotional state of those who prepare the dishes, and also those who eat them. This emotional state holds the keys to a subjective and unique experience of pleasure that escapes the conscience and sets off a mechanism woven with familiar as well as mysterious experiences. And it is in this alchemy where we want to place a fundamental cornerstone for our cuisine. The cuisine Pau Arenós once described as "techno-emotional" is what makes us feel we are doing something special. It helps us to connect dishes to memories or carries us through space and time. We create journeys, in great part thanks to Pere Castells, a brilliant and patient chemist who, from Fundació Alícia, contributes his grain of sand in knowledge to make experimentation in cooking more technically sound.

Therefore, by bringing together cooking, science and technique, and thanks to the Rotaval, we can serve not only the usual ingredients in international or local cuisine, but new products that contribute to creating this link between food and the landscapes of our memory. This is, for example, how the soil distillate was born. When tasted, it creates a bridge between the smells of the earth and the mood they elicit. In what we could call the mathematics of aroma, there is the activation of feelings of nostalgia and melancholy, often associated with the smell of wet soil, to the memories of the earth sprinkled with rain, moss in the manger... All in all, to personal experiences and individual memories from our past or childhood. Thanks to science, we meet again with our most intimate and personal history.

To let our heart beat and our memory travel to a paradise of tasty meanings...

In the dining room...

When we were young we served tables on skates and played jokes on our customers, serving them hot ice cream and fish dishes in a bucket. We did it naturally and blatantly, to add a bit of fun to work. We have always taken the same relaxed approach at the school that was the neighbourhood restaurant where we grew up, amongst regular customers you knew were returning to eat day after day, and with whom you would build a relationship that went far beyond the simple act of putting a plate on their table. This tavern-like character is an important legacy we inherited. Not creating tension, or being inflexible, or setting out parameters of extreme obsequiousness, but sincere, direct, simple and, essentially, honest relationships.

Years ago and up until the 90s, service in big restaurants was very ceremonious, cold and even arrogant, anchored in old-fashioned traditions. It was a nearly aristocratic approach in which the maître d' was king and below came his plebeians, who could not talk to the customer freely. The flow chart was blocked, structured in very separate segments and strict rank categories: maître d', second maître d', chef de rang, server, helper... As our social values change, all this is being transformed, the enjoyment of food is democratised and enriched with principles such as closeness, hospitality and generosity. Hierarchies collapse. That is how we like to work at El Celler.

RUSSIAN SALAD

SERVES 8 PEOPLE

COMPOSITION
Potato spherification
Green olive coulis
Vegetables
Tuna oil air

—POTATO SPHERES
YIELDS 35 SPHERES 9 G EACH

150 g roasted potato purée
75 g water
50 g cream
50 g milk
50 g smoked oil
11 g calcium gluconolactate
Salt

Mix all the ingredients in the Thermomix to a
smooth dough. Run the dough through a fine
sieve and fill 2.5 cm spherical moulds with it.
Freeze.

—POTATO SPHERIFICATION
YIELDS 35 UNITS

Potato spheres (previously prepared)
Calcium alginate bath (basic recipes, p.427)
500 g extra virgin olive oil

Submerge frozen potato spheres into an
alginate bath for 4 minutes. Rinse in a water
bath; drain well any water left and store in
a container. Store submerged in extra virgin
olive oil.

—GREEN OLIVE COULIS
YIELDS 350 G

250 g green olives
150 g water from preserved olives

Place olives and their water in the Thermomix
and blend for 10 minutes.
Run through a fine chinois and reserve.

—VEGETABLES
YIELDS APPROXIMATELY 200 G OF VEGETABLE BRUNOISE

90 g carrots
90 g courgettes
40 g perona beans
Salt
Olive oil

Brunoise the vegetables, blanch each type
separately in water with salt, drain and
season with olive oil. Reserve.

—TUNA OIL AIR
YIELDS 150 G

150 g tinned tuna oil
1 g soy lecithin powder

Mix the tuna oil with soy lecithin. Leave to
stand and reserve.

GARNISHING AND PLATING

Heat water in a casserole at 60°C/140°F with
some of the oil from the tinned tuna. Immerse
the spheres in this water, previously thawed
and spherified, for 2 minutes.

Arrange the brunoised vegetables as a
base on the plate, and on top set the potato
spherification, hot, coating it with green olive
coulis.

Froth the tuna oil with the hand blender,
forming some air on the surface, and drop it on
top of the sphere.

FRIED
CALAMARI

SERVES 8 PEOPLE

COMPOSITION
Calamari
Orly batter pearls
Finger lime

—CALAMARI
YIELDS 40 PORTIONS 6 G EACH

250 g clean squid

Prepare a container suitable for liquid nitrogen.

Cut the squid into irregular slices and freeze in the nitrogen. Remove and blend in the Thermomix. Pour the puréed squid into cylindrical 2.5x1 cm moulds and keep in the freezer.

—ORLY BATTER PEARLS
YIELDS 400 G RAW BATTER / 200 G COOKED BATTER

225 g plain flour
0.5 g baking powder
175 g cold water
Yellow food colouring
1 litre extra virgin olive oil
Salt

In a bowl, mix the flour, baking powder, cold water and, lastly, the food colouring. Leave mixture to stand for 1 hour, refrigerated. Next, transfer to a squeeze bottle.

Heat the olive oil in a casserole until it reaches 170°C/338°F. Using the squeeze bottle, let drops of mixture fall into the oil to form crisp pearls of orly batter. Drain excess oil and adjust salt. Reserve in a dry place.

—FINGER LIME
YIELDS 13 G

1 (30 g) finger lime (*Citrus australasica*)

Cut off the tips of the lime and peel it, cut it in half lengthwise and carefully squeeze out the citrus pearls by applying light pressure to the pith (white part). Separate 16 pearls for this plate and reserve the rest for other recipes.

GARNISHING AND PLATING

1 oblaat sheet 45x32 cm

Cut the oblaat sheet into 9x2 cm strips.

Remove the squid cylinders from their moulds and, while still frozen, half roast them with a blow torch. Wrap them in the oblaat strips leaving 1 cm on top. Fill the remaining space with fried orly batter pearls. Garnish with 1 g of finger lime pearls per serving.

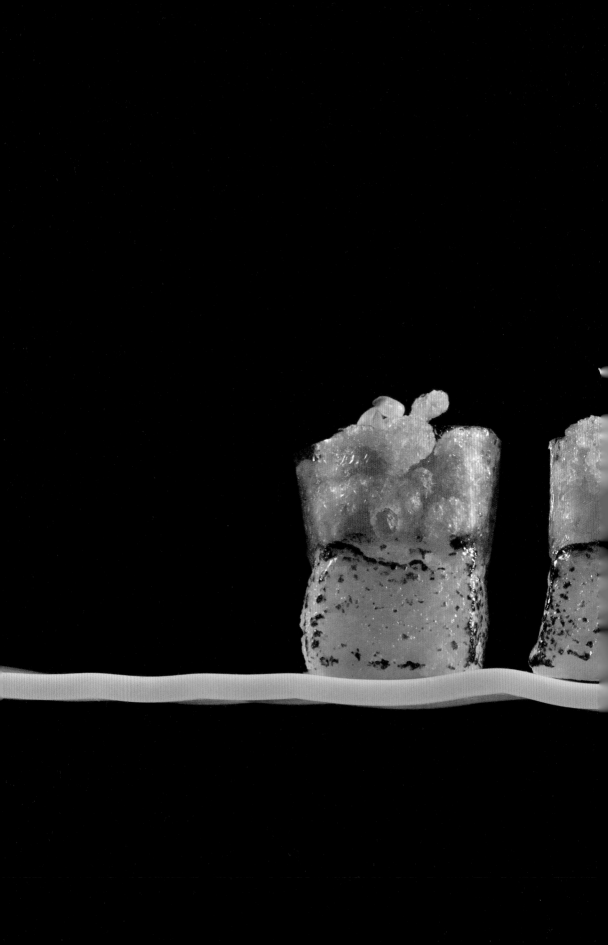

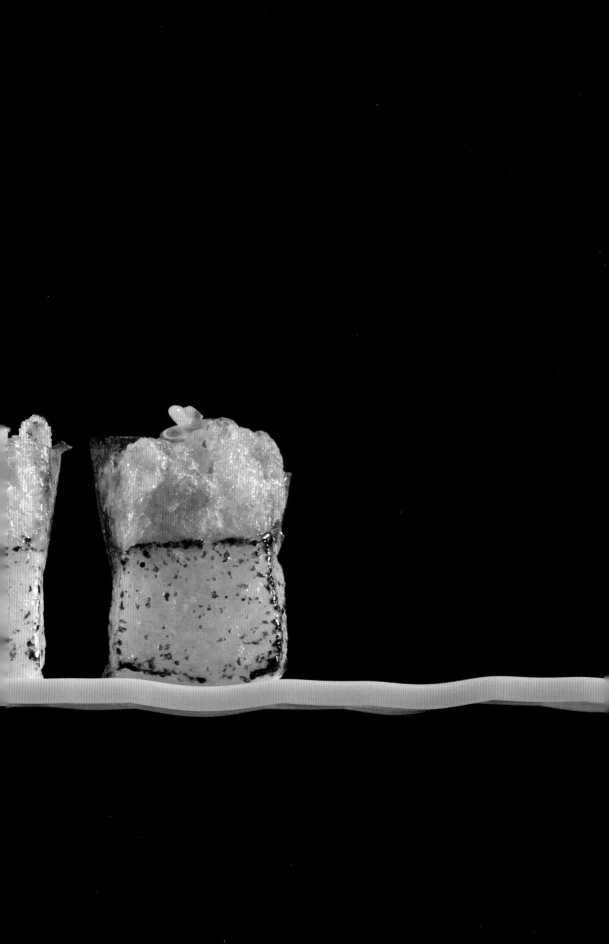

GREAT CHOCOLATE BONBON

COMPOSITION

Chocolate cake
Praline shots
Chocolate coulis
Chocolate shots
Blown sugar sphere
Chocolate coating
Bonbon foam
Chocolate sorbet

—CHOCOLATE CAKE
YIELDS 650 G

100 g butter
240 g couverture chocolate 64%
150 g pasteurised egg yolks
225 g pasteurised egg whites
50 g sugar

Heat the butter and chocolate in the microwave until they reach 45°C/113°F; leave to stand for 5 minutes and blend the mixture. Mix with the egg yolks and reserve.

Whisk the egg whites with the sugar to a smooth froth. Add the mixture previously reserved carefully, without letting it go grainy. Empty in a 25x20 cm baking tin and bake at 180°C/356°F for 5 minutes, then lower temperature to 160°C/320°F and finish baking for 15 more minutes.

—PRALINE SHOTS
YIELDS 250 G

250 g cream
50 g hazelnut praline
1 gelatine sheet
5 g glycerine

Boil the cream with the hazelnut praline and, when the temperature drops to 40°C/104°F, add the gelatine sheet previously hydrated and the glycerine; leave to cool.

Prepare a container with liquid nitrogen.

Put the mixture in squeeze bottles and let drops fall into the nitrogen. Remove the spheres from the nitrogen as they form, and store in a polystyrene foam container in the freezer.

—CHOCOLATE SHOTS
YIELDS 250 G

250 g cream
50 g couverture chocolate 70%
5 g cocoa powder
1 gelatine sheet
10 g glycerine

Boil the cream with the chocolate and cocoa powder, and when the temperature drops to 40°C/104°F, add the gelatine sheet previously hydrated and the glycerine; leave to cool.

Prepare a container with liquid nitrogen.

Put the mixture in squeeze bottles and let drops fall into the nitrogen. Remove the spheres from the nitrogen as they form, and store in a polystyrene foam container in the freezer.

—CHOCOLATE COULIS
YIELDS 800 G

160 g cream
280 g water
400 g sugar
160 g cocoa

Boil the water, cream and sugar until dissolved; then, mix with the cocoa and cook on low heat until the mixture reaches 103°C/217°F. Check the texture when cold, strain and reserve.

—BLOWN SUGAR SPHERE
YIELDS 45 UNITS

500 g fondant
250 g glucose
250 g isomalt
5 drops 50% citric acid solution

Caramelise sugars at 150°C/302°F, add the citric acid and bring temperature to 160°C/320°F. Spread the syrup on a silicone mat and pull 15 to 20 times to homogenise the heat. Cut the sweet while it's still hot and form 2 g balls.

Heat the tip of the blowing pump, insert into the ball, previously heated, and blow until forming a ball of the desired size, trying to stretch the sugar as thinly as possible. Reserve in a moisture-proof cupboard or in an airtight container with silica gel.

—CHOCOLATE COATING
YIELDS 600 G

300 g cocoa butter
300 g couverture chocolate 70%

Melt cocoa butter and couverture, leave to temper and blend the mixture. When the temperature of the mixture has dropped to 30°C/86°F, use it to coat the sugar spheres. Reserve in a moisture-proof cupboard or in an airtight container with silica gel.

—BONBON FOAM

YIELDS 750 G

300 g cream
80 g milk
50 g sugar
0.5 g xanthan gum
60 g pasteurised egg yolks
200 g couverture chocolate 64%
25 g couverture chocolate 70%
25 g hazelnut praline
60 g pasteurised egg whites

Bring the cream and milk to a boil, add sugar, xanthan gum, egg yolks and mix well with a stick hand blender. Pour the mixture over the couvertures and praline; leave to stand for 5 minutes. When the mixture reaches 4°C/39°F, add the egg whites and run again through the hand blender to obtain a smooth cream. Transfer to a 1 litre whipped cream dispenser with 3 chargers. Reserve refrigerated.

—CHOCOLATE SORBET

YIELDS 850 G

700 g water
250 g sugar
40 g inverted sugar syrup
150 g couverture chocolate 64%
150 g cocoa powder
60 g glycerine

Boil the water, sugar and inverted sugar syrup. Pour over the couverture and cocoa powder. Mix and, when the temperature drops to 40°C/104°F, add the glycerine, blend and leave to ripen. Run through an ice-cream maker and store in the freezer.

GARNISHING AND PLATING

Gold leaf

Arrange small pieces of the cake on the plate; spread the praline and chocolate shots around the cake. Insert a chocolate sorbet quenelle in the blown sugar sphere and fill it slowly with bonbon foam.

Lastly, crown the sphere with gold leaf and make different-sized drops of chocolate coulis around it.

LAMB AND PA AMB TOMÀQUET

SERVES 4 PEOPLE

COMPOSITION

Suckling lamb and
*pa amb tomàquet**
Lamb gravy
Curdled lamb gravy
Roasted garlic purée
Tomato sofrito

*Catalan *pa amb tomàquet* is bread rubbed with
ripe tomato, then drizzled with olive oil and a
bit of salt. Very popular for sandwiches and to
accompany cured meats or cheese.

—SUCKLING LAMB AND PA AMB TOMÀQUET

YIELDS 4 SQUARES

2 racks of suckling lamb
4 slices of country bread without the crust
1 tomato
Extra virgin olive oil
Brine for meat (basic recipes, p.429)
Salt

Clean the racks and reserve excess meat for other recipes.

Submerge the rest of the rack in brine for 2 hours. Remove from brine and dry. Seal in a vacuum pack bag with olive oil. Cook at 63°C/145°F in the steam oven for 24 hours. This is a precooking procedure, so cool quickly and reserve. Before serving, regenerate at an equal or lower temperature than that used for cooking it, open the bag, bone and set on a griddle pan with the skin facing down to brown slowly.

Place the slices of bread soaked in a mixture of grated tomato juice, olive oil and salt on top of the rack. Cover with a second rack with the brown side facing up, like an inverted sandwich. Apply pressure, leave a few more minutes on the griddle and remove. Cut into squares and serve.

—LAMB GRAVY

YIELDS 250 G

2 kg lamb bones and trimmings
220 kg mirepoix (basic recipes, p.427)
2.5 kg water
1 bay leaf
45 g kuzu thickening agent (basic recipes, p.427)
Salt

Set bones and trimmings on a baking tray and brown at 180°C/356°F for 45 minutes.

When brown, remove excess fat and transfer into a stockpot together with the mirepoix. Cover with the water, add the bay leaf and cook until only 1 litre remains. Strain and remove the bay leaf, reduce to 250 g and bind with kuzu. Adjust salt, strain and reserve.

—CURDLED LAMB GRAVY

YIELDS 180 G

60 g lamb gravy (previously prepared)
120 g extra virgin olive oil

Place the reduced lamb gravy in a casserole and add olive oil. Reserve in a hot bain-marie until plating.

—ROASTED GARLIC PURÉE

YIELDS 300 G

1 garlic bulb
80 g lamb gravy (previously prepared)
20 g water
220 g extra virgin olive oil
Salt

Charcoal-grill the garlic bulb slowly. Make a charcoal-grilled garlic purée and blend it with the water and reduced lamb gravy. Adjust salt and bind with the olive oil. Reserve.

—TOMATO SOFRITO

YIELDS 200 G

500 g ripe Italian plum tomatoes
1 garlic clove
10 g extra virgin olive oil
Salt
Cumin

Blanch and peel the tomatoes, remove their seeds and reserve them until plating. Cut pulp into small cubes. Peel and chop the garlic clove. In a saucepan with olive oil, brown the garlic, add the tomato, and cook slowly. When soft, season with salt and some cumin. Reserve.

GARNISHING AND PLATING

Fresh curly endive
Chicory leaves

In the middle of a plate, draw a tear shape with the roasted garlic purée and add two dots of tomato sofrito. Next, set the rack 'sandwich' with bread and tomato. Complete the dish with the tomato seeds previously reserved, and a leaf of chicory and some curly endive dressed with hot lamb gravy and olive oil, without emulsifying.

ANCHOVY ESCALIVADA

SERVES 8 PEOPLE

COMPOSITION

Aubergine spheres
Onion spheres
Tomato spheres
Green pepper spheres
Charcoal-grilled pepper juice

—AUBERGINE SPHERES

YIELDS 28 SPHERES

250 g charcoal-grilled aubergine purée, sieved
7.5 g calcium gluconolactate
Calcium alginate bath (basic recipes, p.427)

Blend the aubergine purée with the calcium gluconolactate. With a vacuum sealer, extract 100% of the air.

Pour the mixture into 5 cm spherical moulds and freeze.

When frozen, submerge the spheres in the calcium alginate bath and leave for 4 minutes. Remove the spheres carefully, rinse with water and then leave in the dehydrator for 3 hours at 55°C/131°F.

—ONION SPHERES

YIELDS 28 SPHERES

250 g charcoal-grilled onion purée, sieved
7.5 g calcium gluconolactate
0.5 g xanthan gum
Calcium alginate bath (basic recipes, p.427)

Blend the onion purée with the calcium gluconolactate. When it turns into a smooth dough, add xanthan gum and blend for a few more minutes. Extract 100% of the air in the vacuum sealer.

Pour the mixture into 5 cm spherical moulds and freeze.

When frozen, submerge the spheres in the calcium alginate bath and leave for 4 minutes. Remove the spheres carefully, rinse with water and then leave in the dehydrator for 3 hours at 55°C/131°F.

—TOMATO SPHERES

YIELDS 28 SPHERES

250 g charcoal-grilled tomato purée, sieved
7.5 g calcium gluconolactate
0.5 g xanthan gum
Calcium alginate bath (basic recipes, p.427)

Blend the tomato purée with the calcium gluconolactate. When it turns into a smooth dough, add xanthan gum and blend for a few more minutes. Extract 100% of the air in the vacuum sealer.

Pour the mixture into 5 cm spherical moulds and freeze.

When frozen, submerge the spheres in the calcium alginate bath and leave for 4 minutes. Remove the spheres carefully, rinse with water and then leave in the dehydrator for 3 hours at 55°C/131°F.

—GREEN PEPPER SPHERES

YIELDS 28 SPHERES

250 g charcoal-grilled green pepper purée, sieved
7.5 g calcium gluconolactate
0.5 g xanthan gum
Calcium alginate bath (basic recipes, p.427)

Blend the green pepper purée with the calcium gluconolactate. When it turns into a smooth dough, add xanthan gum and blend for a few more minutes. Extract 100% of the air in the vacuum sealer.

Pour the mixture into 5 cm spherical moulds and freeze.

When frozen, submerge the spheres in the calcium alginate bath and leave for 4 minutes. Remove the spheres carefully, rinse with water and then leave in the dehydrator for 3 hours at 55°C/131°F.

—CHARCOAL-GRILLED PEPPER JUICE

YIELDS 250 G

1 kg red peppers

Arrange the peppers whole on a tray, cover the tray with kitchen foil (the juice should remain on the tray, not evaporate) and place on the grill with the embers at a low temperature until they're extinguished (3-4 hours). When the peppers have cooled down, remove them and reserve the juice.

GARNISHING AND PLATING

16 Cantabrian Sea anchovy fillets
Rosemary flowers
Extra virgin olive oil

Heat the spheres and juice lightly. Place one sphere of each flavour in a bowl, together with two anchovy fillets, some rosemary blossoms and some of the pepper juice as a base. Garnish with a few drops of olive oil.

Put the charcoal embers in a casserole, trap the smoke with a cover and quickly transfer to the escalivada plate.

GRAPEFRUIT
AND CAMPARI BONBON

**SERVES 20 PEOPLE
(2 SNACKS PER PERSON)**

COMPOSITION
Grapefruit and Campari filling
Coating

—GRAPEFRUIT AND CAMPARI FILLING
YIELDS 40 SPHERES

125 g sugar syrup (basic recipes, p.428)
1½ gelatine sheets
125 g Campari
250 g pink grapefruit juice

Heat half of the sugar syrup at 35°C/95°F
and dissolve the gelatine sheets previously
hydrated; add to the Campari and grapefruit
juice. Pour the mixture into 2.5 cm spherical
moulds and freeze.

—COATING
YIELDS 250 G

250 g cocoa butter

Melt down the cocoa butter and cover the
bonbons with a thin layer of it. Leave them
refrigerated so that the filling thaws and
liquefies.

GARNISHING AND PLATING

Gold leaf
Place bonbons on a cold plate and
garnish each of them with a flake
of gold leaf.

ROTISSERIE
CHICKEN TUILE

**SERVES 30 PEOPLE
(1 SNACK PER PERSON)**

COMPOSITION

Rotisserie chicken tuile
Rotisserie chicken cream

—ROTISSERIE CHICKEN TUILE
YIELDS 450 G

100 g plain flour
100 g egg whites
100 g isomalt
250 g rotisserie chicken meat
10 g rotisserie chicken fat

In a bowl, mix the flour, egg whites and isomalt to a smooth paste. Add the chicken meat without removing the fat and blend in the Thermomix for 10 minutes at 50°C/122°F, making sure the result is a very smooth paste. Run through a fine sieve and leave to stand refrigerated for 12 hours in a covered container.

Pre-heat the oven at 175°C/347°F.

Using an acetate stencil, make 5x8 cm rectangles on a silicone sheet. Cook them in the oven for 6 minutes, then top with another silicone sheet and cook for 4 more minutes. Leave to cool and reserve in an airtight container.

—ROTISSERIE CHICKEN CREAM
YIELDS 450 G

120 g chicken stock (basic recipes, p.427)
300 g rotisserie chicken skin
150 g rotisserie chicken meat
45 g cream
Salt

Reduce the chicken stock to half.

Mix and blend all the ingredients together to a fine, smooth paste. Adjust salt and reserve.

GARNISHING AND PLATING

Thyme blossoms
1 lemon

Spread some chicken cream between two tuiles, put the snack together and season with some thyme blossoms and grated lemon zest.

STRAWBERRIES AND CREAM

SERVES 8 PEOPLE

COMPOSITION
Cream base
Strawberry gel
Sorbet base
Strawberry sorbet
Boiled sweet
Strawberry infusion
Milk skin

—STRAWBERRY SORBET
YIELDS 600 G

500 g strawberry purée
250 g sorbet base (previously prepared)

Mix both ingredients with a hand blender, run through the ice-cream maker and reserve at -18°C/0°F.

—CREAM BASE
YIELDS 875 G

750 g cream
125 g dextrose
6 gelatine sheets

Heat the cream and dextrose together; add gelatine sheets previously hydrated, and leave to cool. Whisk and reserve.

—STRAWBERRY GEL
YIELDS 500 G

500 g strawberry purée
12 g agar-agar
3 gelatine sheets

Mix the strawberry purée and agar-agar and bring to a boil, then remove from heat. Next, add the gelatine sheets previously hydrated, leave to set, texturise with a hand blender and remove all the air with the vacuum sealer. Reserve.

—SORBET BASE
YIELDS 480 G

200 g water
40 g glucose powder
200 g sugar
35 g dextrose
20 g inverted sugar syrup
5 g SL-29 stabiliser

Put the water, glucose powder, sugar, dextrose and inverted sugar syrup in a casserole; heat the mixture until it reaches 40°C/104°F. Add the stabiliser and whisk vigorously until it reaches 85°C/185°F. Remove from heat, strain and cool. Reserve.

—BOILED SWEET
YIELDS 400 G

100 g isomalt
100 g fondant
100 g glucose
4 drops of red food colouring

Melt the sugars until they reach 160°C/320°F, add red food colouring and mix well. Stretch the syrup on a silicone mat and pull about 20 times, until it turns satiny. Take a small amount and stretch it, forming a thin string. Wrap the sweet around a 5 cm plastic cylinder. Leave to cool and remove the cylinder. Reserve.

—STRAWBERRY INFUSION
YIELDS 250 G

500 g strawberries
50 g sugar

Seal the strawberries and sugar in a vacuum pack bag. Cook in the Roner at 80°C/176°F for 1 hour. Strain and reserve the resulting liquid.

—MILK SKIN
YIELDS 10 MILK SKINS

1 kg whole milk
Single cream

Pour the milk into a 25 cm frying pan and bring to approximately 60°C/140°F, discarding any bubbles that form. A layer of skin will form on the surface. The first layer takes about 15 minutes to form, the following approximately 8 minutes each. Carefully, take the layer of milk out by grabbing it by the middle. Place it on a tray lined with cling film and brushed with single cream; brush also the surface of the milk skin with cream and cover with cling film. Reserve refrigerated until serving.

GARNISHING AND PLATING

Wild strawberries
Pineberries

On a 10x15 cm acetate sheet draw diagonal lines of strawberry gel 0.5 cm apart. Freeze.

Spread a thin layer of the cream base over the acetate containing the frozen strawberry gel, and roll into a cylinder, leaving a hole in the centre. Freeze again and fill the hole with strawberry sorbet.

Arrange a milk skin at the centre of the plate with a few drops of strawberry infusion. On top of the milk skin, set the boiled sweet spiral and the strawberry ice cream inside it. Garnish with wild strawberries and pineberries.

CARAMEL APPLE

SERVES 8 PEOPLE

COMPOSITION
Sugar apple
Apple foam
Apple sautéed with Calvados
Apple compote
Apple jelly
Calvados ice cream

—SUGAR APPLE
YIELDS 500 G

250 g fondant
125 g isomalt
125 g glucose
10 drops 50% citric acid solution
4 drops of red food colouring

Place the fondant, glucose and isomalt
in a stockpot. Heat to 160°C/320°F, lower
temperature to 150°C/302°F and add the
drops of citric acid and red colouring.

Pour sugar quickly over a silicone mat and pull
approximately 20 times until it turns satiny.
While hot, divide the sugar into approximately
2 cm balls. Heat the tip of the blowing pump,
insert into the ball, previously heated, and blow
until forming a ball of the desired size. Shape it
as an apple and reserve in an airtight container
with silica gel, or in a cupboard for sweets.

—APPLE FOAM
YIELDS 750 G

750 g Golden apples
75 g sugar
60 g butter
250 g egg whites

Clean apples well and quarter. Add the sugar
and bake at 140°C/284°F for 35 minutes.
Remove from the oven, blend, sieve and add
the butter while mixing vigorously to a smooth
purée. Leave to cool and, when cold, add
the egg whites. Fill a 1 litre whipped cream
dispenser with the mixture and add 2 chargers.
Reserve.

—APPLE SAUTÉED WITH CALVADOS
YIELDS 400 G

400 g Golden apples
40 g sugar
1 vanilla pod
20 g Calvados
30 g butter

Peel apples and, with a 1 cm parisienne scoop,
scoop out balls of pulp. Make a caramel with
the sugar. Add the vanilla pod and the apple
balls, cooking until soft. Pour in the Calvados
and flambé. Add the butter at the end and
reserve.

—APPLE COMPOTE
YIELDS 750 G

750 g Royal Gala apples
75 g sugar
150 g butter

Clean and peel the apples, then quarter. Cook
in the oven with the sugar until very soft.
Remove from the oven, purée and mix the
apple with butter. Reserve.

—APPLE JELLY
YIELDS 300 G

300 g natural apple juice
3 gelatine sheets

Put 100 g natural apple juice in a casserole
with the gelatine, previously hydrated, until it
melts. Add the remaining juice, mix well and
transfer the mixture to a container to solidify.

—CALVADOS ICE CREAM
YIELDS 1 KG

541 g whole milk
171 g cream
47 g skimmed milk powder
176 g sucrose
9 g cream stabiliser
5 g buttermilk proteins
51 g Calvados

Mix the milk, cream and milk powder, heat to
40°C/104°F and add the sucrose, stabiliser
and proteins. Pasteurize at 85°C/185°F and
cool to 4°C/39°F. Add the Calvados and leave
to ripen. Run through the ice-cream maker and
keep at -18°C/0°F.

GARNISHING AND PLATING

Royal Gala apple julienne

Serve a base of apple compote on the plate.

Arrange some sautéed apple balls on sides, as
well as some apple jelly cubes and some fresh
apple julienne. Lastly, set the caramel apple
filled with foam and a quenelle of Calvados ice
cream on top of the compote.

muse

The muse of El Celler

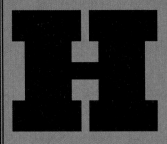

Hanging on the wall at Can Roca is the picture of Àngela Pont Grabuleda, right out of the beauty salon and attired in an evening gown and jewellery. The oil painting is the work of artist Eva Llorens Roca, daughter of Maria Roca, granddaughter of Angeleta, and cousin of Joan, Josep and Jordi Roca Fontané. It was presented to her when the woman, born on 24 August 1912, turned ninety years old; an event celebrated with the whole family.

Angeleta Pont patrolled the burners of Can Roca and strolled around El Celler until her heart gave up on 16 November 2006, at the age of ninety-four. Grandma Angeleta spent nearly her entire life among pots, plates and dining room tables. She either cooked, or served, or picked a random person to chat and explain things to: "I *know* you... your face rings a bell. I've served you food many times." I remember her fried calamari and potato omelette. She never revealed her recipe for the Sunday calamari she made until the very last moment. Her daughter-in-law, Montserrat Fontané, has it; she included it in a book.

Her daughter-in-law, who married Josep Roca i Pont in 1962, gave her three grandsons: Joan, Josep and Jordi. For the youngest, Jordi, "grandma was spontaneity in its purest state." *Pitu*, the middle one, used to play with her: "Grandma was my favourite playmate. We started wars with siphons and flour." For the elder of the three, Joan, she was a source of inspiration, "grandma's presence was enough for me to work joyfully". For the Roca brothers, their grandma was the muse of El Celler. Before she married Joan Roca i Fontané, son of the Reixach family, who owned the Can Reixach tobacconist's shop and inn in Sant Martí de Llémena, Àngela Pont i Grabuleda spent several years of her youth in Can Vador, on the Santa Clara Street in Girona. From the 30s on she worked at the inn owned by her in-laws.

And what did they serve? "At the beginning, in the whole first half of the century, the usual dishes served in inns around the Girona province were blood and liver with onions, tripe and trotters, charcoal-grilled meat, pig's trotters, casserole rice—on Sunday—head and trotters, blood and partridge, lamb with peas, beans with botifarra, or cod in different preparations." She explained they barely got any fresh fish from the sea, except mackerel and sometimes hake. They only had access to river fish: crabs, which they prepared with tomato, and carp and eels they fried or cooked with some sauce.

When her son Josep, a bus driver, and daughter-in-law Montse, a cook who worked with her family in Can Lloret, bought a small establishment in Taialà in 1967, Angeleta was overjoyed to be able to lend a hand in cooking whenever she wanted. That establishment guaranteed the continuation of a hundred-year-old family of restaurateurs and made it possible for El Celler de Can Roca to come into being in 1986. "What did you do for a living, grandma Angeleta?" I asked one day. "Meddling among the burners and feeding people," she replied.

SALVADOR GARCIA-ARBÓS
El Punt. November, 2006

C

—ACADEMIA

C

According to the Roca brothers

Academia offers you a suitcase to start the journey. And then, all of a sudden you realise your luggage is too bulky. It proved useful at the start because when you head into the unknown you always anticipate preventing unwanted surprises, protecting yourself against inclement weather, or any unforeseen shocks. Everything you have in that suitcase at the time of departure is necessary. Later, as you press forward, that luggage becomes too heavy. You drop ballast so that the weight doesn't prevent you from moving on. But there are items you cannot leave behind, that stay with you in spite of the changes and the coming and going of the seasons.

But after all, maybe it was a good idea to depart carrying that entire load. It was necessary that the journey began that way, with so much knowledge, such soundness, and so much history on your back. But it so happens that at El Celler, school has been redesigned, the volume reduced. The essence has remained and the frills disappeared. Now, at the bottom of the suitcase you can still find those pieces you never leave on the side of the road. All the things that endure, that keep you warm when you feel cold, that make you feel comfortable and safe.

Academia facilitates learning and also offers principles with an implicit instruction: they must be subverted. The acquisition of knowledge is only complete when the cook becomes aware that he should not imitate a style, but create his own. "It's very hard work," said Céline. The loftiest challenge.

When we came home from school we helped our parents at the restaurant. When we were children, we stuffed the botifarras, peeled onions for the sofrito, filled flan tins, served, and played with the customers who came so often that they made up a nice family, only bigger than normal. We learnt to respect, share, receive, smile, serve and work while enjoying ourselves. Our childhood passed by among burners and football matches with beer caps and the legs of two chairs as goals, one set at the north end (the main entry to the restaurant) and the other at the south end (the TV stand). It was easy, energetic, spontaneous and exciting.

Going into the Culinary Arts School of Girona proved vital. What we did intuitively at the restaurant of our parents, Can Roca, was something we could actually study! The doors opened to guided knowledge, to the purpose of things. A great deal of what we are now we owe to our academic training, even if only to transgress it later, but from the basis of the knowledge of the subject. It allowed us to nurture our professional education with a solid and structured base and, after much time invested, we gained access to the footprint of bibliographical culture brought about by twenty centuries of gastronomic history. This historical legacy is with us and will remain with us forever, for us to grow and learn from our ancestors and their wisdom. To name them in a hasty order that is likely to be unfair, the books of Pliny the Elder, Apicius, Guillaume Tirel (Taillevent), Eiximenis, Martino, Ruperto de Nola, Savarin, Carême, Scappi and Escoffier are part of the information about taste in Western culinary history we absorbed in school and still revisit.

The richness and literary influence of Catalan cuisine is fascinating. As early as the Middle Ages, we find writings in our language of some of the first and most important European books on the subject. Later, some manuals from the 18th century stand out and, in modern times, *La Cuynera Catalana*, from the 19th century. This is followed by the magnificent 1930s *Llibre de la Cuina Catalana* by Ferran Agulló. Most recently, we cannot ignore the contributions of Manuel Vázquez Montalbán and Josep Pla, the northern Catalan Eliana Thibaut Comelade, the American Colman Andrews, or Néstor Luján, Xavier Domingo, Josep Lladonosa, Jaume Fàbrega, Santi Santamaria, Narcís Comadira, the *Corpus Culinari de Catalunya*, Ferran Adrià and, these days, Pau Arenós and so many others we are failing to include in our list, a list enriched by gastronomic bonanza and good taste.

In school we began the process of shaping our individual personalities and avoided books we then considered somewhat out of sync with the vitality that moved us. We traded the Pellaprat and Escoffier of the first third of the 20th century for Robert Laffont's collection, *Les recettes originales* of the great French cooks of the 70s and 80s: Bocuse, Chapel, and Frédy Girardet's *La cuisine spontanée*. It was a cuisine we saw framed in hotels and the bourgeois atmospheres of the books of the early 20th century, and observed how it looked together with what we were learning: we went to the exhibition of the *nouvelle cuisine française*. We experienced it admiringly and devoured all the books that showed a more direct way of cooking, with a more spontaneous presentation. A live, new, fresh cuisine... We were participants in a splendid era for French gastronomy, the prelude to all the good things we now get to experience in our country's cookery.

In our creative process we have always contemplated closely our academic legacy. Reproductions, reinterpretations, ruptures, inspirations... to enrich a cuisine open to transmitted knowledge. Our TIMBALES OF APPLE AND FOIE (1996) is, in its form, a reproduction of the timbales of Pellaprat, as is the GINGER PEARS TURBAN (2002). The LOBSTER PARMENTIER (1988) has the aesthetics of the French influence of the time, Guérard or Georges Blanc, with whom Joan spent time as an apprentice in the early 90s. The VELOUTÉS, STEAK TARTARE and SOLE MEUNIÈRE are probably some of the clearest examples of reinterpretations of a classical collection of recipes brought up to date, adding technical complexity, craftsmanship, and rich nuances of flavour. This is our way of bringing academic knowledge to the table. This is how we build on what we have read, studied, seen and experimented on.

The footprint of written knowledge endures, as will the latest scientific books on food, like the bible called *On Food and Cooking*, by Harold McGee. Based on our obsession with the research of cooking at low temperatures, we wanted to share our experiences in cooking with the Roner, following conversations and dialogues with Georges Pralus and Hervé This, European examples in the bibliography of food and chemistry, with books like *La Cuisine sous vide* and *Les Secrets de la Casserole*, respectively. That is how we got to the publishing of *Sous-Vide Cuisine* (Joan Roca, Salvador Brugués, Montagud Editores, 2003), a contribution expanded, in the broadest sense of the dialogue between cooking and science, by the absolute *Modernist Cuisine* of Nathan Myhrvold. We must not forget also the accessible dictionary *Léxico Científico Gastronómico* published by Fundació Alícia and the Bulli Taller, a useful tool adapted to understand, from a dialogue with science, the complexity of a whole world no longer foreign to us: the scientific point of view.

In the dining room...

In school we realised that what we had learnt at our
parents' restaurant—that is, having fun while serving—
can also be applied to the study of the reinterpretation
of forms, new eating habits and new serving practices.
This is how we discovered it doesn't end with the fork,
knife and spoon. We let ourselves be surprised by
dessert spoons, cutlery for hors d'oeuvre, meat, fish,
pre-desserts, different utensils and containers... None
of this can be found in a bar. What we learnt at the
Culinary Arts School of Girona served as a foundation,
gave us a soundness that was later seasoned with our
experiences in restaurants around the world, and at the
great establishments we have visited, which have taught
us different working techniques and values from talented
people who are putting forward interesting ideas. And we
bring all this to your table, together with the dishes you
choose, and surrounded by the atmosphere we build for
you day after day.

SOLE MEUNIÈRE

SERVES 4 PEOPLE

COMPOSITION
Sole
Milk skin
Lemon cubes
Fried capers
Caper purée
Beurre noisette
Sole sauce
Sole skin

—SOLE
YIELDS 4 PORTIONS

2 sole (about 400 g each)
Brine for fish (basic recipes, p.429)

Bring water to a boil in a saucepan and submerge the tails of the sole for 2 seconds. Use scissors to cut both lateral fins off and remove the skin by grabbing one end of it with a dry cloth and pulling from the tail towards the head. Blanching facilitates the removal of the skin.

Discard the head and tail of the sole and cut fillets, square off the fillets and immerse them in brine for 5 minutes. Dry well with kitchen towels, join two fillets on the side of the bones. Seal in a vacuum pack bag and cook in the Roner at 55°C/131°F for 4 minutes. Sear on one side on the griddle pan. Cut lengthwise through the middle and reserve.

—MILK SKIN
YIELDS 10 MILK SKINS

1 litre whole milk
Single cream

Pour the milk into a 25 cm frying pan and bring to approximately 60°C/140°F, discarding any bubbles that form. A layer of skin will form on the surface. The first layer takes about 15 minutes to form, the following approximately 8 minutes each. Carefully, take the layer of milk out by grabbing it by the middle. Place it on a tray lined with cling film and brushed with single cream; brush also the surface of the milk skin with cream and cover with cling film. Reserve refrigerated until serving.

—LEMON CUBES
YIELDS 12 CUBES

1 lemon
Sugar

Using a Microplane, grate the lemons as close to the pith as possible, but without touching it. Grate only the outer (yellow) peel of the lemon and reserve the zest in a container with a pinch of sugar to neutralise its acidity.

With a paring knife, pith the lemons and cut the lemon into 3 mm cubes. Before serving, coat these lemon cubes with the mixture of lemon zest and sugar. Reserve.

—FRIED CAPERS
YIELDS 12 FRIED CAPERS

12 preserved capers
500 g sunflower oil

Remove capers from the tin and dry on kitchen towels. Heat a saucepan with sunflower oil and, when the temperature reaches 180°C/356°F, fry the capers until crisp. They should open up like flowers. Reserve.

—CAPER PURÉE
YIELDS 200 G

125 g preserved capers
75 g brine from the preserved capers

Blend the capers in their own liquid. Reserve in a container.

—BEURRE NOISETTE
YIELDS 180 G

250 g butter

Heat the butter in a frying pan over medium-low heat; when the protein separates from the fat, remove the milk solids that accumulate on the surface, and continue cooking the remaining butter until it acquires a golden-brown colour. Run through a cloth filter and reserve.

—SOLE SAUCE

YIELDS 750 G

1 kg sole bones
150 g beurre noisette (previously prepared)
1 kg water
2.3 g xanthan gum
Salt

Clean the bones well and, in a nonstick frying pan with some of the beurre noisette, brown on both sides.

When all the sole bones are brown, weigh and add an equal proportion of water. Bring the water to about 80°C/176°F and add the bones, infusing for approximately 25 minutes. Strain and texturise with xanthan gum (using about 0.3 g xanthan gum for every 100 g sole fish bone stock). Adjust salt if needed.

—SOLE SKIN

YIELDS 8 SKINS

2 sole skins (white/black)
50 g olive oil
Salt

Wash the skins well and, using a paring knife, remove any remaining meat. Cut the skins lengthwise into a 2 cm width.

Place 2 baking trays upside down and line them with greaseproof paper. Wet a brush with olive oil to brush the greaseproof paper, and then arrange the skins on top without overlapping. Add a pinch of salt to each skin and brush again with oil. Cover with greaseproof paper and place another tray on top to press well. Bake at 150°C/302°F for 1 hour with some weight on top, if possible. Next, reserve in a dry place.

GARNISHING AND PLATING

Carnation flowers
Lemon geranium flowers
(*Pelargonium crispum*)

Arrange the milk skin on a rectangular plate, preferably on a dark surface. Alternate 3 lemon cubes and 3 fried capers on top. Draw a few dots of caper purée and add a brushstroke of beurre noisette down the middle. On top of the butter, set the sole, cooked sous-vide and lightly browned on the grill over holm oak embers. Dress the sole with a bit more beurre noisette and the sole sauce.

Serve the sole fish skin on a separate support to keep it crisp. Wet the skin with beurre noisette and caper purée. Garnish with 3 pieces of sugared lemon cubes and the carnation and lemon geranium flowers.

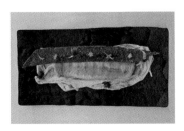

DECLINATION OF HARE
À LA ROYALE 2011

SERVES 8 PEOPLE

COMPOSITION

Beetroot purée
Soil air
Beetroot cubes
Duxelle
Royale
Spoon royale
Hare gravy
Hare sauce
Bacon fat
Civet of hare
Civet of hare gravy
Charcoal-grilled raspberry purée
Loin of hare

—BEETROOT PURÉE

YIELDS 150 G

150 g beetroots
25 g soil distillate (basic recipes, p.428)
0.2 g xanthan gum
Salt

Boil the beetroots until soft. Mash together
with the soil distillate and xanthan gum, and
run through a fine chinois. Adjust salt and
reserve in a squeeze bottle.

—SOIL AIR

YIELDS 250 G

250 g soil distillate (basic recipes, p.428)
1.5 g sucrose ester
3.5 g soy lecithin

Combine all the ingredients, mix well and leave
to stand. Use a hand blender to produce some
air in the mixture. Reserve.

—BEETROOT CUBES

YIELDS 140 CUBES

150 g beetroots

Cook the beetroots whole; when soft, peel and
cut into 0.5 cm cubes. Reserve.

—DUXELLE

YIELDS 250 G

120 g cultivated mushrooms
120 g penny buns (*Boletus edulis*)
120 g shallots
30 g extra virgin olive oil

Clean mushrooms and brunoise; reserve. Peel
the shallots and brunoise, then poach them in
a frying pan with olive oil until soft and slightly
browned. Add the mushrooms, let any excess
water evaporate and cook on very low heat for
20 minutes. Reserve the mixture.

—ROYALE

YIELDS 3 MOULDS 12X12X4 CM EACH

375 g hare meat
185 g pork jowl
10 g black truffle
100 g hare liver
100 g milk
75 g hare blood
20 g Armagnac
50 g pasteurised egg whites
65 g bread crumbs
85 g duxelle (previously prepared)
12 g salt

Mince the hare meat, pork jowl, truffle and liver.

Mix the milk, blood, Armagnac and egg whites,
add the bread crumbs and soak for 15 minutes.
Blend and add to the previous mixture along
with the duxelle; season.

Line a 12-cm-wide by 4-cm-deep square
mould with cling film, smoothing out any
wrinkles, fill with 350 g of the Royale and leave
to cool for 1 hour refrigerated. Seal the mould
with Royale in a vacuum pack bag at 100%.
Cook the terrine in the Roner at 63°C/145°F
for 30 hours. Remove from the Roner and cool
quickly. Cut into approximately 10x1x2 cm
rectangles (they should each weight about 35 g).
Seal in a vacuum pack bag and regenerate
before serving.

—SPOON ROYALE

YIELDS 8 QUENELLES

40 g Royale (previously prepared)

Using a fork, lightly mash the hare Royale.
Use two spoons to form small quenelles,
approximately 4 g each. Reserve.

—HARE GRAVY

YIELDS 200 G

850 g hare bones and trimmings
200 g mirepoix (basic recipes, p.427)
75 g red wine
1.5 kg water

Place the bones and trimmings on a baking
tray and brown at 180°C/356°F. When brown,
remove any excess fat and place in a stockpot;
deglaze the tray and transfer the browned bits
into the stockpot containing the bones and
trimmings. Add the mirepoix and the red wine,
boil and cover everything with very cold water.

Bring to a boil, skim and cook for 3 hours on
very low heat. Next, strain the stock and reduce
to 200 g of hare gravy. Cool and reserve.

—HARE SAUCE

YIELDS 250 G

200 g hare gravy (previously prepared)
20 g kuzu thickening agent (basic recipes,
    p.427)
30 g butter
40 g hare blood

Heat the hare gravy, add the kuzu thickening
agent and butter while stirring vigorously to
obtain a stable, lump-free emulsion; strain.
Before plating, bind the sauce with the hare
blood, stirring to make a fine sauce.

—BACON FAT

YIELDS 55 G

50 g bacon
5 g water
25 g sunflower oil

Cut the bacon into regular 1 cm cubes, using
as much of the fat as possible. Place cubes in
a casserole with water and sunflower oil. Cook
on low heat until all the water has evaporated
and most of the bacon melted. Strain, cool and
reserve.

—CIVET OF HARE
YIELDS 400 G SHOULDER MEAT

150 g leeks
150 g carrots
75 g celery
250 g onion
½ bay leaf
2 thyme sprigs
2 rosemary sprigs
½ cinnamon stick
5 g peppercorns
3 g juniper
½ lemon peel
½ orange peel
4 hare shoulders (200 g each)
1 litre red wine
60 g bacon fat (previously prepared)
Olive oil

Peel vegetables and make a mirepoix. Place all ingredients, except the bacon fat and oil, in an airtight container and marinate for 24 hours.

Next, remove the hare shoulders and wash well any marinade residues. Sear lightly in a frying pan with a little olive oil. Cool and reserve.

Separately, reduce the strained liquid from the marinade to a third of its initial volume, skimming constantly. Reserve.

Remove all the aromatic ingredients (juniper, cinnamon, pepper, orange, lemon, thyme, rosemary and bay) from the marinade and reserve. In a casserole, sweat the marinade vegetables until all the liquid evaporates and they soften. Blast chill and reserve.

Vacuum pack 2 seared hare shoulders, 50 g lightly fried vegetables, 30 g bacon fat and 100 g of the reduced marinade wine per bag. Cook in the Roner at 63°C/145°F for 12 hours. When ready, open the bag, run the cooking juices through a fine chinois and store. Cool and remove any excess fat left. Reserve.

Bone the shoulders, keeping the pieces of meat as big as possible.

—CIVET OF HARE GRAVY
YIELDS 280 G

200 g juices from cooking the shoulders (from previous step)
133 g reduced red wine from the marinade (from previous step)
10 g sugar
Herbs, spices and citrus fruit zest reserved from the marinade
40 g kuzu thickening agent (basic recipes, p.427)

Bring the juices from cooking the shoulders to a boil, skimming. Add the reduced wine and sugar, bring to a boil a second time, and skim. Remove from heat and add the aromatic ingredients. Cover and infuse for 30 minutes. Strain and bind with kuzu thickening agent, strain again and reserve.

—CHARCOAL-GRILLED RASPBERRY PURÉE
YIELDS 180 G

250 g raspberries
10 g extra virgin olive oil

Place the raspberries in a fine sieve. In a separate container, place some glowing hot embers under the sieve containing the raspberries. Sprinkle a few drops of extra virgin olive oil. Cover quickly with cling film and smoke for 5 minutes. Next, remove the raspberries, blend and run through a fine chinois. Reserve the purée.

—LOIN OF HARE
YIELDS 8 PORTIONS

2 loins of hare
Extra virgin olive oil
Salt

Season hare loins with salt and sear on the griddle pan. Reserve.

GARNISHING AND PLATING

Cocoa powder
Crystallised ginger sheets
Fennel sprouts
Juniper berries
Truffle
Beetroot sprouts
Juniper powder
Regenerate the vacuum packed Royale rectangles at 60°C/140°F.

Heat the civet in its own gravy and place a small amount over the Royale. Sprinkle with cocoa powder, add 2 sheets of crystallised ginger, ½ juniper berry peel and 2 fennel sprouts. Next to the civet, place the beetroot-related elements: purée, cubes and sprouts. Heat the spoon Royale quenelle and set next to it. Place a drop of charcoal-grilled raspberry purée and, lastly, add the grilled loin of hare.

Garnish the dish with julienned truffle next to the civet, the soil air and a few drops of hare sauce next to the declination.

CHARCOAL-GRILLED SARDINE CONSOMMÉ

SERVES 8 PEOPLE

COMPOSITION

Charcoal-grilled sardines

Charcoal-grilled sardine
    consommé

Parsley gel

Yellow pepper gel

Rocoto pepper gel

Garlic cream

Apple compote

—CHARCOAL-GRILLED SARDINES
YIELDS 16 FILETS

8 sardines (about 80 g each)
Brine for fish (basic recipes, p.429)
10 g extra virgin olive oil

Clean the sardines and fillet the loins. Bone
and boil them in brine for 3 minutes. Dry loins
well and join them on the meat side, seal with
olive oil in a vacuum pack bag at 100%. Cook
in the Roner for 3 minutes. Remove from the
Roner, open the bag, brush the skin of the
fillets with olive oil, and sear over holm oak
embers. Reserve.

—CHARCOAL-GRILLED SARDINE CONSOMMÉ
YIELDS 200 G

250 g sardine bones with heads
15 g extra virgin olive oil
250 g water
0.6 g xanthan gum

Sprinkle some olive oil over the sardine bones
and sear them over charcoal until they cook
well and acquire a smoky aroma. Place them in
a stockpot with water and heat to 85°C/185°F.
Cover hermetically to infuse for 15 minutes.
Next, run through a fine chinois, strain again
with a sieve, and blast chill. Finally, blend with
the xanthan gum and reserve.

—PARSLEY GEL
YIELDS 160 G

50 g parsley leaves
150 g water
0.48 g xanthan gum
Salt

Blanch parsley leaves in boiling water for about
20 seconds and remove. Cool in iced water and
in a separate container cool the water used for
blanching.

Blend both ingredients cold to a fine, smooth
liquid. Run through a fine chinois, pressing to
obtain as much parsley water as possible.

Texturise with the xanthan gum, adjust salt
and remove all the air in the vacuum sealer.
If a vacuum sealer is not available, leave the
mixture to stand until it releases all the air.
Pour into a squeeze bottle and reserve.

—YELLOW PEPPER GEL
YIELDS 150 G

450 g yellow pepper (150 g juice)
0.3 g xanthan gum

Clean and purée the flesh of the yellow pepper,
texturise it with the xanthan gum and remove
the air. Pour into a squeeze bottle and reserve.

—ROCOTO PEPPER GEL
YIELDS 150 G

450 g rocoto pepper (150 g juice)
0.3 g xanthan gum

Clean and purée the flesh of the rocoto pepper,
texturise it with the xanthan gum and remove
the air. Pour into a squeeze bottle
and reserve.

—GARLIC CREAM
YIELDS 120 G

50 g garlic cloves
100 g water
0.6 g xanthan gum
Salt

Peel garlic cloves and blanch starting with
cold water, then repeat three times. Cut them
in half and remove the germ. Blend with the
remaining ingredients. Strain and pour into a
squeeze bottle.

—APPLE COMPOTE
YIELDS 150 G

200 g Granny Smith apples
10 g sugar
20 g butter
Salt

Cut the apple into small pieces, mix with
the remaining ingredients and cook in the
microwave oven until the apple softens.
Make a very fine purée, cool and reserve.

GARNISHING AND PLATING

Fennel sprouts
Dill sprouts
Chervil sprouts
Rosemary blossoms

Place a grilled sardine at the centre of the
bowl and serve the consommé. Then, carefully
distribute dots of parsley gel, rocoto gel, yellow
pepper gel, garlic cream and apple compote.
Garnish with fennel, dill and chervil sprouts
and rosemary blossoms.

GOOSE ROYALE
WITH APRICOT

SERVES 8 PEOPLE

COMPOSITION
Goose sauce
Filling
Goose Royale
Apricot compote

—GOOSE SAUCE
YIELDS 270 G

1 kg goose bones and trimmings
120 g mirepoix (basic recipes, p.427)
2.5 kg water
15 g Pedro Ximénez
40 g kuzu thickening agent (basic recipes, p.427)

Place the bones and trimmings on a baking tray and brown at 220°C/428°F. When ready, remove excess fat and transfer the bones and trimmings to a stockpot, deglaze the baking tray and add the browned bits to the stockpot. Pour in the mirepoix and cover with very cold water. Boil for 3 hours over very low heat, skimming constantly.

Strain and reduce to 250 g, include the Pedro Ximénez, boil and mix kuzu while stirring constantly. Strain again and reserve.

—FILLING
YIELDS 250 G

120 g shallots
120 g cultivated mushrooms
120 g penny buns (*Boletus edulis*)
30 g extra virgin olive oil
Salt

Chop all the ingredients, cook shallots in oil over low heat and, when soft, add the cultivated mushrooms and penny buns; leave to cook. Remove from heat, adjust salt and reserve.

—GOOSE ROYALE
YIELDS APPROXIMATELY 26 PORTIONS

200 g foie
100 g milk
75 g goose blood
15 g Armagnac
50 g egg whites
50 g breadcrumbs
375 g goose meat
185 g pork neck
60 g foie
40 g truffle
90 g filling (previously prepared)
15 g salt

Cut the 200 g of foie into 1.5-cm-wide strips and reserve.

Mix the milk, blood, Armagnac and egg whites, add the breadcrumbs and soak for 15 minutes; blend.

Mince goose meat, neck, truffle and the 60 g of foie. Mix with the remaining ingredients, blended, and then add the filling and season.

On a piece of cling film, spread a layer of Royale mix; fill the middle with strips of foie. Roll into a very compact 3-cm-thick cylinder filled with foie and cool in the blast cooler. Seal in a vacuum pack bag and cook in the Roner at 63°C/145°F for 30 hours.

When ready, cool the cylinders and cut into 3x3 cm portions. Seal in a vacuum pack bag and regenerate before serving.

—APRICOT COMPOTE
YIELDS 180 G

200 g fresh apricots
50 g sugar
30 g apricot liqueur
10 g butter

Peel the apricots, cut into irregular pieces about 1.5 cm in size and reserve the stones. Heat a casserole with the sugar over low heat and make a light caramel; when it starts to darken, pour in the apricot liqueur slowly. Dissolve well, add the butter, chopped fruit and, lastly, the apricot stones reserved earlier. Cook until making a purée. Remove the apricot stones and mash the compote to make it smoother, then, run through a fine chinois. Reserve.

GARNISHING AND PLATING

Young beetroot sprouts
Beetroot leaves
Borage blossoms
Purple shiso sprouts

Regenerate the pieces of goose at 63°C/145°F; open the bag and dry any liquid it may release.

Set the Royale on the plate and cover with the reduced sauce; paint a tear of apricot compote next to it and garnish with young sprouts and a leaf of beetroot, one borage blossom and some purple shiso sprouts.

STEAK TARTARE

—MUSTARD EMULSION
YIELDS 63 G

10 g egg yolks
45 g extra virgin olive oil
8 g mustard seeds

Beat the egg yolks in a bowl to whip as much air into them as possible, slowly add a stream of olive oil while beating with a wire whisk to emulsify the mixture. Add the mustard seeds, mix and reserve for the steak.

SERVES 8 PEOPLE

COMPOSITION
Mustard emulsion
Steak
Ketchup
Oloroso raisin
Lemon marmalade
Foyot sauce
Mustard shots
Soufflé potatoes
Soufflé potato seasoning

—STEAK
YIELDS 255 G

200 g sirloin steak clear of fat
1.7 g Lea & Perrins Worcestershire sauce
13 g mustard emulsion (previously prepared)
20 g chopped shallots
10 g chopped capers
10 g chopped pickles
Tabasco sauce
Salt
Pepper

Mince the meat finely with a knife, place in a bowl and add all the other ingredients; mix well and reserve the mixture covered and refrigerated.

—KETCHUP
YIELDS 125 G

150 g liquefied tomato
20 g sugar
10 g sherry vinegar
1.5 g Lea & Perrins Worcestershire sauce
0.2 g Tabasco sauce
Salt

In a casserole, cook the blended tomato together with the sugar, vinegar, Worcestershire sauce and Tabasco sauce over low heat for 3 hours.

When the mixture is reduced, adjust salt and reserve.

—OLOROSO RAISIN
YIELDS 127 G (50 UNITS)

500 g water
2.5 g calcium alginate
125 g Oloroso
1.5 g xanthan gum
0.9 g calcium chloride
Sugar

Blend the water and calcium alginate using a hand blender and reserve refrigerated.

Mix Oloroso and xanthan gum and calcium chloride, take small portions with a spoon and drop them in the calcium alginate bath; turn them over to seal them on both sides and leave in the bath for a few minutes. Remove from the calcium alginate bath and rinse with water.

Leave the Oloroso spheres covered in sugar for 4 hours, so that when ready they resemble raisins.

—LEMON MARMALADE
YIELDS 300 G

125 g lemon
100 g sugar
40 g whole capers
35 g chopped capers
25 g lemon juice

Wash the lemon and cut into 0.5-cm-thick slices. Remove any seeds left and chop the lemon finely.

Caramelise sugar to 145°C/293°F, add the chopped lemon and whole capers and cook for a few minutes. Next, add the chopped capers and, lastly, the lemon juice. Cover the mixture and cook for 2 hours on very low heat.

—FOYOT SAUCE

YIELDS 202 G

60 g balsamic vinegar
2.4 g freeze-dried tarragon
100 g beef gravy (basic recipes, p.428)
40 g clarified butter
2 g xanthan gum

Heat the balsamic vinegar and infuse the freeze-dried tarragon. Cool down.

Heat the beef gravy in a bain-marie and emulsify it with the clarified butter; add the infused vinegar and, lastly, the xanthan gum; then, blend everything together until it's free of lumps.

—MUSTARD SHOTS

YIELDS 325 G

250 g cream
50 g egg yolks
25 g mustard seeds
3.7 g gelatine sheets
Salt

In a casserole, mix the cream, egg yolks and mustard seeds, and pasteurize to 85°C/185°F. Remove from heat, add hydrated gelatine and strain the mixture. Adjust salt and blast chill.

Prepare a polystyrene foam container with liquid nitrogen. Transfer the mixture into a squeeze bottle and let drops fall into the nitrogen, then lift the drops with a wire skimmer and reserve them in a container in the freezer.

—SOUFFLÉ POTATOES

YIELDS APPROXIMATELY 45 UNITS

1 (old) medium-size Agria potato
Sunflower oil

Cut the potato lengthwise in half and make 1.5x3 cm rectangles from both halves.

With a mandolin slicer and starting with the widest side, make fine slices out of the potato rectangles and reserve.

Prepare two saucepans with sunflower oil, heat one at 130°C/266°F and the other at 180°C/356°F.

Fry the rectangular potato slices in 130°C/266°F oil until they puff and then, using a wire skimmer, transfer them into 180°C/356°F oil to finish puffing and browning. Place on kitchen towels and reserve.

—SOUFFLÉ POTATO SEASONING

32 soufflé potatoes (previously prepared)
10 g paprika
10 g Sichuan pepper
10 g curry powder
10 g chopped chives
10 g softened butter

Season 8 potatoes with paprika, 8 with Sichuan pepper, and 8 with curry powder and, lastly, butter the last 8 potatoes and cover with chopped chives.

GARNISHING AND PLATING

Hazelnut praline
Mustard leaves

On a rectangular plate, arrange 30 g of steak, forming a 1-cm-thick by 10-cm-long rectangle. On top of it, set in the following order and leaving approximately 1 cm between each ingredient, one Oloroso raisin, one hazelnut praline dot, one lemon marmalade dot, and one ketchup dot. Add a few mustard shots.

On top of the previous elements and in the following order, place one potato seasoned with Sichuan pepper, one with paprika, one with curry, and lastly, next to the ketchup, the soufflé potato with chopped chives. Alternate with a few small leaves of mustard. Dress one corner of the steak with the Foyot sauce.

sauces

**Sauces revisited, the basis
of Joan Roca's cuisine**

"A hot or cold seasoned liquid either served with, or used in the cooking of a dish. The function of a sauce is to add to a dish flavour that is compatible with the ingredients." This is how *Larousse Gastronomique* describes the concept of a sauce, and goes on to classify sauces according to the French canons established by Antonin Carême in the early 19th century. With the passage of time, traditional French sauces began to acquire influences and flavours from other countries and, later on, thanks to Chef Master Auguste Escoffier, they became lighter. Today, vanguard cuisine has made available different ingredients and thickeners that have helped reinvent the world of sauces.

"The basic aim of a sauce is to contribute flavour with a nice consistency. A good sauce stimulates our chemical senses, taste and smell. It must be tasted to check for salt, sweetness, acidity and aroma, and correct the amounts while keeping its general balance. Although in a sauce the most important element is its flavour, texture and density are also essential."

WHAT BRINGS FLAVOUR AND AROMA TO THE SAUCES MADE AT EL CELLER DE CAN ROCA

At El Celler, classic academicism and modernity go hand-in-hand. This explains the use of traditional elements to flavour a sauce, such as stocks, as well as innovative techniques and additives that produce stand-out sauces.

STOCK

MEAT STOCK

Meat sauces start with a stock, generally reduced, made with the bones, meat and skin of the product that will be served with the sauce. When making a stock, the idea is to produce very flavourful liquid and enough gelatine to provide thickness when reduced. Meat is a source of flavour, but is low on gelatine; on the other hand, skin and bones are less flavourful, but very rich in collagen. There should always be more meat than skin and bones. Basic recipes also contain vegetables (especially carrots and onions, which add aroma and a hint of sweetness) or wine (for acidity). There are two types of meat stocks: brown and white.

Brown stock: the bones, meat and vegetables are browned in the oven for colour and to intensify their flavour. The Maillard reaction coagulates the proteins on the surface, prevents the stock from turning murky, and provides the flavour produced by caramelisation.

When the meat and bones are in the stockpot, the same amount of cold water is added. It should be cooked uncovered over low heat, skimming and removing the fat that gathers on the surface constantly. The gradual increase in temperature beginning with cold water allows for soluble proteins to detach from the solid ingredients and slowly coagulate, forming a visible substance that floats up or settles on the sides and bottom of the stockpot, facilitating its removal. This creates a cleaner and clearer stock.

When the stock stops producing foam, add the vegetables, herbs and wine, and cook on low heat until all the flavour and gelatine from the solids is extracted. Then, strain and leave to cool. When cold, the fat that solidifies on the surface can easily be removed.

White stock or blanquette: the only difference to dark stock is that neither the bones nor the vegetables are browned. The result, therefore, is a lighter liquid of smooth flavour that lacks the caramelisation produced by the Maillard reaction.

FISH STOCK

Fish live in a cold environment, so their collagen is less dense and dissolves at lower temperatures. Therefore, fish gelatino can be extracted at temperatures below boiling point and in a relatively short period of time. In the case of cephalopods, collagen requires higher temperatures and longer periods of time to dissolve. When making fish stock, the bones and skin are previously browned in the oven to obtain more flavour.

The Maillard reaction is the result of a series of chemical reactions between amino acids and carbohydrates when applying heat (with the griddle pan, oven, charcoal-grill, etc.) to certain foods, browning them and yielding a characteristic taste.[1]

1 — ALÍCIA & el Bulli taller. *Léxico científico gastronómico. Las claves para entender la cocina de hoy.* Barcelona: Planeta, 2006.

WINE

At El Celler de Can Roca, wine is so important that the aim is to include it in its dishes in its purest state, just as it exists in the glass, without it losing even the slightest amount of character. Wine is very often present in the sauces of classical cuisine, but always subjected to long cooking processes. El Celler, on the other hand, has been able to make wine sauces from reductions achieved at low temperatures in the Rotaval (see box on page 154), keeping its organoleptic properties intact, and thickening them with xanthan gum. The concentration of sugars in the case of sweet wines—a better choice for this process—also improves density.

FRUIT JUICE AND BLENDED HERBS

As with wine, the idea is to make a fruit or herb sauce without sacrificing their original fresh taste. This is a reason to avoid their reduction over heat —it would trigger the Maillard reaction around the walls of the stock pot, altering its flavour. At El Celler, the reduction is made in the Rotaval (see box on page 154). Xanthan gum is used to thicken the liquid, and its added while cold. This way, it becomes unnecessary to apply heat, which in the case of fruit juices would caramelise sugars and alter the original flavour, and in the case of blended herbs would volatilise and oxidise the aroma.

WHAT THICKENS SAUCES AT EL CELLER DE CAN ROCA

Natural gelatine extracted from meat and bone collagen when preparing a reduced stock.

Kuzu or **kudzu** (*Pueraria lobata*), of Chinese or Japanese origin. A vine from the *Fabaceae* family whose root produces a starch that has long been used in Chinese traditional medicine. At El Celler, it is used as a thickener for many hot sauces. It is dissolved with a small amount of cold stock or water, and added when the sauce is ready and the boiling has ceased. One of its great advantages is being flavourless, gluten-free and providing a silky, shiny and gelatinous texture.

Egg yolk is a very efficient protein-based thickener, largely due to the proportion of the concentration of protein: it contains 50% water and 16% protein, finely distributed over a rich and creamy fluid. It is used to thicken white or creamy sauces, veloutés, blanquettes...

Liver is a very flavourful thickener. It must always be previously liquidised—coagulable proteins are concentrated within its cells—and then strained to remove the connecting tissue that bound them together.

Blood, used extensively in traditional cuisine, contains albumin, a protein that thickens liquids when heated above 75°C/167°F.

Shelfish organs are also good thickeners. Liver, oyster beards, or the sexual tissues of sea urchins, have the same advantages and drawbacks as liver, but thicken and coagulate at much lower temperatures. They must be added to sauces at the end of the cooking process, when the temperature is well below the boiling point.

Some **dairy products,** such as cream or butter, are emulsions, versatile ingredients that provide density and a silky quality to sauces.

Xanthan gum is an extracellular polysaccharide produced by the *Xantonomas campestris* bacteria through the fermentation of glucose or sucrose in wheat. It's a thickener that offers the ability to create dense textures both used in cold and hot liquid. At El Celler, it is mainly used to thicken delicate liquids that should not be subjected to heat. From a liquid thickened with xanthan gum, we can make a stable emulsion by adding olive oil.

Olive oil is used to make emulsions from blended herbs, fruit juices and other liquids previously thickened with xanthan gum. It results in stable and very versatile sauces.

THE ROTAVAL: SAUCE MAKING TECHNOLOGY

The Rotaval offers the ability to take a product to a different dimension. It is a still that allows for the vacuum distillation of any ingredient with a certain degree of moisture. The vacuum transforms the atmospheric pressure, so the boiling point is reached at lower temperatures (about 40°C/104°F). The result is the initial separation of alcohol and water—with their volatile aromas—from the main ingredient, which is reduced in the flask. At El Celler, the two parts resulting from this process are used to make sauces:

— Distilled water: is a clear liquid containing all the volatile aromas of the main ingredient. To transform it into a sauce, it must be thickened with xanthan gum to avoid applying heat.

— The reduction of the main product at low temperature: it's a sauce in itself if the initial product is a liquid, since it thickens with distillation. The result is much more interesting than when reduced over heat, because this process does not trigger the Maillard reaction.

EXAMPLES OF SAUCES MADE AT EL CELLER DE CAN ROCA

Brown stock sauce: the stock is reduced in order to concentrate its flavour and density. It is usually bound with kuzu and a knob of butter, emulsified right before using the sauce, is added at the end.

Sardine sauce: prepared from a charcoal-grilled and vacuum infused sardine stock, bound with xanthan gum.

Red mullet sauce: browned bones, carrots and onions are cooked in water (in equal proportions) for six hours over very low heat, like a consommé. The aim here is a baroque and complex sauce. A small amount of lard is added. The binding element is an alioli made from roasted garlic and extra virgin olive oil. Lastly, a little kuzu is added.

Oyster sauce: shallots are cooked in butter and the oyster water is used as the liquid element; the binding elements are the cream and protein from the oyster beards. Freshly grated lime zest is added as a final touch.

Squid sauce: first a sofrito is made with onion, carrot and tomato, cooked in butter. The squid, chopped, is added together with cold water, and reduced over low temperature for several hours. When strained, it is left to stand and, right before use, butter is added to provide some thickness and a foam that will give it a more ethereal effect.

Cava sauce: as a result of a joint research project with Agustí Torelló. Three grams of xanthan gum have been added per bottle at the moment of disgorging the cava, which is then stored for an additional six months. During this time, the xanthan gum hydrates with the cava, transforming it into a sauce without losing its natural carbon dioxide (more information on page 272).

Royale sauce: the goose recipe of El Celler de Can Roca is based on the traditional recipe for Hare à la Royale, thickened with blood, which is added at the last minute (see recipe on page 144).

Pork blanquette: a cut of pork jowl is used to bind this sauce and removed when straining the stock, then blended together with it. The result is an emulsion that adds thickness, consistency and oiliness, and that is lastly stabilised with kuzu.

Soil distillate with the Rotaval: soil and water are infused for 24 hours and distilled in the Rotaval (see box above). The resulting liquid is thickened with xanthan gum.

D

—PRODUCT

The intact essence of the product. What is cooking if not preparation? But, what would cooking be if it wasn't based on unchanging principles, on a nuclear idea that consists of making use of what we have near, at hand, in order to carry out a process that transforms raw material into a creative artefact, or an artifice of craft? The perfect combination of the obvious—natural plant or wild animal —and the mechanism that transforms it is the ideal environment that governs the kitchen.

The chef may make such a crucial contribution, born thanks to creative intervention, that his sublime art rises above the importance of individual parties or the personality of each, and he achieves something that is different. It is then what we might call, a choral performance.

And there may also be solos. That is, the preponderance of one of the elements the cook, and director of the piece, allows to shine through with its own, unique voice. Forcefulness. A chief vector reasserts its dominance over the coordinates of the dish.

We could state that there are combinational dishes—like a game in which the participation of all the elements is the base for success—and explicit dishes that require the decisive intervention of a star ingredient. This is where the product becomes vitally important. This is where El Celler opens up to free expression and acts to control its natural effervescence, assess and analyse it. It has it climb, like ivy, on the wall the cook has drawn.

According to the Roca brothers

What is the product? What must we know about it? How does it fit in a restaurant? In ours it is deeply embedded, with an emphasis on everyday actions, in search of the right way of living, with the ethical involvement of being profoundly connected with nature. We approach the product that comes from nature from an ecological knowledge, or personal eco-philosophy. Because we want to live in this world with an attitude that minimizes our impact on nature and underlines our feelings of reverence, wonderment and belonging.

We are well aware of the extent of our influence at the moment. We know we are prominent and respected in our local surroundings and probably also beyond. This compels us to act responsibly and disseminate a philosophy of care in the selection of products. We have become involved, not from an extreme or fundamentalist point of view, but from rationality and the need to protect. It isn't a brave vision; we act in a natural way. And, from this point, we know we are beginning to build strong ties with a lot people from the vicinity. We are increasingly thankful for the support of nearby artisanal producers. We experiment more and more, we feel more comfortable welcoming people who bring us products with much love, that we know are backed by hard work and history, research, study of genetic proposals, and also cultural habit…

In addition to our relationship with the local producer, we have challenged ourselves to grow our own vegetable garden, which brings us closer to sustainability. We know the vegetable garden will keep us humble, a requirement of anyone who works the earth. It will increase our awareness of our weaknesses and deficiencies, and also of the risks. Like in December of 2011, when the frost destroyed everything… We accepted the fact that we had to start from scratch, that harvesting isn't always guaranteed, and that one must be prepared to face the madness of nature, its uncontrolled strength.

Our power becomes relative and Earth reminds us of its greatness and might, and that we can't control it. The vegetable garden has allowed us to feel the disposition of the farmer. We are learning from agronomists and are carrying out a project with the participation of 10 people and 27 hectares of farmland. The vegetable garden is a space of learning, dialogue and interpretation of the anguish of the farmer, the difficulty to survive, to gain the recognition of the farmers dedicated to growing organic vegetables. Our vegetable garden is located one kilometre away from the restaurant, right on the border of the Llémena Valley, which to us represents the unifying core of our history—our parents come from Sant Martí de Llémena.

Also, we have started studying our most immediate influences, the geography and climate surrounding the restaurant. Botanical specialists have accompanied us to get better acquainted with our surrounding flora and botany, to observe very closely and guided by the wisdom of the experts the countryside we set foot on so many times but never knew how to explore from a culinary point of view until now. This is how we have been able to recover dandelions, rose hips, jujubes... forgotten features of the Mediterranean undergrowth. And the sea fennel and oxalis we used to order from Malaga without realising we had them right under our nose...

A holistic vision

We want to adopt a holistic vision in our connection to the product. To cultivate intuition as well as thought, sensory perception and feeling in our dialogue with sustainability and the knowledge of our immediate surroundings and our Earth. We follow the ideas of James Hutton (1726-1797), who revealed the Earth as a living superorganism; Jean-Baptiste Lamarck (1744-1829), who concluded that all living creatures were only understandable if seen as part of a whole; Johann Wolfgang von Goethe (1749-1832), the representative of a romantic vision; Rudolf Steiner (1861-1925), father of anthroposophy, committed to respecting nature in a way that still reverberates in many environmental experts and those interested in ecology and biodynamics; Alexander von Humboldt (1769-1859), who spoke of the weather as a global unifying force and about the joint evolution of life, the weather and the Earth's crust; and Eduard Suess (1831-1914), who introduced the concept of 'solidarity of life'.

Thought interprets, feelings evaluate, and sense and intuition are perceptive in that they direct our attention to what is happening without interpretation or evaluation. From all those paths we come to a sensitive and deep reflection about how to position ourselves in a world forced to react in the face of climate change, the display of all the embarrassments of an industrial society that has not been able to mature and respect the land, and endangers the life of man on Earth. The Gaia hypothesis by James Lovelock, based on solid observations and detailed descriptions of how the multiple systems on Earth interact to produce a dynamic and emerging unit, is the most meaningful and relevant revolution in the last century, and the platform for the new culture of the current era. It suggests that life and the non-living environment are perfectly coupled like partners in a good marriage. We owe ourselves to the land, respecting its cycles, knowing that the beauty of a product is its transience, and that manure is a source of life. Mark Lynas, author of *Six Degrees: Our future on a hotter planet*, helps us reflect and transform our responsibilities into action starting in the kitchen, with an ethical code of awareness to prevent the apocalyptic future of global warming from catching us off guard.

In the dining room...

We explain our products without making them too obvious, but instead with simplicity, conviction and normality in their use. We are aware that we face a great opportunity to be the ambassadors of our local products. So, our cuisine is international, but has the distinct markings of our land. Our roots in the Girona meadows are, at the same time, the wings we use to fly with stability and awareness of our origins, of belonging. When you come to El Celler, you may not recognise every single product that makes up each dish. But you will savour character, a unique disposition.

We wouldn't be where we are without the fruits of our land. We feel it and respect it to such extent that we even bring it to your table. If you're curious, ask about the SOIL DISTILLATE: you will have the chance to eat the earth, literally but transformed, and let yourself be surprised to rediscover the origin of all products as a product itself.

In the end, everything we eat comes from the land, it is a part of it. We celebrate a liturgy of communion with it. A sacred act of recognition and union. We show the maximum respect without unnecessary tricks. As Stephan Harding suggests in *Animate Earth*[1], we will have done something important if we help you feel, at least for a few minutes, "[...] the love that Earth feels for the very matter that makes up your body, a love that holds you safe [...]."

1. HARDING, S. *Animate Earth. Science, Intuition and Gaia.* Green Books, 2009.

Sensing the round planet

Lie down on your back on the ground in your Gaia place. Relax and take a few deep breaths. Now feel the weight of your body on the Earth as the force of gravity holds you down.

Experience gravity as the love the Earth feels for the very matter that makes up your body, a love that holds you safe and prevents you from floating off into outer space.

Open your eyes and look out into the vast depths of the universe whilst you sense the great bulk of our mother planet at your back. Feel her clasping you to her huge body as she dangles you upside down over the vast cosmos that stretches out below you.

What does it feel like to be held upside down in this way—to feel the depths of space beyond you and the firm, almost glue-like support of the Earth behind you?

Now sense how the Earth curves away beneath your back in all directions. Feel her great continents, her mountain ranges, her oceans, her domains of ice and snow at the poles and her great cloaks of vegetation stretching out from where you are in the great round immensity of her unbelievably diverse body.

Sense her whirling air and her tumbling clouds spinning around her dappled surface.

Breathe in the living immensity of our animate Earth.

When you are ready to get up, breathe deeply, profoundly aware now of the living quality of our planet home.

STEPHAN HARDING
Animate Earth

ARTICHOKE FLOWER

SERVES 8 PEOPLE

COMPOSITION
Artichoke hearts
Artichoke purée
Artichoke hearts brunoise
Foie soup
Artichoke petal chips
Orange and chervil emulsion

—ARTICHOKE HEARTS BRUNOISE
YIELDS 40 G

2 artichoke hearts
Extra virgin olive oil
Salt

Brunoise the artichoke hearts, sauté in olive oil. Adjust salt and reserve.

—ARTICHOKE HEARTS
YIELDS 250 G

1 kg artichokes
1 kg water
1 parsley sprig

Clean the artichokes, removing all their petals and pistils. Only the hearts will be used, cleaned well and reserved in a container with water and the parsley sprig to prevent them from oxidising.

—ARTICHOKE PURÉE
YIELDS 350 G

250 g artichoke hearts (from previous step)
75 g cooking water
5 g salt
45 g pistachio oil

Remove the artichoke hearts from the water with the parsley sprig, transfer them to a pot with fresh water and cook until soft.

Mix the artichoke hearts, while still hot, with the remaining ingredients and purée in the Thermomix until obtaining a silky emulsion free of lumps. Reserve.

—FOIE SOUP
YIELDS 600 G

500 g foie
150 g chicken stock (basic recipes, p.427)
50 g Pedro Ximénez
100 g cream
Salt
Sichuan pepper

Sear the foie on both sides without overbrowning, add the chicken stock, cream, Pedro Ximénez, pepper and salt. Bring to a boil and blend. Run mixture through a fine chinois, cool and reserve.

—ARTICHOKE PETAL CHIPS
YIELDS 50 G

Fresh petals from 6 artichokes
Olive oil

Fry the petals until crisp. Place on kitchen towels and reserve in an airtight container.

—ORANGE AND CHERVIL EMULSION
YIELDS 165 G

100 g orange emulsion (basic recipes, p.427)
2 g chopped chervil

Mix the emulsion with the chopped chervil and reserve.

GARNISHING AND PLATING

Fresh artichoke petals
16 truffle slices *(Tuber aestivum)*
Black truffle oil (basic recipes, p.427)

Place a 6 cm ring in the centre of the plate and fill it half-way with the artichoke purée. Arrange the sautéed artichoke brunoise on top of the purée and crown with a small flower made from the raw petals.

Heat the foie soup and serve it around the ring, spread the artichoke chips and truffle slices on top. Finish with a few drops of orange and chervil emulsion and black truffle oil. Remove the ring and serve.

VANILLA

SERVES 8 PEOPLE

COMPOSITION

Liquorice shots
Caramel jelly
Crystallised olives
Black olive oil
Dehydrated olives
Vanilla sponge cake
Vanilla ice cream
Cocoa crisp

—LIQUORICE SHOTS
YIELDS 1.25 KG

1 kg cream
50 g liquorice root
200 g egg yolks
100 g muscovado
5 gelatine sheets

Boil cream, remove from heat and add the liquorice. Leave to infuse for 10 minutes, strain. Blanch the egg yolks with the sugar, bringing mixture to 85°C/185°F, and add the gelatine. Pour the cream preparation on top of the blanched egg yolks.

Prepare a container with thermal insulation to work with liquid nitrogen, fill it with nitrogen and, using a squeeze bottle, let warm drops of cream fall into the nitrogen. Scoop them out with a strainer and reserve in an airtight container in the freezer.

—CARAMEL JELLY
YIELDS 700 G

200 g sugar
500 g water
7 g kappa carrageenan

Make caramel with the sugar. Interrupt the cooking process by slowly adding the water and the kappa in the end; bring to a boil again and reserve in an airtight container.

When the jelly has set, cut it into tiny cubes and reserve until serving.

—CRYSTALLISED OLIVES
YIELDS 380 G

200 g black olives
200 g water
60 g sugar

Quarter the olives and dry for 12 hours at 60°C/140°F. When dry, reserve 20 g to make the oil.

Make thick syrup with the sugar and water, bringing the syrup to 120°C/248°F; add the dry olives and stir them over the heat until they are coated and then lightly caramelised. Distribute on a tray, leave to cool and reserve in an airtight container.

—BLACK OLIVE OIL
YIELDS 120 G

100 g sunflower oil
20 g dehydrated black olives (from the previous preparation)

Blend the sunflower oil and olives to a black, smooth oil.

—DEHYDRATED OLIVES
YIELDS 160 G

200 g black olives

Quarter the black olives and dry them for 12 hours at 60°C/140°F. When dry, reserve them in an airtight container in a moisture-free place.

—VANILLA SPONGE CAKE
YIELDS 3 KG

600 g butter
740 g sugar
400 g flour
400 g almond flour
20 g baking powder
400 g eggs
160 g egg yolks
6 vanilla pods
400 g egg whites
300 g sugar

Temper the butter until soft and mix with sugar in the food mixer using the spatula.

Sieve the flour; add the almond flour and baking powder. Incorporate the butter and the sugar mixture while stirring constantly. Add the eggs and yolks, and knead until they incorporate into the dough.

Open and scrape the vanilla pods and add the contents to the mixture; finish kneading and reserve.

Make a French meringue with the egg whites and sugar. With a spatula, incorporate the meringue into the previous dough, while keeping it spongy. Spread the dough on a 20x30 cm baking tin, bake at 180°C/356°F for 15 minutes and continue cooking for 30 more minutes at 160°C/320°F.

When baked, remove from the tin, cool and cut into 2x2x0.2 cm squares. Reserve until serving.

—VANILLA ICE CREAM
YIELDS 1.3 KG

500 g whole milk
315 g cream
62 g skimmed milk powder
25 g vanilla powder
100 g dextrose
2.5 g ice-cream stabiliser
125 g pasteurised egg yolks
100 g muscovado
50 g food grade glycerine
11 Tahitian vanilla pods

In a casserole, place the cream, milk, milk powder and vanilla powder, and bring to 40°C/104°F. Add the dextrose and ice-cream stabiliser, and increase the temperature to 85°C/185°F. Remove from heat and stir in the egg yolks with the sugar; purée the mixture with a hand blender. When the temperature drops to 40°C/104°F, add the glycerine and Tahitian vanilla. Leave to stand refrigerated for 24 hours and run through the ice-cream maker.

—COCOA CRISP
YIELDS 400 G

250 g water
5 g gellan gum
75 g glucose powder
75 g sugar
2 g salt
50 g cocoa

In a casserole, place the water and gellan gum, and bring to a boil while stirring constantly. Remove from heat and add the remaining ingredients, previously sieved. Cool until it sets and then run the hand blender through it. Introduce the preparation into pastry bags and draw irregular lines on a silicone mat. Leave to dry at room temperature for 1 hour and bake at 180°C/356°F for 4 minutes. Remove crisps from the oven and, while hot, shape as desired. Leave to cool and reserve in an airtight container with silica gel.

GARNISHING AND PLATING

Cocoa powder

On a rectangular dinner plate, arrange on one side the liquorice shots, caramel jelly, 3 black crystallised olives, 3 dehydrated black olives, black olive oil and a pinch of cocoa powder. On the other side, place the vanilla sponge cake and an ice-cream quenelle on top. Finish by placing the cocoa crisp on top of the shots.

CHARCOAL-GRILLED ELVERS

SERVES 8 PEOPLE

COMPOSITION
Elvers
Roasted garlic foam
Tear peas

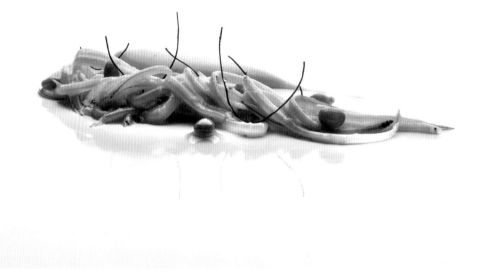

—ELVERS
YIELDS 320 G

320 g live elvers
Extra virgin olive oil
Brine for fish (basic recipes, p.429)

Introduce the elvers in brine for 2 minutes, remove and drain well any excess liquid. Place them in a wide, very fine sieve.

Before serving, place the sieve over the embers and stir the elvers carefully and slowly with a wooden spoon until they turn white. Remove from the embers and serve.

—ROASTED GARLIC FOAM
YIELDS 410 G

40 g whole garlic (1 head)
Extra virgin olive oil
90 g egg yolks
30 g water
6 g salt
270 g sunflower oil

Spray the garlic head with olive oil and wrap in aluminium foil. Place it directly over the embers until the cloves soften. Remove the garlic pulp, run through a fine sieve and reserve.

Separately, beat the egg yolks with water and salt and, when they turn fluffy, pour in the sunflower oil slowly while beating until a mayonnaise is made. Add the roasted garlic pulp and transfer the whole preparation to a ½ litre whipped cream dispenser. Add two chargers and reserve.

—TEAR PEAS

100 g tear peas
Salt

Before plating, blanch the tear peas in water with salt.

GARNISHING AND PLATING

Dry pepper threads
Extra virgin olive oil

Place the freshly grilled elvers in the middle of the plate, garnish with some dry pepper threads and roasted garlic foam on the side. Finish with some tear peas and a few drops of extra virgin olive oil.

CHARCOAL-GRILLED SEA URCHINS

SERVES 8 PEOPLE

COMPOSITION
Charcoal-grilled sea urchin purée
Clarified mantis shrimp
      consommé
Mantis shrimp consommé gelée
Pistillata seaweed purée
Sea urchin roe

—CHARCOAL-GRILLED SEA URCHIN PURÉE
YIELDS 80 G

100 g fresh urchin roe (12 gonads
      approximately)
10 g extra virgin olive oil

Place the sea urchin roe in a fine sieve
preventing them from coming into contact with
each other.

In a separate container, place some hot
embers and the sieve with the sea urchin
roe on top; sprinkle with a few drops of olive
oil. Cover quickly with cling film and leave to
smoke for 5 minutes. Next, remove the smoked
sea urchin roe and blend them with the
remaining oil. Adjust salt. Serve some purée
in each bowl and reserve.

—CLARIFIED MANTIS SHRIMP CONSOMMÉ
YIELDS 200 G

750 g mantis shrimps
50 g extra virgin olive oil
150 g mirepoix (basic recipes, p.427)
1.25 kg water
25 g pasteurised egg whites
Salt

Place the olive oil in a stockpot and brown
the mantis shrimps in it. Add the mirepoix
and fry lightly. Cover with water and set on low
heat until obtaining 500 g of stock. Strain and
transfer to another stockpot to reduce again
to 250 g stock. Blast chill.

Seal the stock in a vacuum pack bag when
it's very cold, together with the pasteurised
egg whites, and submerge in the Roner at
90°C/194°F until the egg whites set. Strain
with a cloth filter and reserve.

—MANTIS SHRIMP CONSOMMÉ GELÉE
YIELDS 160 G

160 g clarified mantis shrimp consommé
      (previously prepared)
1.6 g iota

Mix iota with the clarified consommé
previously prepared and bring to a boil.

Very carefully, pour 20 g of the mixture into the
bowls, on top of the sea urchin purée, and leave
to jellify. Reserve the bowls again.

—PISTILLATA SEAWEED PURÉE
YIELDS 180 G

150 g pistillata algae
100 g water

Clean the algae well and wash with abundant
water to remove any excess salt they may have.
Place in a saucepan with water and bring to
a boil. As soon as they start to boil, remove
quickly from the heat and strain. Purée the
algae in the Thermomix as finely as possible.
Run it through a sieve and reserve in a piping
bag until serving.

—SEA URCHIN ROE
YIELDS 50 G

5 sea urchin

Open the urchin with a pair of scissors, careful
not to break the roe inside. Using a small spoon,
remove the roe and clean off any impurities.
Reserve 4 sea urchin roe for each plate.

GARNISHING AND PLATING

Orange emulsion (basic recipes, p.427)
Fennel sprouts

Heat the bowl containing the jellified mantis
shrimp consommé. When it's very hot, place
the 4 sea urchin roe on top. Add a few drops
of pistillata algae purée and orange emulsion,
and finish with a few fennel sprouts.

IBERIAN
PORK CAPIPOTA

SERVES 8 PEOPLE

COMPOSITION

Pig's cheeks
Pig's tail
Pig's trotter
Pig's ear
Suckling pig gravy

—PIG'S CHEEKS

4 Iberian pork cheeks
Brine for meat (basic recipes, p.429)
Extra virgin olive oil

Immerse pork cheeks in iced water to soak for 6 hours.

Next, remove them from the water and submerge in brine for 2 minutes. Strain and seal in a vacuum pack bag with some olive oil. Cook in the Roner at 63°C/145°F for 24 hours. Cool and reserve.

—PIG'S TAIL

4 Iberian pork tails
40 g carrots
40 g onions
Extra virgin olive oil
Salt

Peel and cut vegetables and toss them in olive oil until they turn soft and brown.

Place the vegetables in a pot with the pig's tails and salt. Cover with water, cook for 4 hours and then remove and bone.

Arrange the boned pig's tails on cling film and roll them to make a cylinder approximately 2 cm thick, pressing to remove any air. Cool and reserve.

—PIG'S TROTTER

2 Iberian pork trotters
40 g carrots
40 g onions
Extra virgin olive oil
Salt

Blanch the pig's trotters by placing them in cold water and bringing them to a boil. As soon as they start to boil, remove from the heat and discard the water. Wash the pig's trotters and reserve.

Peel and cut the vegetables and toss them in olive oil until soft and brown. Place vegetables in a stockpot with the pig's trotters and salt. Cover with water, cook for 5 hours and then remove and bone.

Arrange the boned pig's trotters in a piece of cling film and make a cylinder approximately 3 cm thick, pressing to remove any air. Cool and reserve.

—PIG'S EAR

8 Iberian pork ears
1 litre extra virgin olive oil
Salt

Place the pig's ears in a pot with abundant water and salt. Boil for 4 hours over low heat. Remove from the water and set in the dryer at 60°C/140°F, until they dehydrate completely.

Heat the olive oil at 180°C/356°F and cool the dehydrated pig's ears until they puff and turn crisp. Drain any excess oil and reserve.

—SUCKLING PIG GRAVY
YIELDS 200 G

1.6 kg suckling pig bones and trimmings
210 g mirepoix (basic recipes, p.427)
1.7 kg cold water
32 g kuzu thickening agent (basic recipes, p.427)

Place the bones and trimmings in a baking tray and brown at 180°C/356°F until very crisp.

Remove any excess fat from the bones and place them and the trimmings in a stockpot with the mirepoix, previously browned. Remove any browned bits from the baking tray with cold water and add to the stockpot. Cover with the cold water and cook for 3 hours. Next, strain and reduce until obtaining 200 g of suckling pig gravy. Bring to a boil and add the kuzu mixture, adjust salt and strain. Reserve.

GARNISHING AND PLATING

Orange emulsion (basic recipes, p.427)
Oxalis leaves
Savory blossoms
Dried red chilli
Dried green chilli
Black pepper
Pink pepper
Oregano
Calamondin (*Citrofortunella microcarpa*)

Sear the pork cheeks on the griddle pan.

Cut the cylinder made with the boned pig's tails into 2-cm-thick portions and sear on the griddle pan until they turn brown and crisp.

Cut the cylinder made with the boned pig's trotters into 1-cm-thick portions, sear on the griddle pan until they turn brown and crisp.

Cut the cheeks in half and arrange half on the plate, next the pig's tail cylinder, the pig's trotter and finally, the fried pig's ear.

Arrange 4 oxalis leaves, 2 savory leaves, 3 calamondin segments, some orange emulsion, some suckling pig gravy, and finish with the mixture of spices.

CHARCOAL-GRILLED PRAWN WITH ACIDULATED PENNY BUN STOCK

SERVES 8 PEOPLE

COMPOSITION

Fresh prawns
Penny bun stock
Clarified penny bun stock
Acidulated penny bun stock

—FRESH PRAWNS

8 prawns
Salt

Clean prawns, removing whiskers, legs, tail
and vein. Pierce each prawn with a toothpick to
straighten, salt and charcoal-grill.

—PENNY BUN STOCK

YIELDS 800 G

100 g dehydrated penny buns (*Boletus edulis*)
1 kg water

Boil the water and add the dehydrated penny
buns. Cover and infuse for 30 minutes. Strain,
cool and reserve.

—CLARIFIED PENNY BUN STOCK

YIELDS 600 G

800 g penny bun stock (previously prepared)
80 g pasteurised egg whites

When cold, transfer the penny bun stock into
a vacuum pack bag with the 80 g pasteurised
egg whites. Cook at 90°C/194°F until the egg
white sets. Run through a sieve and reserve
the resulting stock.

—ACIDULATED PENNY BUN STOCK

YIELDS 600 G

600 g clarified penny bun stock (previously
        prepared)
16 g lime juice
0.5 g guindilla pepper oil (basic recipes, p.427)
Salt

Add the 16 g lime juice and 0.5 g guindilla
pepper oil to the 600 g clarified stock. Bring
to a boil, adjust salt and reserve.

GARNISHING AND PLATING

1 finger lime (*Citrus australasica*)
Preserved ginger
2 fresh penny buns (*Boletus edulis*)
Extra virgin olive oil
Mustard leaves
Aptenia cordifolia leaves
Indian cress

Cut the tips of the finger lime and remove the
peel, cut the lime in half and press the pith
lightly to extract its juice vesicles. Separate
16 juice vesicles and reserve the rest for other
recipes.

Cut the preserved ginger into 0.5 cm cubes.
Reserve.

Slice the fresh penny buns thinly and spread
some olive oil on them to keep their moisture.

On the plate, place 4 lime vesicles and 2
preserved ginger cubes. On top, place the
charcoal-grilled shrimp with the tail covered
with penny bun slices and a few leaves of
mustard, *Aptenia cordifolia* and Indian cress.
Finish with the acidulated penny bun stock, hot.

KID BELLY WITH MAJORERO CHEESE

COMPOSITION
Kid belly
Mint gel
Majorero cheese parmentier
Kid gravy
Crystallised pine kernels

—KID BELLY

4 kid bellies
Brine for meat (basic recipes, p.429)
Extra virgin olive oil

Place the kid bellies in brine for 1½ hours.
Remove and dry well of any excess water. Seal
in a vacuum pack bag at 100% with olive oil
and cook at 63°C/145°F for 24 hours.

If parboiling, cool as quickly as possible
and keep refrigerated until regeneration.

—MINT GEL
YIELDS 150 G

200 g mint leaves
50 g blanching water
50 g water
1.2 g agar-agar

Blanch the mint leaves in boiling water with
salt for 10 seconds and cool quickly in a cold
bain-marie. Also, cool the 50 g blanching water.

Blend the blanched mint leaves with the cold
cooking water and the other 50 g water. Strain
and mix with the agar-agar. Bring to a boil and
leave to solidify. Make a smooth purée, reserve
in a squeeze bottle.

—MAJORERO CHEESE PARMENTIER
YIELDS 650 G

200 g milk
50 g whipping cream
150 g majorero cheese
400 g potato purée (basic recipes, p.428)
8 g egg white powder

Heat the milk and cream, add the cheese and
leave to stand for 10 minutes. Next, blend the
mixture well to eliminate any lumps. Let it cool
and mix it with the potato purée and egg white.
Transfer to a 1 litre whipped cream dispenser
with two chargers and reserve in a bain-marie
at 65°C/149°F until serving.

—KID GRAVY
YIELDS 250 G

2 kg kid bones and trimmings
220 g mirepoix (basic recipes, p.427)
2.5 kg water
40 g kuzu thickening agent (basic recipes,
     p.427)

Roast the bones and trimmings in the oven
at 180°C/356°F for 50 minutes until brown.
Remove any excess fat and reserve.

In a stockpot, place the bones and trimmings
and the mirepoix, cover with cold water and
cook. When the liquid has reduced to 1 litre,
strain and reduce again to 250 g. Bring to a
boil, bind with the kuzu mixture, strain again
and reserve.

—CRYSTALLISED PINE KERNELS
YIELDS 30 G

20 g pine kernels
20 g sugar
10 g water

Roast the pine kernels in the oven. Place the
sugar and water in a saucepan, bring to a
boil and, as soon as it starts to boil, add the
roasted pine kernels. Stir continuously until
the sugar crystallises. When the pine kernels
are coated with crystallised sugar, remove
them and leave to cool.

GARNISHING AND PLATING

Cumin powder
Rosemary blossoms
Tarragon leaves

Sear the skin of the kid belly on the griddle pan.

On a plate, place a few drops of mint gel and
a few dots of kid gravy. On top, set the kid belly
with the skin facing up, and the parmentier
next to it with some cumin powder on top.
Finish with the crystallised pine kernels,
3 rosemary flowers and 2 tarragon leaves.

WOODCOCK AND BRIOCHE STUFFED WITH ITS SALMIS

SERVES 8 PEOPLE

COMPOSITION
Woodcock
Brioche
Woodcock duxelle
Woodcock consommé
Woodcock sauce

—WOODCOCK
YIELDS 8 AIGUILLETTES

4 woodcocks

Separate the woodcock breasts and remove their aiguillette. Reserve for plating.

With a knife, cut the heads in half and cook for 3 minutes in the oven at 160°C/320°F before serving.

—BRIOCHE
YIELDS 80 BRIOCHES

30 g sugar
25 g milk
12 g baking powder
125 g eggs
250 g flour
125 g softened butter
3 g salt

In a container, place the sugar, milk, and baking powder, and mix well until it incorporates. Add the eggs.

Sieve the flour and add to the mixture in 2 parts, then stir in the softened butter and salt. Knead the dough until very smooth and elastic, and until it no longer sticks to the container. Place in a bowl, cover and leave to stand for 12 hours refrigerated.

Stretch between 2 sheets of greaseproof paper with a rolling pin and some flour. Cool refrigerated for ½ hour, then divide it into 6g rolls. Refrigerate again. Shape the cold rolls into balls and leave to ferment for 40 minutes at 40°C/104°F. Reserve the fermented brioches.

—WOODCOCK DUXELLE
YIELDS 300 G

250 g onions
25 g butter
125 g mushrooms
50 g woodcock liver
50 g butter
Extra virgin olive oil
Salt

Melt the 25 g of butter and poach the onion, chopped, until very soft; add the mushrooms, brunoised, and toss it all in oil until it incorporates.

Sauté the livers in olive oil and blend with the 50 g of butter. Adjust salt and add the duxelle. Reserve.

—WOODCOCK CONSOMMÉ
YIELDS 225 G

1 kg woodcock bones
110 g mirepoix (basic recipes, p.427)
1 kg water

Place the bones in a baking tray and brown at 220°C/428°F. Remove any excess fat and transfer to a stockpot. Deglaze the baking tray, add the resulting juices to the stockpot with the mirepoix, and cover everything with cold water. Boil for 3 hours on very low heat to obtain a good infusion. Strain and reduce to 225 g of consommé.

—WOODCOCK SAUCE
YIELDS 230 G

1.25 kg woodcock bones
100 g mirepoix (basic recipes, p.427)
50 g extra virgin olive oil
1.25 kg water
15 g woodcock liver
35 g kuzu thickening agent (basic recipes, p.427)
25 g butter

Brown the bones with the vegetables cut up into small pieces, in ¾ of the olive oil. Add cold water and cook for 2 ½ hours.

Strain the resulting broth and reduce it until obtaining 200 g of woodcock stock. Reserve.

Sauté the liver with the remaining oil, add to the sauce and mix everything together. Run through a fine chinois, bind the sauce with the kuzu mixture and finish by emulsifying with butter. Strain again and reserve.

GARNISHING AND PLATING

24 truffle slices
Rosemary blossoms

Place the woodcock liver duxelle in a piping bag. Stuff the brioches and sear on both sides on a griddle pan until brown.

Place the stuffed brioche in the middle of the plate. Heat the woodcock aiguillette in a salamander, without overcooking, and place it next to the brioche, along with the halved woodcock head. Sprinkle it with woodcock sauce and add very thin slices of black truffle and rosemary flower. Accompany with the woodcock consommé served separately.

WHITE AND BLACK TRUFFLE SOUFFLÉ

SERVES 8 PEOPLE

COMPOSITION
Truffle ring
White truffle mousseline

—TRUFFLE RING
YIELDS 15 TRUFFLE RINGS

2 fresh black truffles weighing 50 g each
Egg whites

Slice the truffle thinly with a sharpened mandolin; place one slice on top of the other on an 18x4 cm strip of silicone paper, brush with egg white, and place the strip in a 6-cm-wide and 3-cm-deep metal ring. Reserve.

—WHITE TRUFFLE MOUSSELINE
YIELDS 850 G

500 g cream
150 g fresh white truffle
2.3 g xanthan gum
300 g egg whites
Salt

In a saucepan, bring the cream to a boil, lower the temperature to 80°C/176°F, and add truffle. Infuse for 10 minutes and blend. Add the xanthan gum, blend again until the mixture is very smooth, adjust salt, strain and cool. When the mixture has cooled down, add the egg whites before transferring it to a 1 litre whipped cream container with 2 chargers and reserve in a bain-marie at 65°C/149°F.

GARNISHING AND PLATING

Black truffle oil (basic recipes, p.427)
White truffle slices
10 g holm oak sawdust

Place the metal ring on the salamander and heat the black truffle, lightly brushed with egg white to adhere the slices.

On a plate, serve a dash of truffle oil; then, set the metal ring and the hot white truffle mousseline inside it and covered with some slices of white truffle. Remove the metal ring and the silicone paper, cover and, using a smoking gun, blow smoke inside the cover.

PEARLY RAZORFISH WITH BERGAMOT

SERVES 8 PEOPLE

COMPOSITION
Pearly razorfish
Bergamot foam
Fennel emulsion

—PEARLY RAZORFISH

4 pearly razorfish (*Xyrichthys novacula*)
    weighing 40 g each
Brine for fish (basic recipes, p.429)
100 g plain flour
Extra virgin olive oil

Clean the fish and fillet without scaling.
Immerse in brine for 3 minutes, dry well with
kitchen towels and coat with flour. Fry the fish
fillets in oil until they turn golden brown.

—BERGAMOT FOAM
YIELDS 450 G

150 g pasteurised egg yolks
Salt
300 g sunflower oil
15 g bergamot juice
1 bergamot, grated zest

In a container, place the pasteurised egg yolks
with salt, and emulsify slowly with sunflower
oil. Finish by adding 15 g of freshly squeezed
bergamot juice and grated bergamot zest. Fill
a ½ litre whipped cream dispenser and add 2
chargers. Reserve.

—FENNEL EMULSION
YIELDS 190 G

100 g blended fennel leaves
0.7 g xanthan gum
Salt
100 g extra virgin olive oil

Mix the blended fennel with the xanthan gum
and salt; liquidise with a hand blender for a
few minutes. Emulsify slowly with olive oil and
reserve.

GARNISHING AND PLATING

Orange emulsion (basic recipes, p.427)
Fennel sprouts

On a plate, place a dot of bergamot foam, a
drop of orange emulsion right in the middle of
it, with a drop of fennel emulsion on top. Place
a fried pearly razorfish fillet garnished with
some fennel sprouts.

E

—LANDSCAPE

E

The tomb of Raphael can be found in the Pantheon, in the city of Rome. At its base, praise from Pietro Bembo to the artist. In the times of Sanzio da Urbino, he says, nature was afraid the artist would substitute it. That is, that his powerful recreation would be more compelling, more real, truer than the model. In a couple of verses he summarises the whole history of Western art, what for the Greeks was mimesis, but taken to the extreme. The imitation that captures what it imitates and exceeds it. But on the other hand, as Susan Sontag would put it, we have contemporary convention: art is first of all an object, not an imitation. It all depends on the will to objectivise of both artist and viewer.

But let's return to cooking. We happen to be in the presence of a creation, that is, of an artefact reflected, in this instance, in the nearby landscape. Is it its intention to imitate it? It's a truffle hiding inside a rock like a dark pearl. Or the prawn lying on what could possibly be sand. Pictures, images of these surroundings. But at the same time, aware of its modernity, it isn't only after mimicry (or substitution), but after the game inherent to re-creation.

They are miniatures that evoke and have a different meaning, such as that of the stone (the rock) that breaks and, when open, reveals a new concept as well as a process that both resembles and differs from its model. A stab of pain that goes beyond mimicry; that is a dialogue between those who are fascinated by nature and those who see what has been conceived not as simple imitation, but as an animated object that takes shape on the table. A very different thing.

Mediterranean

The Mediterranean is the land of light. Nothing compares to the glimpse of the infinite that the sea offers. And its strength and character manifest beyond geographical influences. As written by Predrag Matvejevic in his *Mediterranean Breviary*: "Anyone, regardless of place of birth or residence, can become a Mediterranean. *Mediterraneanity* is acquired, not inherited [...]. Being Mediterranean entails more than history or geography, tradition or memory, birthright or belief. The Mediterranean is destiny." This quote, appropriated by cookery writer Óscar Caballero, is the motto of the cookery book, *La Riviera d'Alain Ducasse*.

At the end of the first millennium A.D. there were a multitude of ships coming and going from one culture to another over the Mediterranean sea. Pioneers were the Phoenicians, who invented writing, the computing of their time. The Greeks, for their part, were responsible for two ingenious distillates: wine and oil. The Iberians can be said to have contributed the joy of living: they lived in bright houses in villages facing the sea, and had healthy culinary traditions. They were the Mediterranean towns from which, in spite of Romanisation, we come, even if we present ourselves as descendants of that Romanisation and flaunt it as our main sign of identity in how we are and behave. Flavour and light. We have nourished from them, before and after the Romans. They are the essence inherited from our sea.

Classical *mediterraneanity* in haute cuisine probably began with Roger Vergé's basil sauce with cream. It was then followed by Jacques Maximin when he extolled a courgette flower at the baroque table of Negresco. And Alain Ducasse was his successor, first at La Terrase in the Juana hotel, and then at the luxurious Hôtel de Paris in Monaco. Contemporary *mediterraneanity* will be forever stamped in Ferran Adrià's book, *El sabor del Mediterráneo* (1993), a true historical reference book.

Mediterranean cuisine is a source of inspiration of an extreme richness. Infinite. There is still much to be done. We have to research, go back in history to the time of the Romans. We work with the *garum*, and want to show an update of the concepts of putrefaction, marinating or innards, with approaches such as the BLACK OLIVE GAZPACHO WITH ANCHOVY ICED POWDER, GREEN OLIVE SORBET, PRESERVED OLIVE FLAN, MARJORAM, FENNEL, BLACK OLIVE TEMPURA AND TOASTED BREAD.

To eat the earth

In the kitchen, we are seduced by the idea of 'eating the landscape', a landscape that has given character and essence to our people and that, in a natural way, is present in our burners and our tables. Traditional cuisine incorporates the landscape from local history, roots, generational conveyance of the cookery book and eating habits of the past. From the creative vision of the future, we also want cooking to be 'the landscape to the pot'. This expression, a tribute to Josep Pla, demonstrates perfectly that cooking based on research is not incompatible with cooking from our roots. We have many things in common, such as the essence of our landscape and the memories created by looking at the sea we share.

Landscapes are the key to our cuisine. The revisiting of the products of seasonal changes, the lasting but expected feeling of the ephemeral product. To recapture known smells on a walk by the sea, with samphire and the salty slap of the waves against the slate that cuts into the sea at the Cape of Creus. To go out for the first stroll of spring in the mountain, feeling the earth awaken from its winter silence and witness the sprouting of thyme and rosemary. The aroma of mimosa in February while walking through the botanic garden. The moist borders of the salicornia at the marshlands of l'Empordà. Mushrooms hiding under lush forests, scented with cork oak, pinewood or fern...

The Rotaval helps us consolidate the ties between the kitchen, science and the landscapes of memory. It allows us to bring to the table, almost literally, these scenes of our intimate geography. Through distillation techniques, the Rotaval provides the opportunity to eat impossible things, like soil. We pair it with an oyster, in an authentic surf 'n' turf, without sofritos or minced ingredients. The flavour of the sea and the flavour of the earth, iodine and minerals; the clarity of the colour of the sea and the deep darkness of the earth. Eating the soil distillate generates a very interesting emotional clash. The unknown generates doubts. Our leap into the void when eating this dish makes us question a familiar smell presented in a physical state that is completely unknown. The viscous texture of the soil distillate gives a soft initial impression and an aroma associated with a hard, almost contemptible consistency from the point of view of flavour.

We are also interested in capturing and bringing to the table the memories of the time of country houses: a field of clover, the aroma of the fig tree leaves, even the intense perfume of green tomatoes and the tomato plant. We can recapture this memory of the colour green from a green tomato and tomato plant leaf distillate. It's an approach representing vegetable life, greenness, the humidity of the atmosphere, agriculture, biodiversity and everything involving sustainability, how in danger it is, and this must be the focus of all future efforts.

Our culture of taste

The culture of taste along our Mediterranean Sea has enough elements in common to constitute a single culinary space. We can clearly see ours opening up to other concentric or superimposed culinary spaces: from the obvious that can be seen in a map—like countries—to those present underground in other geographical (or even historical), more subtle spaces such as the Iberian peninsula, the Pyrenees, the Mediterranean, the lands of the Occitania and Southern Europe, as well as in Semitic lands.

There are points in common in our cuisine, of direct Arabic origin. They occur throughout Mediterranean and Latin lands. The raisin and pine kernel garnish, as well as the use of pine kernels and raisins separately, is often present in Mediterranean cuisine, from Catalonia to the Veneto, from Cadiz to Sicily and most countries in the Maghreb. Rice with raisins is Turkish, but also of Valencia. Maghribian couscous is also from Mallorca. Stuffed aubergines are from Mallorca but come from the Arab world. French ratatouille is *pisto* in Spain, *samfaina* in Catalonia, *alboronia* in Murcia… Dried fruits are strongly present in Catalan as well as in Arabic cuisine.

In short, the Mediterranean Sea, its climate and the products of its land result in a gastronomy that, in one way or another, is shared by all the peoples touched by the Mare Nostrum. We look for inspiration in the most traditional techniques of our ancestors; we turn our search to innovative and scientific methods; if we are bathed by the Mediterranean, its breeze is present when we cook and we long for it when we eat.

In the dining room...

We brought the meadows from Girona to the restaurant in the shape of a grove by the table. The team of interior designers surprised us by creating a triangular garden inside the dining area; a poetic, rich and symbolic approach to the brotherhood, reproduced and seen through the trees. We relate this garden to the meadows of Girona, but some see it as a Nordic landscape, and others as a zen landscape... We like the fact that at El Celler people can imagine being in a place that exists in their mind, a place in the world where they would like to be... It is fantastic to have a space that makes us contemplate nature. The landscape is the same for everybody. But each of us experiences a different journey.

THE WHOLE PRAWN

SERVES 8 PEOPLE

COMPOSITION
Charcoal-grilled prawn
Phytoplankton sand
Prawn sand
Prawn head juice
Crisp prawn legs
Prawn stock reduction
Prawn concentrate
Prawn velouté
Phytoplankton velouté
Onion and squid ink sponge cake

—CHARCOAL-GRILLED PRAWN

8 prawns
Salt

Peel the prawn tails and remove the heads, reserving both the heads and legs for other recipes. Adjust salt and sear the tails lightly over holm oak embers to acquire the aroma. Reserve.

—PHYTOPLANKTON SAND
YIELDS 100 G

100 g breadcrumbs
3.5 g powdered phytoplankton
Salt

Toast and dry the breadcrumbs in the oven at 160°C/320°F for 10 minutes unventilated. Leave to cool and mix with the phytoplankton powder and salt. Reserve.

—PRAWN SAND
YIELDS 120 G

75 g prawn oil (basic recipes, p.428)
40 g maltodextrine
Salt

In a bowl, stir in the maltodextrine and salt and add the prawn oil slowly, mixing with a whisk. Reserve.

—PRAWN HEAD JUICE
YIELDS 120 G

8 prawn heads
Salt

Open the prawn heads carefully and extract their juice. Cook it slowly in a frying pan, adjust salt and blend. Strain and reserve in a bain-marie.

—CRISP PRAWN LEGS

Front and back legs of 8 prawns
100 g flour
1 litre extra virgin olive oil

Leave the front and back legs of the prawns
on a baking tray in the oven at 140°C/284°F for
5 minutes. Next, coat them with flour and fry in
olive oil at 160°C/320°F until crisp. Reserve
in a dry place.

—PRAWN STOCK REDUCTION
YIELDS 500 G

1 kg prawn stock (basic recipes, p.428)

Reduce half of the prawn stock over low heat.

—PRAWN CONCENTRATE
YIELDS 80 G

250 g prawn stock reduction
    (previously prepared)

Introduce the prawn stock in the Rotaval
at 56°C/133°F Bt (bath temperature) and
45°C/113°F Dt (distillation temperature) for
6 hours at 30 rpm. The result is an airy, clear
and subtle prawn distillate, leaving in the first
flask a very flavourful prawn juice that results
from the evaporation produced by boiling at
very low temperature. Reserve the concentrate.

—PRAWN VELOUTÉ
YIELDS 500 G

250 g prawn stock reduction
    (previously prepared)
260 g cream
10 egg yolks
Salt

In a casserole, place the prawn stock reduction
together with the cream, and bring to a boil.
As soon as it comes to a boil, pour it quickly
over the egg yolks and mix with a hand blender.
Transfer the mixture into a covered terrine
and place it in a bain-marie in the oven at
160°C/320°F for 45 minutes. Next, remove
from the bain-marie and blast chill. Divide the
mixture into two 250 g portions: blend and
adjust salt one portion and reserve in a bain-
marie until plating; reserve the other half for
the phytoplankton velouté.

—PHYTOPLANKTON VELOUTÉ
YIELDS 250 G

250 g prawn velouté (previously prepared)
4 g phytoplankton
Salt

Mix the velouté and phytoplankton with a
hand blender, adjust salt and reserve in a bain-
marie until plating.

—ONION AND SQUID INK SPONGE CAKE
YIELDS 450 G

125 g pasteurised egg whites
120 g onion confit
80 g pasteurised egg yolks
80 g isomalt
20 g flour
7 g squid ink
2 g baking powder
Salt

Blend all the ingredients in the Thermomix and
run through a fine chinois. Pour the mixture
into a ½ litre whipped cream dispenser with
2 chargers and reserve refrigerated for 24 hours.

GARNISHING AND PLATING

Pistillata seaweed

Arrange the prawn and phytoplankton sands
on a plate. Place the crisp prawn legs on top.
Pour 20 g of onion and squid ink sponge cake
into a plastic cup, set it in the microwave on
the highest setting for 1 minute, remove from
the mould and coat with the prawn head
juice. Stick 2 pieces of pistillata seaweed
in the sponge cake and place it on one side
of the plate, next to the sands. Add a dot of
phytoplankton velouté, another of prawn
velouté, and one of prawn concentrate. Heat
the prawn, previously charcoal-grilled, on the
salamander and serve.

MEDITERRANEAN GARDEN

SERVES 8 PEOPLE

COMPOSITION

Lavender sugar
Orange blossom cream
Orange blossom jelly
Cantaloupe melon granita
Fennel sauce
White peach and juniper sorbet

—LAVENDER SUGAR
YIELDS 1.080 G

1 kg sugar
80 g lavender

Mix the sugar with the lavender in the Thermomix until it is a uniform colour. Reserve.

—ORANGE BLOSSOM CREAM
YIELDS 520 G

250 g milk
250 g cream
50 g sugar
40 g cornflour
30 g orange blossom water

Make a crème pâtissière by heating the milk and cream with sugar; in the meantime, mix the cornflour with the orange blossom water. When the milk comes to a boil, add the mixture of cornflour and orange blossom water and stir until obtaining a creamy texture. Strain and leave to cool before reserving in an airtight container.

—ORANGE BLOSSOM JELLY
YIELDS 195 G

200 g orange blossom water
1 g agar-agar

Mix the agar-agar with ⅓ of the orange blossom water and bring to a boil. Add the remaining water and spread the mixture on a 1.5-cm-deep tray. When it has set, cut the jelly into 1.5 cm cubes.

—CANTALOUPE MELON GRANITA
YIELDS 550 G

500 g cantaloupe melon juice
25 g inverted sugar syrup
25 g dextrose
2 gelatine sheets

Heat the inverted sugar syrup with the dextrose and some cantaloupe juice; while still hot, add the gelatine sheets previously hydrated and, lastly, the remaining cantaloupe juice. Reserve at -18°C/0°F.

—FENNEL SAUCE
YIELDS 100 G

100 g blended fennel leaves
20 g sugar
1 g agar-agar

Bring all the ingredients to a boil and leave to solidify. When the mixture has set, break its texture with the hand blender to a sauce-like consistency. Reserve in a piping bag.

—WHITE PEACH AND JUNIPER SORBET
YIELDS 1.5 KG

200 g water
20 g inverted sugar syrup
0.5 g juniper
200 g sugar
50 g dextrose
30 g glucose powder
7.5 g sorbet stabiliser
1 kg white peach purée

Heat the water with the inverted sugar syrup and juniper berries. Just before it comes to a boil, add the remaining dry ingredients, previously mixed, and increase temperature to 85°C/185°F. Then, add white peach purée and leave the mixture to ripen for 24 hours. Next, run it through the ice-cream maker and reserve in the freezer at -18°C/0°F.

GARNISHING AND PLATING

Marigold petals
Basil leaves
Calamondins (*Citrofortunella microcarpa*)
Fresh almonds
Gooseberries

Spread a base of lavender sugar on the plate and rake like sand. On top of it, distribute in a balanced way the cantaloupe melon granita, two dots of orange blossom cream, a couple of orange blossom jelly cubes, three dots of fennel sauce, a small quenelle of white peach and juniper sorbet and, lastly, the marigold petals, basil leaves, a few calamondin segments, one fresh almond and a couple of gooseberries.

ST. GEORGE'S MUSHROOM BONBON

**SERVES 25 PEOPLE
(1 SNACK PER PERSON)**

COMPOSITION

St. George's mushroom cream

—ST. GEORGE'S MUSHROOM CREAM
YIELDS 200 G

200 g St. George's mushrooms
20 g butter
50 g shallots
100 g cream
100 g cocoa butter
Olive oil
Salt

Sear mushrooms in a frying pan with
olive oil until brown; remove and reserve.

Heat the butter and poach the brunoised
shallots very slowly with a pinch of salt,
then add the previously seared mushrooms
and cream, and cook.

When the cream has reduced to half, blend
the mixture and run through a fine chinois.
Pour into mushroom-shaped moulds made
with liquid silicone (see process on page 429)
and freeze.

When the bonbons have frozen, remove them
from the mould and puncture the base of
the mushroom stalk; coat completely with
a fine layer of melted cocoa butter.

Reserve refrigerated so that the inside thaws
and becomes creamy.

GARNISHING AND PLATING

Freeze-dried moss

Place a small amount of freeze-dried moss
on the plate, from where a few St. George's
mushrooms will 'sprout'.

SEA SNAILS WITH FENNEL

SERVES 8 PEOPLE

COMPOSITION
Fennel foam
Squid soil
Fennel soil
Sea snails
Slow-cooked sea snails
Sea snail sofrito

—FENNEL FOAM
YIELDS 560 G

500 g bulb fennel
40 g onion
5 g anise seeds
500 g cream
1.5 g xanthan gum
Olive oil

Sweat the onion well until very soft; add the fennel, previously washed and julienned. Fry lightly and add the anise seeds. Add the cream and cook for approximately 20 minutes. Remove from the heat and blend in the Thermomix, add xanthan gum and continue blending for 5 minutes. Run the mixture through a fine sieve and transfer to a ½ litre whipped cream dispenser, adding 2 chargers. Reserve in a bain-marie.

—SQUID SOIL
YIELDS 125 G

100 g butter
100 g flour
50 g sugar
5 g salt
10 g squid ink

Cut the butter into small irregular cubes and leave to soften at room temperature. Mix the sugar and salt with the butter and add the flour, previously sieved. Lastly, add the squid ink. Spread the mixture on cling film and roll; freeze. When frozen, grate the roll with a fine Microplane over a baking sheet lined with greaseproof paper and bake at 180°C/356°F for 15 minutes. Remove from the oven, leave to dry and crumble by hand. Reserve.

—FENNEL SOIL
YIELDS 120 G

100 g butter
100 g flour
50 g sugar
5 g salt
5 drops of fennel essence
3 g dehydrated fennel powder

Cut the butter into small irregular cubes and leave to soften at room temperature. Mix the sugar and salt with the butter and add the flour, previously sieved. Lastly, add the fennel essence and dehydrated fennel powder. Spread the mixture on cling film and roll; freeze. When frozen, grate the roll with a fine Microplane over a baking sheet lined with greaseproof paper and bake at 170°C/338°F for 15 minutes. Remove from the oven, leave to dry and crumble by hand. Reserve.

—SEA SNAILS
YIELDS 500 G

500 g sea snails

Wash the snails several times to eliminate any possible impurities and dirt left. Place them in a large stockpot covered with water and paint the rim of the pot using a brush dipped in a water and salt solution to prevent them from escaping. Bring to a boil starting with cold water. When all the snails are cooked, strain and reserve.

—SLOW-COOKED SEA SNAILS
YIELDS 375 G

2 garlic cloves
100 g sunflower oil
50 g bulb fennel
500 g cooked sea snails (previously prepared)
30 g shallots
3 g salt
5 peppercorns

Crush garlic cloves and fry them lightly in a stockpot with a dash of sunflower oil. Wash the bulb fennel well and julienne as finely as possible. Add it to the crushed garlic and julienned shallot and toss everything in oil until the fennel is very soft. Add the cooked snails and the remaining sunflower oil, cover and cook for 2 hours on a heat diffuser over very low heat, stirring every half hour. Strain the liquid left and cool down before deglazing. Remove the snails from their valves and reserve with the fennel.

—SEA SNAIL SOFRITO
YIELDS 220 G

3 garlic cloves
6 shallots
150 g tomato concasse
45 g sea snail cooking juices
    (from previous preparation)
60 g slow-cooked sea snails
    (previously prepared)
75 g bulb fennel (from previous preparation)
Extra virgin olive oil

In a frying pan with a dash of olive oil, sauté the garlic cloves, brunoised, then add chopped shallots and lastly, the tomato. When everything is gently fried, deglaze with the snail cooking juices and bring to a boil. Then, add the cooked snails and bulb fennel previously prepared. Mix and reserve.

GARNISHING AND PLATING

Fennel sprouts

On a dinner plate, place a spoonful of poached sea snails previously heated in a frying pan with a dash of oil. Add a few dots of sofrito on top and cover with hot fennel foam. On top of it, add a few crumbs of squid soil and fennel soil. Distribute a few sea snails around the plate and on the foam. Lastly, stick a few fennel sprouts into it.

TRUFFLE

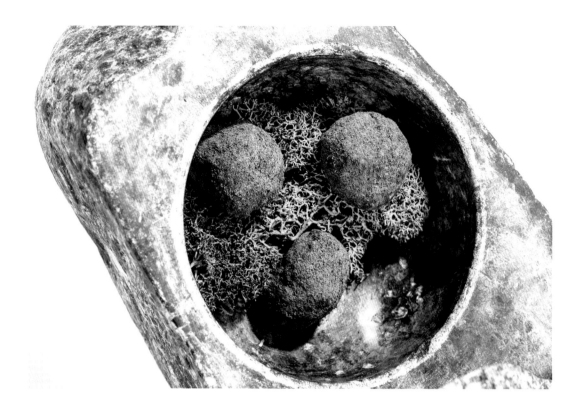

**SERVES 25 PEOPLE
(1 SNACK PER PERSON)**

COMPOSITION

Truffle and black
    chanterelle powder
Black truffle cream
Cocoa butter coating

—TRUFFLE AND BLACK
CHANTERELLE POWDER
YIELDS 180 G

200 g fresh black chanterelles
200 g truffle skin

Prepare a baking sheet with a silicone mat.

Finely chop both ingredients and distribute
over the baking sheet. Introduce in the
dehydrator at 60°C/140°F for 24 hours. When
dehydrated, crush and reserve in an airtight
container.

—BLACK TRUFFLE CREAM
YIELDS 250 G

230 g cream
20 g grated truffle
15.5 g black truffle oil (basic recipes, p.427)
10 g truffle juice
0.5 g xanthan gum
Salt

Place all the ingredients in a container and
blend to a smooth cream. Fill silicone moulds
shaped as truffles (see process on page 429)
and freeze.

—COCOA BUTTER COATING
YIELDS 200 G

200 g cocoa butter

Prepare a container with the black chanterelle
and truffle powder.

Melt the cocoa butter and coat the truffles
while frozen and pierced by a toothpick. Coat in
the black chanterelle and truffle powder.

GARNISHING AND PLATING

Freeze-dried moss

Leave the truffles to temper and place in the
stone over a layer of moss.

AUTUMN SALAD

—PUMPKIN JUICE
YIELDS 250 G

250 g liquefied pumpkin
0.25 g xanthan gum

Churn the pumpkin juice with xanthan gum, strain and reserve refrigerated.

—PENNY BUN STALKS
YIELDS 24 STICKS

4 medium-sized penny buns (*Boletus edulis*)

Separate the caps of the penny buns and reserve them for other recipes. Clean the stalks and cut them into small 3x0.3 cm sticks. Reserve them refrigerated in a covered container.

—PUFFED PUMPKIN SEEDS
YIELDS 85 G

250 g sunflower oil
75 g pumpkin seeds
Salt

In a container, mix the pumpkin seeds and sunflower oil while cold and heat to 180°C/356°F. Using a wire skimmer, remove the seeds from the oil as they puff, and transfer them quickly to kitchen towels. Adjust salt and reserve.

—PUMPKIN SEED SAND
YIELDS 172 G

114 g maltodextrine
11.5 g salt
103 g oil from frying seeds
    (from previous preparation)
65 g puffed pumpkin seeds
    (previously prepared)

Mix the maltodextrine and salt and slowly add the oil from frying seeds, mixing well with a whisk. Using a knife, chop the puffed seeds and add them to the previous mixture. Reserve in a covered container.

—WALNUT SAND
YIELDS 250 G

114 g maltodextrine
3.5 g salt
85.5 g walnut oil
50 g walnuts

Mix the maltodextrine and salt and slowly add the walnut oil, mixing well with a whisk. Using a knife, chop the walnuts and add them to the mixture. Reserve in a covered container.

—PENNY BUN OIL
YIELDS 280 G

10 medium-sized penny buns (*Boletus edulis*)
200 g sunflower oil
100 g penny bun powder

Clean the mushrooms, cut them into thick slices, and brown them on both sides in a frying pan with a dash of sunflower oil. When brown, add the remaining oil and cook for 2 hours at 70°C/158°F. Remove from heat, add powder and blend. Run through a fine chinois and blast chill. Reserve refrigerated and well covered.

—MUSHROOM SAND
YIELDS 230 G

2 g dehydrated black chanterelles
27 g penny bun powder
100 g maltodextrine
3.5 g salt
105 g penny bun oil (previously prepared)

Place the black chanterelles in the Thermomix and crush to a fine powder. Add the penny bun powder, salt and maltodextrine. Blend on medium speed while pouring the oil slowly until obtaining a fine sand texture. Reserve in an airtight container until plating.

—ENOKI MUSHROOMS

24 fresh enoki mushrooms

Remove the mushroom caps leaving a 1.5 cm stalk. Reserve them refrigerated in a covered container.

—GOLDEN ENOKI MUSHROOMS

24 golden enoki mushrooms

Remove the mushroom caps leaving a 1.5 cm stalk. Reserve them refrigerated in a covered container.

—PERSIMMON PURÉE
YIELDS 180 G

250 g persimmon
2.5 g agar-agar

Peel persimmons and purée. In a container, mix the persimmon and agar-agar and bring to a boil. Strain and blast chill.

When set, blend the mixture with a hand blender and reserve refrigerated in squeeze bottles.

—FRITTER ROOTS
YIELDS 350 G

145 g plain flour
100 g eggs
65 g water
30 g sugar
27 g honey
1.5 g baking soda
Extra virgin olive oil
Salt

Mix all the ingredients making sure it's free of lumps, and leave the mixture to stand for 12 hours refrigerated.

Heat the olive oil to 180°C/356°F, insert two toothpicks in the dough and let strings of dough fall into the hot oil; cook until golden brown. Drain any excess oil on kitchen towel and reserve.

—JERUSALEM ARTICHOKE SKIN
YIELDS 10 FRIED SKINS

200 g Jerusalem artichokes
Sunflower oil
Salt

Cook the tubers in the oven at 170°C/338°F until soft. Remove and peel them carefully avoiding breaking the skin. Clean the skin well and leave to dry in the dehydrator at 65°C/149°F. When dry, fry it in sunflower oil at 180°C/356°F, remove from heat and shape quickly by hand before it cools down, rolling it. Adjust salt and reserve in an airtight container in a dry place.

—QUINCE PURÉE
YIELDS 170 G

250 g quinces

In the oven, cook the quinces unpeeled and wrapped in aluminium foil. When cooked, peel, purée with the water they released in the oven, and reserve refrigerated in a covered container.

—TANGERINE CELLS
YIELDS 80 G

2 tangerines

Peel the tangerine segments and freeze by immersing them for a few seconds in liquid nitrogen. Place the frozen segments between two sheets of kitchen paper and tap carefully until the cells break off. Reserve them in a container in the freezer until serving.

—SOIL AIR
YIELDS 250 G

250 g soil distillate (basic recipes, p.428)
3.5 g soy lecithin

Combine both ingredients, mix well and leave to stand. Liquidise with a hand blender, forming some air in the mixture. Reserve.

—PERSIMMON SORBET
YIELDS 700 G

10 g inverted sugar syrup
18 g dextrose
100 g water
100 g sugar
20 g glucose
2.5 g sorbet stabiliser
500 g persimmon purée

In a container, place the inverted sugar syrup, dextrose and water. Cook on low heat until it reaches 40°C/104°F and then add the remaining ingredients except the persimmon purée. Continue cooking until it reaches 85°C/185°F. Remove from heat and leave to stand refrigerated for 24 hours.

Next, blend the sorbet base with the persimmon purée. Place in a Pacojet beaker and freeze. Churn before serving.

—SWEET POTATO PURÉE
YIELDS 200 G

250 g sweet potatoes
25 g butter
10 g extra virgin olive oil

Charcoal-grill the sweet potatoes and, when cooked, peel and mash the flesh with butter and oil. Reserve in piping bags.

—APPLE
YIELDS 20 SHEETS

60 g water
30 g sugar
1 Royal Gala apple

Bring the water and sugar to a boil in a casserole until the sugar dissolves. Remove from heat and cool.

Slice the Royal Gala apple finely and seal 10 slices per vacuum pack bag at 100% together with some syrup. Reserve until ready to use.

—CHANTERELLES
YIELDS 16 UNITS

4 small chanterelles

Clean the chanterelles well and quarter. Reserve.

GARNISHING AND PLATING

Beetroot sprouts

Draw a line through the centre of the plate with the sweet potato purée, and arrange penny bun strips on it. Cover with the sands in the following order: seed sand, walnut sand and mushroom sand.

Over the last sand, set randomly 2 puffed pumpkin seeds, 3 golden enoki mushrooms and 3 enoki mushrooms. On each end, place 2 fritter roots. In the middle of the sand, stick the fried Jerusalem artichoke skin, beetroot sprouts and 2 quarters of chanterelle.

Form a very small quenelle with the quince purée on one side of the plate, and distribute the tangerine cells, a few dots of persimmon purée and a few drops of pumpkin juice. Air the soil distillate and place it on one side of the dish with the rolled apple sheet. Garnish with a quenelle of persimmon sorbet.

F

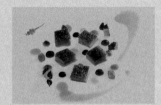

—WINE

One cannot stress enough the importance attributed to wine after visiting the sanctuary Josep built as a wine cellar at El Celler. The *wine server*, as he defines himself, works hard not only to learn everything there is to know, but makes a conscious effort to share it with any friend or stranger who enters this box of boxes—the structure that is both relaxation and effervescence, peace and vitality—to enjoy a unique moment: the ceremonial consecration of the wine cellar. Each of the chapels has a specific purpose because each of them is a stage, a liturgy —because it is religion.

But wine is more, a lot more, than the liquid element that remains static on the table. Wine is not a reminder or a footnote, but here it is transformed into an essential component of gastronomy. It doesn't watch the play from the gallery. It makes no brief comments or lively exclamations from a distance. Instead it participates, just like any other actor. And its transformation, from the changing room that is the wine cellar to the stalls, is not only thanks to Josep's restlessness to discover new coded messages, but the tripartite will to transform food, or the construction of that food, into a shared adventure.

In *Els fruits saborosos*, Carner said that the poet, just like the grape, does not seek the crown but leaves for future generations, "a little sunshine of my distant love, / locked in the cellar, buried in cobwebs". What is achieved here is that the transition is not made from privacy but from involvement. The wine leaves the web to become the breath which invades the kitchen.

According to the Roca brothers

In his work *Natural History*, Pliny the Elder chose to refer to the vine with the "seriousness of a Roman when dealing with arts and sciences". In fact, the relationship between culture, agriculture and science can hardly be ignored. Being so close to our land, we also cannot forget our connection to wine, omnipresent in our gastronomic heritage. A historical outline suffices to show that our enjoyment of wine and food comes from afar. Our culture has made a fundamental contribution to the culture of wine. The first book published on wine is said to be *Liber de vinis,* by Arnau de Vilanova, in the 13th century. In the *Llibre de Sent Soví,* an anonymous Catalan cookery book from the 14th century, it is said that the culture of wine and gastronomy are "courtesies one must know, men and women of any social class". Master Ruperto de Nola wrote treatises about how to serve wine; and examples of harmony between dishes and wines are found as early as the beginning of the Middle Ages in the section 'Com usar bé de beure e menjar' [How to drink and eat well] of *Lo Terç de Lo Crestià* [The third volume of The Christian], from the 14th century, written by Francesc Eiximenis, a priest born in Girona, considered the first wine critic and the most valued and regarded from the Middle Ages. Also, Ramon Llull illustrated our love of good food and drinks when he said "we want exquisite delicacies and we want to drink noble wines".

Wine in vanguard cuisine

So we come from a tradition that is closely linked to wine. But in recent years few great chefs have ventured to contribute their knowledge to cooking with wine. The article 'El vino y la gastronomía molecular' [Wine and molecular gastronomy] by French physicist and chemist Hervé This, published by *ACE Revista de Enologia*, explains the experiments carried out in this area by French chef Pierre Gagnaire, who in March 2008 suggested to "control the release of flavour through processes such as the extraction of odoriferous hydrophobic molecules from wine in oil, temperature control, and the use of several components present in wine to release flavour only at specific moments". Hervé This says that, in order to achieve it, "we used to resort to molecular associations with polymers such as gelatine. Clearly, the higher the association, the lower the molecule release." In May 2005, Gagnaire's suggestion was "not using wine for sauces, but resorting to the phenol extracted from wine or grapes. These completely synthetic sauces resulting from the addition of said ingredients, were called *Wöhler sauces,* in honour of Friedrich Wöhler (1800-1882), the first chemist to obtain synthetic organic molecules." And in 2004, it was Gagnaire again who made wine gelatines, "although phenols cloud the liquid when adding the gelatine", as This explains.

Science and mysticism. Body and soul

So we confirmed that wine opens the doors to experimentation in cooking because it "contains molecules that arouse great interest in physics and chemistry", as the French scientist explained. Wine is already interesting for its spiritual, mystical, customary, geologic, and geographic background. But it is even more attractive when its composition is valued.

Wine is life. It may seem like a poetic statement, and it is, but it is also charged with an empirical discourse when we take into account the series of physical and chemical reactions that make up wine. Science and mysticism. Body and soul... We approach cooking with wine from customary observation. Also academic. From transgression, tasting, personal or interpretation of the landscape. And again, from a dialogue with science. So, by making the most of our synergy with Fundació Alícia and the Guivaudan Company, we come closer to the molecular connection of wine as a starting point for the creation of new dishes. Therefore, we make a tripartite cuisine in which wine enters with all its generosity through a wide open door.

Sweet wine: spoonfuls of pleasure

Sweet wine is the result of unique actions, as this sugary creation of oenology is unique. Often times, when we reach the height of tasting great sweet wines, we understand they can be considered desserts in and of themselves, due to their aromatic complexity and gustative body. The enormous play of nuances sweet wines offer entails a special type of seduction. Frequently, when we face the peak of taste and an emotional and moving communion, we have the feeling that we don't need a dessert to accompany a great sweet wine. We recall the day when Joan and Jordi were served a wine in a soup dish, having to eat it with a spoon (instead of drinking it). The aim was to verify the complexity of a wine and change the classical concept of container and tasting. Thus, with a spoon, the wine is presented as a dessert, transformed into a half-congealed soup, served in a soup dish and accompanied by a sorbet made with the same wine. The wine chosen for this experiment was a Riesling from the clayey area of Rheingau (Germany), of crystallised density and fresh acidity, an essence of raisin seasoned with noble rot, sweet, low alcohol content, and extraordinarily arrogant.

To eat it with a spoon signifies a new way of enjoying wine, of unhurried enjoyment and a complete conceptual twist on tasting. The sorbet adds texture and a refreshing temperature. Wine in a dish is accompanied by a glass of a drink made from some of the aromatic descriptors of the wine: hints of honey and lemon, orange and saffron, basil, mint and raspberry. Even if only once, how interesting it is to wink an eye at the history of blends and travel the road in the wrong direction!

Non-alcoholic wine?

Why is alcohol so important in a wine? Because it has a direct and crucial influence. It provides sweetness, oiliness, and fills the mouth… It is volatile, releasing a bouquet that contributes to the aromatic and tasty function of the wine. Alcohol is a platform from where an aromatic range unfolds. It is also crucial when creating tactile sensations. It creates an enveloping sensation… Why not say it: alcohol is the soul of wine.

We are currently working with a more open, pragmatic and permissive mind. And in spite of the importance of alcohol in wine, its removal has become common practice. The methods employed more frequently are:

— **Reverse osmosis**: a molecular filtering system to trap the alcohol, water, and volatile components of wine.

— **Cold evaporation (Spinning Cone Column)**: uses the centrifugal force of cones installed on large columns to evaporate alcohol.

— **Distillation of alcohol through pressure at low temperatures**: as done with the Rotaval.

We are all aware that removing alcohol from wine from the beginning means losing an important amount of the aromas that define its essence. Also, wine evolves with time and therefore, to deprive it of alcohol from the beginning hinders this evolution.

There is another path that needs to be researched: the membranes of reverse osmosis and nanofiltration at the end of the process, after bottling. We need to establish the operating conditions to design a versatile and practical device that facilitates reducing the alcohol content of a beverage at a small scale, without it losing its essential organoleptic qualities and maintaining the highest level of the volatile substances necessary to preserve such properties. This device would be very useful in the restaurant business and also at home. Its aim is to reduce the alcohol content of the wine before drinking, or we could say, 'alcohol à la carte'.

Apart from these techniques, we can obviously dilute its alcohol content by simply adding water. In any case, the challenge will continue to be finding the right balance, whether through technology or by natural means. The latter are worked on more intensely on the vine or are subjected to new areas of research, such as finding new yeasts that can transform sugar with a lower content of alcohol.

De-alcoholisation with the Rotaval

Our approach with the Rotaval revolves around working selectively and concretely with specific wines. Our experiences have led us to see interesting changes in wines. De-alcoholisation with the Rotaval is performed through distillation at very low temperatures (20-30°C/68-86°F); therefore, the product is not affected. The interesting game consists of diluting a wine by two to three degrees at a time until all the alcohol has been removed.

The results of our research until now show that the appearance of dry wines with a high percentage of alcohol and a good density level remains unchanged during this process. Dry wines with a low alcohol content and less structure tend to go lean. Sweet wines from white grapes produce a large amount of liqueur and alcohol-free wine of outstanding qualitative value. The absence of alcohol in this case is replaced by residual sugar, a vital component to maintain its viscous and pleasant feel. Although tannin determines their flavour, sweet wines from red grapes maintain a good tactile balance, diluted but still interesting. Pedro Ximénez, Muscatel, Mistelle and other wines of similar characteristics and that possess a high density of sugar and caramelisation, offer very interesting results. Pedro Ximénez, sugar content of which reaches 500 grams per litre, continues to seduce without being affected by the injustice of having extracted its spirit. The alcohol resulting from it has a special magic. Its performance, memory and the associations of its aroma remind us of red wine in spite of its obvious clearness. It is, in fact, a liqueur of Pedro Ximénez that bears no similarities with the barrel-aged brandy of the same company. There is nothing like it in the market. One of the games we can suggest is serving alcohol-free Pedro Ximénez and a grappa made from its extract with the Rotaval. Two paths to pleasure on the table. A divertimento.

Clearly, wine is a source of enjoyment and infinite pleasure. Between the burners and high technology, we pretend to be alchemists, extracting its true essence and transforming it into a thousand different and surprising experiences to bring to your table. We want to honour this fruit of the earth and tradition by raising it to the throne of privilege it deserves and approaching it with all the tools we have available, from the knowledge of our distant past, to the most revolutionary of scientific instruments. Because cooking at El Celler is not understood without a passion for wine.

In the dining room...

We have always tried to avoid ostentation, from symbolising luxury and money in a label. At some point we started to find other things about wine that were more interesting to us. We have been able to enjoy multiple experiences in these open tastings, to witness expressions enriched by the senses, and we have tried to bring to the restaurant whatever has seduced us and made us fall in love, to share our way of experiencing wine.

We hope that the people who come to El Celler get to know better the person who keeps the wine; we want to create interaction, a reflective approach of respect for nature, of dialogue with wine makers. We want to feel like the ambassadors of those who make the wine, to be close to people, who don't have to find rigidity in the habit and consumption of wine. We want to show that wine is not only to be tasted and sniffed, but that it can be felt, or even heard. We want for the visit to the cellar to be as pleasant for the wine enthusiast as for the teetotaller. We want to invite children and the elderly, and for all of them to find a recreational sense in the cellar, of entertainment but also reflection over the fascinating dialogue between man and nature: to know that when man intervenes, nature will put him in his place. In short, we want to show wines we like with frankness, in five chapels or spaces dedicated to five varieties and exhibit the landscapes and feelings evoked by each of them.

A special suggestion: the wine region of Empordà

Wine possesses the magic power to make us dream and transport us to enrapturing landscapes where we can read, contemplate or explore the pleasures of the senses in depth. Our society lacks, now more than ever, events that bring us closer to nature by offering us a healthy pleasure, that stretch time by creating an emotional connection with the people we value, that can bring a positive outlook to the world we get to live, shaping it, indulging it, delving into the feelings of reverence, wonder and belonging. Empordà, a cultural cradle of wine, sheltered by beautiful spots and natural parks, attests to it.

To explore the wine of Empordà is a preface to associate wine with other sensory and cultural domains. I suggest you discover routes transformed into passionate dialogues with the vine tendrils of Empordà, and cellars that will open their doors to you.

You will be amazed by the linear kilometres of dry stone caressing the coiled vines. You will stroll through clay dreams, red, black and bituminous slate chips, through sandstone, granite, coarse sand, clayey mud, gravel, potter's clay, marl, clayey lime, pebbles, silicic rocks and black basalt.

You will travel through time; from the Greek Emporion and the Roman city built on top, to the summit of Benedictine wisdom, the magnanimous monastery of Sant Pere de Rodes.

To wander round the villages of Empordà, seeing lights and colours and listening to the sound of the changing environment. Routes through plains or mountains. Routes through cabins, monasteries, phylloxera, history, cooperative businesses, pipeclay. Even a literary and pictorial route. And the sea route, enjoying a sea bordered by vineyards from Cap de Creus to Gavarres.

To stop and breathe in. To perceive the aromas of a walk by the sea, with samphire, mastic, gorse and heather; and the salty stampede of the waves lashing at the slate that cuts into the sea at Cap de Creus... The first walk of spring through the mountain, feeling how the earth awakens from its mineral silence and begins to beat, distilling therapeutic perfumes. The white bursting of blossoming almond trees, following the routes of dolmen and menhirs. The scent of February's lethargic yellow mimosas while strolling through a vineyard. To run your fingers through the humid borders of the glasswort from the marshlands of Empordà while stocks on barren land can be seen in the distance.

To pay attention to the grape cycle, stroke the earth, understand the cry of the vine, the ephemeral moment of flowering, the resonance of the aestival force on the vine, how it unfolds its tendrils until they fully become the smooth fruit that creates the art work. A natural fascination within hand's reach, a landscape arranged to linger in your memory.

Prepare yourselves to savour wines that are delicate, flavourful, generous, reflective, serious, accessible, smiling, dressed of authenticity and seasoned by a sky traversed by the north wind. You will taste the entrepreneurial vitality that flows from the enotouristic Empordà, reinforced by the gastronomic excellence of the basic and luminous cuisine that comes with it, today more than ever before.

JOSEP ROCA

Cooking with wine at El Celler de Can Roca

Technique, imagination and dialogue with science have created a great area of improvement in the applications of wine in the kitchen. Reflection and the evolution of wine as an ingredient lead us to a revolution, thanks to the methods and products we now have available.

These are some examples of how we cook with wine at El Celler de Can Roca:

— **Wine reduction:** we reduce wine without cooking it directly, because we perform cold reduction with the Rotaval, which distills at low pressures.

— **Thickening:** xanthan gum makes it possible to thicken wine while cold without altering its aromatic particles when changing its texture. It allows us to make wine sauces by only changing its thickness.

— **Shaved ice:** the Pacojet yields an interesting texture. But adding a fixer such as xanthan gum, gelatine or agar-agar, makes shaved ice at a temperature higher than normal, at around 0°C/32°F; this way, there is no hardness or painful thermal sensation.

— **Vacuum impregnation:** we marinade any fruit with a smooth and generous wine and introduce the wine into the voids generated in the fruit, producing very interesting results.

— **'Perfume-cooking' or volatile fixation:** we have the ability to cook from the volatile elements of wine and liqueur in the manner of the traditional flambé.

— **'Perfume-cooking' in front of the diner:** we 'cook' the dish at the table by pouring the perfume over glowing rocks to instantly flambé the main product.

— **Spheriphications:** smooth or sparkling wine bubbles.

— **Spheriphications and sugar dehydration (osmosis):** dehydration allows us to make grapes that look like raisins.

— **Plain sorbets:** xanthan gum acts as a stabiliser.

— **Candy sugar** (minimum 40% vol.), or wine liqueur stones.

— **Nitrogen:** viscose wines. Instant sorbets. Wine mousse from the whipped cream dispenser.

— **Venturi effect:** ambient aromas from wines or liqueurs.

— **Freeze-drying:** wine powder and rocks.

— **Wine and its components:** anthocyanin powder. Flavonoid powder. Natural tartrates. Wine lees. Grapes with endogenous carbon at the starting stage of carbon fermentation. Grapes with exogenous carbon. Oak wood to scent, perfume and smoke ingredients. Grape syrup. Juice from different grape varieties. Grapes as a seasonal product.

— **Integral harmony (with vintage wines):** turbot with Xarel·lo. Grape juice from Xarel·lo and fennel. Air from its lees. Grapes with exogenous carbon. Tartaric acid and hazelnuts and toast symbolising autolysis.

— **Interpretation of the earth:** we make a traditional association from an avant-garde point of view. We interpret the land, native soil, type of wine, and its gastronomic surroundings. The area where wine is produced is an inspiration when cooking. A Chardonnay from Chablis, a Savagnin from the Jura region, or an Alsatian Gewürztraminer, all French wines, help us create recipes with universes and landscapes that are markedly different. With their own personalities.

— **Grape variety:** we use aromatic nuances from grape varieties as a starting point to create and recreate dishes. Galician Albariño, Riesling from the Rhine, Castillian Verdejo, or the French Sauvignon Blanc from Sancerre and Gamay from Beaujolais inspire us in different ways and invite us to create in their honour.

— **Wine sauces:** we use cava as a sauce. In order to achieve the appropriate viscosity, we apply xanthan gum when disgorging the sparkling wine, just before the end of the traditional production process. And so we obtain a sauce-like texture you can eat with a spoon, with a maximum respect for the product and minimum intervention. We also do this with Viognier or Monastrell.

— **Saturation of wine with kappa:** as in the case of PALO CORTADO OYSTER and ying yang of white and black garlic (page 213).

— **Wine aromas:** we transform them into a dish, as is the case of ecological vintage aromas that permeate the SCAMPI IN TEMPURA, FRESH ALMONDS, CURRY COMPOTE AND MUSHROOMS, or the aromas of dried figs in the FIGS WITH FOIE and Pedro Ximénez jelly (page 94). The dish emerges from wine and its aromatic hues, and the remaining ingredients seek to create total affinity: spice bread, toffee biscuit, date compote, coffee and chocolate, with the rebellious counterpoint of ginger.

— **Wine landscapes:** wine is grape, the vine, and also the soil in which it sinks its roots. Like the white sand of the vines of Jerez, known as *albariza*. Or the crumbled black sand over which the Priorat vine grows. We have reproduced both of them on the plate, with recipes such as PRAWNS WITH TEXTURISED WHITE GARLIC OIL SAND, GRAPE, FRIED GARLIC, AJOBLANCO, APPLE AND FRESH AND SALTED ALMOND COMPOTE; or the PARTRIDGE FROM THE PRIORAT with truffle slate, blackberries, pepper, pomegranate, black olives and violets (page 208).

— **Grappa à la carte:** thanks to the Rotaval we can extract the alcohol from wine and obtain a specific grappa from a specific wine. We can build a personalised and unique product. The offer is almost infinite...

— **Wine as a main ingredient:** this is the wine to eat with a spoon mentioned before, an extreme exercise we put into practice in the WINE ON A PLATE AND DESSERT IN A GLASS (page 376). We inverted the terms and exchanged textures with a Riesling by Peter Jakob Kühn, Oestrich Lenchen Beerenauslese Goldkapsel of 2002, accompanied with an infusion of honey and lemon, orange and peach, basil and eucalyptus, raspberries and white flowers.

PARTRIDGE FROM THE PRIORAT

SERVES 8 PEOPLE

COMPOSITION

Partridge breast
Black truffle rock
Strawberry infusion
Priorat wine reduction
Berry compote
Wine pearls
Partridge sauce

—PARTRIDGE BREAST

8 partridge breasts
Brine for meat (basic recipes, p.429)
Extra virgin olive oil

Submerge the breasts in brine for 6 minutes and dry any excess water remaining. Seal them in a vacuum pack bag with olive oil and cook in the Roner at 62°C/144°F for 25 minutes.

—BLACK TRUFFLE ROCK

YIELDS 8 UNITS

250 g cream
25 g truffle juice
25 g dextrose
2 gelatine sheets
Salt
15 g grated fresh truffle

Mix the cream, truffle juice and dextrose, bring to a boil and remove from heat. Next, add the gelatine, previously hydrated, stir the mixture until smooth and reserve refrigerated.

When it has completely cooled down, whip, adjust salt and, lastly, add grated truffle slowly. Place the mixture on a silicone mat and, with a spatula, form peaks with it. Freeze.

—STRAWBERRY INFUSION

YIELDS 200 G

500 g strawberries
50 g sugar

Seal both ingredients in a vacuum pack bag and cook in the Roner at 80°C/176°F for 1 hour. Strain and reserve the resulting liquid.

—PRIORAT WINE REDUCTION

YIELDS 100 G

1 litre Priorat wine
30 g sugar

Heat both ingredients in a casserole and reduce to 100 g. Reserve.

—BERRY COMPOTE

YIELDS 250 G

200 g strawberry infusion
    (previously prepared)
20 g Priorat wine reduction
    (previously prepared)
24 pomegranate seeds
8 raspberries
8 redcurrant berries
4 cranberries

Mix all the ingredients and bring to a boil, remove from heat and leave to stand for a few minutes.

—WINE PEARLS

YIELDS APPROXIMATELY 500 PEARLS

50 g Priorat wine
0.1 g carrageenan

Prepare a metal tray with ice and place another tray on top, lined with a silicone mat.

Mix the Priorat wine with the carrageenan, both cold. Pour them into a saucepan and bring to a boil. Fill some pipettes with the mixture and slowly let drops fall on the trays lined with a silicone mat prepared previously. When they have set, pick the drops up with a spatula and reserve refrigerated in an airtight container.

—PARTRIDGE SAUCE

YIELDS 390 G

2.5 kg partridge bones
250 kg mirepoix (basic recipes, p.427)
2.5 kg water
40 g kuzu thickening agent (basic recipes, p.427)
50 g butter
Salt

Place the bones on a baking tray and brown at 220°C/428°F. Remove any excess fat and place the bones in a pot, deglaze the tray and add the browned bits to the stockpot containing the bones. Add the mirepoix and water.

Simmer for 5 hours on very low heat to obtain a good infusion, strain and reduce to 300 g of partridge sauce. Boil the partridge sauce again, add the kuzu mixture and finish by binding with butter. Adjust salt, strain and reserve.

GARNISHING AND PLATING

Remove the aiguillette from the breast, slice on the bias and arrange it on a plate; break a piece off of the truffle rock and place on the side.

Set one raspberry, half a cranberry, 2 redcurrant berries and 3 pomegranate seeds from the berry compote. Lastly, place a few Priorat wine pearls over the truffle rock and garnish with a few touches of partridge sauce.

SUCKLING PIG BLANQUETTE WITH RIESLING PFALZ

SERVES 8 PEOPLE

COMPOSITION

Suckling pig belly
Black garlic purée
Onion purée
Orange purée
Beetroot purée
Melon with beetroot cubes
Onion oil
Clear suckling pig stock
Cooked suckling pig skin
Suckling pig blanquette
Mango terrine

—SUCKLING PIG BELLY
YIELDS 48 BELLY CUBES

2 Iberian suckling pig bellies
Brine for meat (basic recipes, p.429)
Extra virgin olive oil

Clean the suckling pig skin and submerge the bellies in brine for 2 hours. Vacuum pack separately with olive oil and cook in the Roner at 63°C/145°F for 24 hours.

Open the cooking bags and bone the bellies. Sear on the griddle with some weight on top so the skin browns evenly and turns crisp. Cut into 1.5 cm squares; reserve.

—BLACK GARLIC PURÉE
YIELDS 110 G

50 g black garlic
70 g water
0.2 g xanthan gum
Salt

Blend all the ingredients and run the resulting purée through a fine chinois. Reserve in a squeeze bottle.

—ONION PURÉE
YIELDS 350 G

300 g onions
30 g butter (cooking)
20 g butter (emulsifying)
50 g water
0.4 g xanthan gum
Salt

Julienne the onion and toss it in oil with 30 g of butter for cooking until it softens but without overbrowning. Blend with the remaining ingredients, run through a fine chinois and adjust salt. Reserve in a squeeze bottle.

—ORANGE PURÉE
YIELDS 300 G

450 g oranges
400 g sugar syrup (basic recipes, p.428)
0.6 g xanthan gum

Wash the orange peel and blanch 3 times in a stockpot, starting with cold water. The fourth time, place in the stockpot with the sugar syrup and cook for 15 minutes. Next, remove and blend with 100 g of the cooking syrup and xanthan gum. Run the resulting purée through a fine chinois and reserve in a squeeze bottle.

—BEETROOT PURÉE
YIELDS 150 G

150 g beetroots
25 g soil distillate (basic recipes, p.428)
0.2 g xanthan gum
Salt

Boil the beetroot whole until soft. Blend it together with the soil distillate and xanthan gum, run through a fine chinois, adjust salt and reserve in a squeeze bottle.

—MELON WITH BEETROOT CUBES
YIELDS 30 CUBES

100 g melon
1 beetroot

Cut melon into 0.5 cm cubes and reserve.

Blend the beetroot and cook the melon cubes together with the liquid sous-vide for 3 hours before serving, so that the flavour and colour of the beetroot soak in.

—ONION OIL
YIELDS 120 G

100 g onions
120 g extra virgin olive oil

Julienne the onion and toss it in oil over low heat for about 30 minutes. Leave to cool and strain. Reserve in a covered container.

—CLEAR SUCKLING PIG STOCK
YIELDS 200 G

1 kg Iberian suckling pig bones
200 g onions
2 kg water

Soak the suckling pig bones in cold water for
12 hours. Next, place the bones in a stockpot
and add julienned onion and water. Boil for
2 hours and skim to obtain a clear stock. Cool
and reserve.

—COOKED SUCKLING PIG SKIN
YIELDS 150 G

240 g Iberian suckling pig skin
200 g onions
150 g carrots
Cold water

Place all the ingredients in cold water and boil
for 4 hours. Next, strain and reserve the skin
for the sauce.

—SUCKLING PIG BLANQUETTE
YIELDS 250 G

200 g clear suckling pig stock (previously
    prepared)
0.4 g xanthan gum
20 g cooked suckling pig skin (previously
    prepared)
40 g onion oil (previously prepared)

With a hand blender, mix the xanthan gum
together with the clear suckling pig stock for a
few minutes. Add the cooked suckling pig skin
and continue blending. Lastly, bind it with the
onion oil and strain. Reserve in a bain-marie.

—MANGO TERRINE
YIELDS APPROXIMATELY 400 CUBES

2 ripe mangos
40 g butter
3 g agar-agar

Peel and thinly slice the mango. Place it in a
10x12.5 cm mould, adding some of the butter
and sprinkling agar-agar in between slices.
The result should be a 0.7-cm-thick terrine.
Bake it in the oven at 160°C/320°F for
30 minutes. When cooked, cut into 0.5 cm
cubes and reserve.

GARNISHING AND PLATING

Black truffle
Purple shiso
Apricot sprite hyssop flowers

Arrange 5 cubes of suckling pig belly on the
plate. Place 3 dots of black garlic purée, onion,
orange and beetroot. Alternate them with
3 cubes of melon soaked in with beetroot juice
and 3 cubes of mango terrine with 1 small
sheet of truffle on top. Add 2 leaves of shiso
and 1 apricot sprite hyssop flower on the side.
Season with the blanquette of suckling pig.

CHABLIS OYSTER

COMPOSITION

Oyster
Granny Smith apple purée
Acacia honey liqueur candies
Mushroom air
Fennel and oyster soup

—OYSTER

4 oysters

Open the oysters with a paring knife and remove the beard. Reserve.

—GRANNY SMITH APPLE PURÉE

YIELDS 150 G

1 Granny Smith apple
200 g water
20 g sugar

Cut the apple without peeling. Heat the water with the sugar and apple. Cool, blend and reserve.

—ACACIA HONEY LIQUEUR CANDIES

YIELDS APPROXIMATELY 125 CANDIES

120 g sugar
40 g water
25 g acacia honey liqueur
Cornflour

Make a syrup by bringing the water and sugar to 109°C/228°F. Remove from the heat and let the temperature drop a bit. Add the liqueur very carefully. The ideal way to do this is by letting the syrup slide very slowly down the sides of one container into the one with the liqueur and back, until both liquids and both densities integrate. Reserve.

Fill a baking sheet with cornflour and leave to dry for a few hours at 80°C/176°F. Flatten, smooth out and make small holes to be filled with the syrup and liqueur mixture. Dust the surface lightly with some dry cornflour and leave for 24 hours at approximately 40°C/104°F.

Next, remove the candies from the cornflour, dust with a brush and reserve. Each candy weighs approximately 1 g.

—MUSHROOM AIR

YIELDS 220 G

500 g fresh cultivated mushrooms
30 g butter
Salt
3 g lecithin

Cut the mushrooms into thin slices and add to the melted butter. Salt and cook on very low heat in a covered container in order for the mushrooms to release water with the heat. Strain, squeezing them to eliminate as much water as possible. Emulsify them with lecithin to obtain a foamy air.

—FENNEL AND OYSTER SOUP

YIELDS 300 G

250 g liquidised fennel leaves
100 g single cream
40 g salted egg yolks
4 oysters

Mix liquidised fennel and cream and salted egg yolks. Heat to 85°C/185°F, remove from heat, lower temperature to 65°C/149°F and add oysters. Blend until obtaining a very smooth soup; strain and reserve in a bain-marie.

GARNISHING AND PLATING

Soil distillate (basic recipes, p.428)
Fine fresh cultivated mushroom julienne
Black truffle oil (basic recipes, p.427)
Apple julienne

Divide the oyster into three parts and form a circle on the plate, then place the soil distillate and the fresh mushroom julienne on top. Surround it with four dots of truffle oil, apple purée with julienne and acacia honey liqueur candies. Garnish with the mushroom air and, when serving, pour the fennel and oyster soup.

PALO CORTADO OYSTER

SERVES 4 PEOPLE

COMPOSITION

Oyster
Palo Cortado coating
Black garlic sauce
White garlic shots
Oyster sauce

—OYSTER

YIELDS 700 G

4 oysters
500 g sea water

Open oysters with a paring knife and remove them from their shells carefully. Cut the beard off with a paring knife and blanch oysters in boiling sea water for 15 seconds. Remove them from the water and place them on a baking sheet to blast chill. Reserve.

—PALO CORTADO COATING

YIELDS 150 G

100 g water
50 g Palo Cortado
1.5 g kappa carrageenan

Mix the water with the Palo Cortado and kappa and bring to a boil. Coat the oysters with a layer no thicker than 2 mm. Place them on baking sheets and reserve.

—BLACK GARLIC SAUCE

YIELDS 550 G

250 g peeled almonds
500 g water
7.5 g Gran Reserva sherry vinegar
12.5 g extra virgin olive oil
3 black garlic cloves
3.75 g salt
20 g squid ink
0.25 g xanthan gum (for 100 g sauce)

Crush the almonds, peeled, with water and leave to stand for 24 hours refrigerated. Run through a cloth filter, applying pressure to squeeze out as much water as possible. Mix it with the remaining ingredients, blend, strain and keep the resulting sauce very cool until serving.

—WHITE GARLIC SHOTS

YIELDS 700 G

250 g almond paste
250 g water
½ garlic clove
166.5 g water
15 g Gran Reserva sherry vinegar
20 g extra virgin olive oil
Salt
3 gelatine sheets

Hydrate almond paste for 12 hours with 250 g water. Cut the garlic clove in half and remove the germ if necessary. Mix all the ingredients except for the gelatine and blend in the Thermomix.

Separate a third of the mixture, heat it while keeping it below 35°C/95°F and dilute gelatine sheets, previously hydrated. Add in the remaining mixture and transfer it into a squeeze bottle. Let drops of the mixture fall into a container with liquid nitrogen to make frozen spheres; remove with a strainer and reserve in a container in the freezer until serving.

—OYSTER SAUCE

YIELDS 550 G

10 oysters
50 g shallot
5 g butter
35 g oyster water
20 g Asian oyster sauce
625 g cream
Salt

Open the oysters and reserve their water. Julienne the shallot finely and toss in butter with a pinch of salt over very low heat until it cooks well. Add the oysters and sear them on both sides to brown them lightly; use the oyster water to deglaze, add the oyster sauce, cook for 1 minute and add cream. Simmer the mixture on very low heat for 5 minutes, remove and place in the Thermomix. Blend the mixture and run it through a fine chinois. Reserve in a bain-marie at 65°C/149°F.

GARNISHING AND PLATING

Cut the oysters coated in Palo Cortado in half and, using a paring knife, cut a small base at the tip of each oyster, so that they stand on the plate.

On a small soup dish, set one spoonful of very cold black garlic sauce on one side and white garlic shots on top of it, as well as half a cold oyster coated in Palo Cortado. On the opposite side, with both sauces touching but not mixing, arrange the hot oyster sauce and the other half of Palo Cortado coated oyster on top of it, previously set on the salamander to heat it slightly. This way, a play with cold and hot temperatures is created with both the oysters and the sauces.

MUSSELS WITH RIESLING

SERVES 4 PEOPLE

COMPOSITION

Mussels
Riesling sauce
Bergamot mousseline
Apple compote
Lemon infusion
Lemon infusion gel
Rose preserve
White truffle emulsion
Crystallised roses

—MUSSELS

24 rock mussels
Brine for fish (basic recipes, p.429)

Clean the mussels and immerse them in brine for 10 minutes. Rinse and remove excess water. Seal in a vacuum pack bag at 100% and cook in the Roner at 85°C/185°F for 7 minutes. Cool quickly in a cold bain-marie. Open the bags and remove the mussels from their valves. Reserve refrigerated.

—RIESLING SAUCE
YIELDS 200 G

200 ml Riesling
0.5 g xanthan gum

Mix the Riesling and xanthan gum using a hand blender. Leave to stand to release the air and reserve refrigerated.

—BERGAMOT MOUSSELINE
YIELDS 300 G

250 g sunflower oil
50 g pasteurised egg yolks
50 g water
5.5 g bergamot essential oil
Salt

Make a mayonnaise with all the ingredients and fill a ½ litre whipped cream dispenser, adding 2 chargers. Keep at 50°C/122°F in a bain-marie when serving.

—APPLE COMPOTE
YIELDS 200 G

200 g Granny Smith apple purée
2 drops of jasmine essence
0.2 g xanthan gum

Mix all the ingredients and thicken with the xanthan gum. Leave to stand to eliminate the air and reserve refrigerated.

—LEMON INFUSION
YIELDS 100 G

120 g lemon peel
120 g water
8 coriander seeds
3 green cardamom seeds
2 white cardamom seeds

Heat the water to 80°C/176°F and infuse with the lemon peel, coriander, and white and green cardamom for 20 minutes, covered. Strain and reserve.

—LEMON INFUSION GEL
YIELDS 100 G

100 g lemon infusion (previously prepared)
0.8 g xanthan gum

Blend the xanthan gum with the infusion. Reserve.

—ROSE PRESERVE
YIELDS 150 G

4 g pectin
120 g sugar
100 g rose water
20 g rose petals

Mix the pectine with 20 g sugar.

Heat the rose water with the remaining sugar and chopped rose petals in a casserole.

When the sugar has dissolved, add the mixture of sugar and pectin. Cook for 10 minutes and leave to cool.

—WHITE TRUFFLE EMULSION
YIELDS 160 G

2 g xanthan gum
120 g water
60 g white truffle oil
Salt

Run the xanthan gum and the water through a hand blender. Emulsify, pouring in the truffle oil slowly, and adjust salt. Reserve.

—CRYSTALLISED ROSES
YIELDS 20 CRYSTALLISED PETALS

100 g sugar
100 g water
20 rose petals

In a casserole, place the sugar and water and bring to a boil. When the water boils, add the rose petals and cook for a few seconds until they change colour. Strain and stretch the petals cooked in the syrup over a baking sheet lined with greaseproof paper. Dry in the cooker at 50°C/122°F for 12 hours, until crisp. Reserve.

GARNISHING AND PLATING

Jasmine blossoms
Grated lemon zest with sugar
Lemon verbena leaves
Nectarine cubes
Soil distillate (basic recipes, p.428)
White truffle

On a plate, arrange the Riesling sauce and 6 mussels aligned vertically. On top of each, and in the following order, place: the bergamot mousseline, the apple preserve with a jasmine blossom on top, the lemon infusion gel with some sugared lemon zest on top, and a lemon verbena leaf, some rose preserve with 2 nectarine cubes and one crystallised rose on top, the soil distillate and, lastly, the white truffle emulsion with a small slice of white truffle.

BREAD ICE CREAM
WITH GREEN WHEAT JUICE,
SARDINE AND GRAPE

SERVES 8 PEOPLE

COMPOSITION

Country bread ice cream
Sardine
Grape jelly
Grape
Yeast air
Green wheat juice

—COUNTRY BREAD ICE CREAM
YIELDS 1.75 KG

200 g country bread
1.14 kg milk
200 g cream
130 g sugar
260 g dextrose
40 g milk powder
10 g ice-cream stabiliser
Olive oil
Salt

Charcoal-grill the bread with oil and salt.

Heat the milk and cream with the sugar,
dextrose and powdered milk to 85°C/185°F.
Leave to cool to 40°C/104°F and add ice-cream
stabiliser. Lastly, add the toasted bread, infuse
for 5 minutes. Blend, strain and leave to stand
for 6 hours. Run through the ice-cream maker
and reserve in the freezer at -18°C/0°F.

—SARDINE
YIELDS 8 FILLETS

4 sardines (about 80 g each)
Brine for fish (basic recipes, p.429)

Scale the sardines, fillet and remove as many of
the bones as possible. Immerse for 3 minutes in
cold brine, then dry with kitchen towels.

Arrange the sardine fillets in a container with
holes without overlapping. Place the container
inside another. Cover both very tightly with
cling film and introduce smoke with a smoking
gun; cover the small hole left by the gun by
wrapping the container with more cling film.
Leave to smoke for 15 minutes. Uncover, cut
into 2 cm squares and reserve refrigerated.

—GRAPE JELLY
YIELDS 100 G

250 g red grapes
1.5 g agar-agar

Blend the red grapes, and add the agar-agar.
Bring the mixture to a boil and leave to jellify for
at least 3 hours. When set, blend and reserve.

—GRAPE
YIELDS 32 QUARTERS

8 white grapes

Using a paring knife, peel the grapes leaving
the pulp intact. Quarter and remove the seeds.
Reserve.

—YEAST AIR
YIELDS 300 G

200 g milk
50 g fresh yeast
1.3 g sugar
50 g water
2.5 g soy lecithin
1.5 g sucroester
1 g salt

Warm the milk and mix it with the sugar
and fresh yeast, crumbling it by hand. Leave
to stand for 2 minutes.

Add the remaining ingredients, blend and leave
to stand 2 more minutes. Reserve.

—GREEN WHEAT JUICE
YIELDS 350 G

500 g French beans
500 g green wheat sprouts
0.4 g xanthan gum
150 g extra virgin olive oil
Salt

Blanch the French beans and liquidise them
together with the green wheat sprouts. Adjust
salt, texturise with the xanthan gum and, lastly,
emulsify with olive oil.

GARNISHING AND PLATING

Extra virgin olive oil

As the base for the plate, serve the green
wheat juice and, around the border, arrange
4 pieces of sardine, 4 dots of grape jelly,
and 4 grape quarters. Place a quenelle
of bread ice cream in the centre, crowned
with the yeast air.

COMTÉ AND ONION SOUP

SERVES 8 PEOPLE

COMPOSITION
Onion gel
Comté and curry cream
Rosemary gel
Bay leaf gel
Thyme gel
Sherry gel
Onions
Walnut sponge cake
Caramelised walnuts

—ONION GEL
YIELDS 250 G

1 kg onions
500 g water
2 g xanthan gum
Salt

Julienne the onion and toss in oil until it turns golden brown. Add the water, boil over low heat and reduce to half. Strain, add the xanthan gum, run through the blender and adjust salt. Reserve.

—COMTÉ AND CURRY CREAM
YIELDS 400 G

125 g comté cheese
35 g walnut paste
250 g chicken stock (basic recipes, p.427)
0.2 g curry powder
1 g iota
Salt

Place comté cheese, chopped, and the walnut paste in the Thermomix, add boiling chicken stock and blend to a smooth cream. Adjust salt, add the curry and cool down. Reserve 200 g for plating.

Add the iota to the remaining cream, mix and bring to a boil. Fill the bottom of a bowl or soup dish with 20 g of this cream, leave to set and reserve.

—ROSEMARY GEL
YIELDS 100 G

120 g water
100 g rosemary
0.7 g xanthan gum
Salt

Heat water in a casserole to 80°C/176°F, remove from heat and add rosemary. Infuse covered for 20 minutes; strain. Blend the infusion with xanthan gum and adjust salt. Reserve in a squeeze bottle.

—BAY LEAF GEL
YIELDS 100 G

120 g water
100 g bay leaf
0.7 g xanthan gum
Salt

Heat the water in a casserole to 80°C/176°F, remove from heat and add bay leaves. Infuse covered for 20 minutes; strain. Blend the infusion with xanthan gum and adjust salt. Reserve in a squeeze bottle.

—THYME GEL
YIELDS 100 G

120 g water
100 g thyme
0.7 g xanthan gum
Salt

Heat the water in a casserole to 80°C/176°F, remove from heat and add thyme. Infuse covered for 20 minutes; strain. Blend the infusion with xanthan gum and adjust salt. Reserve in a squeeze bottle.

—SHERRY GEL
YIELDS 100 G

100 g sherry
0.7 g xanthan gum

Blend the sherry with the xanthan gum and reserve in a squeeze bottle.

—ONIONS

4 shallots
1 Figueres onion
4 spring onions
Salt

Cook the shallots unpeeled, starting with cold water, and bring to a boil; then, cook for 5 minutes and cool in a cold bain-marie. Peel the shallots, cut them in half with a paring knife and reserve half a shallot for each plate.

Blanch the Figueres onion 5 times, starting with cold water, and cook in a pressure cooker with abundant water for 5 minutes, adding salt to taste. Remove from the cooker and cool in a cold bain-marie. Peel and cut the onions into 0.3x1-cm-long strips. Reserve 3 strips for each plate.

Blanch spring onions (only the white part) in boiling water, adding salt to taste. Cool them in a cold bain-marie, cut in half to use one half for each plate, and reserve.

—WALNUT SPONGE CAKE
YIELDS 360 G

120 g eggs
75 g sugar
60 g flour
60 g walnut paste
50 g inverted sugar syrup
20 g softened butter
1 g salt

Mix all the ingredients, emulsify using a hand blender, run through a fine strainer and transfer to a ½ litre whipped cream dispenser with 2 chargers.

Fill the bottom of a disposable plastic cup with 20 g of dough and cook in the microwave for 1 minute on the highest setting. Reserve.

—CARAMELISED WALNUTS
YIELDS 110 G

100 g water
60 g sugar
100 g walnuts
40 g icing sugar
Sunflower oil

Place the water and sugar in a saucepan and bring to a boil, add the walnuts and cook over low heat until very soft, almost translucent. Strain and leave to dry on a silicone mat. Cut each walnut in four and dust with icing sugar. Fry them in sunflower oil at 180°C/356°F until brown and crisp. Remove the walnuts from the oil and place them on kitchen towels; then reserve.

GARNISHING AND PLATING

Rosemary blossoms
Curled chives
Chervil sprouts
Dill sprouts
Fennel sprouts

Let the comté cream set on the plate, then cover it with the onion gel and place a dot of each aromatic gel. Stick into the onion gel one half a shallot, three slices of Figueres onion and half a spring onion. Heat everything on the salamander. When very hot, arrange a piece of walnut sponge cake, and two caramelised walnuts, then finish with the rosemary blossoms, a sprig of curled chive and the sprouts of fennel, chervil and dill.

On the table (in front of the guest), cover it with very hot comté and curry cream.

wine cellar

A sensory wine cellar

El Celler de Can Roca today offers a very unique interpretation of the world of wine.

While at their previous establishment, Josep didn't feel the need to show his wine cellar: to show the bottles to his customers, it seemed to him, would excessively reduce the world of wine. But after the relocation, their new installations facilitate not only the display of his collection, but go further and convey to the public a personal and moving, multisensory and absolutely global view of this world.

Once the difficulties in terms of storage were overcome, the new Celler de Can Roca grew to have 260 square metres of its surface dedicated to WINE in capital letters, distributed over five 'chapels' where Josep can share his way of experiencing this world. *"I choose five wines that are particularly appealing to me—Champagne, Riesling, Burgundy, Priorat and Sherry—and try to show my respect for these lands, for the wisdom of the fields, for the work of the people of each region."*

Through the senses, each of the five sanctuaries expresses the spirit of a region or grape variety. In every chapel there are photographs of the land taken by Quim Turón, accompanied by a tactile and a musical element that transport visitors and submerge them into a sea of stimuli.

Josep pays homage to the landscape and nature, but also to the men who take care of the land, the wine growers who participate in achieving the final result. *"To me, it means to open the doors for people to reflect and think that, when we drink wine, there is a history behind it, a traditional approach, a cultural habit and a dialogue between man and nature, where man intervenes and nature puts him in his place."*

A sensory space where Joseph bares his soul, *"but I do it convinced that wine can project itself much beyond basic flavours and eagerness to share. In short, a dreamland where we act out our feelings."* An invitation to 'feel' directly the essence of his five favourite wines.

CHAMPAGNE

We put our hand in a large bowl full of hundreds of tiny steel spheres, we pick some up and they tinkle as they drop, reproducing the effect of bubbles. *"It may be the first time Champagne bubbles have been captured."* Mozart's *Piano concerto No. 20* plays in the background.

"I'm fascinated by the taste association between the two opposite worlds that are Champagne and Sherry. Two contrasting lights. Wines for contemplation and meditation. Fun and complexity. Wines of second chances. Brothers of limestone. Accomplices in controlled aging in semidarkness.

"The beauty of the Champagne fields lies in the difficulty associated with the harvesting of a wiry, gaunt, perpetually adolescent grape from plains with little soil above a calcareous mass. The extreme conditions in wild, cold, freezing weather of growing grapes demands a great deal of dedication, and that is where the reward of the second fermentation comes from. I'm interested in this close view of the work of over 4,000 small producers creating their small revolution, beyond the glamour often associated with this world. I should also mention that in the nearby world of cava, lucid and skilful work is also being carried out. Thanks to the generation that has taken over, we will enjoy like never before the expression of the land and our mild southern, Mediterranean climate."

Champagne is an effervescent wine, but especially a wine that evokes optimism. Clear and exultant. That is why at El Celler metallic spheres symbolise the fun, optimism and celebration of bubbles. *"One can hardly drink a sparkling wine when sad,"* reflects Josep.

RIESLING

A dynamic and bright, long, shimmering-golden green silk cloth wrapped around a sturdy slate centrepiece. The 3rd movement (minuet) of Mozart's *Eine Kleine Nachtmusik*, an expression of nobility; the features of exuberance in bloom, the richness of the fruit and mineral depth of Riesling.

Josep is especially devoted to Riesling, particularly from Germany. It's an eye-catching variety, a playful palate. *"It rejects ornaments or excessive manipulation, it wants to present itself immaculately and clearly, but also with an acidity that allows for long aging. It symbolises an approximation to enthusiasm. It's a cheerful variety—direct, sincere, effusive, and smiling, but restrained. It exhibits all of its attributes spectacularly but also with rigour, rigidity and precision, like no other variety,"* explains Josep.

Riesling is a variety grown in partially sunny vineyards and difficult conditions, requiring inclines that facilitate good water drainage. The ricochet effect of sunlight on the river water, as in the case of the Moselle, the Rhine, or the Nahe, has an added value: it creates a thermo-regulating effect and confers aromas that interact and intertwine with the grape in a natural way better than anywhere else. *"These aromatic precursors will explode in fermentation, yielding powerful wines; wines born from worshiping the sun and, often, southern exposure."*

As a result of aging and a consequence of the progressive process of degradation and reduction of aromas and mineral elements, Riesling tends to present some interesting tasting notes of hydrocarbons or spices, all the way to the omega of aroma. *"Seduction for those who are new to the world of wines, as well as for the more experienced."*

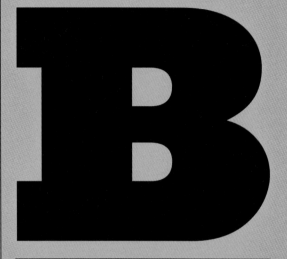

BURGUNDY

We run our fingers through small red velvet bags while listening to a tense and vibrant violin that conveys femininity without frailty. It is the *Méditation de Thaïs* by Jules Massenet.

Burgundies require attention, require one's full intention to perceive their character because, a priori, they are not simple. *"This variety, pinot noir, is suggestion, it's ethereal, enveloping, framed by the sum of magical imperfection and brilliant youth."*

The extreme division of plots is the general rule, and the diversity of the soil—with four hundred different types—is evidence that the results are the origin of the concept of *terroir*. Farmers demonstrate that each field, each village and each interpretation can be the same in appearance, but entirely different. *"It's a difficult land where the sun doesn't always shine, where the grape develops a thin skin and fragile juice. It shows the land in a way that cannot be found anywhere else in the world."*

A land of fully enclosed fields, walls, monoliths and monuments. In the background, a powerful discourse of quality, wine growers who make over fifty different wines. *"They explain without arrogance they do nothing special, only work the earth and pass the baton from one generation to the next."* And they do it successfully: this soil has been yielding great wines and earning respect for over ten centuries. Those who work it follow nature with humbleness and let it take its course; it's the wise smallholding of Burgundy, looking into the future with eyes always set on acknowledging the past.

SHERRY

SHERRY / JEREZ WINE

Miguel Poveda provides the musical component to the poem *Boca seca*, by Narcís Comadira. We feel a gypsum stone lying on the straw, in an esparto grass basket symbolising the dryness and sun of Andalusia, and the blinds that cover the doors of wine cellars in that region, providing airflow and ventilation.

"Sherry is wine that astonishes; unusual, rich and generous. Unique. To me it symbolises concentration, ennobled oxidation, reduction, essence of sun and salt, the force of permanent history that goes from one place to another and is ennobled in oblivion."
This is a wine born out of neglect, from the watery palomino grape, a very simple variety when new, but one that spends years in barrels, influenced by the breeze of Sanlúcar de Barrameda and Puerto de Santamaría. In its journey from one place to another, it slowly acquires its spirit in semidarkness. The grape juice is reduced and its essence concentrated. *"Its caustic rotundity is fascinating, sometimes painful and extreme, like being stabbed on the tongue. I like this abrasive part of great vintages preserved like hidden treasures. Sherry has the ability to seduce with broad, proud and prolonged wines like few others in the world."*
The world of sherry generates a fascinating game of words. *Finos Antiguos, Palmas, Dos Palmas, Tres Palmas, Manzanillas Amontilladas, Manzanillas Pasadas, Amontillados, Amontillados Finos, Amontillados Pata de Gallina, Palo Cortado, Sobretablas, Rocío, Soleo, Raya y Punto, Punzante, Chico, Andana, Cachón.* These words make sense there, but exist nowhere else. *"It's the unique jargon of wine cellars around Andalusia, but it's also part of my vocabulary. Everything Jerez represents feels close to me."*
At El Celler de Can Roca, sherry also symbolises an approach to the childhood of the three brothers: it stands for their closeness to the memories of the neighbourhood, its connection with a welcoming land—the poorest neighbourhood in the city of Girona, where people in the 50s and 60s arrived from Southern Spain. They accept and experience living together with total normality and feel comfortable. To exhibit sherry is a sort of homage to the people who arrived in those years and have stayed. *"This corner devoted to sherry in the wine cellar allows me to show the wine like a cultural bridge, as an example of fraternity, warmth, involvement and brotherhood. From Girona to Jerez, from poetry to Andalusian cante."*

PRIORAT

A sharp, ridged slab of slate drops heavily onto an olive wood container, symbolising the tactile hardness of barren land. Pau Casals' cello plays *Carnaval des animaux* by Camille Saint-Saëns.

"Priorat captivates me, leaves me flabbergasted. It comes from a land of influence that I began to discover in the early nineties, when I saw foreigners who loved this region, who fell in love with it and devoted their bodies and souls to it. They encouraged the locals, who worked thoroughly, dignifying the work of the farmer and preserving its historical heritage."
It's an austere, barren land of twisted vines where the knowledge of wine was disrupted by phylloxera, when a plague struck Catalonia in the 1880s. Lack of understanding, uncertainty, disenchantment, emptiness and oblivion existed for two to three generations. *"This is heroic wine growing. The movement of the nineties resurrected the territory and gave way to a revolution that brought together an old vine and young people to work it, with an eclectic, enthusiastic, optimistic, vital and responsible view. The short-sighted, lazy and close-minded views of the past have been sidestepped to make way for the fight to shine again, to return to field work and prove it's possible to be a farmer. Priorat symbolises a new beginning after hard times."*
At El Celler de Can Roca, Josep hopes to communicate the mark left on him by Porrera with images of a hidden, shrunken village, left empty. *"When I was there for the first time in March I found blossoming almond trees. This flowering element in a harsh land of steep paths impacted on me in a symbolic and powerful way with regard to what can flourish in a barren land."*
Vast historical wine-producing regions have long been linked to a religious approach, and this is also reflected on the image of the Carthusian monastery of Escaladei, where the monks, who possessed great knowledge, passed on the culture of wine.
"Priorat is a great stimulus and a wonderful example for other regions, like Empordà, to restore themselves and cast out into the world with their own uniqueness."

G

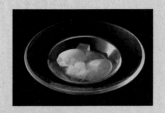

—CHROMATISM

G

— CHROMATISM

According to the Roca brothers

Chromatism is a concept that applies to colours, their variety and multiplicity, but also to music, semitones, notes that derive a certain unity from their smallest differences. That is why when we speak of chromatism, we also refer to the will to bring minor discrepancies together, to build a scale in which everything has a position, where there is value in blurring and in the slight variations around a whole that we want both aligned and scattered at the same time, almost chaotic. We experiment with the importance of nuances and, thanks to the apparent accumulation of the differences, we reach a universe that is visually the complete opposite of that hazy fluidity: coherence in tonality.

Research about the unity found in variety consists, at El Celler, of two types. It is an intellectual, inductive process, because of its significance in the rebuilding of a universe that has never existed (the search for a scattered subtlety that withdraws thanks to creative will). And it's craftwork, a deductive effort, because it stems from the intuition of a harmonious whole that demands almost the skills of a goldsmith that brings every single miniature into life.

Musical variations from known elements that transform and acquire a new nature. Illusion of the colour that leads us to admire the palette of a painter who lives obsessed with minimalist alterations. A whole world hides behind the elegance of the nuance.

Colours become an element of culinary selection that derives from evocative combinations. They awaken psychological associations depending on the chromatic affinity of the ingredients. White demands rice and almond. Yellow leads to egg yolk and saffron. A sauce of oatmeal porridge with plum confit brings us to black. As does, evidently, black garlic... Today, at El Celler, we have started a creative line that originates from colour and its resonance in our mood. Monochromatic dishes are an exercise we have been carrying out since 2003, consisting of bringing together different flavours of the same chromatic range, and suitable to the power suggested by the colour. Now, Jordi is moving deeper into our research of colour: he develops the idea that every colour evokes a mood and, therefore, the elements placed in a recipe are orchestrated around producing that mood.

RED CHROMATISM seeks to arouse excitement, euphoria, energy and—why not—a bit of aggressiveness. It is made from a mixture of infusions and spices, like the flax-leaved daphne of the Pyrenees, hibiscus, rose, pink pepper; and other ingredients such as Campari, blood orange, raspberries, strawberry and wild strawberries.

WHITE CHROMATISM suggests purity and is composed of distilled ingredients. Ingredients that are nonetheless not white in their natural state. The challenge is to snatch the fragrant soul of perfumes such as cocoa, coffee, lemon, cinnamon or aniseed, and turn it into the colour of snow.

ORANGE CHROMATISM contains, in our latest version, a game of draughts that suggest autumn, with ingredients such as orange, quince, egg yolk, carrot, carrot shaved ice and orange sugar.

GREEN CHROMATISM introduces the more soothing version. It brings together green apples, the French liqueur Chartreuse, and herbs: mint, basil, fennel, eucalyptus, dill, and green shiso.

At El Celler, recipes do not end with a version of the dish, they often reincarnate into various evolutions. For instance, we went back to this idea of a dessert— chromatisms are usually desserts—and transformed it into a starter in the shape of a peculiar GREEN SALAD the composition of which also stems from chromatism and the meeting of fruit and plants, vegetables and the culture of olive oil. The refreshing juice from blended cucumber, the oiliness of avocado, the spirit of the lime compote, and the saltiness of the manzanilla olive sorbet bring complexity of taste to the herb and fruit dressing that form this salad version of coloured cuisine. It is said that, par excellence, green represents nature, harmony, growth, exuberance and freshness. In this actual instance, it is a calming vision of cooking, conceived as a dessert and finally served as a starter. Because in our kitchen, ends meet. This is an example.

In the dining room...

In the dining room, we have looked for chromatic associations that convey warmth, emotion and the organic element, which creates comfort. Wood and nature go beyond colours and suggest a new meeting with the beauty of the essential. Our vision of colour in the dining room is of naturalness, discreetness, clarity of shapes and chromatic simplicity, so that the colours do not distort the show coming from the kitchen. On the plate you will find all the colours, shapes and risky compositions. You will savour the adventure at the table. When you look up, you will feel calm, relaxed and comforted.

GREEN SALAD

SERVES 4 PEOPLE

COMPOSITION
Kumato seeds
Mini cucumber
Lime jelly
Avocado cream
Green olive ice cream
Chartreuse candies
Cucumber skin juice

—KUMATO SEEDS

1 kumato

Cut the kumato in half and remove its seeds carefully. Divide them in three parts and reserve.

—MINI CUCUMBER
YIELDS 50 SHEETS

1 mini cucumber

Wash the skin well and slice it thinly with a mandolin. Reserve in a closed container.

—LIME JELLY
YIELDS 90 G

75 g water
20 g sugar
1.2 g agar-agar
20 g lime juice

Bring the water and sugar to a boil until the sugar dissolves. Leave to cool and add the agar-agar, boil again and remove from the heat. Add the lime juice, mix and pour into a mould to set. When cold, blend to obtain a silky gel.

—CHARTREUSE CANDIES
YIELDS 74 UNITS

20 g water
60 g sugar
12 g green Chartreuse
Cornflour

Make syrup by bringing the water and sugar to 109°C/228°F. Remove from the heat and let the temperature drop slightly. Add the Chartreuse carefully. The ideal way to do this is by letting the syrup slide very slowly down the sides of one container into the one with the alcohol and back, repeating until both liquids and both densities integrate. Reserve.

Fill a baking sheet with cornflour and leave to dry for a few hours at 80°C/176°F. Flatten, smooth out and make small holes to be filled with the syrup and liqueur mixture. Dust the surface lightly with some dry cornflour and leave for 24 hours at approximately 40°C/104°F.

Next, remove the candies from the cornflour, dust with a brush and reserve. (Each candy weighs approximately 1 g).

—CUCUMBER SKIN JUICE
YIELDS 200 G

330 g cucumber
0.4 g xanthan gum
Salt

Peel the cucumber including approximately 1 cm of pulp. Run it through the blender and adjust salt on the resulting juice; blend it with xanthan gum. Using the vacuum machine, remove any air produced when liquidising, then reserve.

—AVOCADO CREAM
YIELDS 154 G

140 g ripe avocados
14 g lime juice
Salt

Blend the pulp of the avocado, mix it with lime juice and adjust salt. Reserve refrigerated in a piping bag.

—GREEN OLIVE ICE CREAM
YIELDS 440 G

375 g green olives
145 g brine from the preserved olives
25 g dextrose
2 g cream stabiliser
2 g salt
37 g glycerin

Blend the olives with their brine until obtaining a very fine cream, free of lumps. Run the mixture through a fine chinois and mix the resulting juice with dextrose. Heat to 40°C/104°F while stirring; then, add the remaining ingredients, stir with a whisk and pasteurise at 85°C/185°F. Cool, place in a Pacojet beaker and freeze. Churn before serving.

GARNISHING AND PLATING

Arugula sprouts
Watercress sprouts
Salad burnet leaves
Extra virgin olive oil

Arrange all the ingredients on a plate together with the sprouts and leaves. Dress with a few drops of olive oil.

ORANGE

SERVES 8 PEOPLE

COMPOSITION

Carrot jelly
Passion jelly
Quindim
Tangerine jelly
Orange jelly
Carrot granita
Carrot oil
Clove oil
Tangerine sugar

—CARROT JELLY
YIELDS 750 G

500 g carrot juice
5 g iota
250 g sugar

Blend the carrot juice with iota, then add the sugar and bring to a boil.

Place the mixture, while still hot, on a 1-cm-deep baking tray. Cool refrigerated and reserve.

—PASSION JELLY
YIELDS 750 G

500 g passion fruit juice
10 g iota
250 g sugar
4 g trisodium citrate

Blend the passion fruit juice with iota, then add the sugar and trisodium citrate and bring to a boil.

Place the mixture, while still hot, on a 1-cm-deep baking tray. Let it cool down while refrigerated and reserve.

—QUINDIM
YIELDS 645 G

215 g cream
215 g sugar
215 g egg yolks

Boil the cream and sugar and pour the egg yolks on top. Mix vigorously to prevent egg yolks from curdling. Strain and pour the mixture into a 1-cm-deep baking tray, cover with cling film and bake in the steam oven at 110°C/230°F for 35 minutes. Cool down refrigerated and reserve.

—TANGERINE JELLY
YIELDS 750 G

500 g tangerine juice
7.5 g iota
250 g sugar

Blend the tangerine juice with iota, then add the sugar and bring to a boil.

Place the mixture, while still hot, on a 1-cm-deep baking tray. Cool refrigerated and reserve.

—ORANGE JELLY
YIELDS 750 G

500 g orange juice
8.5 g iota
250 g sugar

Blend the orange juice with iota, then add the sugar and bring to a boil.

Place the mixture, while still hot, on a 1-cm-deep baking tray. Cool refrigerated and reserve.

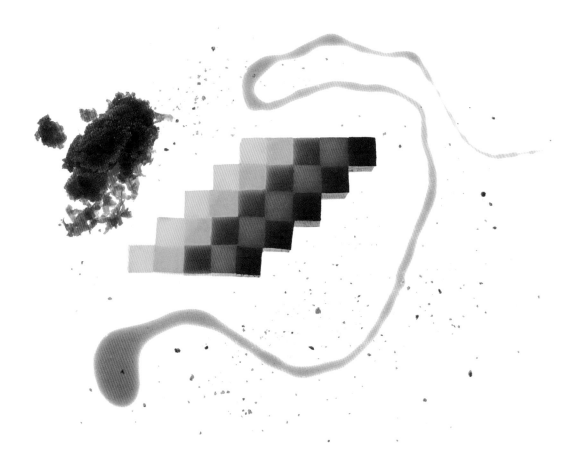

—CARROT GRANITA
YIELDS 600 G

500 g carrot juice
50 g inverted sugar syrup
50 g dextrose
2 gelatine sheets

Boil half of the carrot juice with the inverted sugar syrup and dextrose. Remove from heat; add the gelatine sheets previously hydrated and the remaining carrot juice. Transfer to a container and freeze.

—CARROT OIL
YIELDS 400 G

200 g carrot juice
100 g sugar
100 g pumpkin seed oil
0.8 g xanthan gum

Heat the carrot juice with sugar, emulsify with the pumpkin seed oil and, lastly, stabilise the emulsion with xanthan gum. Reserve.

—CLOVE OIL
YIELDS 150 G

150 g sunflower oil
4 cloves

Seal the oil and cloves in a vacuum pack bag, infuse in the Roner at 40°C/104°F for 30 minutes. Store the oil in the bag and hermetically sealed.

—TANGERINE SUGAR
YIELDS 200 G

100 g sugar
100 g tangerine zest

Mix the sugar with the tangerine zest and blend. Spread the mixture on a silicone mat and dry in the dehydrator. When dry, blend lightly. Reserve.

GARNISHING AND PLATING

Grated carrot

Cut the jellies and quindim into 1 cm cubes and form five lines, alternating in the following order: carrot jelly, passion jelly, quindim, tangerine jelly, and orange jelly.

Shave the granita and serve a spoonful next to the jellies; on top, arrange the grated carrot and a few drops of carrot oil and clove oil. Finish with a pinch of tangerine sugar.

WHITE

SERVES 8 PEOPLE

COMPOSITION
Tonka bean cream
Coffee jelly
Passion fruit granita
Cocoa sorbet

—TONKA BEAN CREAM
YIELDS 110 G

100 g tonka bean distillate*
10 g sugar
0.5 g salt
1 g agar-agar

*FROM AN INFUSION OF 250 G WATER AND 50 G TONKA
BEANS, AND FOLLOWING THE SAME PROCESS USED TO
MAKE THE SOIL DISTILLATE AS EXPLAINED IN THE BASIC
RECIPES SECTION, PAGE 428.

Mix the sugar, salt and agar-agar, dissolve in
50 g of tonka bean distillate and bring to a boil.
Then, mix quickly with the other half of the
distillate and leave to set in another container.
When solid, mix with a hand blender and
reserve refrigerated.

—COFFEE JELLY
YIELDS 110 G

100 g coffee distillate*
10 g sugar
0.5 g agar-agar

*FROM AN INFUSION OF 250 G COFFEE AND 50 G COFFEE
BEANS, AND FOLLOWING THE SAME PROCESS USED TO MAKE
THE SOIL DISTILLATE AS EXPLAINED IN THE BASIC RECIPES
SECTION, PAGE 428.

Mix the sugar and agar-agar, dissolve in 50 g
coffee distillate and bring to a boil. Then, mix
quickly with the other half of the distillate and
leave to set in a 1-cm-deep container. When
solid, cut into 0.5 cm cubes.

—PASSION FRUIT GRANITA
YIELDS 110 G

100 g passion fruit distillate*
15 g dextrose
½ gelatine sheet

*FROM AN INFUSION OF 250 G PASSION FRUIT JUICE AND
FOLLOWING THE SAME PROCESS USED TO MAKE THE SOIL
DISTILLATE AS EXPLAINED IN THE BASIC RECIPES SECTION,
PAGE 428.

Dissolve the dextrose and gelatine with a part
of the distillate and then mix with the rest of it.
Reserve in a container in the freezer.

—COCOA SORBET
YIELDS 170 G

100 g cocoa distillate*
25 g glucose powder
15 g dextrose
0.6 g sorbet stabiliser
30 g water

*FROM AN INFUSION OF 250 G WATER AND 50 G COCOA
BEANS, AND FOLLOWING THE SAME PROCESS USED TO
MAKE THE SOIL DISTILLATE AS EXPLAINED IN THE BASIC
RECIPES SECTION, PAGE 428.

Mix the glucose, dextrose and stabiliser with
water and bring to 85°C/185°F; mix with the
distillate and freeze in a Pacojet beaker.

GARNISHING AND PLATING

Churn the sorbet and arrange the ingredients
for the dessert in the middle of a soup dish.

H

—SWEETNESS

FOIE TURRON

246

SOIL BEETROOT

247

MELON WITH HAM

250

SQUAB BONBON

252

WHITE ASPARAGUS
VIENNETTA

253

APRICOT

254

SUCKLING PIG
CUT WITH MELON

256

H

—SWEETNESS

We associate sweetness with fluffy and savoury with sharpness. That almost childish and basic difference has set limits that have been difficult to breach because they are part of the culture and education our taste buds —which at the tip of the tongue detect the characteristics of flavour—have received for centuries.

So we face two seemingly opposing and separate universes. And nothing is more absurd than this confrontation through indifference. In fact, traditional cuisine brings the two into harmony. The contribution of El Celler is not to incorporate their sporadic relationship into the menu, with more or less distortion or convergence of concepts, but to destroy; to blow up the borders. It is not about seeing desserts and the rest of the meal as two different worlds, with a pause in the middle, but about incorporating sweetness into the main course and have it interfere continuously in the slow succession of the menu. Moreover, it is about transforming desserts, the kingdom of sweetness, into something beyond an extra or a celebration ending. Today, they are the final act of the show, the closing of the circle, the outcome of the play that reveals the conclusions we ought to make. Worn out frontiers, continuity, free movement of ideas and tastes.

According to the Roca brothers

Stuffed apples, a typical fiesta delicacy still prevalent in villages of Alt Empordà, where it's called *pomes de relleno*, is a solemn and magnificent dish served as a dessert and the inspiration for our APPLE AND FOIE GRAS TIMBALE WITH OIL AND VANILLA. The mixture of fruit and meat and the combination of sweet and savoury are common in our cuisine. It is frequently interpreted as a connection between the modernity and the meeting of the worlds of Joan and Jordi, but it responds to the most delicious tradition. The generous use of sugar in meat dishes can be found in our medieval, Renaissance cuisine, as we can see for example in the *Llibre del Coch* by Master Ruperto de Nola. In the well-to-do gastronomy of the time, the abundant and excessive use of sugar—a very expensive ingredient in those days—probably represented a symbol of power.

Today, we are pleased to incorporate that atavistic culinary habit. Some time back we had already reinterpreted it by proposing a menu with pre-desserts, conceived as a special starter to the world of sweet. Thus, we have created organised menus arranged like a unique theory of chaos, with an established and continuous rhythm that breaks the rigidity of the structure of the last hundred years, and the sweet always precedes the savoury.

The concept of chaos is relatively recent and became widely known thanks to the valuable contributions and body of writings by scientists and researchers of different disciplines that have made possible the development of the *theory of chaos*. It states that while there is order within chaos, there is also chaos within order. And it aims to describe the behaviour of nonlinear dynamics, as the antithesis of a stable and foreseeable reality. For us, the theory of chaos is the starting point of a way of structuring a menu that breaks with the dominant academic rigidity from the days of Georges Auguste Escoffier (1846-1935), father of French cuisine methods and highly influential around the world.

Sweet before savoury. Or mixed. Never pushed over the edge. This is our interpretation of the theory of chaos. A silent revolution. Breaking away from preconceptions. A divertimento for palates... The last become the first and the pyramid of culinary power is turned upside down.

In the dining room...

"The true voyage of discovery consists not in seeking new landscapes but in having new eyes," said Marcel Proust. When we serve our Chaos Theory Menu we hope to present you with the challenge of adopting this novel perspective. We want to create a mess. To cause a stir. To kick up a hell of a row and have you participate in it. To use disorder to build a sense of recklessness. We invite you to enjoy a dance of textures, tastes, accompaniments and main ingredients that seem to be out of step, out of rhythm. Sweet as appetiser, between dishes in the middle of the meal, and as a pre-dessert.

An unpredictable and disconcerting carousel. An amazing journey. A meal to remember...

Chaos Theory Menu. A palindromic menu (2009)

Razorfish skin
Smoked black tea distillate with caviar and sheep yogurt
Hazelnut and foie turrón with soy
Dry Gambini
Melon with Iberian ham
Chablis Oysters
Mussels with white tea
Figs with fig tree leaf
Dorsal fin of turbot, juice of its essence and 'dry egg' powder with citrus fruits
Prawn with amontillado
Green olive coulant with potato, tuna air, vegetables and sprouts
Endives with coffee ice cream
Cod
Kid head. Cheeks with their gravy, brains with mustard leaves and jowl with goat milk and ashes
Summer truffle soufflé
Caramelised raspberries with squab aiguillette
Spider crab with snails and chocolate
Apple, vanilla and foie timbale
Anarchy

FOIE TURRON

**SERVES 30 PEOPLE
(1 PER PERSON)**

COMPOSITION
PX reduction
Foie turron
Turron paint

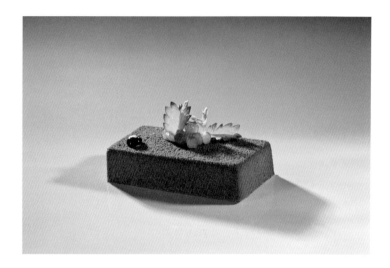

—PX REDUCTION
YIELDS 85 G

200 g Pedro Ximénez

Place the sweet wine in a casserole over heat
and reduce to 85 g.

—FOIE TURRON
YIELDS 300 G

200 g foie gras
50 g hazelnut praline
50 g hazelnut paste
15 g butter
30 g cocoa butter
10 g white truffle oil
10 g PX reduction (previously prepared)
Salt

Sauté the foie, searing it on both sides; place
it in the Thermomix with the praline, hazelnut
paste, softened butter, melted cocoa butter,
truffle oil, Pedro Ximénez reduction and salt.
Blend well and run through a fine chinois. Place
the mixture in a metal bowl, prepare a cold
bain-marie and emulsify the paste with a hand
blender until it turns a lighter colour and its
density changes. Fill some 2.5x5x1-cm-deep
moulds shaped as ingots and freeze. (10 g
of the mixture goes into each ingot.)

—TURRON PAINT
YIELDS 200 G

100 g cocoa butter
100 g couverture chocolate 70%

Melt and mix the couverture chocolate with the
cocoa butter; when the mixture is 40°C/104°F,
strain and fill the airbrush with it.

Activate the compressor and paint each turron
with a thin coat of paint; reserve again in the
freezer.

GARNISHING AND PLATING

Soybean sprouts
Soy sauce
Salad burnet leaves
Rosemary blossoms
Gold leaf

Cut the soybean sprouts to the size of grains
of rice, marinate in soy sauce for about
30 seconds, then strain any excess sauce and
set on the turron. Also, arrange a salad burnet
leaf, rosemary flowers and, on a corner, a dot of
PX reduction crowned with a piece of gold leaf.

SOIL BEETROOT

SERVES 8 PEOPLE

COMPOSITION
Blown sugar beetroot
Beetroot foam
Cocoa meringue
Soil distillate gel

—BLOWN SUGAR BEETROOT
YIELDS 25 UNITS

500 g isomalt
5 g water
20 drops 50% citric acid solution
10 g red food colouring

Place the isomalt sugar in a container and cook until it reaches 180°C/356°F. Remove from the heat and add the water, citric acid and red food colouring; leave to stand for a few minutes and pull the sugar on a silicone mat.

Heat a small amount of sugar under the heat lamp and gloss by kneading it about 20 times. While the sugar is still hot, form small uniform balls and, with a blowing pump, inflate slowly to shape them as beetroots. Make a small hole to fill them in later. Reserve in a moisture-free place.

—BEETROOT FOAM
YIELDS 700 G

500 g beetroots
200 g pasteurised egg whites
5 g salt

Boil beetroot until soft, blend it to a fine purée and leave to cool. Mix with the egg whites and salt. Transfer into a whipped cream dispenser and reserve.

—COCOA MERINGUE
YIELDS 110 G

100 g pasteurised egg whites
10 g cocoa powder
5 g squid ink
Salt

Beat egg whites with a pinch of salt until soft peaks form. Slowly, add the sieved cocoa and squid ink; stretch over a silicone mat and leave to dry for 24 hours. When it is completely dry, crush and reserve in an airtight container.

—SOIL DISTILLATE GEL
YIELDS 100 G

100 g soil distillate (basic recipes, p.428)
0.5 g xanthan gum

Mix the distillate with the xanthan gum and run a hand blender through it until it acquires a thick texture. Leave to stand to eliminate the air.

GARNISHING AND PLATING

Beetroot
Beetroot leaf sprouts

On a plate, place a spoonful of soil distillate gel and cover it with cocoa meringue, dried and crushed. Fill the blown sugar beetroot with foam and place it on top of the sand imitated by the meringue. Garnish with a beetroot leaf and a few slices of raw beetroot.

MELON WITH HAM

SERVES 4 PEOPLE

COMPOSITION
Tarragon water
Melon rind
Melon pulp
Iberian ham consommé
Iberian ham consommé jelly

—TARRAGON WATER
YIELDS 250 G

300 g tarragon leaves
75 g cooking water
75 g water
Salt

Blanch the tarragon leaves in boiling water with salt, cool quickly in a cold bain-marie. Reserve 75 g of the cooking water and blast chill to use very cold. Blend the blanched tarragon leaves with this cooking water and the remaining 75 g of water. Run through a fine chinois, adjust salt and reserve.

—MELON RIND
YIELDS 3 HALF-MELON COATED MOULDS

100 g tarragon water (previously prepared)
20 g sugar
2 g agar-agar
2.5 gelatine sheets

Place some 16x8.5x6.5-cm-deep moulds in the shape of half-melons in the freezer.

Mix the ingredients and heat until they come to a boil, remove and add gelatine sheets previously hydrated. Leave to cool to solidify and blend to obtain a very fine purée.

Pour the mixture in each of the moulds that were in the freezer, tilt so the mixture coats the sides, turn the mould over on a sheet to eliminate any excess liquid and freeze again.

GARNISHING AND PLATING

Iberian ham

Remove the melon from the mould and cut into wedges.

Accompany with thin slices of Iberian ham and Iberian ham jelly grated with a Microplane.

—MELON PULP

YIELDS PULP FOR 4 HALF-MELON MOULDS

330 g melon pulp
30 g sugar
3.5 gelatine sheets
Raw pine kernels

Reserve half the melon pulp refrigerated.

Heat the other half of the pulp with sugar until the sugar dissolves, remove from heat and add the gelatine, previously hydrated, mixing it all well and placing it in the mixer bowl. Slowly, add remaining pulp and mix until the preparation cools completely.

Refill the moulds that contained the tarragon jelly with the mousse obtained, insert a few pine kernels on the surface, imitating the seeds, and freeze.

—IBERIAN HAM CONSOMMÉ

YIELDS 600 G

1.5 kg water
1 kg Iberian ham bones
2 pig's trotters
250 g carrots
250 g onions

Boil the pig's trotters, bones and lightly cooked vegetables for 2 hours on low heat. Strain and reserve.

—IBERIAN HAM CONSOMMÉ JELLY

YIELDS 550 G

600 g Iberian ham consommé (previously prepared)
6 g agar-agar

Add consommé and agar-agar to a casserole and mix well. Bring to a boil, strain and leave to set. Reserve.

SQUAB BONBON

SERVES 8 PEOPLE

COMPOSITION

Squab liver parfait
Bristol Cream coating
Spice bread sheets

—SQUAB LIVER PARFAIT
YIELDS 180 G

200 g squab livers
200 g butter
25 g Harvey's Bristol Cream
5 g salt
1 g Sichuan pepper
Orange peel confit cubes (basic recipes,
    p.427)

Soak the squab livers in a container with
abundant iced water. When soaked, strain well
and dry with kitchen paper. In a frying pan with
some butter, cook the livers on both sides and
deglaze with half the Bristol Cream. Place this
mixture in a Thermomix bowl and blend with the
remaining ingredients and the rest of the Bristol
Cream. Run the mixture through a fine chinois
and use piping bags to fill semi-spherical
moulds of 2.5 cm diameter by 1 cm depth; then,
place 1 caramelised orange cube inside each
bonbon. Soften what will be the base of the
bonbons with a spatula and freeze.

—BRISTOL CREAM COATING
YIELDS 200 G

200 g Harvey's Bristol Cream
2 g kappa carrageenan

Remove the squab bonbons from the previous
preparation from their moulds.

Mix the kappa and cold Bristol Cream, bring
to a boil and coat the frozen bonbons lightly.
Reserve refrigerated so they thaw inside.

—SPICE BREAD SHEETS
YIELDS 15 SHEETS

500 g spice bread (basic recipes, p.428)

Freeze the spice bread and, using a meat slicer,
cut thin sheets. Stretch the sheets over a
baking sheet lined with greaseproof paper and
dry then in the cooker at 70°C/158°F until the
bread is crisp. Reserve in an airtight container
in a dry place.

GARNISHING AND PLATING

Pine kernel paste
Juniper powder

Temper the bonbons and top with a dot of pine
kernel paste, the juniper powder and a small
sheet of spice bread.

WHITE ASPARAGUS VIENNETTA

SERVES 8 PEOPLE

COMPOSITION
Asparagus ice cream
Asparagus viennetta
Asparagus tips
Black truffle powder

—ASPARAGUS ICE CREAM
YIELDS 1 KG

570 g white asparagus
250 g cream 35%
60 g skimmed milk powder
60 g dextrose
50 g glycerin
5 g ice-cream stabiliser
7 g salt

Peel the asparagus and boil them until soft.
Purée them and run through a fine chinois.
Reserve.

Mix the cream, milk powder and dextrose in
a casserole, heat until the mixture reaches
40°C/104°F. Add the glycerine and ice-cream
stabiliser. Mix with the hand blender to prevent
lumps from forming, pasteurise at 85°C/185°F.
Add salt, mix and leave to cool to 40°C/104°F.
Add the asparagus purée and blend to smooth
the mixture. Leave to ripen for 24 hours
refrigerated and reserve.

—ASPARAGUS VIENNETTA
YIELDS 10 PORTIONS 2 CM WIDE EACH

1 kg asparagus ice cream
     (previously prepared)
30 g black truffle

Run the ice cream through the ice-cream
maker and transfer to a piping bag with a star
nozzle.

Pipe in a layer approximately 8 cm thick, forming
curly 'waves' as seen in the image. Cover it with
truffle sheets and top with a second layer of
ice cream, cover with another layer of truffle
sheets and finish with a third layer of ice cream.
Reserve in the freezer until serving.

—ASPARAGUS TIPS
YIELDS 16 TIPS

16 white asparagus tips
1.6 g salt
0.3 g sugar

Cut the tips of the asparagus about 5 cm long,
seal in a vacuum pack bag with salt and sugar
and cook at 85°C/185°F for 30 minutes.

—BLACK TRUFFLE POWDER
YIELDS 75 G

200 g black truffle skin

Chop the truffle finely and sprinkle over a
sheet lined with a silicone mat. Place it in the
dehydrator at 60°C/140°F for 24 hours. When
dehydrated, crush and reserve in an airtight
container.

GARNISHING AND PLATING

Black garlic purée (basic recipes, p.427)
Chicory leaves
Extra virgin olive oil

Draw a line with the truffle powder on a cold
plate. Cut a 2-cm-thick piece of Viennetta, and
place over the truffle line, then sprinkle more
truffle powder on top.

Next to it, serve hot asparagus tips with a dot
of black garlic purée on top and a chicory leaf.
Finish with extra virgin olive oil.

APRICOT

SERVES 8 PEOPLE

COMPOSITION

Blown sugar sphere
Apricot foam
Apricot sauce
Vanilla shots

—BLOWN SUGAR SPHERE
YIELDS 20 SPHERES

500 g sugar
70 g water
100 g liquid glucose
20 drops 50% citric acid solution
Orange food colouring
Icing sugar

In a saucepan, bring the water and sugar to a boil. When it begins to boil, add liquid glucose and let it boil without stirring. Continue cooking at 158°C/316°F, remove from heat and add the orange colouring (amount to taste) and 20 drops of the citric acid and water solution. Set the mixture aside for 1 minute and heat it lightly to remove the sugar from the saucepan and pour it on a silicone mat. While hot, stretch the sugar and join its ends 15-20 times to distribute the small air bubbles inside it, give it a satin texture and allow it to blow up more uniformly.

Using a pair of scissors, cut the caramel into sections and reserve them in an airtight container with silica gel to prevent moisture. A suitable heat lamp is needed to work the sugar. Soften the caramel again under the heat lamp, insert an air pump into it and blow to form a sphere. While hot and using a paring knife, shape it like an apricot. Remove the sphere from the pump by heating the metallic section with a blow-torch; at the same time, heat a tube with the blow-torch to make a hole on the base of the sphere. Using an airbrush, paint one side of the ball faintly to create the effect of the apricot skin. Sprinkle with icing sugar and reserve.

—APRICOT FOAM
YIELDS 500 G

500 g apricots
50 g sugar
20 g albumin powder

Peel and cut up the apricots, blend and mix the pulp with sugar and albumin powder. Run the hand blender through the mixture and leave to stand refrigerated for 12 hours. Transfer to a whipped cream dispenser and reserve.

—APRICOT SAUCE
YIELDS 250 G

50 g sugar
100 g apricot liqueur
100 g apricot pulp
20 g butter

Place the sugar in a casserole until it starts to caramelise. When it turns a reddish colour, add the apricot liqueur, stirring well to mix. Then add the apricot pulp and lastly the butter. This sauce must be prepared for each meal and right before serving, otherwise the butter separates (it must be warm).

—VANILLA SHOTS
YIELDS 550 G CREAM, 300 G SHOTS

250 g cream
250 g milk
½ vanilla pod
25 g sugar
2 gelatine sheets

Bring the cream and milk to a boil with the vanilla pod. When it has come to a boil, add the sugar and gelatine sheets previously hydrated. Strain the mixture and reserve in a squeeze bottle. When it cools down, let drops fall into a container with liquid nitrogen and scoop out the shots as they form.

GARNISHING AND PLATING

Apricot
Fresh almonds

In the middle of the plate, serve some apricot liqueur sauce with the vanilla shots, a piece of apricot, a fresh almond, and the blown sugar apricot filled with apricot foam.

SUCKLING PIG CUT WITH MELON

SERVES 8 PEOPLE

COMPOSITION
Suckling pig belly
Melon
Suckling pig gravy
Suckling pig sauce
Orange coating
Orange and clove sorbet

—SUCKLING PIG BELLY

2 Iberian suckling pig bellies
Brine for meat (basic recipes, p.429)
Extra virgin olive oil

Heat and keep the Roner at 63°C/145°F. Clean the skin of the suckling pig and immerse the belly in brine for 2 hours. Seal in a vacuum pack bag with olive oil and cook in the Roner for 24 hours. Next, remove and cool quickly.

—MELON
YIELDS 35-40 SQUARES 3X3 CM EACH

1 melon
200 g orange juice

Cut 1-cm-thick melon slices, peel and cut into 3 cm squares.

Seal 8 squares per vacuum bag at 100% with orange juice, without overlapping. Reserve refrigerated.

—SUCKLING PIG GRAVY
YIELDS 200 G

1.6 kg suckling pig bones and trimmings
210 g mirepoix (basic recipes, p.427)
1.7 kg cold water

Place the bones and trimmings in a baking tray and brown at 180°C/356°F until well toasted. Then, remove any excess fat and transfer to a stockpot together with the mirepoix. Deglaze the juices that may be left on the tray with cold water and add to the cooking stockpot. Cover everything with cold water and cook for 3 hours. Next, strain and reduce to 200 g of suckling pig gravy.

—SUCKLING PIG SAUCE
YIELDS 200 G

200 g suckling pig gravy (previously prepared)
20 g butter

Heat the suckling pig gravy and add butter, stirring vigorously to bind the sauce. Reserve.

—ORANGE COATING

YIELDS 270 G

250 g orange juice
25 g sugar
2.5 g agar-agar
2 gelatine sheets

Set some silicone moulds in the shape of acorns (see page 429) in the freezer.

Hydrate the gelatine sheets in cold water.

Mix the juice, sugar and agar-agar and bring to a boil. Remove from heat and add gelatine previously hydrated. Pour the mixture into the cold moulds; a small amount in each hole will suffice to form a layer along the walls of the mould. Reserve in the freezer face down to eliminate any excess juice.

—ORANGE AND CLOVE SORBET

YIELDS 450 G

2.5 g sorbet stabiliser
130 g water
65 g dextrose
50 g sugar
1 g orange zest
0.5 g clove
250 g orange juice

Mix the stabiliser with some of the sugar from the ingredients. Reserve.

Mix the water and dextrose, put in a stockpot and heat to 40°C/104°F. When that temperature is reached, add the remaining sugar, orange zest, clove and mixture of stabiliser and sugar. Mix well to prevent lumps from forming and pasteurise at 85°C/185°F.

Remove from heat, strain and cool. Leave to ripen refrigerated for 12 hours before using.

Blend the orange juice with the sorbet base and run through the ice-cream maker. When it acquires the desired texture, transfer the sorbet into piping bags and fill the acorn moulds previously prepared with the orange coating; smooth out the surface and keep in the freezer until serving.

GARNISHING AND PLATING

Orange emulsion (basic recipes, p.427)
Baby mustard leaves

Regenerate the bellies in the Roner at 60°C/140°F, remove them from the bag and sear on the griddle pan until the skin turns brown and crisp. Cut the suckling pig belly exactly the same size as the orange soaked melon and sandwich together, with the belly as a biscuit and the melon as ice cream.

Arrange the slice on the plate with some dots of orange emulsion and suckling pig sauce. Garnish with the orange and clove acorn and the baby mustard leaves.

I

—TRANSVERSAL CREATION

I

—TRANSVERSAL CREATION

A transversal line crosses or cuts through a system of recipes. That is, it escapes from convention, from the line drawn. It ignores the rules and moves forward on an unknown road. The adventure can be undertaken alone (with the risks involved in walking alone down an unmarked road) or accompanied (with the chance to move on with the help of friendly forces). To be transversal also means to be humble, because you're aware that in order to find what you're looking for —that obscure object of desire barely in sight—your strength alone will not suffice. Better yet: the desire will be more complete and corporeal when another person joins the journey.

At El Celler there are aromas that translate into the language of taste. Also desserts that rise up to the cloud without the perfume. Back and forth from solidity to the nebula, from evanescence to touch. To get here, Jordi sought the company of an experienced man who didn't work with spatulas or sugar, but with the still and essences. This is the start of the perfume that arises from the dish, the straight line it crosses, and the oblique shape that escapes the expected. The same happens with the cava that solidifies after a process of concentration.

Combining disciplines, symbioses born to bring the venture to fruition. Once this ship is boarded, there is the implicit need to work together to unfold all the sails at the same time and with a single purpose.

According to the Roca brothers

We are not artists, but goldsmiths. In the vastness of messages that can come out of cuisine, there is always an element of arrogance, or even vanity about the earnestness to know and show. It is inherent in our conscience... The Roca brothers are curious by nature and this curiosity is the foundation of creativity. Creativity understood as an act of therapy, healing, and reconciliation. There is a type of creativity that is an attitude, a point of view, a way of existing in life: pure creation. The way to creation is a perpetual adventure that begins day after day. We acknowledge that the perfect work of art does not exist, but we must seek the unprecedented dish we haven't found yet.

If there is anything enriching about the sweet moment we are experiencing from the creative point of view, we want to increase its glory with the collaboration of open-minded people that approach our world with freshness and innocence. We take those synergies and grow and enrich our discourse within beauty, conveying a fresh and well seasoned message.

We want to attract the sort of talent that can boost the engine of creativity. Dialogue, permeability and the flow of ingenuity fertilize our creative field. Craftsmen, industrial engineers, painters, photographers, directors, musicians, chemists, poets, writers, illustrators, psychologists, physicists, perfumiers, anthropologists of the senses, artists of all sorts increasingly permeate our fertile imagination. To receive and to give. To give and to receive. We feel capable of driving forward this two-way feedback, of promoting a breeding ground for open thought in the broad sense, of favouring a cocktail of nonconformity, intentional and transversal.

We want to be proactive in this exchange, to create instants of beauty and at the same time gather tools with a cultural, educational and social purpose. Collaboration will become increasingly necessary. We need to open new frontiers in science, art and thought that cooking can use in enriching ways.

In the dining room...

The design of new supports, utensils and tableware is considered from a transversal point of view, the same as in the kitchen, with a team structure. Aesthetics at the table, their sense and coherence with an idea, build bridges to dialogue and materialise the finished work of seduction. We can use this symbiosis and link those brainstorming sessions with specific objects or dishes. We want to prove the goodness of interdisciplinary dialogue with facts. We hope to facilitate the expansion of ideas.

We also interact with the world of wine and the world of science and ask wine experts and scientists, physicists and chemists to explain the reason for things in order to reflect upon the harmony between wines and dishes, or go a little further. We try to understand *terroir...*
We want to know the 'mineral' smell, pay attention to the innovations of the sensory sciences. To go deeper into the nature of sensory perception with the help of anthropologists of the senses. To know whether instrumental sensometry can help us distinguish aromas and become a great complement in the sensory analysis of foods. As experts in its complexity, we try to make an objective validation of human olfactory and tasting perception, as demonstrated by Werner Heinsenberg, Nobel Prize winner in 1932: the uncertainty principle that expresses essentially that "the process of observation is not foreign to the observed reality, but an inevitable component of it. We are more than simple participating observers." In any case, it is said that what we see is what is reflected in our brain. It is our will to remain close to the interpretation of the sensory approach. To be sponges and absorb, to then share it with you.

NÚVOL DE LLIMONA

SERVES 4 PEOPLE

COMPOSITION
Bergamot jelly
Lemon pith
Lemon pith syrup
Lemon cream
Lemon sponge cake
Lwmon distillate
Lemon sorbet
Milk cloud

—BERGAMOT JELLY
YIELDS 715 G

500 g water
100 g sugar
8 g agar-agar
100 g lemon juice
Bergamot essence

Bring the water and sugar to a boil, blast chill and boil again with the agar-agar, starting at cold temperature. Remove from heat and add the lemon juice and bergamot essence. Smooth with a hand blender to make a gel and reserve refrigerated in piping bags.

—LEMON PITH
YIELDS 500 G

500 g water
100 g sugar
500 g lemon pith

Place the 500 g water and 100 g sugar with the lemon pith in a casserole. Bring to a boil and cool down. Repeat 4 times and, lastly, reserve the dry piths.

—LEMON PITH SYRUP
YIELDS 500 G

500 g sugar syrup (basic recipes, p.428)
500 g lemon pith (previously prepared)

Mix sugar syrup and blanched piths and leave to stand for 24 hours.

—LEMON CREAM
YIELDS 750 G

500 g lemon pith syrup (previously prepared)
70 g cream
25 g butter
100 g lemon juice

Remove the piths from the syrup and blend them in the Thermomix for 5 minutes at 65°C/149°F, incorporating the cream, butter and lemon juice.

If necessary, thin with some of the syrup used to settle the piths to obtain a creamy texture. Reserve refrigerated in piping bags.

—LEMON SPONGE CAKE
YIELDS 1 KG

200 g butter
4 lemons, grated zest
245 g flour
120 g icing sugar
10 g baking powder
3 g salt
50 g milk
245 g eggs
130 g inverted sugar syrup

Melt the butter and the grated zest of the 4
lemons. Add the dry ingredients, mix well and
add the remaining ingredients before leaving
the dough to stand for 24 hours. Place in a
buttered baking tin and bake at 180°C/356°F
for 15 minutes. Leave the sponge cake to cool
on a rack and cut it into 1 cm cubes. Reserve in
an airtight container in a dry place.

—LEMON DISTILLATE
YIELDS 350 G

350 g lemon peel
400 g water

Clean well and infuse the lemon peel,
refrigerating for 6 hours (all the pith must be
eliminated to prevent any bitterness). Leave
the infusion in the Rotaval at 45°C/113°F for
1 hour and 45 minutes. Reserve the resulting
distillate.

—LEMON SORBET
YIELDS 100 G

100 g lemon distillate (previously prepared)

Place the lemon distillate from the previous
preparation in a bowl suitable for liquid
nitrogen. Mix the distillate with a whisk, adding
the liquid nitrogen slowly until forming a
smooth sorbet.

—MILK CLOUD
YIELDS 250 G

250 g skimmed milk

Run the hand blender through the skimmed
milk until it is full of air. Scoop the resulting
mixture out and submerge it for a few seconds
in a container with liquid nitrogen. Quickly
reserve in the freezer.

GARNISHING AND PLATING

Beurre noisette (basic recipes, p.427)
Lemon
Carnation flowers

Make a spiral with the bergamot gel, leaving
an approximately 1 cm hole in the middle. In
that space, draw another spiral with the lemon
cream to alternate the ingredients. Set 3 cubes
of lemon sponge cake around the edge and one
knob of beurre noisette.

Serve the lemon sorbet next to it and the milk
cloud on top. Grate some lemon zest on it and
garnish with carnations of different colours.

OYSTER WITH CAVA

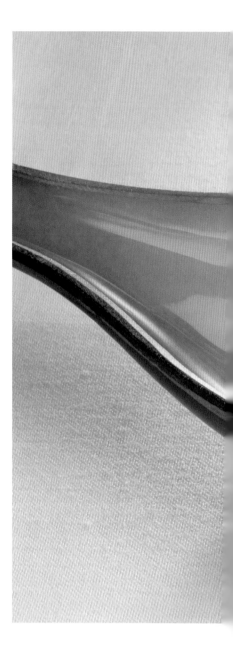

SERVES 4 PEOPLE

COMPOSITION
Oysters
Apple compote
Spice bread slices
Solid cava

—OYSTERS

8 oysters

Open the oysters with a paring knife and
remove from their shell without damaging
them. Cut off the beard with a paring knife
and reserve cold until serving.

—APPLE COMPOTE
YIELDS 100 G

100 g Royal Gala apple juice
1 g agar-agar

Leave the juice to decant to eliminate its pulp;
then add the agar-agar, boil and leave to set.
When cold, purée finely. Reserve.

—SPICE BREAD SLICES
YIELDS 15 SLICES

50 g spice bread (basic recipes, p.428)

Freeze the spice bread and, using a meat slicer,
cut it into thin slices. Distribute the slices over
a baking sheet lined with greaseproof paper
and dry on the cooker at 70°C/158°F until
the bread turns crisp. Reserve in an airtight
container in a dry place.

—SOLID CAVA
YIELDS 400 G

400 g cava
1.6 g xanthan gum

Mix the cava with the xanthan gum with a hand
blender and transfer the mixture to a whipped
cream dispenser with 2 chargers.

RECENTLY, EL CELLER DE CAN ROCA, IN A JOINT RESEARCH
PROJECT WITH CATALAN CAVA PRODUCER AGUSTÍ TORELLÓ,
HAS BEEN ABLE TO ADD 3 G OF XANTHAN GUM PER BOTTLE AT
THE MOMENT OF DISGORGING, AFTER WHICH TIME IT IS LEFT TO
STAND FOR 6 MORE MONTHS. DURING THIS TIME, THE XANTHAN
GUM HYDRATES WITH THE CAVA, TRANSFORMING IT INTO A
SAUCE AND KEEPING ITS NATURAL CARBON DIOXIDE WITHOUT
HAVING TO ADD ANY MORE GAS.

GARNISHING AND PLATING
Lemon peel confit (basic recipes, orange peel,
    p.427)
Pineapple
Preserved ginger
Curry powder
Cumin powder

Serve the apple compote on a plate; set
2 oysters, 4 preserved lemon cubes,
8 pineapple cubes, and 4 preserved ginger
cubes on top. Season with a pinch of curry
and cumin, and finish with a slice of spice
bread. Pour the solid cava when serving.

ex-
change

The creative exchange

TRANSVERSAL CREATIVITY

Creativity is a form of therapy, healing and reconciliation.

Creativity at El Celler is not necessarily related to the science of eating, but to a different point of view: pure creation. A dish can be born from an experience. Or not. Creativity gives shape to a work-river of many tributaries: at El Celler they are mainly brotherly, although they don't want to do without the creative input from their brilliant team and from transversal creation.

They want to be proactive. They know shared values mobilise and expand. The examples of cross-cutting collaboration they describe next are only an illustration of the conciliatory will and ability of the Roca brothers to maintain an active dialogue.

SÒLID, A CAVA SAUCE

El Celler de Can Roca
Agustí Torelló
Alícia Foundation

Jaume Coll suggested creating a dish to describe live while the book *Una Sinfonía Fantástica* (2006) was being written. He suggested *Huîtres au Champagne* from *Larousse Gastronomique* (ed. Robuchon, 1996). That moment set into enthusiastic motion the machine of creative fun and it did not stop until obtaining a transversal view and until the circle was completed with the advantageous connection with Alicia Foundation, a research centre devoted to technological innovation in cuisine, and cava producer Caves Agustí Torelló Mata. The challenge was to make full use of the essence of both products (oyster and cava) at room temperature and with minimum handling. The idea was to avoid exposing the oyster to liposoluble ingredients such as butter or cream, and aim for a fresh and water-soluble combination. We quickly opted for xanthan gum (cold thickener), newly introduced in vanguard cuisine. All we needed was to combine it with the cava and blend the mixture.

It all began in early November 2005, when we first mixed cava and xanthan gum in a whipped cream container, producing cava that contained and held exogenous gas. After some conferences about cava, we set the challenge to try to keep the endogenous carbon from its own gas. By late 2005, our friendship with Agustí Torelló led us to begin to introduce xanthan gum in the *liqueur d'expedition* when disgorging the cava (second fermentation). In our experiments between 2006 and 2008, we noticed problems with the thickness, the increase of pressure and the spontaneous release of gas and fluid. After multiple tests the method was perfected and, by late 2008, Sòlid Brut and Sòlid Rosat went out on the market. Straight from the cellar to the plate, in an innovative format ready for serving. We finally closed the circle of ideas around using cava in cuisine. A product that revolutionised using cava and champagne in cooking. The highest degree of integrity, more density, more flavour retention, better preservation of endogenous carbonic gas. The possibilities for recipes are endless, but the first, a classic from El Celler, is OYSTER WITH CAVA and apple compote, spice bread, cumin, curry, oyster leaf, cava bubbles and cava sauce served in a bottle of Kripta by Agustí Torelló (page 268).

The product of a three-sided effort: two families —El Celler de Can Roca and Agustí Torelló Mata— and the bridge of knowledge we will always be thankful for—Alícia Foundation.

HIGH PRESSURE

El Celler de Can Roca
Alícia Foundation
Institute for Food and Agriculture
Research and Technology (IRTA)

There are no words to describe our gratitude to Ferran Adrià and his generosity in his bid to bring science into the kitchen. Thanks to the personal closeness of Ferran and the educational ability and professionalism of the members of Alícia Foundation, we have found fundamental support for many of the projects that have been bubbling away in our heads.

The first idea was to experiment, through the distillation process, with extracting 'clear smells'. We thought that separating body and soul in a product could be thought-provoking. To smell a clear liquid, in this instance from condensation after the distillation process of a strawberry and black pepper infusion was the starting point of a research project that is still underway. The Rotaval allows us to set hints of smells, but also to recover the reflux in the base flask with a visible and concentrated intensity.

One of the latest aspects of research arising from the productive collaboration of El Celler with Alícia, studies the application of high pressure in order to comply with food safety.

The consumption of bivalves can be a source of food poisoning or infections. Cooking these products reduces the risks, but it also means modifying their sensory attributes. Because of these risks, in gastronomy it is impossible to offer these products with the required guarantees of food safety. That is why many establishments exclude fresh bivalves from their menus.

With support from Alícia Foundation and IRTA, we have studied an alternative treatment to clean the product without modifying its sensory properties: high pressure.

High pressure can be a method of cold pasteurisation with water. The product, vacuum packed, is placed in a cavity; water is introduced to the desired pressure (water has the ability to compress). It is important to emphasise that the pressure applied reaches every part of the product uniformly and almost immediately, regardless of its composition, size or shape. This prevents the product from misshaping in spite of the high pressure level. Meanwhile, microorganisms are in fact affected by pressure, making pasteurisation possible.

The pressure generally used to treat foods is usually between 100 and 1,000 MPa. The time needed to apply pressure ranges from a few minutes to a few hours, and the temperature for treating the product can go from -20°C/-4°F to 90°C/194°F. In the collaborative research carried out by El Celler and Alícia, we have worked with the following parameters:

450 MPa at 7°C/44.6°F input water temperature for 300 seconds. The high pressure equipment was operating with all 3 pumps

The sensory and nutritional impact on products from applying high pressure is minimal, and it's used to sell products highlighting their 'fresh flavour'.

NÚVOL DE LLIMONA, THE PERFUME

El Celler de Can Roca
Agustí Vidal

The power of perfume traps us, its richness overcomes us and encourages us to keep generating new ideas, improving the technique and reinventing the concept. From desserts based on perfumes... we suggest the opposite. We move to the next stage and, instead of finding inspiration, we stimulate expiration. We leave the kitchen to create a perfume from a dessert. In reverse. And why not?

The base of creativity is poetry, grace, courage, nerve, breaking away from rigidity. It is a way of thinking. It cannot be measured. It is also the illusion of closing the circle. We first made a dessert: NÚVOL DE LLIMONA (Lemon cloud, page 264). Then its perfume, with perfumer Agustí Vidal.

NÚVOL DE LLIMONA, THE DESSERT

"Lemon pith cream,
lemon water sorbet,
bergamot jelly, toasted
and emulsified butter,
milk air and lemon sponge cake"

The first sensation after tasting the dessert NÚVOL DE LLIMONA, is the lemon pith water, together with the tenderness of a lemon milky air and a crystalline and subtle sorbet, cooked sous-vide in the Rotaval and then frozen. Lightly toasted lactic references prolong its flavour. The lemon pith cream helps it settle on the palate. Its flavour is deep and pure, almost bitter. The lemon sorbet leads to a refreshing sensation. And the bergamot jelly shoots the essential oils into space, joyful and crystalline.

A PERFUME OUTSIDE THE KITCHEN, WITH AGUSTÍ VIDAL

We used the most common elements employed in the ranges of fresh perfumes: bergamot, tangerine and lemon zests. The key is a very precise combination of these three ingredients. Although the idea came from a children's perfume, we have taken the concept to a perfume for the family that is deeper and more expressive, and doesn't affect the complexity of its tender and clean aspects.

Nuances of lily of the valley and Indian sandalwood in the perfume's base constitute its serious and deeper side. A reference to baby powder with hints of rose petals is the first impression, the first road to tenderness. The warm sensation is reached with the sweetness of the heliotrope and the aromatic warmth of vanilla. Its caress comes from the powdery sensation of one's own clean skin after using a moisturising soap. Clearness and depth for a totem perfume, of family well-being.[1]

---

1 — Based on an article written by the Roca brothers, published in *El País* by Rosa Rivas.

INDUSTRIAL DESIGN ON THE TABLE

El Celler de Can Roca
Andreu Carulla

Bringing ideas to fruition. Shaping illusion. This is how we convey our collaboration with Andreu Carulla. We seek to bring emotions to the stage, to reproduce landscapes, choose atmospheres... Andreu devises and builds the base of our fantasies.

So, the dream comes to the table as a GOAL BY MESSI (PAGE 414)—half an inverted football with a piece of turf that becomes stage for a dessert in which the diner takes part in the play and relives the excitement of the goal scored by the football idol. Or through the sensations and memories evoked by a landscape drawn from nature and served in our restaurant. Andreu Carulla is responsible for the hooks to hang the caramelised olives filled with anchovy from the bonsai tree that imitates a Mediterranean OLIVE TREE (PAGE 337), in our approximation to our origins. And for the nets that hold the ANCHOVY BONE TEMPURA (PAGE 336); the same nets that can still be spotted around our coastal landscape.

And the lantern painted as a world map that opens like a window to THE WORLD (PAGE 352) and takes the diner on a trip around the globe through five delicious extracts of gastronomic culture.

One of the latest results of working with Andreu is *Roca on Wheels* (page 404), the dessert cart that, after many years of absence, returns to our dining room. This cart attempts to recapture the spirit and style of the cuisine of El Celler. Illusion, surprise, fascination. The cart, collapsible and covered with drawers and trays full of all sorts of coloured sweets, would amaze kids of every age. And not only children... because the cart amazes everybody, young and old. As if taken from the stills of *Charlie and the Chocolate Factory,* the incredible black lacquered vehicle with red wheels and red and white metallic bars unfolds all its charm in an unexpected visit at the end of the meal. A magical moment to bring the experience to a close.

J

–PERFUME

J

Perfume comprises essential oils and aromatic substances, and alcohol and balsams. Perfume is chemistry, hydrocarbons. And unhurriedness. Perfume is distillation, a purification process, meant to reach the essence. It is extracting, macerating, dissolving. And structure, molecules coming together, a thought that spins, retouches, misleads nature. And, after all, there is nothing like the dictionary definition to explain what a perfume is: smoke or vapour made by cooking aromatic substances. In other words, evanescence. Present that becomes past in the blink of an eye.

And on the other hand, what remains? What other memory can we consider more lasting than this subtlety? When it returns to us it transports us, it takes us back to the moment we perceived it for the first time. And it solidifies, it turns into a tangible substance. A substance that can be tasted.

The challenge for El Celler is to make perfume edible. It is about building the opposite road from that sought out by synthesis, the concentration of a substance in a drop. Here, it is about finding the secret to make it visible, to make that palpability completely real. In every dish perfume, concentration, becomes a new exuberance of its origins. And then, the miracle: in this reconstruction process the synthesis is not lost, but magnified. The atmosphere becomes fixed thanks to the puzzle that is encapsulated again in the excitement of a drop.

According to the Roca brothers

It all began with the arrival of the bergamot, the absolute essence of El Celler. We were captivated by its noble scent and thick and aromatic zest.

We wanted to make aroma edible. We had to decipher the formula of a perfume, to capture its head, heart and base notes and compare them with the ingredients expressed by the perfumier. Then, we had to transfer them to an edible reality and measure out their intensities. It was a stimulating adventure. We started out from a concept that at the time was unprecedented in gastronomy: to capture the volatile soul of a perfume. We felt like Grenouille in *Perfume* by Patrick Süskind (1985) and we shared his fascination: "Odours have a power of persuasion stronger than that of words, appearances, emotions, or will. The persuasive power of an odour cannot be fended off, it enters into us like breath into our lungs, it fills us up, imbues us totally. There is no remedy for it."

The first adaptation was Eternity, by Calvin Klein. We deconstructed the aromatic notes of perfume: bergamot, basil, tangerine, vanilla, orange. The trick in the process of making something volatile palatable is how much the dish can mimic it. We were seized by the idea, the ability of the chef to translate a language as powerful as that of perfume into another, equally powerful language, a language in which aromas combine with the edible. The sense of smell looks for flavours as a natural complement and transforms into flavour while keeping its constructive strength intact. To translate aroma into a sapid language is an eternal desire of man: "All a rose needs to be perfect is to be edible," said Josep Pla. Making it a reality is not impossible.

Jordi's adaptations are interpretations of perfumes. They do not aim to be an exact replica of the perfume, which is impossible to materialise, but to suggest its disappearance into edible ingredients. The objective is to hint, not to highlight the obvious.

Perfumes branch out, are powerful, and expand the record of reconstructions with over twenty-five interpretations taken to Jordi's world of sweets. Some examples are:

ETERNITY BY CALVIN KLEIN, TRÉSOR BY LANCÔME, MIRACLE BY LANCÔME, POLO SPORT WOMAN BY RALPH LAUREN, ANGEL BY THIERRY MUGLER, CAROLINA BY CAROLINA HERRERA, LOLITA LEMPICKA BY PARFUMS LOLITA LEMPICKA, HYPNOTIC POISON BY DIOR, L'EAU D'ISSEY BY ISSEY MIYAKE, ENVY BY GUCCI, EXTRÊME BY BULGARI, INCANTO BY SALVATORE FERRAGAMO, CONCENTRÉ D'ORANGE VERTE BY HERMÈS, EAU PARFUMÉE AU THÉ BLANC BY BULGARI, FEMME INDIVIDUELLE BY MONTBLANC, DKNY BY DONNA KARAN, UN JARDIN EN MÉDITERRANÉE BY HERMÈS, TERRE D'HERMÈS, EAU PARFUMÉE AU THÉ VERT BY BULGARI.

The practice of transforming a perfume into a recipe is a challenge, a game, another somersault in the art of cooking. It is to tackle a chimera that, with work, technique and passion, finally becomes a reality. A reality, however, that would not be complete if we didn't also tackle its opposite. Therefore, the following step was inevitable, and our curiosity and desire to create led us to making a perfume from a dessert. Because, just like Grenouille, we are excited by "this procedure for using fire, water, steam and a cunning apparatus to snatch the scented soul from matter". We had to close the circle and did so by first creating a dessert, NÚVOL DE LLIMONA [Lemon cloud, page 264], and then its perfume with the help of perfumier Agustí Vidal. Its flavour consists of lemon pith cream, lemon water sorbet, bergamot jelly, emulsified noisette beurre, milk air and lemon sponge cake. Its feel is that of bergamot, tangerine and lemon, memories of muguet and Indian sandalwood, a reference to baby powder with hints of rose petals, heliotrope and vanilla... Closed circle. Joy.

In the dining room...

If you ever wear one of these perfumes, imagine how it could transform into a dish, a recipe... Play, like us, with this magic. And when you come to our house, you will finally be able to conclude the adventure and try our interpretation of these aromatic jewels. Before you come, scent your skin with the fragrance we will later serve at your table. We will bring the perfume to the dining room and try to experiment and show complicity, while making sense of the impossibility of creating a dessert from a perfume. We will show you the product, exhibit the result of our work, divertimento, research... And we will serve it in its own package. Just like a perfume in its bottle...

THÉ VERT
BY BULGARI

SERVES 8 PEOPLE

COMPOSITION

Frozen bergamot cream
Tonka bean and vanilla jelly
Lime sorbet
Lime meringues
Royal icing
Basil gel

—FROZEN BERGAMOT CREAM
YIELDS 520 G

500 cream
50 g dextrose
3 gelatine sheets
1 bergamot, grated zest

In a casserole, heat the cream and dextrose and remove from the heat when it comes to a boil. Add then the gelatine sheets, previously hydrated, and the grated bergamot zest. Leave to infuse for about 5 minutes, strain and cool. Reserve the mixture refrigerated in an airtight container for 12 hours before whipping. Next, whip with a hand blender to a Chantilly cream and, using a piping bag with a star tip, pipe 5 cm dots. Reserve in the freezer at -18°C/0°F.

—TONKA BEAN AND VANILLA JELLY
YIELDS 200 G

200 g water
30 g sugar
½ vanilla pod
½ tonka bean, grated
1 g agar-agar

Heat the water with sugar until it comes to a boil, add the vanilla pod and grated tonka bean and infuse for 5 minutes. Strain the infusion, add the agar-agar and increase the temperature until it boils again. Leave the resulting jelly to temper and reserve refrigerated in an airtight container.

—LIME SORBET
YIELDS 750 G

100 g water
24 g dextrose
100 g sugar
3.5 g sorbet stabiliser
16 g glucose powder
10 g inverted sugar syrup
2 limes, grated zest
500 g lime juice

In a casserole, heat the water and dextrose; when it reaches 60°C/140°F, add the sugar, stabiliser, glucose powder, inverted sugar syrup and lime zest. Bring the mixture to 85°C/185°F whisking constantly. Cool quickly to 4°C/39°F, pour in lime juice and run a hand blender through it to accelerate homogenization. Next, churn in the ice-cream maker and reserve the sorbet in an airtight container at -18°C/0°F.

—LIME MERINGUES
YIELDS 110 G

100 g sugar
60 g egg whites
1 lime, grated zest

Place the sugar and egg whites in a bowl, heat in a bain-marie and, when the sugar has dissolved, whip the meringue. When stiff, add the lime and transfer into piping bags to make small dots of meringue on a baking tray. Leave to dry on the cooker at 50°C/122°F for at least 12 hours. Reserve in an airtight container.

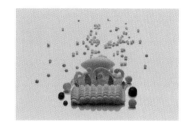

—ROYAL ICING
YIELDS 100 G

20 g egg whites
75 g icing sugar
10 g lime juice
½ vanilla pod

Mix the egg whites in a bowl with the sugar and lime juice, then add the vanilla and stir until obtaining a creamy and smooth texture. Transfer to a piping bag with a plain nozzle and form small parallel swirls with the icing. Dry on the cooker at 50°C/122°F for 12 hours.

—BASIL GEL
YIELDS 200 G

50 g basil
250 g blanching water
30 g sugar
3 g agar-agar

Heat the water in a stockpot and blanch the basil leaves for 20 seconds; remove them and refresh in iced water. In a separate container, cool the indicated amount of blanching water. When cold, place it in the Thermomix with basil and blend until obtaining a very fine liquid; strain.

Heat the resulting basil water with sugar and agar-agar while stirring constantly until it comes to a boil. Reserve the mixture and, when the agar-agar sets, run through a hand blender until it acquires a sauce-like texture. Reserve the gel in a piping bag.

GARNISHING AND PLATING

Mint leaves
Basil leaves

In the middle of a dinner plate, serve the frozen bergamot cream. Surround it with some dots of basil gel and tonka bean and vanilla jelly, some swirls of icing with mint and basil leaves, some lime meringue dots and the lime sorbet.

ANGEL
BY THIERRY MUGLER

SERVES 8 PEOPLE

COMPOSITION
Toffee cream
Berry and Tahitian vanilla sorbet
Rose jelly
Bergamot sauce
Honey jelly
Violet preserve
Caramel threads

—TOFFEE CREAM
YIELDS 250 G

200 g sugar
500 g cream
2 gelatine sheets

Hydrate the gelatine sheets in cold water.

Heat the sugar up to 150°C/302°F, add the cream and, when the caramel has dissolved, add the gelatine. While it's still hot, serve in a soup dish and leave to cool refrigerated until it sets.

—BERRY AND TAHITIAN VANILLA SORBET
YIELDS 1.2 KG

1 kg berries
200 g water
20 g inverted sugar syrup
1 Tahitian vanilla pod
200 g sugar
50 g dextrose
30 g glucose powder
7.5 g sorbet stabiliser

Purée the berries and reserve.

Heat the water with the inverted sugar syrup and vanilla pod. Before it comes to a boil, add the remaining dry ingredients, already mixed, and bring to 85°C/185°F. Then, add the berry purée and leave to ripen for 24 hours. The following day, run the mixture through the ice-cream maker and reserve in the freezer at -20°C/-4°F.

—ROSE JELLY
YIELDS 190 G

200 g rose water
1 g agar-agar

Boil some of the rose water with agar-agar to incorporate it well, pour in the rest of the rose water and spread on a tray 0.5 cm deep. Leave to set and cut into 0.5 cm cubes.

—BERGAMOT SAUCE
YIELDS 190 G

50 g water
50 g sugar
2 g agar-agar
1 bergamot, grated zest
100 g bergamot juice

In a casserole, put the water, sugar, agar-agar and bergamot zest and bring to a boil. Mix with the juice, leave the mixture to set and, when cold, run the hand blender through it to make a sauce.

—HONEY JELLY
YIELDS 190 G

150 g honey
50 g water
1½ gelatine sheets

Hydrate the gelatine in cold water. Strain and reserve.

Boil the honey, add water and dissolve the gelatine. Pour into a container with a 0.5 cm thickness and leave to set refrigerated.

—VIOLET PRESERVE

YIELDS 195 G

100 g water
20 g fresh violets
100 g sugar
10 g pectin

Boil the water, violets and 75 g sugar.

In a separate container, mix the 25 g sugar remaining with pectin and add slowly to the mixture while stirring constantly. Leave to reduce until it acquires the texture of a preserve, considering it will become denser when it cools down. Reserve.

—CARAMEL THREADS

Sugar

In a saucepan, heat the sugar, without fat or liquids. Leave over medium heat until it melts, stirring with a spatula to help it blend. When it liquidises and is somewhat caramelised, remove from the heat and leave to stand until the caramel gains some elasticity. Then, insert a fork or a whisk with the tip cut off into the caramel and stretch the filaments by hand to form the threads that will crown the dish.

GARNISHING AND PLATING

Raspberries and blackberries

Run the raspberries and blackberries though liquid nitrogen to freeze and make them easy to crumble.

On the dish with the set toffee cream, place 4 dots of each jelly (diced rose jelly, bergamot sauce, honey jelly and violet preserve), alternating them around the perimeter of the cream. Place the frozen raspberries and blackberries in the centre and, on top, a quenelle of berry and vanilla sorbet. Finish with the caramel threads, which will add volume to the dish.

ETERNITY
BY CALVIN KLEIN

SERVES 8 PEOPLE

COMPOSITION

Vanilla cream
Orange blossom water jelly
Basil sauce
Maple syrup jelly
Tangerine granita
Bergamot ice cream

—VANILLA CREAM
YIELDS 650 G

500 g cream
1 vanilla pod
100 g egg yolks
50 g sugar
42 g cornflour

Boil the cream with the vanilla and add egg yolks, sugar and cornflour. Pasteurise the mixture while stirring until it's set and smooth. Cool and reserve.

—ORANGE BLOSSOM WATER JELLY
YIELDS 195 G

200 g orange blossom water
1 g agar-agar

Mix the agar-agar with one third of the water and bring to a boil; add the remaining water and spread on a tray with a thickness of 1.5 cm. When solid, cut jelly into 1.5 cm cubes.

—BASIL SAUCE
YIELDS 190 G

100 g water
50 g sugar
50 g fresh basil
3 g agar-agar

Boil 50 g water with the 50 g sugar. Reserve.

Separately, bring to a boil with the remaining 50 g water and blanch basil leaves for 20 seconds; cool quickly by submerging in iced water. When the blanching water has cooled down, place it with the syrup and leaves in the blender, liquidise and strain. Mix some of the mixture with the agar-agar, boil, add the rest of the mixture, leave to set and, lastly, run through the hand blender to break the structure and make a sauce. Reserve.

—MAPLE SYRUP JELLY
YIELDS 190 G

150 g maple syrup
50 g water
1½ gelatine sheets

Dissolve the maple syrup with water and heat to 40°C/104°F. Add the gelatine sheets, previously hydrated, and when they dissolve, pour the whole mixture in a tray with a thickness of 1.5 cm. Leave to solidify refrigerated and, when set, cut the gel into 1.5 cm cubes.

—TANGERINE GRANITA
YIELDS 650 G

500 g tangerine juice
100 g dextrose
100 g inverted sugar syrup
3 tangerines, grated zest
4 gelatine sheets

Boil some of the juice to dissolve the dextrose and inverted sugar. Then, add the tangerine zest and cover for 5 minutes to infuse. Add the gelatine sheets, previously hydrated, strain and pour in the rest of the juice. Reserve in the freezer at -20°C/-4°F.

—BERGAMOT ICE CREAM
YIELDS 950 G

600 g milk
300 g cream
90 g inverted sugar syrup
90 g dextrose
60 g sugar
36 g milk powder 1% fat content
6 g ice-cream stabiliser
4 bergamots, grated zest
120 g bergamot juice

Heat the milk, cream and inverted sugar syrup to 40°C/104°F.

Separately, mix the dextrose, sugar, milk powder and ice-cream stabiliser, and add to the previous mixture. Pasteurise until it reaches 85°C/185°F. Strain the mixture, add the grated bergamot and blast chill. Leave to ripen refrigerated for 12 hours.

Next, strain the mixture again and run through the ice-cream maker. When it reaches -1°C/30°F, pour in the bergamot juice while the ice cream churns. Reserve at -20°C/-4°F.

GARNISHING AND PLATING

8 tangerine segments, peeled including the pith

On the plate, place 3 dots of vanilla cream, 5 dots of basil sauce, 3 orange blossom jelly cubes, 3 maple syrup jelly cubes, and 1 tangerine segment. Serve the tangerine slush on top and garnish it with a bergamot ice cream quenelle.

HYPNOTIC POISON
BY DIOR

SERVES 8 PEOPLE

COMPOSITION
Toffee cream
Rose jam
Fresh almond water
Fresh almond sorbet
Crystallised rose petals
Coconut marshmallow

—TOFFEE CREAM
YIELDS 650 G

200 g sugar
500 g cream
2 gelatine sheets

Hydrate gelatine sheets in cold water.

Heat the sugar to 150°C/302°F, add cream and, when the caramel is melted, stir in the gelatine. Leave to cool at 4°C/39°F for at least 12 hours to stabilise. Next, whip the cream in the mixer and reserve in a piping bag with a star nozzle.

—ROSE JAM
YIELDS 200 G

100 g water
20 g fresh roses
100 g sugar
10 g pectin

Boil the water, roses and 75 g of sugar.

In a separate container, mix the other 25 g sugar with pectine and slowly add it to the mixture while stirring. Reduce until it acquires the texture of a jam, considering it will turn denser when cold.

—FRESH ALMOND WATER
YIELDS 1 KG

1 kg water
500 g fresh almonds

Blend the almonds with the water, marinate refrigerated for at least 8 hours. Strain and reserve.

—FRESH ALMOND SORBET
YIELDS 1.4 KG

200 g water
20 g inverted sugar syrup
1 vanilla pod
200 g sugar
50 g dextrose
30 g glucose powder
7.5 g sorbet stabiliser
1 kg fresh almond water (previously prepared)

Heat the water with the inverted sugar syrup and vanilla pod. Before boiling, add the remaining dry ingredients, previously mixed, and increase the temperature to 85°C/185°F. Pour in the fresh almond water, leave to ripen for 24 hours. The following day, run the mixture through the ice-cream maker and reserve in the freezer at -20°C/-4°F.

—CRYSTALLISED ROSE PETALS
YIELDS 30 G

100 g water
100 g sugar
30 g fresh rose petals

Boil the water with sugar, pour hot over the rose petals, leave to temper and flatten the petals on a silicone mat. Leave them to dry at 50°C/122°F for 12 hours, then reserve in an airtight container.

—COCONUT MARSHMALLOW
YIELDS 200 UNITS

250 g sugar
50 g water
90 g coconut purée
5½ gelatine sheets
30 g egg whites
Grated coconut

Make an Italian meringue: boil the water with the sugar until it reaches 121°C/250°F, cleaning the brim of the casserole with a wet brush to prevent the syrup from crystallising. While it's still hot, add the coconut purée and previously hydrated gelatine. Pour this mixture slowly over the egg whites while beating them carefully, until they acquire some volume. Then, spread the mixture over a 1-cm-deep baking tray, leave to set and cut into 1 cm cubes that will then be coated in grated coconut. Reserve.

GARNISHING AND PLATING
Strawberries
Fresh rose petals

Pipe some curly tips of toffee cream onto a dinner plate and accompany them with rose jam, a couple of coconut marshmallows and some crystallised rose petals. Set the sorbet on top and garnish with strawberries and fresh petals.

TERRE D'HERMÈS

SERVES 8 PEOPLE

COMPOSITION
Patchouli ice cream
Milk chocolate mousse
Cocoa biscuit
Soil distillate
Jasmine tea air

—PATCHOULI ICE CREAM
YIELDS 1 KG

500 g milk
200 g cream
200 g dextrose
50 g milk powder
100 g sugar
6 g ice-cream stabiliser
20 g dry patchouli roots
Milk chocolate 35% cocoa

Mix milk and cream with the dextrose and
milk powder, heat. When the mixture reaches
approximately 70°C/158°F, add the sugar and
stabiliser and, stirring constantly, increase to
85°C/185°F. Then, and when it's still hot, add
the patchouli and leave to infuse while it cools
down. Reserve.

After about 6 hours, churn the ice cream.
Reserve at -18°C/0°F.

When the ice cream has a better structure,
make small balls and freeze again to coat them
later in melted milk chocolate. Reserve
in the freezer.

—MILK CHOCOLATE MOUSSE
YIELDS 900 G

120 g cream
80 g egg yolk
20 g sugar
500 g cream
260 g milk chocolate 44% cocoa

Make a pâte à bombe by mixing the cream, egg
yolks and sugar, and heating to 85°C/185°F.
When still hot, whip it in a mixer until its
volume triples and it cools down. Reserve.

In a separate container, whip the 500 g of
cream. Reserve.

Mix the pâte à bombe slowly with the
chocolate couverture and finish by adding the
whipped cream. Reserve refrigerated in an
airtight container.

—COCOA BISCUIT
YIELDS 300 G

200 g butter
50 g icing sugar
20 g egg yolks
275 g flour
40 g cocoa powder

In a bowl, mix all the ingredients, starting
with the softened butter, sugar and egg yolks,
then add the flour and cocoa sieved together.
Reserve. Stretch the dough to 0.5 cm on a
baking tray lined with a silicone mat. Cook
at 180°C/356°F for 5 minutes. Reserve in an
airtight container.

—SOIL DISTILLATE
YIELDS 430 G

430 g soil distillate (basic recipes, p.428)
1 g xanthan gum

Mix both ingredients with a hand blender and
reserve cold.

—JASMINE TEA AIR
YIELDS 500 G

500 g skimmed milk
10 g jasmine tea

Heat the milk to 80°C/176°F and infuse the
tea for 4 minutes. Then, strain and reserve
the milk refrigerated. When serving, whip with
hand blender.

GARNISHING AND PLATING

Orange segments
Beetroot leaves
Purple shiso leaves
Grated grapefruit zest

In a dessert bowl, serve a quenelle of milk
chocolate mousse. Top it with three balls of
patchouli ice cream, a few orange segments,
some crumbled cocoa biscuit, a few drops of
soil distillate, the beetroot and purple shiso
leaves, a pinch of grated grapefruit zest and,
lastly, the jasmine tea air on the side.

K

—INNOVATION

K

Every cuisine is sophistication. The first fire, the first cooking time, were conscious acts that upset what until then was the natural order of things. It was the first step that distanced us from necessity and brought us closer to purification. The rest has been the evolution of a technique that first exceeded immediacy and later came to the palate. The technique as a tool for progress but also as a mechanism that reveals, at a specific moment, new forms of pleasure, a new way of observing the product. Revolution at the service of pleasure. That is why the masterly innovations of Joan—'perfume-cooking' and sous-vide cuisine—cannot be confined to the collection of inventions whose purpose is explained in their instruction manual. They must be shelved where we store those things that will help us achieve a goal that has already been described and foreseen. Instruments are useful because they were a previous answer to a well thought out plan. They are not knives for cutting, but engraver's chisels that come into contact with a plate to carry out the engraving the artist had planned.

We are talking about steam, distillation, temperatures, events and wonders based on great technical complexity. Innovation, however, isn't having them close at hand, but having thought that they would help fulfil an idea.

According to the Roca brothers

Technological innovation: its tools

From technocracy to feeling. We feel very close to 'techno-emotional' concepts. It's a way of growing, improving, feeling fellow citizens in a society that wants to know and understand. We want to approach research as a vital attitude but with conceptual maturity, in order to maintain the tone and entrepreneurial drive. We love having a discreet influence. The dimension of what isn't obvious but a sign of curious involvement. The greatness of seduction and the analysis behind it. To hide the technique in order to boost flavour. Smoke and mirrors between the hidden technique and the overt flavour...

Our link to technology is part of the research and obsession to improve known and ancestral cooking techniques. The chance to reinforce our academic education after the Culinary Arts School of Girona, led us to contact Georges Pralus, inventor of sous-vide cuisine, in 1988. With his help and our background we were able to develop the formal work on precision cooking at low temperatures thanks to the Roner. This device [patented by Joan Roca and Narcís Caner—its name derives from joining the first and last syllables of both surnames] pioneered this cooking technology. The book *Sous-Vide Cuisine*[1] was the first to deal with cooking sous-vide for immediate consumption.

1. ROCA, J.; BRUGUÉS, S. *Sous-Vide Cuisine*. Barcelona: Montagud Editores S.A., 2004.

This first research led us to contact different companies that manufactured machines for laboratories and we got in touch with very interesting institutions necessary to develop the path of technological progress. Fundació Alícia became our most fascinating and fruitful collaborator. We feel very fortunate for the treatment received from its scientific researchers. They are modest and have a profound knowledge of their formal discourse. It's a pleasure to learn from educated, sober and humble people. It's a luxury strongly related to our growth and the areas of improvement in our cooking. The Rotaval is another device created by us as a result of this collaboration. It's a distillation device, a product of our obsession with cooking with volatile elements, something we have called 'perfume-cooking,' obtaining flavour (the combination of aromatic, flavourful and tactile properties perceived when tasting) from food and the extraction of natural essential oils. Finally, we have the lyophilizer, a tool also used at El Celler to make cubes of stock in the shape of pills, oyster shells, and other applications related to dehydration.

Being in contact with industries associated with aroma and food has facilitated our approach to new technologies that are not always successful; nonetheless it informs us how the industry may influence our eating habits in the future. The technique of encapsulating aroma, for example, is fascinating. The technical support of IRTA (Institute for Food and Agriculture Research and Technology) on high-pressure cooking, provides deeper knowledge about food poisoning and information on viruses in molluscs and oysters (see more on page 273). Contact with experts in the field of the senses and emotional marketing also brings complexity and aromatic transcendence to our kitchen. Our links with the university, giving an endless source of mutual relations, are important connections to manage innovation and continue our technological research.

Emotional innovation: its values

One aspect we have strengthened recently at the restaurant is connected to our need to slow down and talk to the team. Managing success and its destructive pull can distort the quality due to the burden of routine sometimes misunderstood as arrogance, or the lack of stimuli to make us smile and be positively empathetic.

As managers of a team, we understand we must adapt with innovation, interest our employees and amaze continuously. We go for good and normal people. We like to surround ourselves with young people capable of moving ahead. We want to be proactive. We know shared values mobilise and widen. We work on letting our team know about our goals, and we analyse them together and plan together... Tuesday mornings we gather and give ourselves some time for internal emotional management: we sacrifice some time and money in order to continue learning.

In the dining room...

With Andreu Carulla we create containers for specific dishes. We go through a whole thought process and, when necessary, we make a new mould for a new creation. Or we think of cutlery in a different way: we talk about whether it should weigh less when a dish is more ethereal, or if its touch should be different because it suits the culinary offering. Cutlery, trays, plates, utensils to lift with your fingers... It's an open road and a long way ahead. An important contribution to offer our customer is a comprehensive experience in which all the senses partake.

AMONTILLADO
STEAM OYSTER

SERVES 4 PEOPLE

COMPOSITION
Oyster
Oloroso abocado reduction
Oyster soup
Manzanilla pasada steam

—OYSTER
4 oysters

Open the oysters before serving, remove the beard and reserve.

—OLOROSO ABOCADO REDUCTION
YIELDS 200 G

500 g Oloroso Abocado

Place the Oloroso Abocado in the Rotaval and distill at a 45°C/113°F bain-marie temperature. Retrieve the reduction and reserve.

—OYSTER SOUP
YIELDS 550 G

10 oysters
50 g shallots
5 g butter
35 g oyster water
20 g Asian oyster sauce
625 g cream
Salt

Open the oysters and reserve 35 g of their water. Julienne the shallot finely and sweat it with butter and a pinch of salt over very low heat until cooked. Add the oysters and sear on both sides, browning them lightly, deglaze with the oyster water previously reserved, add the oyster sauce, cook for 1 minute and add the cream. Boil the preparation over low heat for 5 minutes, remove from heat and place in the Thermomix. Blend and strain with a fine chinois. Reserve in a bain-marie at 65 °C/149°F.

—MANZANILLA PASADA STEAM
150 g Manzanilla Pasada

Reserve this wine for serving the oyster, which will be steamed in front of the guest.

GARNISHING AND PLATING
4 stones

Heat the stones over high heat. Place one very hot stone in a bowl and a sieve on top, to set the oyster as soon as it's opened.

In a spoon, place a drop of Oloroso Abocado reduction. In front of the guest, pour a dash of Manzanilla Pasada over the hot stone, and keep it covered for 20 seconds to generate the steam that will scent and cook the oyster lightly. In the meantime, serve a small glass with 30 g oyster soup, very hot.

DRY GAMBINI

COMPOSITION
Prawn
Prawn powder
Prawn cocktail

—PRAWN

8 large prawns

Separate the heads from the prawns and reserve. Blanch the prawns in boiling water with salt to taste and peel to the beginning of the tail.

—PRAWN POWDER
YIELDS 5 G

8 prawn heads

Mash the prawn heads in the Thermomix to a smooth paste. Spread the paste on a baking sheet lined with greaseproof paper and place it in the oven at 120°C/248°F for 12 minutes. Remove and leave to dry on the cooker at 60°C/140°F for 12 hours.

When the paste is completely dry, crush it with a grinder to a fine powder. Reserve in an airtight container in a dry place.

—PRAWN COCKTAIL
YIELDS 125 G

500 g prawn stock (basic recipes, p.428)
0.5 g xanthan gum
25 g vinic alcohol

Put the prawn stock in the Rotaval at a 56°C/133°F bath temperature (Bt) and 45°C/113°F distillation temperature (Dt) for 6 hours at 30 rpm. The result will be a light, clear and subtle prawn distillate, and an intensely flavoured prawn juice will remain in the first evaporating flask as a result of the evaporation produced by boiling at a low temperature. Reserve the distillation concentrate for plating.

Mix 100 g of the distillate with the vinic alcohol and thicken with the xanthan gum. Reserve refrigerated.

GARNISHING AND PLATING

Distillation concentrate (from previous preparation)

Frost part of the rim of a cocktail glass with the dehydrated prawn powder and, on the opposite side, set a drop of the distillation concentrate. Temper the prawn and lean it against the rim so that the body is inside and the tail sticks out of the glass. Finish by serving the cocktail cold.

TRIP TO HAVANA

SERVES 4 PEOPLE

COMPOSITION

Rum candies
Lime jelly
Mint water
Mint granita
Cigar base
Tempered chocolate cylinder

—RUM CANDIES
YIELDS 74 UNITS

20 g water
60 g sugar
12 g rum
Cornflour

Prepare some syrup with the water and sugar and bring to 109°C/228°F. Remove from heat and let its temperature drop slightly. Carefully, pour the rum into the mixture. The ideal way to do this is by transferring the syrup slowly back and forth from the rum container into the other, letting it slide slowly until both liquids and densities combine. Reserve.

Cover a baking sheet with cornflour and leave it to dry at 80°C/176°F for a few hours. Press, smooth and make small holes to fill with the syrup and rum mixture. Sprinkle the surface slightly with some more dry cornflour and bake for 24 hours at approximately 40°C/104°F.

Next, remove the candies from the cornflour, brush clean and reserve.

—LIME JELLY
YIELDS 100 G

75 g water
20 g sugar
1.2 g agar-agar
20 g lime juice

Bring the water with sugar to a boil until it dissolves. Let it cool down and add the agar-agar, bringing it once again to a boil. Remove from the heat. Pour in the lime juice, mix the preparation and transfer it to a mould to cool and solidify.

When set, blend the mixture to a silky gel.

—MINT WATER
YIELDS 100 G

75 g mint leaves
50 g cold blanching water
50 g water

Bring a stockpot full of water to a boil. Blanch the mint leaves for about 20 seconds and remove from heat. Cool in iced water.

Place the blanched mint leaves together with the blanching water, cold, and the water indicated above, and blend to a fine, smooth liquid. Run through a fine chinois and press to obtain as much mint water as possible. Reserve refrigerated.

—MINT GRANITA
YIELDS 150 G

25 g water
12.5 g inverted sugar
25 g dextrose
½ gelatine sheet
100 g mint water (previously prepared)

In a casserole place the water together with the inverted sugar and dextrose and bring to a boil. Remove from the heat and add the gelatine, previously hydrated and strained; next, blast chill. Mix the cold syrup, with the mint water and freeze.

—CIGAR BASE
YIELDS 1 KG

750 g cream
150 g dextrose
4 gelatine sheets
1 Partagás Serie D No. 4 Cuban cigar

Mix the cream and dextrose in a casserole and bring to a boil. Remove from the heat and add to the previously hydrated gelatine, stirring well. Leave to cool refrigerated for 6 hours. With a mixer, whip the cold cream mixture while incorporating the cigar smoke with an air pump. This process, in addition to generating air by whipping, also introduces the smoke of the cigar, producing a taste that closely resembles the scent of the cigar. When whipped, remove the cream and cool down.

—TEMPERED CHOCOLATE CYLINDER

200 g dark couverture chocolate
Cigar base (previously prepared)

Cut some 5x10 cm rectangles of greaseproof paper. Temper the couverture chocolate and, with a palette knife, spread a very fine layer on each paper rectangle leaving 1 cm free on one end. Roll into regular tubes so that the clean end of the paper sticks out like a flap that can be pulled to remove when serving. Leave the couverture chocolate to dry and fill the cylinders with cigar base with a piping bag. Freeze and cover one end of the cigars with the same couverture chocolate. Reserve in the freezer.

GARNISHING AND PLATING

Sugar coal
Mint flowers

With a Microplane, grate the sugar coal and sprinkle a small amount in a cigar ashtray. Dip the tip of the cigar that hasn't been covered by dark chocolate into the coal simulating the ash of the cigar. Set the cigar on the side.

Fill ¾ of a shot glass with lime gel, then arrange the mint slush, rum candies, and finish by placing the mint flowers on the surface.

CURRY-SMOKED SCAMPI

SERVES 8 PEOPLE

COMPOSITION
Curry-smoked scampi
Crustacean velouté
Comté air
Poached onion
Shallots and spring onions

—COMTÉ AIR

YIELDS 380 G

125 g comté cheese
35 g walnut paste
250 g chicken stock (basic recipes, p.427)
Salt
0.3 g curry powder
1 g soy lecithin
0.5 g sucroester

Place chopped comté cheese, and walnut paste in the Thermomix, boil the chicken stock, add to the comté and walnut mixture and blend everything to a smooth mixture. Run through a fine chinois and adjust salt, add curry powder, lecithin and sucroester. Cool and reserve.

—CURRY-SMOKED SCAMPI

8 fresh scampi (20-25 cm)
Brine for fish (basic recipes, p.429)
10 g curry powder

Peel scampi and remove their intestines. Submerge them in brine for 3 minutes, remove and dry well. Pierce with a toothpick lengthwise to prevent them from curling up when cooking.

Heat a stockpot on low heat, add the curry powder and immediately place a sieve inside it, on which to place the scampi, previously submerged in brine. Cover the container, leave to smoke for 5 minutes, remove from heat and reserve.

—CRUSTACEAN VELOUTÉ

YIELDS 260 G

112 g prawn stock (basic recipes, p.428)
130 g cream
5 egg yolks
Salt

Place the prawn stock and cream in a stockpot, boil and remove from heat. Add to the egg yolks while stirring constantly with a whisk. Run through a strainer and pour into a mould. Cover it with aluminium foil and place it in a bain-marie in the oven at 160°C/320°F for 20 minutes.

When the preparation has set, remove it from the mould and run it through the Thermomix to obtain a smooth and uniform cream. Adjust salt, cover and reserve.

—POACHED ONION

YIELDS 150 G

250 g Figueres onions
25 g butter
10 g extra virgin olive oil
Salt

In a casserole, heat the olive oil with the butter until it melts. Add the onion, previously julienned, and adjust salt. Sweat until soft. Reserve.

—SHALLOTS AND SPRING ONIONS

8 shallots
16 spring onions

Cook the shallots unpeeled, starting with cold water and bringing to a boil; cook for 5 minutes and cool in a cold bain-marie. Peel shallots, cut into three parts with a paring knife and reserve.

Cut the spring onions 1.5 cm long (only the white part of the onion will be used) and blanch them in boiling water with salt. Cool in a cold bain-marie and reserve 2 spring onions per plate.

GARNISHING AND PLATING

Olive oil
Green shiso sprouts
Purple shiso sprouts

Brown both sides of the curry-smoked scampi on the griddle pan with the olive oil.

Place the poached onion on a plate and draw two tears with the hot crustacean velouté. On top of the poached onion, arrange the griddle-seared scampi, and around it, 2 spring onions and the shallot cut in three. Churn the compté mixture to fill it with air, and draw small dots of it around the plate. Finish with the green and purple shiso sprouts.

sous vide

An update to sous-vide cooking

An update
to sous-vide
cooking

The sous-vide technique consists of "modifying the atmosphere of a container to impede the growth of certain existing micro-organisms or to impede oxidation reactions in vacuum-sealed food."[1] The increasing use of sous-vide has been so spectacular in the last decade that many chefs currently exercise it on a daily basis as normally as any other technique in the trade. The percentage of potential uses for this technique has been growing and it currently isn't just a means of preservation (or arranging), but also a very comprehensive tool that includes a range of uses that go far beyond the original intent of preserving.

Uses of the sous-vide technique in the kitchen:

1. Cooking

To cook applying heat to a product previously vacuum-packaged. This type of cooking is characteristically carried out at lower temperatures and for longer periods of time than common cooking processes, which helps preserve the product's organoleptic qualities to the maximum. Spearheading this technique was French Chef George Pralus, who cooked a foie gras terrine for the first time in 1974.

2. Preservation

To prolong the life of a product by preventing the spread of micro-organisms that require oxygen to live and are the main causes of food decay. It is important not to mistake this technique with preserving food by applying heat, since sous-vide does not destroy micro-organisms.

3. Permeation

To scent products. The process entails transferring the aroma of one product to another. Sous-vide facilitates the permeation of a liquid of a specific flavour into solids of different degrees of porosity (aniseed syrup and pineapple), or for a solid to release its aroma inside another product (dill and oil), with or without the use of heat.

4. Compacting

To make terrines and other preparations using the vacuum pressure on the different ingredients. In the case of certain fish, this technique can be used to join fillets together and obtain different results by adding new elements (see RED MULLET STUFFED WITH ITS LIVER, SUQUET AND FENNEL, ORANGE AND SAFFRON GNOCCHI, PAGE 84) or to obtain pieces that are twice their original size and have a tender and sweet texture.

Sous-vide cuisine is a "method of cooking raw foods vacuum-sealed, with or without other semi processed products, at precisely controlled times and temperatures. It is a cooking technique that generally involves low temperatures for varying periods of time, depending on the product cooked."[2] It is used both in restaurant and social catering and, in recent years, its use in haute cuisine—whose most important aim is to preserve the maximum quality of the product in organoleptic and textural terms—has made great advances.
There are two main types of sous-vide cooking methods:

—**Direct cooking** (immediately served). Using very low temperatures (between 40°C/104°F and 60°C/140°F), the optimal cooking point is right on the verge between raw and cooked.

—**Indirect cooking** (reserved before serving). Using low temperatures (between 60°C/140°F and 70°C/158°F) for prolonged periods of time.

1 — ROCA, J.; BRUGUÉS, S. *Sous-Vide Cuisine*. Barcelona: Montagud Editores S.A., 2003.
2 — *Guia per a l'aplicació del sistema APPCC en cuina al buit*. Alicia Foundation, jointly with the Catalan Agency for Food Safety, 2012.

The beginning of sous-vide at El Celler de Can Roca

Sous-vide made its first appearance at El Celler as part of the menu in 1995, with its LUKEWARM COD WITH SPINACH, IDIAZABAL CHEESE CREAM, PINE KERNELS AND A REDUCTION OF PEDRO XIMÉNEZ. Improvements in the technique led to the publication in Spanish of *Sous-Vide Cuisine* in 2004, written jointly by Joan Roca and Salvador Brugués. The book sets the theoretical basis for this new method in haute cuisine, revolutionising many restaurants.

Narcís Caner, a friend of Joan and Salvador and promoter of the new technique, was responsible for arousing their interest in sous-vide cooking. El Celler then turned into a laboratory for his culinary innovations, and a machine for cooking bain-marie became increasingly necessary, including the ability to control temperature and provide water flow to guarantee an even temperature. They came into contact with a manufacturer of scientific materials of the desired characteristics and from there the **Roner**, a machine that revolutionised the technique, was born. Next, with the emergence of new machines and accessories such as the **Rotaval** or the **Gastrovac**, sous-vide went through a series of technical and practical improvements.

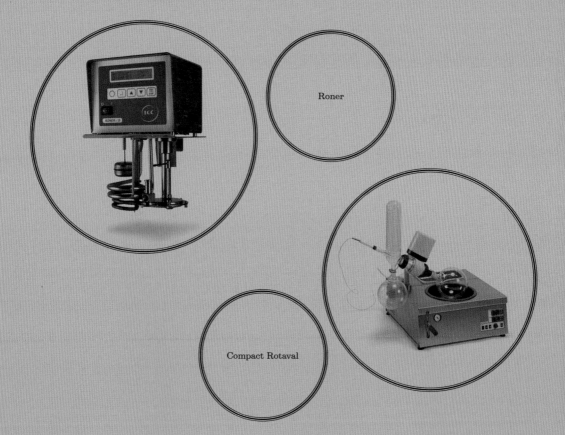

Roner

Compact Rotaval

Evolving toward precision

The most important contribution of El Celler de Can Roca in sous-vide cooking in recent years, has been adjusting cooking temperatures. With time they have learnt that, in order to fully respect the properties of products and make the best of them, one must find the optimal balance of temperature and time. Often, this temperature directly defies the sanitary rules established by public health authorities. Therefore, responsible sous-vide cooking demands a balance between both time and temperature.

Lately, the expression 'precision cooking' is used to complement every definition of sous-vide cooking. It explains why many restaurants are increasingly using this technique to guarantee a positive end result. A more objective cuisine that has found a very effective tool in sous-vide. Now more than ever, we must underline the importance of mastering this technique and insist on one idea:

KNOWLEDGE = RESPONSIBILITY

Since the first cooking charts were established at El Celler, they have been able to adjust temperatures with the highest precision in order to achieve the best quality, while observing their sanitary obligations and responsibility in matters of food safety.

All in all, the search for precision doesn't have to be overly complex, but on the contrary. The evolution and consolidation of the use of this technique has led to the simplification of guidelines for sous-vide cooking: thus, endless temperature charts give way to a range that establishes the minimum and maximum temperatures for each group of products:

MEAT: 60-65°C/140-149°F

FISH: 50-55°C/122-131°F

VEGETABLES: 82-85°C/180-185°F

El Celler improves on the idea of cooking at low temperatures, a wider concept that includes processes beyond sous-vide. The appearance of steam ovens that incorporate highly precise technology for cooking at low temperatures has a lot to do with it. It is smaller-sized equipment that facilitates its installation and has a very precise mechanism to control moisture that allows for cooking at low temperature with or without sealing the product in a vacuum-pack. El Celler, pioneer since the start of the research and promotion of low-temperature cooking, has been supporting the creation of the TekTherm ovens by Distform that bear its name.

TekTherm Compact
oven by Distform

perfume cooking

**Perfume cooking,
aroma permeation**

After pondering on the old way of throwing herbs or spices into the fire to aromatise a product being cooked on the charcoal-grill, El Celler de Can Roca went a little further and developed a new gastronomic technique: 'perfume-cooking'. That is, cooking a product with the aroma of a different one. In the same way smoked salmon is 'cooked' with smoke, the Roca brothers cook meat and fish with herbs and spices.

The process consists of fitting a sieve into a casserole so as to leave some space at the bottom, under the net. The spices, herbs, citrus fruits, tea or liqueur that will release their aroma are placed at the bottom of the container, and the product that is to be cooked goes on the sieve. By heating the base of the casserole, all the aromatic particles are released and permeate the product as it cooks.

'Perfume cooking' is especially recommended for crustaceans and the fattier parts of fish, like the loin, which absorb aromas well. One of the first dishes that resulted from this idea was the SAFFRON-SMOKED LOBSTER (2004); other examples are the SCAMPI PERFUMED WITH CARDAMOM AND CITRUS FRUITS (2005) and the PRAWN WITH AMONTILLADO (2007).

—INTERNAL
MOTIVATION

L

–POETRY

L

Poetry is also distillation, the purification of an experience. An action than can have a universal reach and can be boundless is possible thanks to concrete and specific materials and a set framework. Not everything is meant to be said, but rather suggested with uniform grammar and the discipline of rhythm and syntax applied to the immense variety of life. The cuisine of El Celler is pursuing a similar objective. Because dishes speak not only about what we see, but also about what they evoke, about abstract concepts, or emotions we have stored somewhere in our memories.

Beyond swallowing, or even tangible beauty, the poetry of this cuisine seeks a strong metaphor and metonymy. The welcome sign is an inviting olive tree that offers shelter: the bones tell us of the ability to face difficulties, the powerful light of the Mediterranean is explained with a still equilibrium. The parts—the accumulation of milky textures, for example—transport us to a whole, to the return to tenderness.

Poetry is an intellectual process through which, thanks to its constant treatment and transformation of the language, we acquire a deeper knowledge of ourselves. Wordsworth said that poetry is "recollection in tranquillity", emotion seen from a distance. We may not be able to express everything the present makes us feel at the time we feel it. It is later, when we take a break, when we experience poetry, and because of the mechanisms provided by language, that we can extract moral lessons, memories that solidify. Like in gastronomy.

Often when we bring a dish to the table we remain silent. The stimulus that drove us to create the dish is implied and very few times do we explain the reasons behind it. It is better to leave the door open to seduction. Thus, the same way poetry beautifully summarises the essence of an idea, in gastronomy we can often suggest dishes with poetic evocations.

Cooking as poetry begins where words end, where they are not suitable to voice our thoughts. The art of poetry consists of expressing ourselves following a rhythm, an idea, a feeling that can pierce through language and become a physical gesture symbolised as something elevated or emotional.

The symbol. It is also very important to us. An olive tree is a symbol. It represents the landscape at the table. The possibility of picking a fruit, an olive. A welcoming feature in the form of sweet and savoury, the essence of the cuisine of Jordi and Joan. All this is present when we serve you the olive and sugar that envelops it. A surf 'n' turf with an olive stuffed with anchovies. This is our OLIVE TREE. A dish. A symbol. Possibly a poem…

And beyond the symbol there is transformation and creativity. Using local products, enjoying the ingenuity in times of shortage, or transforming the commonly discarded product into an extraordinary delicacy. These are also forms of poetry in the kitchen.

In the end, what becomes poetry is food. Poetry in the mouth. Embellished and elevated at times, and at others, routine. If, as a wise man would say, everyday speech is a poem worn by use, everyday cuisine can be also considered a forgotten poem... If so desired, it can also be transformed into a marvellous recital.

In the dining room...

Poetry in the dining room is the ability to seduce. Seduction is important when serving: there is a message and we all know it; our interaction at the table determines whether we can deepen our ability to show more than what is being eaten.

It is essential to interpret correctly the rhythms and pauses of the table. To become tellers of stories, dishes and wines. Wisdom is essential for physical and mental decompression. Not surprisingly study and knowledge are in part where our conceit lies, clothing the professional movements we perform. The pillars are the study, perseverance and curiosity. All this is very important, but not vital. The values of the waiter of the future go beyond his/her knowledge and specific training: they are rooted in generosity and knowing how to manage emotional intelligence.

In service there is a great deal of respect for silence and privacy. Gastronomy enjoys such elevated social status that we sometimes exhibit an excessively arrogant attitude when talking to our submissive customers. We must be able to hint rather than inform. Excessive explanations can border on the hyperbolic or even break the dialectical harmony at the table. It is a courtship in which we must know how to act and, only if the diner opens up in conversation, then we can contribute our poetic and creative sense.

ELDERBERRY
AND CHERRY SOUP

—ELDERBERRY INFUSION
YIELDS 1.030 G

1 kg water
80 g sugar
40 g elderberries

In a casserole, heat the water and sugar to 85°C/185°F. Remove from heat, add the elderberries and cover. Leave to infuse for 30 minutes. Strain, cool and reserve.

SERVES 8 PEOPLE

COMPOSITION

Elderberry infusion
Elderberry sauce
Cherry sauce
Amaretto cherry
White base for the ice cream
Ginger ice cream
Cherry gel
Mimetic cherry
Fresh almond
Candied ginger
Sardine
Smoked sardine
Thin slices of cherry

—ELDERBERRY SAUCE
YIELDS 480 G

500 g elderberry infusion (previously prepared)
1.5 g iota

Mix the iota with the elderberry infusion in a saucepan and bring to a boil. Remove from heat, strain and leave to set refrigerated. Reserve.

—CHERRY SAUCE
YIELDS 625 G

500 g cherry pulp
1 g xanthan gum
125 g olive oil
4 g Chardonnay vinegar

Blend the cherry pulp with the xanthan gum. When the mixture is smooth, slowly add the olive oil and vinegar until the sauce emulsifies completely. Reserve refrigerated in a squeeze bottle.

—AMARETTO CHERRY
YIELDS 8 CHERRIES COATED IN AMARETTO

8 cherries
200 g amaretto
2 g kappa

Wash cherries and cut a slice off the base to remove the stone. Remove the stem and, using a skewer, perforate the cherry exactly at that point. Place the amaretto in a casserole with the kappa and bring to a boil. Envelop the cherries with a coating of amaretto. Reserve refrigerated.

—WHITE BASE FOR THE ICE CREAM
YIELDS 2.45 KG

1.36 kg milk
430 g cream
342.5 g dextrose
97.5 g milk powder
252.5 g sugar
17.5 g ice-cream stabiliser

Heat the milk, cream, dextrose and milk powder to 40°C/104°F and slowly add the sugar mixed with the stabiliser, until the mixture reaches 85°C/185°F. Churn, strain and blast chill. Reserve this base for making the ginger ice cream.

—GINGER ICE CREAM
YIELDS 500 G

750 g white base for ice cream (previously prepared)
30 g fresh ginger juice

Mix the white base and ginger juice well and leave to ripen refrigerated for 24 hours. Next, run through the ice-cream maker and reserve in the freezer at -18°C/0°F.

—CHERRY GEL
YIELDS 500 G

500 g cherry pulp
5 g agar-agar
3 gelatine sheets

Bring the cherry pulp and agar-agar to a boil; when the temperature lowers slightly, separate a third of the mixture to dissolve the gelatine sheets, previously hydrated. Reintegrate to the mixture and leave to set.

—SMOKED SARDINE
YIELDS 2 SMOKED SARDINE FILLETS

2 salted sardine fillets (previously prepared)

Arrange the sardine fillets in a container with holes without overlapping. Place this container inside another. Cover both containers tightly with cling film and introduce smoke with a smoking gun; cover the small hole left by wrapping the container with more cling film. Leave to smoke for 15 minutes. Uncover and reserve the fillets refrigerated.

—MIMETIC CHERRY
YIELDS 45 MIMETIC CHERRIES

500 g cherry gel (previously prepared)
Ginger ice cream (previously prepared)

Submerge the cherry-shaped moulds made with liquid silicone (see process on page 429) in liquid nitrogen to cool well. With a hand blender, break the structure of the cherry gel and reheat in a casserole. Fill the holes with this mixture, very hot, and empty them to form a cherry gel lining. Leave to set in the freezer and finish by filling them with the ginger ice cream using a piping bag. Smooth their surface and keep them in the freezer. Remove the mimetic cherries from their mould before serving and always reserve in the freezer at -18°C/0°F.

—THIN SLICES OF CHERRY
YIELDS 24 THIN SLICES

4 cherries

Slice the cherries thinly and form groups of three slices for each plate. Reserve refrigerated.

GARNISHING AND PLATING

Red shiso
Elderflowers

In a soup dish, serve some elderberry sauce. With a squeeze bottle, make several dots of cherry sauce on the surface of the elderberry sauce. Next, place the amaretto coated cherry crowned with red shiso. Next to it, place the mimetic cherry and a few slices of fresh almond. Finish with 2 cubes of candied ginger, 3 slices of cherry, 3 small slices of smoked sardine and the elderflowers.

—FRESH ALMOND
YIELDS 50 THIN SLICES

5 fresh almonds

Peel the fresh almonds and slice them thinly with a paring knife. Reserve cold and covered with a wet cloth.

—CANDIED GINGER
YIELDS APPROXIMATELY 15 CUBES

8 g candied ginger

Cut ginger into regular 3 mm cubes. Reserve them cold and well covered.

—SARDINE
YIELDS 2 FILLETS

1 sardine
Brine for fish (basic recipes, p.429)

Scale and fillet the sardine. Bone the fillets and submerge them in a container with brine for 2 minutes. Remove from the brine, dry well and reserve.

MEDITERRANEAN SOLE

SERVES 4 PEOPLE

COMPOSITION

Sole

Fennel emulsion

Bergamot gel

Bergamot emulsion

Pine kernel emulsion

Manzanilla olive emulsion

Olive oil sweets

—SOLE
YIELDS 4 PORTIONS

2 sole (400 g each)
Brine for fish (basic recipes, p.429)
Extra virgin olive oil

Bring the water to a boil in a small saucepan and submerge the tail of the soles for 2 seconds in the water. Remove both lateral fins with a pair of scissors and, using a dry cloth, remove the skin by pulling from the tail toward the head. Blanching the tail facilitates separating the skin from the bone.

Remove the head and tail of the sole and fillet. Then, square off and immerse the sole in brine for 5 minutes. Dry the fillets well with kitchen towels and join them in pairs on the meat side that was in contact with the bones. Seal in a vacuum pack bag with the oil and cook in the Roner at 55°C/131°F for 4 minutes. Reserve.

—FENNEL EMULSION
YIELDS 190 G

100 g blended fennel leaves
0.7 g xanthan gum
Salt
100 g extra virgin olive oil

Mix blended fennel and xanthan gum and salt; mix with a hand blender for a few minutes and, lastly, emulsify it slowly with olive oil. Reserve.

—BERGAMOT GEL
YIELDS 150 G

125 g water
25 g sugar
½ bergamot zest
2 g agar-agar
25 g bergamot juice

Bring the water and sugar to a boil in a saucepan, remove from heat and infuse the grated bergamot zest for 15 minutes well covered. Cool, strain and mix with the agar-agar, bring to a boil and add the bergamot juice. Remove from heat and leave to set refrigerated.

—BERGAMOT EMULSION
YIELDS 180 G

150 g bergamot gel (previously prepared)
50 g extra virgin olive oil

Using a hand blender, mix the bergamot gel and emulsify it slowly with the olive oil. Reserve.

—PINE KERNEL EMULSION
YIELDS 120 G

75 g pure pine kernel paste
20 g extra virgin olive oil
40 g water
Salt

Blend the pine kernel paste together with the olive oil with a hand blender. Emulsify slowly with water to a smooth dough. Adjust salt and reserve.

—MANZANILLA OLIVE EMULSION
YIELDS 260 G

125 g manzanilla olives pitted
75 g olive water
0.5 g xanthan gum
100 g extra virgin manzanilla olive oil

Blend the olives with their own water to a smooth and uniform texture. Run the purée through a fine strainer, then blend with the xanthan gum for a few minutes and emulsify slowly with olive oil. Reserve.

—OLIVE OIL SWEETS
YIELDS 20 SWEETS

100 g isomalt
Extra virgin olive oil

In a small saucepan, cook the isomalt until it melts. When melted, submerge the tip of a pastry nozzle to create a fine membrane, inside which a small amount of olive oil will be dropped. The weight of the oil will close this membrane, creating a sweet filled with oil. The sweets can be stored submerged in olive oil to prevent moisture.

GARNISHING AND PLATING

Extra virgin olive oil
Orange emulsion (basic recipes, p.427)
Fennel sprouts
White baby sage flowers
Orange peel confit (basic recipes, p.427)
Fresh pine kernels

Open the bag where sole has been cooked and remove the fillets, which will have adhered to one another and will be very juicy. Sear over holm wood on the grill with a dash of olive oil.

On a rectangular plate, arrange one dot of each emulsion in the following order: fennel, bergamot, orange, pine kernel and olive. Place the sole parallel to the dots. On top of the fillet, place the following elements, complementary to the emulsions, in this order: fennel flower, white baby sage flower, preserved orange peel, fresh pine kernels and one olive oil sweet.

TRUFFLE-STEAMED BRIOCHE

SERVES 8 PEOPLE

COMPOSITION
Brioche
Escudella stock
Escudella stock with truffle
Truffle mayonnaise

—BRIOCHE
YIELDS 80 BRIOCHES

30 g sugar
25 g milk
12 g baking powder
125 g eggs
250 g flour
125 g softened butter
3 g salt

Place the sugar, milk, and baking powder in a container and mix well until everything integrates. Add the eggs. Sieve the flour and add to the mixture in 2 parts, then add the softened butter and salt. Knead the dough until it's very smooth, elastic and no longer sticks to the container. Place it in a bowl, cover and leave to stand for 12 hours refrigerated.

Stretch the dough between 2 sheets of greaseproof paper with the rolling pin and some flour. Refrigerate for ½ hour, cut into 6 g rolls and refrigerate again. Shape the rolls into balls when they are very cold and leave them to ferment for 40 minutes at 40°C/104°F. Reserve proved brioches.

—ESCUDELLA STOCK
YIELDS 2 KG

2 chicken thighs
2 pig's trotters
1 pork snout
500 g pork backbone bones
5 litres water
100 g parsnips
70 g celery
100 g turnips
70 g savoy cabbage
200 g onions
100 g carrots

Bring all the cuts of meat to a boil starting with cold water, skim when it starts to boil. Add the vegetables, peeled and chopped, and cook for 6 hours. Strain and reserve.

—ESCUDELLA STOCK WITH TRUFFLE
YIELDS 1.02 KG

1 kg escudella stock (previously prepared)
20 g truffles

Clean truffle and brunoise. Add to the stock and reserve to cook the brioches.

—TRUFFLE MAYONNAISE
YIELDS 150 G

25 g egg yolks
10 g water
80 g black truffle oil (basic recipes, p.427)
45 g extra virgin olive oil
15 g truffles
Salt

Mix egg yolks and water and beat until they start to foam. Add the oils slowly while beating, until the texture turns thick. Brunoise the truffle and add to the mayonnaise, adjust salt. Transfer to piping bags and reserve.

GARNISHING AND PLATING

Black truffle in thin slices

Place fermented brioches on a bamboo steamer over the steam of the escudella and truffle stock for approximately 20 minutes or until they cook. Stuff them with truffle mayonnaise (3 g per brioche), and crown with some thin sheets of black truffle, sliced when serving.

ANCHOVY BONE
TEMPURA

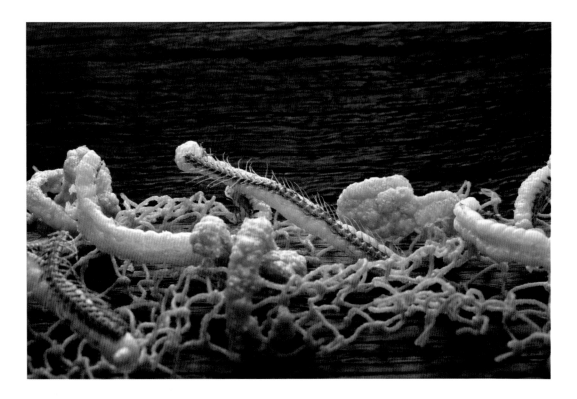

SERVES 8 PEOPLE

COMPOSITION
Cooked rice paste
Anchovy bone tempura
Seaweed tempura

—COOKED RICE PASTE
YIELDS 330 G

100 g Senia rice from Pals
300 g water
Salt

Place rice in a saucepan with water, cover and cook on low heat. Blend the rice with the remaining water in the Thermomix and sieve. Reserve.

—ANCHOVY BONE TEMPURA
YIELDS 16 UNITS 12 G EACH

165 g cooked rice paste (previously prepared)
16 salted anchovy bones
1 litre extra virgin olive oil

Transfer the rice paste to a piping bag and make 6x1 cm strips over a baking sheet lined with a silicone mat. Place one anchovy bone on top of each strip of paste and dry in the cooker at 40°C/104°F for 12 hours.

Remove the dry rice strips with the bones and fry them in olive oil at 180°C/356°F until the rice puffs. Remove any excess oil with kitchen towels.

—SEAWEED TEMPURA
YIELDS 18 UNITS 9 G EACH

165 g cooked rice paste (previously prepared)
3 g phytoplankton
1 litre extra virgin olive oil

Mix rice paste and phytoplankton and place it in a piping bag. On a baking sheet lined with a silicone mat, draw shapes imitating small algae with the dough. Dry in the cooker at 40°C/104°F for 12 hours.

When dry, fry it in olive oil at 180°C/356°F until they puff. Remove any excess oil with kitchen towels.

GARNISHING AND PLATING

Salt

Season the bones and seaweed to taste with salt and serve.

OLIVE TREE

**SERVES 8 PEOPLE
(2 SNACKS PER PERSON)**

COMPOSITION

Green olive caramel
Caramelised olives

—GREEN OLIVE CARAMEL
YIELDS 250 G

500 g green olive purée
100 g fondant
50 g glucose
50 g isomalt

Spread the green olive purée over silicone mats
and place in the dehydrator at 60°C/140°F,
until the purée is completely dry. Crush and
store in an airtight container.

In a separate container, place the fondant,
glucose and isomalt, heat until they melt and
reach 160°C/320°F, lower the temperature to
150°C/302°F and add the dry olive purée. Stir
the resulting caramel to smooth it out and pour
it on a silicone mat, place another mat on top
and flatten with a rolling pin. When the thickness
is uniform, remove the silicone mat and, with
a wheel dough divider, cut into approximately
4x4 cm squares. Leave to cool and reserve in an
airtight container in a dry place.

Arrange 2 caramel squares on a silicone mat
and melt in the oven at 180°C/356°F, place
another silicone mat on top and stretch with a
rolling pin until obtaining a very fine caramel
sheet. Cut again with the wheel dough divider
into 4x4 cm squares and leave to cool. Reserve
in an airtight container.

—CARAMELISED OLIVES

Green olive caramel (previously prepared)
16 green anchovy stuffed olives

Arrange the olives on a baking sheet and place
a fine caramel square on top of each. Bake at
180°C/356°F so that the caramel melts and
envelops the olive.

GARNISHING AND PLATING

Prick each olive with a hook to hang on the
olive bonsai tree.

LACTIC

SERVES 4 PEOPLE

COMPOSITION

Dulce de leche
Guava gel
Ripollesa sheep milk ice cream
Ripollesa sheep cottage cheese foam
Guava sheet
Sugar candyfloss
Ripollesa sheep yogurt
White caramel

—DULCE DE LECHE
YIELDS 2.5 KG

3 kg sheep's milk
1.5 kg sugar
450 g glucose
4 cloves
4.5 g baking soda

Boil the sheep's milk with sugar, glucose, cloves and baking soda; reduce until it acquires a caramel-like colour and a thick texture when cold. Reserve.

—GUAVA GEL
YIELDS 580 G

250 g guava purée
35 g inverted sugar syrup
35 g glucose
7.5 g apple pectine
250 g sugar
7 g citric acid

Mix the purée and inverted sugar syrup, glucose and pectine, boil and then add the sugar, previously mixed with citric acid. Stir to prevent lumps from forming and bring to a boil until it reaches 104°C/219°F. Cool and transfer the gel to piping bags.

—RIPOLLESA SHEEP MILK ICE CREAM
YIELDS 1.25 KG

87.5 g Ripollesa sheep milk
205 g cream
25 g milk powder
170 g dextrose
128 g sugar
8.7 g cream stabiliser
625 g Ripollesa sheep cottage cheese

Heat the cream, milk, and milk powder to 40°C/104°F; then slowly add the dextrose, sugar and stabiliser, until the temperature rises to 85°C/185°F. When the mixture is pasteurised, blend and blast chill to 20°C/68°F. Once this temperature is reached, add the cottage cheese, leave to rest refrigerated for 24 hours, churn and run through the ice-cream maker. Keep the ice cream at -18°C/0°F.

—RIPOLLESA SHEEP COTTAGE CHEESE FOAM
YIELDS 600 G

300 g Ripollesa sheep cottage cheese
300 g cream

Mix sheep cottage cheese and cream, transfer into a whipped cream dispenser with 3 chargers. Reserve in cold storage.

—GUAVA SHEET
YIELDS 200 G

250 g guava purée
1 gelatine sheet

Heat a small amount of the guava purée to 50°C/122°F to dissolve the gelatine sheet previously hydrated in iced water, and then mix with the remaining guava. Spread a thin layer on silicone paper and freeze.

—SUGAR CANDYFLOSS
YIELDS 7 CANDYFLOSSES

20 g sugar

Place sugar in the candyfloss maker, pick up sugar threads with a whisk and reserve in an airtight container, or make them when plating.

—RIPOLLESA SHEEP YOGURT
YIELDS 200 G

200 g Ripollesa sheep yogurt

Mix yogurt with a whisk and transfer it to a squeeze bottle.

—WHITE CARAMEL
YIELDS 125 G

125 g isomalt
5 g white food colouring

Place the isomalt in a saucepan to melt and bring to 160°C/320°F, then lower its temperature to 140°C/284°F, add the white colouring and smooth out. Spread it over a silicone mat with a rolling pin to obtain thin sheets of caramel. Cut it into irregular pieces and reserve in an airtight container in a dry place.

GARNISHING AND PLATING

Set the dulce de leche on the base of a soup dish and accompany it with some dots of guava gel on each side. In the centre, on top of the dulce de leche, add a quenelle of sheep's milk ice cream, cover it with cottage cheese foam, stick a sheet of guava and place the candyfloss on the surface of the foam. Finish with some dots of sheep yogurt surrounding it, and chunks of white caramel over the candyfloss.

dining room

Poetry and seduction
in the dining room

A WONDERFUL DINING ROOM

Go is a marvellous Chinese board game played all over the East. In it, two players face each other by moving white and black pieces. Some have even compared it to chess, in which two worlds divided into black and white figures also meet, maybe like cooks and waiters. In chess you have to kill in order to win. In *go*, you need to construct in order to live. The aim isn't to eat one another, but to expand one's territory. That is a good way to look at the complicity between the kitchen and dining room staff in the future of gastronomy. Constructing and proposing strategies for seduction. The dining room in a restaurant is a unifying space like few others. It's a universe of emotional connections enriched by the feedback of proximity. We must reinvent our profession by making the most of the current good times in cooking to grow with them, with the people in the white jackets. Seducing so that they also seduce. We must be able to connect emotionally with chefs and better prepare our approach to the diner. To serve with a deliberate and calm expression. To draw from Eastern knowledge and its rituals. The spell of the tea ceremony is an example of service for the West. To feel well, comfortable, clean; it's said that those who wear perfume—us, subtly—have a better opinion of themselves. To explore fashion trends and update our uniforms. To know how to ask. To think about our tone of voice. To display a natural and sincere smile. Forcing things may lead to ridicule, obsequiousness frightens and overwhelms. Simplicity, please, simplicity and normality as a rule.

Reconstructing gastronomy in the dining room and putting forward new changes and concepts can be fascinating. Knowing how to read the rhythms and pauses at a table. Becoming storytellers that can also tell about dishes and wines and more and more... Wisdom is essential. Our pillars are study, perseverance, constancy and curiosity to increase our confidence and assertiveness. This is, in effect, important, but not fundamental.

I feel very fortunate for the support and involvement of my team in the dining room. I owe to all of them an important part of our success. We enjoy extraordinary circumstances of positive energy and it's a true luxury to be able to show the magic of our cuisine with the loyalty, precision, predisposition and love with which my team welcomes and captivates. I hope this positive energy can transmit its brilliance beyond our walls.

Sebastià Serrano reminds us that hominids are here to woo. I encourage you to woo your customers by being friendly and holding out your hand.

Luckily, in its celebration of plates and glasses the vocation of the waiters, like a tree full of nests, intertwines with customers eager for shelter and warmth. Every contact with people is a chance to improve their life, according to Alex Rovira and Francesc Miralles in their book *El laberinto de la felicidad*[1] [The Maze of Happiness]. In it, they narrate the findings of a man who worked as a waiter for forty years:

—I have calculated that the contact of a waiter with each customer that asks for a coffee on average isn't more than a bare minute. It's the total time including the greeting and the question "What would you like to drink?" what the customer asks for, when you put the cup on the table, the time to add up the bill and saying goodbye when he leaves. These are many different moments, but the real contact between the waiter and the customer isn't more than a minute.

—And what does this mean?

—It means it's an opportunity! Apart from the quality of the coffee, which is the least important thing, in that minute the waiter has before him three options, or better put, three possible results that depend on his attitude.

After saying this, the waiter paused briefly to look for the most adequate words. Then he continued.

—At that minute you can make the person leave in a worse state than when he arrived if you're rude. Or, perhaps, he can leave in the same way he came if you treat him with indifference. But you also have the opportunity that he can go out of the café in better spirits than when he entered if you treat him to a little friendliness.

—And that's all?—said Ariadna without hiding her disappointment—But what's this got to do with the meaning of life?

—That IS precisely the MEANING OF LIFE! And not only for waiters. Every day we have hundreds of short and long moments in contact with others. Our challenge is to obtain the third result: that your life is a little better after being with us. That's the challenge, the gold prize of every encounter!

On hearing this Ariadna stood still, pensive. The waiter then winked at her and said goodbye in this way:

—And now I have to go: we have to improve many lives.

Dear colleagues, awaited diners, admired chefs; the dining room is not at risk: like good, generous wines, brave and shaded, it never dies, but reinvents itself and today it can be better than ever. Welcome seduction.

JOSEP ROCA

1 — MIRALLES, F.; ROVIRA, A. *El laberinto de la felicidad*. Madrid: Aguilar, 2007.

M

–FREEDOM

— FREEDOM

In the creative process, absolute freedom does not exist. Creation demands a framework, containment will allow precisely the rigour that we pour into it, a conceptual leap. But at the same time, without a spirit that rises, breaks rules, experiments with the processes, and is able to establish the need for an engine of imagination, creation is barren.

It is in this sense that we can understand the freedom in the world of the kitchen of El Celler. It is subject to strict mechanisms, as an essential component is uncovered. It shows its presence beyond the usual protocol, beyond anything planned and scheduled. Precision is its key but this does not have the role of a corset, but is at the service of enthusiasm and the possibility of experimentation. If it were not so, the journey of flavours from around the world in the shape of a Chinese lantern would not exist. If we talk about a landscape setting, the evocation of our surroundings, it allows us to undertake a longer, more intense journey toward a world that is within reach. The tasting adventure in the universe presented when the sphere opens up (in The World dessert p.352) is the exact metaphor for a desire not to have any limits. Freedom does not question strict approaches, technical advances, moderation and control. It does not exclude them. It takes advantage of them when proposing an imaginative act that is not superfluous. There is no room for frivolity, but a capacity of the mind to take flight, to make possible what seems unachievable.

According to the Roca brothers

Cooking is a branch of geography. Of physical geography and political geography. It speaks to us about climates and landscapes, geology and humidity, but also about cultural habits, religions, wealth and poverty. All of which is understood at the table.

Our fare is Mediterranean cuisine, synthesizing mountain and sea. It is also the cuisine of the Pyrenees. Overtly from Girona. And friend of other cuisines of the Mediterranean coastline. Our cuisine assimilates, is open, plural, integrating, accepts the influence of migratory flows, absorbs the inspiration that comes with travelling. Fusion is natural, like the slow transformation of society. Like the adaptation to gastronomic habits that have seasoned our cuisine throughout the years, helping it evolve. Integrating ingredients cannot change our identity, on the contrary, it enriches it. Evolution doesn't affect the essence, but brings it closer to us, makes it more ours by the minute. Our approach to cooking, therefore, begins with respect for the past, integrating influences, and with the freedom to transform. Freedom nurtures creativity and travels on established paths, sometimes deviating and, other times, returning to them. We create new roads, routes and detours that expand the original map, but never destroying it or erasing it from our memory. Geography changes, but our planet is always, essentially, immutable.

By travelling around THE WORLD we want to show our more
open vision. We embrace a living, gastronomic and social
world in which we feel active participants. We watch
the world spin and see that is not as big as some say.

The fact that the main ingredient in Catalonia and Italy
is the tomato, that the Spanish dish par excellence
is the potato omelette, or that the French use corn to
fatten ducks to make foie gras, are as much clear signs
of fusion as the fact that Argentina exports meat and
wheat (two European contributions). We could go on with
the gratin dauphinois, French fries with mussels, or the
Kartoffelsalat made in France, Belgium and Germany;
or the gazpacho from Andalusia, or the pepper used in
Basque and Hungarian cuisines. Back and forth. Fusing
and exchanging. Freedom to reinterpret. We share a world,
enjoy it and respect the seasonal cycles and their beauty.
A world so rich and complete with colours that it cannot
be interpreted but from the spirit of freedom. With open
doors. With broad-mindedness. That is how we eat up THE
WORLD. And in this spirit, we serve it to you at the table.

In the dining room...

There is a part of service that needs to free itself from rigidity and rules in order for the whole dining room staff to become fully involved, starting with the first server. In this manner, the customer can see the professional and personal growth of each one of us. We must help each employee grow, motivate them, and bring out their abilities and interests so that, when helping the customer, they can offer more confidence and closeness. For us, there is no difference between how maîtres, sommeliers or the top waiters should treat the customer. This unity prevents anyone from feeling under valued: on the contrary, everyone feels important. This is how we break with the old approach of serving customers and achieve a simple environment.

At El Celler there are no rigid instructions for matching dishes and wines, because we understand that no two customers are alike, no two people know wine the same way, and in every instance, there can be more agreement about acidity, more agreement about freshness, more agreement about maturity, less intensity placed on persistence... We want to have the freedom to reinterpret one pairing according to how it merges at the moment of the tasting; even to show that the perfect pairing is not always the best.

We must maintain our ability to improvise, even if everything is well planned, conceptualised and organised. Only from previous study, knowledge and order can one improvise. Improvisation cannot exist in absolute chaos. And without the ability to improvise we are not truly free. We need to plan to change everything, if necessary. That is how we understand freedom.

THE WORLD

SERVES 8 PEOPLE (SNACKS)

COMPOSITION

Mexico
Avocado cream
Tomato water

Peru
Sole fish stock
Leche de tigre
Cooking for the spheres

Morocco
Almond nougat
Orange blossom sphere
Rose water jelly

Korea
Fritter dough
Fermented soybean paste centre

Lebanon
Hummus
Bath for hummus spheres

MEXICO

—AVOCADO CREAM
YIELDS 290 G

15 g lime juice
3 g Tabasco sauce
1½ gelatine sheets
260 g avocados
12 g extra virgin olive oil
Fresh tomato seeds

Heat the lime juice and Tabasco sauce and dissolve the gelatine, previously hydrated.

Remove the pulp from the avocado and purée until it's very creamy. Add the dissolved gelatine and oil, and blend again to prevent lumps from forming.

Place a piece of cling film on a flat surface, in the centre, place 3 g of avocado cream and 4 to 5 tomato seeds in the middle; cover the seeds with a dot of avocado cream and close by pressing together the corners of the cling film to shape it like a tomato. Each pocket must weigh approximately 6.5 g. Freeze.

—TOMATO WATER
YIELDS 500 G

500 g tomato water (basic recipes, p.428)
5 g kappa carrageenan

Remove the cling film from the avocado pockets and prick lightly with a toothpick. Keep them in the freezer.

Mix kappa and cold tomato water, bring to a boil, skim and submerge the small avocado cream tomatoes while the tomato juice is still hot. Reserve refrigerated.

GARNISHING AND SERVING THE SNACK

Coriander sprouts

Garnish with a coriander sprout leaf and place the snack on the metal structure.

PERU

—SOLE FISH STOCK
YIELDS 800 G

1 kg sole fish bones
1 kg water

Soak sole fish bones in iced water for 6 hours.

Strain bones and seal in a vacuum pack bag with the water from the recipe; cook in the Roner at 80°C/176°F for 30 minutes. Strain and reserve the resulting stock.

—LECHE DE TIGRE
YIELDS 750 G (70 UNITS)

750 g sole fish stock (previously prepared)
55 g onion
35 g lime
25 g yellow pepper
18 g red pepper
7.5 g salt
5.5 g lime peel
1.1 g Tabasco sauce
7 g xanthan gum

Mix all the ingredients, except the xanthan gum, in a container and marinate for 24 hours.

Next, strain the mixture, blend with the xanthan gum, fill 2.5 cm spherical moulds with it and freeze.

—COATING FOR THE SPHERES
YIELDS 200 G

200 g cocoa butter
1 lime

Prick the leche de tigre spheres with a toothpick and keep them in the freezer.

Melt the cocoa butter and coat the spheres, covering them completely with a layer of butter. Remove the toothpick from the sphere and, with a Microplane, grate some lime zest on the surface, covering the hole from the toothpick. Reserve refrigerated.

GARNISHING AND SERVING THE SNACK

Green shiso

Arrange a leave of green shiso on the metal structure and the coated sphere on top.

MOROCCO

—ALMOND NOUGAT
YIELDS 150 G

45 g isomalt
45 g glucose
95 g fondant
55 g toasted almonds

Mix the sugars and heat to 145°C/293°F. Remove from heat and let the temperature drop to 140°C/284°F; then, add the almonds, previously crushed, and spread the preparation on silicone mats to cool. When cold, crush the caramel in the Thermomix and sprinkle a very thin layer of the resulting powder on a silicon mat. Melt again in the oven at 180°C/356°F and, while still hot, draw 4 cm squares.

—ORANGE BLOSSOM SPHERE
YIELDS 250 UNITS

55 g molasses
167 g water
12 g orange blossom water
6 g calcium lactate gluconate
9 g xanthan gum
Calcium alginate bath (basic recipes, p.427)
Saffron strands

Heat the molasses slightly to dissolve with the water. Mix with the orange blossom water and reserve half of this mixture to store the spheres. Blend the remaining half with xanthan gum and lactate gluconate and let some drops fall into calcium alginate bath. Before sealing the spheres that will form, place a saffron strand inside them. Leave them in the bath for 3 minutes, remove and rinse with water. Immerse the spheres in the reserved mixture.

—ROSE WATER JELLY
YIELDS 225 G

125 g rose water
50 g sugar
50 g water
0.8 g agar-agar

Mix all the ingredients and bring to a boil. Pour the resulting jelly in a 0.5-cm-deep container and, when it solidifies, cut into 0.5 cm squares. Reserve.

GARNISHING AND SERVING THE SNACK

Toasted almond powder
Ras el hanout
Salt
Mint leaves
Goat yogurt

Place an almond nougat square on a 2-cm-wide cylindrical pastry cutter; heat it on the salamander to soften the caramel and so that it becomes shaped like the container. In it, place ingredients in the following order: toasted almond powder, ras el hanout, a pinch of salt, 2 rose jelly cubes, toasted almond powder, a mint leaf, and an orange blossom sphere. Garnish with a dot of goat yogurt.

KOREA

—FRITTER DOUGH
YIELDS 345 G

145 g flour
1.5 g baking soda
7 g honey
30 g sugar
100 g eggs
65 g water

Mix all the ingredients, stirring well to prevent lumps from forming. Leave to stand refrigerated for 24 hours.

—FERMENTED SOYBEAN PASTE CENTRE
YIELDS 440 G (90 UNITS)

125 g cream
4 gelatine sheets
21 g water
250 g fermented Korean soybean paste
25 g rice vinegar
0.6 g yuzu
Extra virgin olive oil

Heat a small amount of cream to dissolve the gelatine leaves, previously hydrated. Reserve.

Heat the water slightly; mix with the fermented soybean paste, vinegar, yuzu, and all the cream. Place the mixture in 1.5 cm semi-spherical moulds, 1 cm deep, and reserve in the freezer.

Prepare a container with liquid nitrogen. Remove the fermented soybean paste spheres from their moulds and finish freezing in the nitrogen (if this process is not performed, the fritter dough will not bind and cooking will be difficult).

Prepare two containers with olive oil, one at 150°C/302°F and another at 180°C/356°F. Stick a needle in the fermented soybean paste centres and fill them with the fritter dough, drain any excess dough and fry first in 150°C/302°F oil until the dough sets and its inside thaws, then in 180°C/356°F oil to finish browning.

GARNISHING AND SERVING THE SNACK

10 g fresh ginger

Peel ginger and cut it into 1-mm-thick by 0.5-cm-wide squares.

Arrange the sphere in the metal structure and place the ginger square on top.

LEBANON

—HUMMUS
YIELDS 250 G

250 g cooked chickpeas
35 g clarified butter
15 g water from cooking the chickpeas
3 g olive oil
1 g sesame oil
1 g chopped garlic
0.6 g lemon juice
0.5 g cumin powder
Salt

Place all the ingredients in a container and purée them to a very smooth cream. Use it to fill moulds shaped as chickpeas and freeze.

—BATH FOR THE HUMMUS SPHERES
YIELDS 200 G

200 g cocoa butter
White sesame seeds
Chopped parsley
Cumin powder

Toast sesame seeds and reserve. Melt cocoa butter and add toasted sesame seeds.

Remove hummus chickpeas from their mould and insert a toothpick in them to help coating with the mixture of cocoa butter and sesame seeds. Sprinkle some of the cumin powder and chopped parsley while the butter is still soft.

GARNISHING AND SERVING THE SNACK

Place the mimetic chickpea on the metal structure.

THE WORLD

The selection of destinations for this gastronomic world tour is in response to the most recent trips taken by the Roca brothers. These 'capsules' of concentrated flavour culture emerge from the tastes pervading in their memory. Their aim is to diversify their journey and discover new culinary destinations in time and with the arrival of every new season. Currently, four new snacks are in the making: Brazil, Japan, Thailand and Iceland.

CUTTLEFISH
AND PEA DIM SUM

SERVES 8 PEOPLE

COMPOSITION
Cuttlefish
Cuttlefish stock
Pea purée
Dim sum

—CUTTLEFISH
YIELDS 2 SQUARES 8 CM EACH

1 cuttlefish

Clean the cuttlefish and remove its skin, cut
into approximately 8 cm squares and freeze.
Reserve the trimmings for the stock.

—CUTTLEFISH STOCK
YIELDS 500 G

300 g onion
30 g extra virgin olive oil
500 g cuttlefish trimmings (from previous
    step)
150 g celery
1 kg water

Julienne onion and toss it in olive oil, then
add the cuttlefish trimmings, celery and water.
Simmer until it reduces to half. Strain and
reserve.

—PEA PURÉE
YIELDS 250 G

250 g peas
75 g cooking water
30 g beurre noisette (basic recipes, p.427)
50 g tear peas
Salt

Boil the peas in water with salt, purée with 75 g
of the cooking water and butter, run through a
fine sieve and cool. Mix the purée with the tear
peas, previously blanched.

—DIM SUM
YIELDS 16 FILLED POCKETS

2 cuttlefish squares (previously prepared)
Pea purée (previously prepared)

Cut the cuttlefish in a meat slicer to make very
fine sheets, stretch and, in the centre of each
sheet, serve a spoonful of pea purée. Close the
sheets by joining their corners on top to form a
pocket, like filled pasta. Reserve.

GARNISHING AND PLATING

Pea flowers

Before serving, arrange the cuttlefish dim sum
in a steamer to cook lightly with the steam
from the cuttlefish stock. Serve in a bamboo
steamer with a cup of the stock served under
it. Lastly, add the pea flower.

CAVIAR OMELETTE

COMPOSITION

Calcium alginate
and egg yolk bath
White caviar base
Fennel gel

—CALCIUM ALGINATE AND EGG YOLK BATH
YIELDS 600 G

500 g water
7.5 g calcium alginate
125 g pasteurized egg yolks

Churn the water with the calcium alginate, add the egg yolks and create a smooth mixture. Remove the air with a vacuum-packing machine.

—WHITE CAVIAR BASE
YIELDS 450 G (APPROXIMATELY 22 OMELETTES)

250 g milk
250 g cream
10 g salt
6 gelatine sheets
1 g xanthan gum
10 g calcium lactate gluconate
75 g caviar
8 g chopped chives

Place the milk and cream with salt in a casserole and heat. Remove from the heat before adding the remaining ingredients. Smooth with the hand blender; let it cool down a bit and add the chives and caviar.

Fill some silicone moulds with 20 g white caviar base and cool to jellify. Remove from the moulds and submerge in the calcium alginate and egg yolk bath for 10 minutes, turning the omelettes over after 5 minutes. Remove from the bath and drain well any excess egg yolks, so that the surface stays smooth and free of edges. Reserve.

—FENNEL GEL
YIELDS 250 G

300 g fennel leaves
75 g blanching water
75 g water
2.5 g xanthan gum
Salt

Blanch fennel leaves in boiling water with salt, cool in a cold bain-marie and reserve 75 g of this water, as indicated. When cold, mix with the blanched fennel and 75 g of additional water and blend. Run the mixture through a fine sieve, adjust salt and add the xanthan gum, mix with hand blender to prevent lumps from forming. Strain the gel again and reserve.

GARNISHING AND PLATING

Dill sprouts
Tarragon sprouts
Chervil sprouts
Chives

Sear the omelette on the griddle pan on both sides.

On a rectangular plate, place the hot omelette and make 5 dots of fennel gel, finish with 3 dill sprouts, 2 tarragon sprouts, 2 chervil sprouts, and some chives.

SQUAB WITH ANCHOVIES

SERVES 8 PEOPLE

COMPOSITION
Squab breasts
Anchovy emulsion
Blackberry coulis
Black olive oil
Blackberry drupelets
Squab sauce

—SQUAB BREASTS
YIELDS 8 BREAST FILLETS

4 squab breasts
Brine for meat (basic recipes, p.429)
Extra virgin olive oil

Soak the squab breasts in brine for
10 minutes. Place a perforated tray on top
of a normal tray. Arrange the breasts on it
and cover with cling film. Make a small hole
to introduce sawdust smoke with a smoking
gun. Lastly, cover the hole and leave to smoke
refrigerated for 2 hours.

Next, seal the breasts with oil in a vacuum
pack bag and cook in the Roner at 63°C/145°F
for 22 minutes. Remove, blast chill and reserve
refrigerated.

—ANCHOVY EMULSION
YIELDS 130 G

50 g anchovies
50 g anchovy oil
30 g water

Blend anchovy fillets into a very smooth paste,
add the oil slowly while blending and, lastly,
add the water to make an emulsion. Strain
and reserve.

—BLACKBERRY COULIS
YIELDS 154 G

125 g fresh blackberries
0.4 g xanthan gum
50 g extra virgin olive oil

Blend blackberries and run the resulting purée
through a fine chinois. Add the xanthan gum
and mix well. Lastly, emulsify with the olive oil
and reserve the resulting sauce.

—BLACK OLIVE OIL
YIELDS 120 G

100 g sunflower oil
20 g dehydrated black olives

Blend the sunflower oil and black olives well
into a black and smooth oil.

—BLACKBERRY DRUPELETS
YIELDS 20 G

4 blackberries

Freeze blackberries. When frozen, place them
between two sheets of greaseproof paper
and crush with a rolling pin to separate the
drupelets. Reserve.

—SQUAB SAUCE
YIELDS 180 G

1.25 kg squab carcases
20 g extra virgin olive oil
160 g mirepoix (basic recipes, p.427)
1.25 kg water
24 g kuzu thickening agent (basic recipes,
        p.427)
25 g butter
Salt

Brown the carcases in oil and add the mirepoix.
Cover them with cold water and cook for
3 hours. Next, strain the stock and reduce
to 150 g.

Bring to a boil and add the kuzu mixture, finish
with the butter and, if necessary, adjust salt.
Strain and reserve.

GARNISHING AND PLATING

Anchovies
Black truffle julienne
Beetroot sprouts

Regenerate the squab breast fillet in the Roner
at 63°C/145°F. Remove from bag and sear
the skin on the griddle pan until brown. Leave
to stand for 2 minutes on the salamander.

On a dinner plate, alternate some dots of
blackberry coulis with some of the anchovy
emulsion, squab sauce and black olive oil.
Set a few blackberry drupelets and 2 anchovy
squares. Finish by serving the squab breast
with the black truffle julienne on top and some
beetroot sprouts around it.

N

—BOLDNESS

N

—BOLDNESS

According to the Roca brothers

One of the bases of creation is to break away from the expected. It is also resisting what seems predictable, the constant struggle against boring the spectator, the observer, and the diner with the sensation that everything they see in front of them follows a specific, immutable order. This is where boldness must win the game. To dare is to defy and offer a challenge to pre-established laws. The acrobat who walks the tight rope between two buildings knows there is only one certain ending: ahead are emptiness, falling and failure. But is it the only ending? If nobody had ever carried out such a risky and senseless act, what would the acrobat achieve other than proving he can do it? Nothing, except proving it; showing there was another possibility against all odds and the law of gravity. The boldness of acknowledging danger and preventing it from swallowing you up.

Such actions, applied to the kitchen, respond to an intuitive mechanism that can only be conceived from the generosity of unbridled passion. It is the desire to go boldly, a path that is not marked, which has no landmarks or signposts, a path that moves away from convention. If there is an indication that there must be a harmonious whole, why not try to synthesize chaos and in an almost circus-like act, commit the 'crime' of making it even more difficult : to teach that anarchy can also be a scheduled movement?

At El Celler boldness means letting go, giving an example of generosity, the desire to flirt with the absurd so that there is always proof that even poor balance is a source of knowledge.

The adage for an entrepreneur is: 'if it cannot be done, do it. If you don't, it doesn't exist.' Refusal inspires action. The challenge is to transform a 'no' into a 'yes'. Boldness means to avoid the most accepted base of knowledge. Knowledge comes from the past, and this is why it's safe and verifiable. Experience is just the opposite of daring creativity. We can resort to experience, but we must adapt it to new challenges, new solutions. We must open our minds and take risks by going to the limits of the ethical code, which makes us feel alive and consistent with an avant-garde philosophy. *Boldness* is to add a pinch of salt and a pile of acid when cooking. If there were no ethical boundaries, a dish like the BLOODY OF MARY (an underground dish rumoured to have been eaten or drank late at night at El Celler...) would be offered in the menu.

What is the acceptable creative limit for a diner? We have heard Ferran Adrià state in conferences after returning from China: "there are no weird foods, there are only weird people!" It is a way to explain clearly and overtly the influence of cultural eating habits in the human race through the years. From habit, we can eat rabbit with snails, a traditional dish in Catalonia that would probably not become popular among Anglo-Saxons. Just like many people would have a hard time eating the popular Icelandic hákarl, a shark-based dish cured by a fermentation method rich in uric acid, which the natives advise to wolf down with your nose covered to try to avoid its strong smell of ammonia. Escamoles, giant black ant larvae—*Liometopum apiculatum*—considered a luxury in the state of Hidalgo, Mexico, might also be hard to swallow. And crickets on a stick can seem an extreme frivolity if our mind is not open to this common snack in Beijing or Bangkok. There is nothing odd, then, in their cuisine, but in the different cultures and established prejudices when eating. However, dishes should not necessarily lead to a pompous transgression in order to show boldness. We don't need to ask our customers to take leaps in the dark against their will. Boldness can also be shown by the simple but transgressive act of serving a suquet of fish without the fish... Along these lines, we recall the fun and contrasting CUBAN RICE AND CURRY CHICKEN served at El Bulli.

We open the door to boldness once in a while. For no reason. Only because we want our troublemaking and mischievous spirit to stay alive. To show that cooking can also offer extreme dishes such as the daring OYSTER AND SOIL, the radical ANARCHY, the fantastic TREASURE ISLAND, the WINE ON A PLATE AND DESSERT IN A GLASS or the PEDRO XIMÉNEZ DISTILLATE IN TWO SERVINGS: BODY AND SOUL.

OYSTER AND SOIL is an important act of boldness, but also a way to reconstruct a basic surf 'n' turf. Surf 'n' turf to the maximum power, done like never before. To eat soil without the feel of soil but with the emotional shock of a familiar aroma with a fluid and clear appearance, astonishing. A minimalist and poetic vision that has gained both passionate supporters and critics. In an opera performance at La Scala in Milan in which he had participated, artist Franc Aleu celebrated the fact that people whistled and clapped at the same time. Its success consisted of provoking and stirring up debate, acknowledgement and controversy because of the daring path it had taken. It is the same for us.

ANARCHY, one of the most radical desserts ever seen, originated as a reaction by Jordi. He was annoyed by having to justify each dish or every move of an ingredient in a dish. The boldness of the dessert ANARCHY lies in the thought that knowledge is in the past, is obsolete, and that there is no need to justify everything. A surprising, mysterious dish, experimentation with chance, without obstacles or prejudices. Everything is possible. An orgy of flavours, in the shortest amount of time in the mouth. Flavours to the limit, fitting to large celebrations, lunatics, the daring and the brave. Everybody having a separate experience but sharing the fascination of each bite. To celebrate with anticipation a quick journey to a place where habits aren't stored away, they are blurred. The game of anarchy. Liberating happiness.

With the Rotaval we have defied the limits of flavour and experimented with volatile elements, the results trapped in the flask. Moulds that break when introducing a wine like Pedro Ximénez VORS in a bottle split in half; an iodine-coloured wine we place in the flask, distil, and whose vapour and alcohol we use to make a grappa of Pedro Ximénez and serve it with alcohol-free wine: body and soul of a wine at the table, in two servings. Boldness.

Boldness will persist in our creative spirit like the tide that bathes the Rocas. Because if we don't make it, it will not exist.

In the dining room...

Josep has combined two wines in one glass. If a cocktail is allowed, why not a wine cocktail? In ANGEL BY THIERRY MUGLER, he was surprised by Jordi combining toffee, roses, violets and berry compote with vanilla in one dish. There was not a single wine that had all of that, so Josep put together a Mataró wine from Alella (that provided wooden, vanilla and berry notes) and a Gewürztraminer (aromatic, floral, surprising). Until he discovered the Moscato Rosa of Alto Adige, made by a winemaker from Northern Italy, and another black Muscatel from California. That is, red wines from a black Muscatel grape!

There is also boldness in the harmony of some specific products such as truffle with tea. A truffle soufflé, for example, is so ethereal, subtle and delicate that the hardness and alcohol of the wine produce extremely marked feelings of corrosion. In this case, the dish can be combined with fifteen, twenty or thirty year-old teas from China and Taiwan, aged in caves, which contribute to an earthy and ethereal harmony.

The WINE ON A PLATE AND DESSERT IN A GLASS is boldness in the dining room, as Josep explains: "I brought my brothers a Beerenauslese wine (of very late harvest) of a Riesling grape with very low natural alcohol content in a soup dish. I told them: 'try this soup'. I surprised them by having them drink and eat a wine at the same time. This brought about the idea of making sorbets only adding xanthan gum and breaking all the preconceptions about sorbets, while keeping the purity of wine at its highest.
It is the boldness that comes from cooking with wine and wine in gastronomy."

OYSTER AND SOIL

SERVES 4 PEOPLE

COMPOSITION
Oyster
Soil distillate

—OYSTER

4 oysters

Open the oysters and remove them from their shell carefully. Remove the beard with a paring knife and reserve refrigerated until plating.

—SOIL DISTILLATE
YIELDS 430 G

300 g soil
500 g water
0.2 g xanthan gum
Salt

Mix soil and water, cover the container and infuse for 12 hours refrigerated.

Introduce the infusion in the evaporating flask with a 0.22 μm sterilisation membrane filter between the flask and the outlet towards the cooler. Distil the soil at 30-35°C/86-95°F (bath temperature) for 1-2 hours, and finish at 40-45°C/104-113°F for 30 minutes. Remove the distillate and seal it in a vacuum pack bag to conserve its aroma. To keep it for days or weeks, freezing is recommended.

When plating, thicken the distillate with xanthan gum and adjust salt.

GARNISHING AND PLATING

Place the oyster in the middle of the plate and pour soil distillate on it.

ANARCHY

"The idea came to me one day when Joan and Pitu [Josep] were talking about a dish of avocados, about the reason for each element to be in the dish, its concept, doing a comprehensive analysis of the reasons behind choosing one thing or another… At that moment, I thought: why not make something to prove that it isn't always necessary to give a specific meaning
to a dish or a combination of flavours? ANARCHY is rebelling against order, leaving the concept open to the perception of each individual diner."

JORDI ROCA

COMPOSITION
Creams
Jellies
Sauces
Spheres
Sponge cakes
Crisps
Ice creams

—CREAMS
Vanilla, green cardamom, white cardamom, milk chocolate, 70% chocolate, Sichuan pepper, pink pepper, Javanese long pepper, green tea, white tea, bitter almonds, cumin, curry, liquorice.

—JELLIES
Campari, orange blossom, rose, coffee, rum.

—SAUCES
Basil, mint, strawberry, fennel, tarragon, cocoa, dulce de leche, violet jam, jasmine jam.

—SPHERES
Saffron, sheep milk, chocolate.

—SPONGE CAKES
Chocolate, vanilla, citrus fruits, pistachio, muffin.

—CRISPS
Cocoa, milk, pistachio, chocolate, toasted corn.

—ICE CREAMS
Yogurt, ginger, honey, Chartreuse.

GARNISHING AND PLATING

Flowers
Leaves
Sprouts

Assembling this dish should stay true to its name: without a pre-established order and a composition that changes with the passage of time and the changing seasons. It is therefore impossible to pin it down in time and describe it in detail. That would be going against its essence. From one day to the next, its ingredients may change depending on their availability, but there should always be a vast variety of processes, flavour contrasts, plays of textures, and chromatic richness.

FIGS WITH BARIDÀ CHEESE

SERVES 8 PEOPLE

COMPOSITION

Baridà cheese cream
Fig purée
Fig seeds
Guava gel
Asparagus and rocket air
Fig sorbet
Baridà coating

—BARIDÀ CHEESE CREAM
YIELDS 270 G

150 g Baridà cheese (Alt Urgell)
150 g cream

Cut the cheese into small cubes, reserve.

Boil the cream and pour it over the cheese, leave the mixture to stand and use a hand blender to make a thick cream. Strain and blend again if necessary. Reserve.

—FIG PURÉE
YIELDS 480 G

500 g fresh figs
1.7 g agar-agar

Peel figs, discard their skin and purée the pulp. Run through a very fine sieve to separate the seeds and reserve them in a separate container. In a separate container, mix the seedless purée with the agar-agar. Bring the mixture to a boil and leave to cool to solidify. When it sets, mash it with a hand blender to a fine purée. Reserve.

—FIG SEEDS

Fig seeds (from previous purée)

Clean the seeds well to remove any pulp left. Place them in the dehydrator at 60°C/140°F. When dry, toast them lightly on the salamander. Reserve.

—GUAVA GEL
YIELDS 580 G

250 g guava purée
35 g inverted sugar syrup
35 g glucose
7.5 g apple pectin
250 g sugar
7 g citric acid

Mix the purée and inverted sugar syrup, glucose and pectin; bring to a boil and then add the sugar, previously mixed with the citric acid. Stir to prevent lumps from forming and boil to 104°C/219°F. Leave to cool and transfer the gel into piping bags.

—ASPARAGUS AND ROCKET AIR
YIELDS 250 G

500 g asparagus
250 g rocket
2.5 g soy lecithin
1.5 g sucroester
Salt

Blanch the asparagus and rocket separately, cool and liquefy each ingredient.

Mix the rocket and asparagus juices with the soy lecithin and sucroester. Adjust salt and reserve.

—FIG SORBET

YIELDS 1.2 KG

150 g sugar
0.6 g sorbet stabiliser
150 g water
38 g dextrose
25 g glucose powder
13 g inverted sugar syrup
800 g fig purée

Mix the stabiliser with a pinch of sugar from the recipe. Reserve.

Mix the water with the remaining ingredients except the fig purée and heat to 50°C/122°F; then, add the sugar and stabiliser mixture reserved previously, mixing with a hand blender to eliminate any lumps. Pasteurize this sorbet base to 85°C/185°F, strain and cool. Leave to ripen refrigerated for 24 hours.

The following day, blend the fig purée with the sorbet base and run through the ice-cream maker; when the sorbet achieves the desired texture, place in piping bags and fill some moulds shaped like figs made with liquid silicone (see process on page 429). Reserve in the freezer for 2 hours until they take the shape of the mould.

Next, remove the figs from the mould and stick a needle in them. Keep them in the freezer until coating.

—BARIDÀ CHEESE COATING

YIELDS 400 G

300 g milk
150 g Baridà cheese (Alt Urgell)
4.5 g agar-agar
2.5 gelatine sheets

Grate cheese and reserve in a container. Boil milk and pour it over the grated cheese. Leave to stand for 15 minutes and blend to eliminate any lumps. When cold, run through a strainer and add the agar-agar; boil the mixture and, when it has been removed from the heat, add the gelatine sheets, previously hydrated.

Coat the sorbet figs with this mixture and place them again in the freezer.

GARNISHING AND PLATING

Cut the frozen figs in half and reserve.

In the middle of the plate, serve a spoonful of fig purée, half a frozen fig on top, and some dots of Baridà cream on the side.

Using the hand blender, air the asparagus and rocket mixture and place three spoonfuls around the fig. finish with some dots of guava gel and sprinkle some fig seeds.

TREASURE ISLAND

SERVES 4 PEOPLE

COMPOSITION
Oyster
Woodcock gravy
Woodcock bath
Soil foam
Sea stock
Ink sand

—OYSTER

4 Gillardeau no. 1 oysters

Open oysters with a paring knife; remove the beard and save their water. Reserve cold.

—WOODCOCK GRAVY
YIELDS 200 G

1.25 kg woodcock bones
30 g extra virgin olive oil
100 g mirepoix (basic recipes, p.427)
1.25 kg water
15 g woodcock liver
20 g extra virgin olive oil
25 g butter

Brown woodcock bones well in a stockpot with the 30 g of olive oil and then add the mirepoix. Cover with water and cook for 2 ½ hours.

Strain the stock and reduce to 200 g of woodcock gravy.

Sauté woodcock livers with the 20 g olive oil, add to the gravy and blend. Run the liquid through a fine chinois, add the butter and bind. Reserve.

—WOODCOCK BATH

YIELDS 200 G

150 g woodcock gravy (previously prepared)
50 g chicken stock (basic recipes, p.427)
2 g carrageenan

Mix gravy and stock well when cold, together
with the carrageenan. Introduce the mixture in
a saucepan and bring to a boil. Reserve to coat
the oysters.

—SOIL FOAM

YIELDS 350 G

350 g soil distillate (basic recipes, p.428)
½ gelatine sheet
3 g egg white powder

Hydrate gelatine in iced water, drain well
and heat to 35°C/95°F with 30 g soil distillate.
When dissolved, mix it with the remaining
distillate and add the egg white powder.
Transfer into a ½ litre whipped cream
dispenser and add 2 chargers. Reserve.

—SEA STOCK

YIELDS 200 G

500 g purple basil
300 g mineral water
50 g kombu seaweed
100 g oyster water
1.5 g agar-agar

Blanch basil leaves in abundant boiling water
with salt for 10 seconds. Remove and cool in
iced water. When cold, remove from the water
and dry with kitchen towels. Reserve.

In a casserole, place the mineral water and
kombu seaweed and bring to a boil. Cover and
infuse for 30 minutes. Strain and cool.

Blend blanched basil leaves with the kombu
water, strain through a fine chinois, applying
pressure to extract as much of the liquid
as possible, and add to the oyster water,
previously strained. Leave to cool.

Mix 200 g basil water with agar-agar and bring
to a boil (skim if necessary). Serve some water on
a plate and cover it with a circle of greaseproof
paper of the same size as the plate. When it
comes into contact with the water, the paper
will wrinkle and create the illusion of sea waves
on the surface of the jelly as it cools down.

—INK SAND

YIELDS 250 G

100 g butter
10 g squid ink
120 g flour
15 g sugar
3 g salt

Mix the softened butter and the squid ink.

In a separate bowl mix the flour, sieved, with
the salt and sugar, and add the mixture to the
butter preparation, stirring well until the dough
is smooth. Place the dough on cling film, stretch
and roll tightly to make a compact roll. Freeze.

Grate the frozen dough with a Microplane over a
baking sheet lined with greaseproof paper, and
bake at 180°C/356°F for 15 minutes. Remove
from the oven and cool. Chop with a knife if
necessary, and store in an airtight container.

GARNISHING AND PLATING

Purple shiso

Use a toothpick to help immerse the oyster in
the hot woodcock stock 3-4 times until forming
a coating approximately 2 mm thick.

Serve on the plate containing the sea stock.
Cover the oyster with soil distillate foam and
this, in turn, with squid ink sand. Garnish by
sticking a few leaves of purple shiso in it.

WINE ON A PLATE AND DESSERT IN A GLASS

SERVES 8 PEOPLE

COMPOSITION
Wine compote
Wine sorbet
Citrus and honey infusion
Basil and mint infusion
Berry infusion

—WINE COMPOTE
YIELDS 350 G

350 g Riesling (2002 Oestrich Lenchen
      Beerenauslese, VDP Rheingau, by Peter
      Jakob Kühn)
1 g xanthan gum

Emulsify the wine and xanthan gum with
a hand blender. Transfer the mixture into
an airtight container and remove the air by
activating the vacuum sealer repeatedly until
it turns clear. Reserve.

—WINE SORBET
YIELDS 400 G

400 g Riesling (2002 Oestrich Lenchen
      Beerenauslese, VDP Rheingau, by Peter
      Jakob Kühn)
0.7 g xanthan gum

Emulsify the wine and xanthan gum with a
hand blender. Run the mixture through the ice-
cream maker and reserve at -18°C/0°F.

—CITRUS AND HONEY INFUSION
YIELDS 160 G

100 g orange juice
50 g lemon juice
30 g honey
1 lemon peel
1 orange peel
0.2 g xanthan gum

Heat the orange and lemon juices with honey
and the peel of one orange and one lemon.
Strain the mixture and add the xanthan gum
before emulsifying with the hand blender.
Introduce the mixture into an airtight container
and remove the air by activating the vacuum
sealer repeatedly until it turns clear. Reserve.

—BASIL AND MINT INFUSION
YIELDS 200 G

25 g mint
125 g water used for blanching mint
25 g basil
125 g water used for blanching basil
20 g sugar
0.1 g xanthan gum

Heat the water in a stockpot and blanch the
mint leaves for 20 seconds; remove and cool
in iced water. In a separate container, cool the
indicated amount of blanching water. When
cold, mix the water and mint in the Thermomix
and blend to a very fine liquid; strain. It yields
100 g of mint water.

Repeat the same process to make 100 g of
basil water.

First, heat 50 g of the mint water with sugar
and then add the rest of the liquids together
with the xanthan gum, and emulsify with
a hand blender. Transfer the mixture to an
airtight container and remove the air by
activating the vacuum sealer repeatedly until
it turns clear. Reserve.

—BERRY INFUSION
YIELDS 200 G

200 g berries
20 g sugar

Seal both ingredients in a vacuum pack bag
and cook in the Roner at 80°C/176°F for 1 hour.
Strain and reserve the resulting liquid.

GARNISHING AND PLATING

Pineapple sage flowers
Apricot sage flowers
Fennel sprouts
Mint sprouts
Basil sprouts

In a bowl, serve a spoonful of wine compote with a quenelle of wine sorbet on top.

Next to it in a wine glass, serve a spoonful of citrus and honey infusion; on top and carefully to prevent the soups from mixing, serve the berry infusion. Lastly, pour the mint and basil infusion on top. The three superimposed layers are later mixed in the mouth. Garnish with flowers and sprouts on the surface.

O

—MAGIC

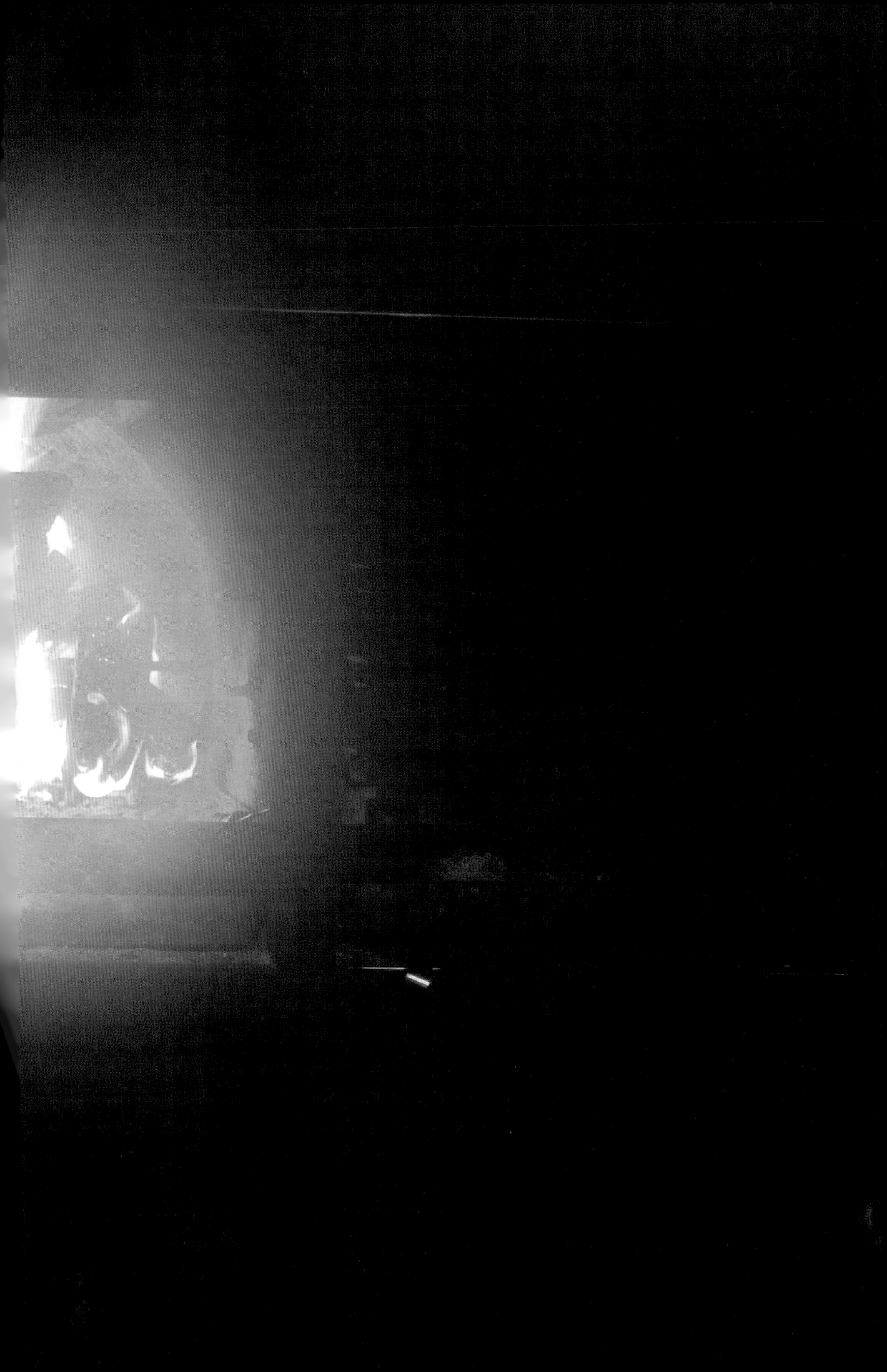

—MAGIC

It has been said that ten percent of magic is the trick, the technique. The rest, the remaining ninety per cent, is based on the ability to create an illusion, the ability to make others believe in something that isn't there. Sharing a stage—and rightly so, as El Celler is a theatre where the full production takes place—are those who try to amaze and those open to amazement. Behind this symbiosis is the secret of pleasure, in the shared will to make the show possible and watch the performance while aware of witnessing an ephemeral event that will end up being embedded in our memories.

Magic is the catalyst of this formula. The customer gives time and receives happiness. The Roca brothers agree to the idea and offer a conjuror's trick in exchange for the generosity of those who step away from convention and wish to catch a few moments of a gift that won't wither. The trade is enjoyable because both the seducer and the seduced win. Throughout the gastronomic process and, particularly, under the light in the dining room when each act meant to dazzle takes place. It's something of an Epiphany, a discovery, going beyond the limits. The rules of physics, or what we try to understand, are dissolved when a liquid becomes solid right in front of your astonished eyes. You shouldn't try to discover the mechanisms of the magic trick, but let yourself be carried by the shared will to participate.

Magic as a synonym for explosion, for astonishment.
A bubble we inhabit through the duration of the show
—a lasting moment.

According to the Roca brothers

A wise saying is that science is wonderful if you don't have to make a living from it. We, who approach it from the back door, approach it innocently. For cooks, science is an open door to empirical knowledge. Science excites us because it allows us to redefine, question, parody and find new ways of seeing things. It facilitates our continuation in the research of products and forms. What we want is to find out more in order to provide as many of our own original answers as we can. The relationship between art, craft and science has existed since time immemorial. They are absolute complementary concepts, beyond any discrepancies or controversy. And it is thanks to science, the transformations it lets us carry out, trying out construction and deconstruction, and pure alchemy that we end up submerged in a true game of magic. Both for us, as the curious and daring researchers, as well as for our customers, who participate in the staging and watch the show. And they end up eating the product of the magic; a privilege unlike that of traditional magic acts.

We like to have the chance to show a deep glass dish with cling film stretched over it like a drum, over which we place a quenelle of parmentier with floating baby octopuses: the pressure of the spoon on the food magically raises the rings of smoke, scented of smoked paprika, hidden underneath. Or have the diners return to their childhood, when they played with Plasticine, that are now silicon moulds to make ice cream and structures from delicious imaginable and imitated forms (figs, walnuts, St. George's mushrooms, truffles, penny buns, tangerines,...). Even to take advantage of an instant of icy friction to create a solid and growing stalactite right in front of the diner.

The word *magic* is a fantastic word. Magic symbolises pleasant surprises, and the dishes that have made magic are not always the most imaginative or the most spectacular. Often, we find magic in simplicity and modesty. We create magic from implying or appealing to primal feelings like tenderness. We strive fully to create the emotional charge that can come from an instant of magic.

In the dining room...

There is magic in the new Celler because its surroundings make it possible. When it's dark, the fascinating play of mirrors lets our diners discover something interesting wherever they look. That is where luxury in the cuisine of the future lies: in entertainment, fun, movement, staging, acting, the theatrical approach of the play.

The perfect combination of external and internal stimuli generated by food constitutes yet another fragment of magic. It's like the moment of silence. And the proper tempo in which each act and each scene are performed. Or the ability to create a dramatic effect followed or preceded by subtle surprises, controlled emotions, hints caught in the air...

EUCALYPTUS

SERVES 8 PEOPLE

COMPOSITION
Avocado cream
Lime sauce
Chartreuse candies
Eucalypt leaf distillate
Green shiso sugar
Basil jelly
Granny Smith apple cubes

—AVOCADO CREAM
YIELDS 400 G

300 g avocado
75 g sugar
40 g lemon juice

Mix the ingredients in a container and blend to a smooth and sticky cream. Reserve well covered to prevent it from oxidizing quickly.

—LIME SAUCE
YIELDS 500 G

125 g water
125 g sugar
2 lime peels
5 g agar-agar
250 g lime juice

Boil the water with sugar and infuse the lime peel for a few minutes. Strain and add the agar-agar; bring to a boil and remove from heat. Lastly, add the lime juice and leave the mixture to cool and solidify. When solid, use a hand blender to liquidise to a silky cream.

—CHARTREUSE CANDIES
YIELDS 40 UNITS

40 g water
120 g sugar
25 g green Chartreuse
Cornflour

Make syrup with the water and sugar, and bring to 109°C/228°F. Remove from the heat and let the temperature drop slightly. Very carefully add the green Chartreuse. Ideally, the syrup should be transferred slowly, letting it slide through the sides of the casserole into the container with the liquor and back, until both liquids and both densities integrate. Reserve.

Spread cornflour on a baking sheet and leave to dry at 80°C/176°F for a few hours. Press, smooth and create small holes to fill with the syrup and Chartreuse mixture. Sprinkle the surface lightly with some dry cornflour and bake for 24 hours at approximately 40°C/104°F.

Next, remove the candies from the cornflour, brush them clean and reserve.

—EUCALYPT LEAF DISTILLATE
YIELDS 1 KG

1 kg water
200 g fresh eucalypt leaves

Break leaves and mix them with water; place the mixture in the Rotaval and distil at 40°C/104°F, until all the water decants into the receiving flask. Reserve in bottles in the freezer at -5°C/23°F.

—GREEN SHISO SUGAR
YIELDS 30 G

15 green shiso sprouts
15 g sugar

Place both ingredients in the Thermomix and crush to a smooth mixture. Store this sugar covered to keep its aroma.

—BASIL JELLY
YIELDS 120 G

50 g basil
250 g blanching water
20 g sugar
2 g agar-agar

Heat the water in a pot and blanch the basil leaves in it for 20 seconds; remove and cool in iced water. In a separate container, cool the indicated amount of blanching water.

Place the basil and 250 g of blanching water in the Thermomix and blend to a very fine liquid; strain. Mix half of the resulting basil water with the agar-agar and sugar and bring to a boil. Next, mix it with the other half of the reserved water and transfer it to a container to solidify. When solid, blend it well to a very fine purée.

—GRANNY SMITH APPLE CUBES

1 Granny Smith apple
100 g lime juice

Peel the apple and cut it into 1 cm cubes. Submerge the cubes in the lime juice and reserve.

GARNISHING AND PLATING

Green shiso sprouts
Melon slices

Prepare a container with liquid nitrogen and immerse the melon slices and the green shiso sprouts in it for a few seconds.

In a soup bowl, arrange a spoonful of avocado cream, a few dots of lime sauce, 3 Chartreuse candies, 3 dots of basil gel, a pinch of shiso sugar, a few cubes of Granny Smith apple, and lastly, 1 thin slice of melon and about 8 sprouts of frozen shiso over the cream and candies.

To finish, pour some eucalypt distillate at -5°C/23°F on top of the melon, and the frozen shiso to form a distillate stalagmite.

FROM SOLID TO LIQUID

The change from solid to liquid takes place at the fusion point, but the change from liquid to solid requires a specific order: first, it is necessary to bring the liquid to freezing temperature until an ice crystal appears and acts as a trigger. In this instance, those triggers are the melon and shiso leaves at -18°C /0°F.

This is why it is common to keep liquids below the freezing point but without freezing. The lower the temperature of the liquid and the ice crystal acting as a catalyser are, the faster the freezing effect takes place.

FLOWER BOMB

SERVES 8 PEOPLE

COMPOSITION
Blown sugar sphere
Rose foam
Camomile sorbet
Violet preserve
Honey jelly
Violet sugar candyfloss

—ROSE FOAM
YIELDS 650 G

500 g cream
100 g egg yolks
30 g sugar
40 g rose water

Prepare some custard by heating the cream. Mix the yolks with sugar separately and then pour them onto the cream. Stir the mixture until it reaches 85°C/185°F. Remove from heat, strain and add the rose water. Reserve the cream refrigerated for 12 hours before transferring it into a whipped cream dispenser.

—BLOWN SUGAR SPHERE
YIELDS 20 SPHERES

500 g sugar
70 g water
100 g liquid glucose
20 drops of 50% citric acid and water solution

In a casserole, bring the water and sugar to a boil. When the boiling starts, add liquid glucose and let it boil without stirring. Continue cooking at 158°C/316°F, remove from heat and add 20 drops of a 50% solution of citric acid and water. Reserve the mixture for 1 minute, heating it lightly to remove the caramel from the saucepan, and then pour it over a silicone mat. While still hot, pull the sugar 15-20 times to distribute the small air bubbles inside, give it a satin colour, and make the blowing uniform.

Use a pair of scissors to cut the caramel and reserve the slices in an airtight container with silica gel to prevent moisture. To shape the caramel, an appropriate light is needed to facilitate working with the sugar. Soften the caramel under the heat lamp, insert an air pump into it, and blow to form a ball as spherical as possible. Detach the sphere from the air pump by heating the metallic part with a blow torch; at the same time, heat a tube with the blow torch to puncture a hole in the base of the sphere. Reserve.

—CAMOMILE SORBET
YIELDS 950 G

750 g water
20 g inverted sugar syrup
5 g camomile
200 g sugar
40 g glucose powder
36 g dextrose
5 g sorbet stabiliser

Heat the water, inverted sugar and camomile. Before it comes to a boil, add the rest of the dry ingredients, previously mixed together, and increase the temperature to 85°C/185°F. Leave the mixture to ripen, strain and run it through the ice-cream maker. Reserve at -18°C/0°F.

—VIOLET PRESERVE
YIELDS 200 G

100 g water
100 g sugar
20 g fresh violets
10 g pectin

Boil the water, violets and 75 g of sugar.

In a separate container, mix the remaining 25 g of sugar with the pectin and slowly add them to the mixture, stirring constantly. Reduce it to the texture of marmalade, aware that it will thicken as it cools down.

—HONEY JELLY
YIELDS 120 G

100 g water
50 g honey
1 g agar-agar

Heat all the ingredients together, stirring constantly, and bring to a boil. Pour the mixture into a tray to make a thin sheet of jelly. Let it cool before cutting.

—VIOLET SUGAR CANDYFLOSS

50 g violet sugar

Before serving, run the sugar through the candyfloss machine.

GARNISHING AND PLATING

Lychees
Flowers: pansy, sage, mallow, marigold...

Turn the sphere upside down and fill it first with the flowers, then a quenelle of camomile sorbet, the honey jelly, some chopped lychees, violet preserve and rose foam. Serve the sphere enveloped by violet sugar candyfloss.

CHARCOAL-GRILLED PENNY BUN ICE CREAM

SERVES 8 PEOPLE

COMPOSITION

Preserved penny bun carpaccio
Penny bun oil
Charcoal-grilled penny bun ice
  cream
Caramel sphere

—PRESERVED PENNY BUN CARPACCIO
YIELDS 120 G

200 g penny buns (*Boletus edulis*)
200 g extra virgin olive oil

Clean the fresh penny buns and cook them
submerged in oil until soft.

Drain any excess oil and freeze them
separately to keep their shape. Before serving,
use a meat slicer to cut them into very
fine slices.

—PENNY BUN OIL
YIELDS 300 G

10 penny buns (*Boletus edulis*)
300 g sunflower oil
100 g penny bun powder

Clean penny buns and cut them into thick
slices. Brown on both sides in a frying pan with
some sunflower oil. When brown,
add the remaining oil and cook on low heat
for 2 hours at 70°C/158°F. Remove from heat,
add the penny bun powder and blend. Run
through a fine chinois and blast chill. Reserve
refrigerated and sealed.

—CHARCOAL-GRILLED
PENNY BUN ICE CREAM
YIELDS 1 KG

150 g penny buns (*Boletus edulis*)
462 g whole milk
124 g cream (35% fat)
54 g skimmed milk powder
176 g dextrose
20 g sugar
6 g salt
4 g ice-cream stabiliser

Sauté penny buns and infuse them
with half the milk; when the infusion reaches
60°C/140°F, add the remaining liquids,
milk powder, dextrose, sugar, salt and ice
cream stabiliser. Pasteurise the mixture at
85°C/185°F, blend with a hand blender and
leave to ripen refrigerated for 12 hours. Next,
strain, run through the ice-cream maker and
store at -15°C/5°F.

—CARAMEL SPHERE
YIELDS 220 G

100 g fondant
67 g isomalt
67 g glucose
5 drops of 50% citric acid and water solution

Caramelise the sugars until they reach
150°C/302°F, add the citric acid and increase
their temperature to 160°C/320°F. Spread
the caramel on a silicone mat and pull
15-20 times to satin and distribute the heat.
Cut the caramel while it's still hot and form
2 g balls.

Soften one of the caramel balls under a heat
lamp, heat the tip of the air pump, insert it into
the sphere, and blow to the desired shape and
size, keeping the layer of caramel as thin as
possible. Reserve in a moisture-free cupboard
or an airtight container with silica gel.

GARNISHING AND PLATING

Toasted pine kernels
Salt

Arrange some penny bun slices in the middle.
Season the carpaccio with penny bun oil and
salt. Cut some toasted pine kernels in half
and place them on the slices of mushroom.
Set a ball of penny bun ice cream on top.
Using a smoking gun and sawdust, fill the
caramel sphere with smoke and set it on top
of the ice cream.

BABY OCTOPUSES
SMOKED WITH PAPRIKA

COMPOSITION
Baby octopuses
Squid chessboard
Ink oil

—BABY OCTOPUSES

16 baby octopuses
Brine for fish (basic recipes, p.429)
Extra virgin olive oil

Clean the baby octopuses, submerge them
in brine for 2 minutes. Remove from the water,
dry well and sauté in a frying pan with olive oil.
Serve immediately.

—SQUID CHESSBOARD

2 squids
Spanish smoked paprika from La Vera

Clean squids well, remove their skin
and cut lengthwise into 0.5-cm-wide strips.

Sieve the smoked paprika over the squid strips
and roll them with cling film, forming a cylinder
no thicker than 4 cm. Freeze.

With a meat slicer, cut 1-mm-thick discs and
reserve refrigerated until serving.

—INK OIL
YIELDS 60 G

1 garlic clove
10 g extra virgin olive oil
5 g flour
50 g water
5 g squid ink

Chop and fry the garlic clove in olive oil, add
the flour and make a roux. Add the water
and squid ink and bring to a boil. Remove from
the heat, run through a fine chinois before
reserving in pipettes.

—PREPARING THE DISH

4 glass bowls
Spanish smoked paprika from La Vera
Cling film

Set a spoonful of smoked paprika in a bowl.
Cover the bowl with cling film, tightening (the
plastic must be smooth and imperceptible).
With a very hot skewer, cut any excess cling
film from the rim of the bowls and make a
small hole in the tense wrap to introduce the
smoke through it. Reserve the bowls with
the punctured cling film until serving.

GARNISHING AND PLATING
Potato purée (basic recipes, p.428)
50 g beech sawdust

Place a quenelle of potato purée and two discs
of squid chessboard on the cling film. On the
purée, arrange some freshly sautéed baby
octopuses. Draw a few dots of ink oil next to
the purée.

Lastly, using a smoking gun and beech
sawdust, introduce smoke through the hole
in the film.

smoke

**The creative sequence
around smoke by Jordi Roca**

Ice creams

J ordi Roca became deeply involved in ice-cream making techniques under the wing of the Sicilian Angelo Corvitto. One of the rules the master continuously repeats is that the work atmosphere has to be completely pure, as ice cream is an emulsion in which air is a very important ingredient. An ice cream is a sponge for scents. This golden rule is what sparked Jordi's imagination. What would happen if smoke was added in on purpose? Until then he had heard of tobacco-flavoured ice creams, made from an infusion, and thought that perhaps working with direct smoke would improve the final result. To carry out the first experiments he had to blow the smoke of a cigar directly into the ice-cream maker. He obtained satisfactory and surprising results, but also realised that the method was neither practical, nor good for his health.

With the help of his father, Jordi put together a **water pump** that blows smoke automatically without human intervention. On one end, it draws smoke directly from the cigar that hangs from it (joined hermetically by a balloon), and blows it into the ice-cream maker from the other end. The result of this new technique is the PARTAGÁS CIGAR SERIES D NO. 4 ICE CREAM in 2001, presented as a cylinder made of dark chocolate, filled with ice cream of a neutral base infused with Havana cigar smoke. This cigar, together with the MOJITO, would come to constitute the dessert named TRIP TO HAVANA (PAGE 306).

El Celler has included in its dishes fruits made of blown sugar, a very fragile product with a great degree of difficulty in the making that must be handled with extreme care. Once while making blown sugar apples, one of the fruits was overblown and became deformed, as well as too thin. As usual in creative processes, mistakes lead to new thoughts: what could go into that frail sugar bubble without moistening or breaking it? The answer was smoke.

From that point on, Jordi began to think about how this process could be carried out in a more practical way with such an oversized pump. He found the solution in a **mechanical pipe,** a device that smokes, with a fast and controlled combustion, and that offers the ability to introduce smoke into a caramel bubble. From the application of this new tool derived the CHARCOAL-GRILLED PENNY BUN ICE CREAM (PAGE 390), a penny bun carpaccio with a penny bun ice cream quenelle on top, which is brought to the table covered by a caramel bubble filled with fresh olive wood smoke. Thanks to this recipe, El Celler de Can Roca was awarded sixth place award for Dish of the Year at the Spanish conference Lo Mejor de la Gastronomía. It was the first of a series of dishes prepared around the same concept, like the SMOKED CUTTLEFISH TARTARE, the SARDINES MARINATED WITH CHARCOAL-GRILLED AUBERGINES, or the BABY OCTOPUSES SMOKED WITH PAPRIKA (PAGE 392).

Blown sugar

Embers

Sometimes returning to tradition serves as an inspiration to create new methods: once Jordi had experimented with different techniques to introduce smoke into his dishes, he took a look back at the embers of the past. What could result from capturing the smoke in a container and serving it directly to the diner? In an attempt to reproduce the smoky effect created when fat drips on glowing embers, he applied a controlled amount of oil drops. When enough smoke is produced, he quickly traps it inside a cover and covers the plate with it. It's a return to tradition. It's the origin of the LAMB WITH CHARCOAL-GRILLED PEPPER AND TOMATO, or the ANCHOVY ESCALIVADA (PAGE 120).

Volcano

But Jordi kept pondering on smoke and discovered the Volcano, a vaporiser that worked with air at a controlled temperature. A hot air current vaporised the active principles, as well as the aromas of herbs, spices, plants, flowers, seeds or resins. This scented air was stored in a container bag that could then be emptied on top of a product or a dish. The possibilities of this new utensil were put to the test, but in the end it was never used for the dishes of El Celler.

rocam-bolesc

The desserts of El Celler become ice cream

This was the origin of Rocambolesc, the ice-cream parlour that features the desserts of El Celler. The three brothers wanted to surprise the customer by introducing a moment of magic and unexpectedness at some point during the meal. To start, they needed a vehicle to carry out the delicacies, so they commissioned designer Andreu Carulla, responsible for a handful of containers and utensils used at the restaurant. Amongst his drawings was a collapsible cart full of drawers they loved and had them dreaming about the idea of going around Girona with the most emblematic desserts in the history of El Celler. They could see themselves driving down Rambla de la Llibertat or Plaça del Vi as salesmen of illusion, but they put their feet back on the ground when they found out that legislation would prevent them from selling food on the streets except during official holidays and sports events. They refused to give up on the project, so they started to seek alternatives for moving their products, and came up with a minimalist establishment where they can park the cart and that looks like some sort of garage. One step leads to the next and the question arises: why not open an ice-cream parlour based on the desserts of El Celler?

Rocambolesc is the democratisation of the desserts of the restaurant. Anyone can taste Jordi's creations at an affordable price, transformed into cones or terrines for take away. So, the LACTIC dessert becomes a sheep milk ice cream with sheep milk dulce de leche, guava preserve and candyfloss; the ORANGE chromatism took the shape of an orange and mandarine ice cream with orange segments, bladder cherry and crystallised passion fruit; and the BAKED APPLE (his mothers' recipe) was transformed into baked apple ice cream with butter biscuit and fresh and caramelised apple. The flavours will change with the season and surprise on special occasions, like Sant Jordi.

But they go a bit further. They want customers to participate in the excitement of creation and propose a LACTIC kit, consisting of sheep cottage cheese ice cream, vacuum-packed candyfloss and a piping bag with sheep dulce de leche, guava and sheep yogurt, to prepare at home following a simple set of instructions. As Jordi would say, *"We offer an Ikea-like game for desserts".*

Rocambolesc also sells an assortment of high-quality ice cream in basic flavours like vanilla and chocolate that let customers put their imagination to work by making their own combinations with the different toppings offered, called *additions*.

Sandra Tarruella is responsible for the interior design, which pays homage to old ice-cream parlours and the imaginary world of Willy Wonka in *Charlie and the Chocolate Factory*, or the comics of professor *Franz de Copenhague*. With a fun touch in every element, the front wall looks like the machine that is making the ice cream, covered with tubes, spirals, lights and gears surrounding the six levers that serve the soft product. The machinery behind it can churn ice cream on the spot to prevent ice from crystallising, therefore producing much creamier, freshly made ice cream. So the old cart that is also the counter and was used to display ice-cream containers in classic Italian ice-cream parlours, here is only used to keep the toppings. The side wall, with its display of toy tubes, becomes a dispenser for terrines, spoons and napkins. Many years ago, the dessert cart disappeared from El Celler as its sweet cuisine evolved into much more complex techniques and due to the need to finish each dish right before serving. But now, Rocambolesc brings back the spirit of that cart. *"We didn't bring back the cart, but the fascination about what is in it,"* explains Jordi.

P

—SENSE
OF HUMOUR

P

—SENSE OF HUMOUR

Aristotle said that the difference between man and animal is that the first has a sense of humour. And Rabelais spoke of the agelasts, those who are incapable of laughter. Later, Kundera returned to them by saying that "they think truth is clear, but are mistaken since man becomes an individual only when he loses the certainty of that truth". In other words, when we laugh we are wiser. Laughing entails not believing in absolute and eternal truths, it means admitting our own limitations, lying in wait for the undulations of life, as Montaigne suggested.

All of these reflections converge in part of the cuisine of El Celler, which does not see itself with the seriousness of those who believe themselves in possession of indestructible arguments, but of those who accept doubt as an unquestionable form of knowledge. To laugh is to let go, to remove oneself from convention, to practise the dynamics of intelligence that refer us to distant things, to acquire a different perspective. And laughing, exercising our sense of humour, is also sharing experiences, an invitation to play. To eat at El Celler is also to participate in a show not as spectators, but as part of the performance, also responsible for the party. It is to admit that, for a moment, you are the citizen of a country where rigidity is nonexistent and where the walls of convention are there to be breached. Humour equals involvement; it means to share a code that invites us to understand in order to let ourselves be astonished. This differentiates us as human beings. The ability to understand that the distance provided by laughter is not a separation, but an act that brings us closer to knowledge.

According to the Roca brothers

There is one dish that symbolises the sense of humour we share in our establishment: GOAL BY MESSI. It hopes to add a pleasant effect, after a long menu where rigour, sensuousness, sensibility, tradition, slow and deliberate creativity, respect for the product, 'techno-emotion' and intellectuality are stressed. GOAL BY MESSI symbolises the quest for the impossible, with a kind and fun face. It is an expression of joy, fun, surprise, radicalism, magic, games and smiles. It is an exciting, visual, acoustic and tasty laughter. Cooking must exist within the framework of transcendence, but this dessert emulates uninhibited relaxation. An absolute and jubilant expansion. The same feeling we get when Messi scores with Barça. That is why this dish is dedicated to him. Because we are his fans. Because he's our idol and we have his signed jersey as the main feature in our kitchen. Because he gives us joy, smiles and happiness.

We serve GOAL BY MESSI in a dish that is half a football, with an artificial pitch to which we add an essential oil distillate from grass freshly cut for the occasion. On the grass we place a flat zigzag shape made of methacrylate, with three points along the trajectory with the signs I+ I+ I+, and on top of which we set a series of soft meringues with violet caramel (could they be the players of Real Madrid?). At the end of the methacrylate path there is a white ball made of Argentine dulce de leche. Next to it, a white bowl covered with a net made of icing sugar that simulates the goal. While the recorded voice of famous football reporter Joaquim Maria Puyal is heard broadcasting the mythical goal Messi scored against Getafe (in which he dribbled eight players of the opposite team from the midfield), the diner must participate in the game, follow the zigzag, eat the meringues and, lastly, 'kick' the ball into the net and enjoy the feeling of scoring a goal, with an explosion of mint powder, lemon cream, passion fruit cream, Pop Rocks balls with chocolate and soft mousse made of dulce de leche. Joy, elation, excitement, passion and well-being are the ingredients of this dessert.

GOAL BY MESSI is ecstasy, fascination, a possible dream and, never better said, a game. It brings individual interpretations of victory to the table. Each person visualises their own goal. After eating it, the dish continues on its tasty trajectory, and the ball goes from mouth to mouth... When it is all over, a smile. End of the menu.

In the dining room...

There are dishes that can be daring, brave, scandalous or radical, and that require complicity at the table. In the dining room, we try to transmit the younger, more innocent and playful vision of Jordi, and convey its value. But always with respect and sensibility, interpreting rhythms and moods. We must observe and know how to translate the verbal and non-verbal language at the table, how our customers talk to us, how they act. We have to look them in the eye and watch their hands. We even have to pay attention to their watch, shoes or other elements that can provide information about the person we have in front of us. We must know when to act, or when a table may be going wrong and may need more involvement. We must have the psychological ability to sense if a dish may not be suitable. There are elements of subjectivity in the approach of a humorous touch. The show, therefore, is never the same. Just like the public is never the same. Like a good clown, we try to understand if a joke is appropriate or silence is preferable.

SMILE

COMPOSITION

Citrus fruit cream
Lemon jelly
Coffee jelly
Lime rock
Sorbet base
Lime sorbet

—CITRUS FRUIT CREAM

YIELDS 850 G

166 g yuzu juice
166 g passion fruit juice
166 g lemon juice
125 g egg yolks
125 g sugar
2½ gelatine sheets
222 g butter

In a casserole, mix the fruit juices and bring to a boil. In a separate container, blanch the egg yolks with sugar and add the juices, hot. Stir constantly and heat again to pasteurise at 85°C/185°F. When that temperature is reached, remove from the heat; add the gelatine, previously hydrated, and the butter, cold and cut into cubes. Reserve.

—LEMON JELLY

YIELDS 300 G

2.5 g iota
200 g water
50 g sugar
50 g lemon juice

Hydrate the iota with water, add the sugar and bring to a boil; remove from heat, stir in the lemon juice and leave to solidify in the fridge.

—COFFEE JELLY

YIELDS 600 G

500 g brewed coffee
100 g sugar
6 g agar-agar

Mix the coffee, sugar and agar-agar, bring to a boil and leave to set in a container. When it has cooled down, run the gel through a hand blender and reserve.

—LIME ROCK

YIELDS 600 G

500 g sugar
150 g water
100 g Fizzy (effervescent tablets) from
  Texturas
2 limes, grated zest

Place the water and sugar in a container and cook until reaching 127°C/261°F. Separately, crush the effervescent tablets with the lime zest and add to the water and sugar mixture. Pour the result in a 20x25 cm mould and leave to cool.

—SORBET BASE

YIELDS 750 G

500 g water
10 g sorbet stabiliser
50 g sugar
100 g glucose powder
75 g dextrose
40 g inverted sugar syrup

Mix all the ingredients in a container and pasteurise at 85°C/185°F; remove from heat, cool and reserve.

—LIME SORBET

YIELDS 750 G

250 g sugar syrup (basic recipes, p.428)
250 g lime juice
250 g sorbet base (previously prepared)

Mix all the ingredients with a hand blender and run through the ice-cream maker. Store the sorbet at -18°C/0°F.

GARNISHING AND PLATING

1 finger lime (*Citrus australasica*)

Cut the tips of the finger lime and peel, cut it in half and apply light pressure to the pith (white membrane) to carefully extract its juice vesicles. Reserve.

On a silicone mat, draw a happy face with the coffee gel and freeze. Place a 2 mm layer of citrus fruit cream on top of it and freeze again.

Cut a 5 cm circle around the face and reserve in the freezer.

On a plate, set some lemon gel, lime rock and lime sorbet, and place the happy face on top. Garnish with some citrus vesicles.

GOAL BY MESSI

SERVES 8 PEOPLE

COMPOSITION

Passion fruit cream
Lemon tablet
Dulce de leche mousse
Mint and lime pitch
Sugar net
Dulce de leche ball
Violet sugar marshmallow

—PASSION FRUIT CREAM
YIELDS 860 G

400 g passion fruit purée
80 g egg yolks
100 g eggs
100 g sugar
2 gelatine sheets
180 g butter

Pasteurise the passion fruit pulp with
egg yolks, eggs, and sugar until it reaches
85°C/185°F, then add the gelatine sheets,
previously hydrated. Stir the mixture well and,
when the temperature drops to 40°C/104°F,
add the butter. Run through a hand blender to
a smooth cream. Reserve cold.

—LEMON TABLET
YIELDS 450 G

150 g lemon juice
1 lemon, grated zest
150 g water
75 g dextrose
75 g inverted sugar syrup
1½ gelatine sheets

Mix all the ingredients except the gelatine
and heat to 50°C/122°F. Add the gelatine,
previously hydrated, cool down and freeze
in 2-cm-deep moulds.

—DULCE DE LECHE MOUSSE
YIELDS 375 G

125 g dulce de leche
250 g cream

Introduce all the ingredients in a whipped
cream dispenser with 2 chargers and
reserve cold.

—MINT AND LIME PITCH
YIELDS 40 G

200 g mint leaves
5 limes

Blanch mint leaves, strain any excess water
and dehydrate.

Grate the lime peels over a silicone mat
and dehydrate.

Mix both ingredients and crush to a very
fine powder. Reserve in an airtight container.

—SUGAR NET
YIELDS 150 G

150 g icing sugar
8 g egg whites
3 citric acid drops

Sieve icing sugar, add the egg whites and
drops of citric acid. Smooth the mixture
and, using a piping bag, draw a net on a
silicone mat. Dehydrate and reserve.

—DULCE DE LECHE BALL
YIELDS 400 G

250 g cream
125 g dulce de leche
125 g cocoa butter
125 g white chocolate

Whip the cream, mix it with the dulce de leche and transfer into 5 cm spherical moulds. Freeze.

Melt cocoa butter, mix it with the white chocolate, also melted, and use it to coat the dulce de leche bonbons. Reserve refrigerated.

—VIOLET SUGAR MARSHMALLOW
YIELDS 630 G

100 g water
65 g glucose
330 g sugar
100 g egg whites
20 g sugar
15 g gelatine
Icing sugar
Violet sugar

Make syrup with the water, glucose and 330 g sugar. Increase temperature to 121°C/250°F.

Start to slowly whisk the egg whites with 20 g sugar.

When the syrup is ready, add it slowly to the whisked egg whites, continue whisking until the temperature drops slightly and add the gelatine, previously hydrated. Continue whisking until it cools down.

Transfer the mixture into piping bags and make cylinders with a 1 cm nozzle. Sprinkle with icing sugar and leave to dry. Cut the cylinders in 1 cm pieces and, when serving, coat one end with violet sugar.

GARNISHING AND PLATING

Chocolate Pop Rocks
Mint flowers

Serve the passion fruit cream in a bowl shaped as half a football, designed specifically for this dessert; set the lemon tablet in the middle, and the chocolate Pop Rocks and dulce de leche mousse covering everything. Flatten the surface to make it smooth and sprinkle the mint and lime pitch on it. Add the mint flowers, cover with the net and finish by setting the marshmallows and dulce de leche ball on their corresponding spots.

RAZOR CLAM
MACARONI AL PESTO

SERVES 8 PEOPLE

COMPOSITION
Razor clams
Pesto

—RAZOR CLAMS
YIELDS 24 RAZOR CLAM MACARONI

12 razor clams
Brine for fish (basic recipes, p.429)

Soak razor clams in brine for 10 minutes,
remove, rinse and dry any excess water. Seal
the razor clams in a vacuum pack bag and cook
in the Roner for 4 minutes at 63°C/145°F. Take
the razor clams out of the bag, remove them
from their shell and cut the central muscle
in the shape of two macaroni (separate the
rest of the body and use to make the pesto).
Reserve.

—PESTO
YIELDS 310 G

25 g pine kernels
60 g basil leaves
30 g water
½ garlic clove
10 g Parmesan cheese
15 g Pecorino cheese
20 g cooked razor clam (previously prepared)
150 g sunflower oil
Salt

Toast pine kernels in the oven at 160°C/320°F.
Blanch the basil leaves in boiling, salted water
for 10 seconds and cool quickly in a cold
bain-marie. Remove the leaves, draining any
water left. Blend together with the 30 g water,
½ garlic clove, Parmesan, Pecorino, cooked
razor clam and toasted pine kernels. Whip the
mixture with the sunflower oil. Adjust salt and
strain. Reserve in a hot bain-marie.

GARNISHING AND PLATING

Basil flowers
Purple basil sprouts
Parmesan cheese

Heat the razor clams lightly with a hot spatula,
draw a tear with the pesto in the middle of
the plate. Place 3 razor clam macaroni on the
pesto tear and garnish with flowers, sprouts
and a tip of grated Parmesan.

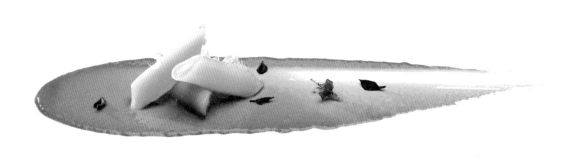

BLOOD ORANGE
AND BEETROOT SORBET

SERVES 8 PEOPLE

COMPOSITION
Beetroot sauce
Crumbled blood orange segments
Honey and orange blossom ice cream
Blood orange sorbet
Beetroot tuile
Blood orange sugar

—BEETROOT SAUCE
YIELDS 300 G

200 g blended beetroot
100 g sugar syrup (basic recipes, p.428)
0.3 g xanthan gum

Mix all the ingredients cold and emulsify
the mixture with hand blender. Reserve.

—CRUMBLED BLOOD ORANGE SEGMENTS

Blood orange segments

Submerge the blood orange segments in a
container with liquid nitrogen and remove.
Break them with one sharp blow to crumble
to extract the vesicles. Reserve in the freezer.

—HONEY AND ORANGE BLOSSOM ICE CREAM
YIELDS 700 G

420 g milk
200 g cream
40 g milk powder
130 g dextrose
75 g honey
50 g sucrose
5 g ice-cream stabiliser
70 g orange blossom water

Heat the milk, cream, milk powder and
dextrose to 60°C/140°F, add the honey and
the remaining dry products quickly. Bring the
mixture to 85°C/185°F, then cool to 4°C/39°F.
Add the orange blossom water and emulsify
it with a hand blender. Leave to ripen, run
through the ice-cream maker and reserve
the ice cream at -18°C/0°F.

—BLOOD ORANGE SORBET
YIELDS 900 G

735 g blood orange juice
180 g dextrose
60 g glucose
20 g sucrose
5 g sorbet stabiliser

In a saucepan, mix 200 g blood orange juice
with the dextrose and heat to 70°C/158°F.
Then, add the remaining dry ingredients
and increase the temperature to 85°C/185°F.
Remove from heat, cool at 4°C/39°F and add
the rest of the orange juice before emulsifying
everything with a hand blender. Leave to ripen,
run through the ice-cream maker and reserve
at -18°C/0°F.

—BEETROOT TUILE
YIELDS 110 G

100 g blended beetroot
100 g sugar
1 oblaat sheet, 20x30 cm

Make syrup by boiling the blended beetroot
with sugar and reserve.

Line a baking tray with a silicone mat and
brush it with beetroot syrup. Place the oblaat
sheet on top and add a second layer of
beetroot syrup. Bake it at 120°C/248°F for
40 minutes. Remove the oblaat sheet, crumble
the resulting beetroot tuile lightly, and store
in an airtight container with silica gel to
prevent moisture.

—BLOOD ORANGE SUGAR
YIELDS 240 G

200 g sugar
40 g blood orange peel

Blend the orange peel and sugar well in
a blender until the mixture turns smooth.
Spread the contents over a tray and leave
to dry at room temperature. Reserve in an
airtight container.

GARNISHING AND PLATING

On a dinner plate, make an irregular splash
of beetroot sauce to simulate blood splatter.
Arrange the crumbled segments in the middle,
top them with a swirl of honey and orange
blossom ice cream and blood orange sorbet.
Garnish by sticking beetroot tuiles in the ice
cream and sprinkling them with blood orange
sugar.

III.

—APPENDIX

III.

1.
BASIC
RECIPES

—BEURRE NOISETTE
YIELDS 180 G

250 g butter

Heat the butter in a frying pan over medium-low heat; when the protein separates from the fat, remove the milk solids that accumulate on the surface, and continue cooking the remaining butter until it acquires a golden-brown colour. Run through a cloth filter and reserve.

—BLACK GARLIC PURÉE
YIELDS 110 G

50 g black garlic
70 g water
0.2 g xanthan gum
Salt

Liquidise all the ingredients and run the mixture through a fine chinois. Reserve.

—BLACK TRUFFLE OIL
YIELDS 110 G

20 g fresh black truffle brunoise
100 g extra virgin olive oil

Mix the truffle and olive oil, and seal in a vacuum pack bag. Infuse in the Roner at 60°C/140°F for 2 hours. Remove from bag and reserve.

—CALCIUM ALGINATE BATH
YIELDS 1 KG

1 kg water
5 g calcium alginate

Blend ingredients with a hand blender, strain and reserve. Leave this bath to stand at least 6 hours before using.

—CHICKEN STOCK
YIELDS 8.5 L

11 kg chicken bones
1 kg mirepoix (basic recipes, p.427)
15 litres water

Place the carcases on a baking tray and brown in the oven at 180°C/356°F for 40 minutes. Next, transfer to a stockpot and deglaze with water any browned bits from the bottom of the baking tray. Add the resulting juice to the stockpot and, lastly, add the mirepoix and water. Boil for 5 hours and strain.

—GARLIC OIL
YIELDS 150 G

3 garlic cloves
150 g extra virgin olive oil

Peel the garlic cloves and split them in half to remove the germ. Chop finely and mix with the oil; cook at 90°C/194°F for 3 hours. Strain and reserve the oil.

—GUINDILLA PEPPER OIL
YIELDS 100 G

3 dried guindilla peppers
100 g extra virgin olive oil

Cook the guindilla peppers in a casserole with the olive oil at 65°C/149°F for 3 hours. Cool and reserve.

—KUZU MIXTURE FOR THICKENING SAUCES
YIELDS 400 G

150 g kuzu (*Pueraria lobata starch*)
250 g cold water

Mix both ingredients and reserve. Stir the mixture every time before using.

—LOBSTER STOCK
YIELDS 2 L

7 kg lobster heads
100 g extra virgin olive oil
1.2 kg mirepoix (basic recipes, p.427)
15 litres water
8 g sugar

Brown the lobster heads in olive oil and transfer to a stockpot together with the mirepoix. Cover with cold water and bring to a boil. Skim, add sugar, and continue cooking over low heat until obtaining 2 litres of stock. Reserve.

—MIREPOIX
YIELDS 12 KG

13 kg onions
2 kg carrots
1.75 kg leeks
200 g extra virgin olive oil

Finely chop vegetables for mirepoix and cook in a casserole with oil for 12 hours over low heat. Reserve.

—ORANGE EMULSION
YIELDS 160 G

200 g orange juice
2 g glucose
100 g extra virgin arbequina olive oil

Mix the juice and glucose in a casserole and reduce to a third of its initial volume (approximately 70 g) over low heat. Temper and, when the mixture reaches room temperature, transfer into a bowl. Trickle the oil while constantly stirring with a whisk to emulsify. Reserve.

—ORANGE REDUCTION
YIELDS 90 G

375 g strained orange juice
5 g liquid glucose

Mix both ingredients and reduce to the indicated amount over very low heat.

—ORANGE PEEL CONFIT
YIELDS 140 G OR 20 STRIPS 1 CM EACH

2 oranges
700 g sugar syrup (basic recipes, p.428)

Peel the oranges, removing the peel together with the pith as well as some of the pulp. Cut peel into 1 cm strips and transfer into a casserole with cold water. Heat and, as soon as they come to a boil, remove from the heat. Transfer again to cold water and bring to a boil a second time. Repeat this process 5 more times.
When blanched, immerse the strips of peel in the sugar syrup and boil on very low heat for 3 hours.

Remove from the sugar syrup and set on a rack to dry. Reserve.

—POTATO PURÉE
YIELDS 450 G

500 g Mona Lisa potatoes
70 g butter
30 g extra virgin olive oil
6 g salt

Peel and wash the potatoes. Cut them into cubes and seal them in a vacuum pack bag with the butter, oil and salt, then cook at 85°C/185°F in the Roner for 4 hours. Remove from the bag, mash and reserve.

—PRAWN OIL
YIELDS 300 G

150 g prawn heads
300 g sunflower oil

Brown the prawn heads lightly in a casserole with a dash of sunflower oil. When brown, cover with the remaining oil and cook for 6 hours at 65°C/149°F. Strain and cool. Reserve.

—PRAWN STOCK
YIELDS 2 L

7 kg prawn heads
100 g extra virgin olive oil
1 kg mirepoix (basic recipes, p.427)
13 litres water

Brown the prawn heads in olive oil and transfer to a stockpot together with the mirepoix. Cover with cold water and bring to a boil. Skim and continue cooking over low heat until obtaining 2 litres of stock. Reserve.

—SCAMPI STOCK
YIELDS 2 L

7 kg scampi heads and claws
100 g extra virgin olive oil
1.2 kg mirepoix (basic recipes, p.427)
14 litres water
12 g sugar

Brown the scampi heads and claws in olive oil and transfer to a stockpot together with the mirepoix. Cover with cold water and bring to a boil. Skim, add sugar, and continue cooking over low heat until obtaining 2 litres of stock. Reserve.

—SOIL DISTILLATE
YIELDS 480 G

300 g soil
500 g water

Mix the soil and water, cover the container and infuse refrigerating for 12 hours.

Transfer the mixture into an evaporating flask and place a 0.22 µm filter membrane for sterilising between the evaporating flask and the outlet into the cooler.

Distil the soil at 30-35°C/86-95°F (bath temperature) for 1-2 hours, and finish at 40-45°C/104-113°F for 30 minutes. Remove the distillate and seal in a vacuum pack bag to conserve its aroma. To keep for days or weeks, freezing is recommended.

—SOUFFLÉ POTATOES
YIELDS APPROXIMATELY 45 UNITS

1 (old) medium-size Agria potato
Sunflower oil

Cut the potato lengthwise and cut each half in 1.5x3 cm rectangles.

With a mandolin slicer and starting with the flat side, make fine slices out of the potato rectangles and reserve.

Prepare two casseroles with sunflower oil, aiming to keep one at 130°C/266°F and the other at 180°C/356°F. Fry the rectangular potato slices in 130°C/266°F oil until they puff and then, using a wire skimmer, immerse them into 180°C/356°F oil to finish puffing and browning. Place on kitchen towels and reserve.

—SPICE BREAD
YIELDS 1.34 KG DOUGH

200 g honey
200 g sugar
150 g butter
300 g water
500 g flour
90 g almond powder
45 g baking powder
2 g spice mix

Place the honey, sugar, butter and water in a container and dissolve over low heat. Put the remaining ingredients in the food mixer, trickle the liquid in and mix until obtaining a smooth and thick dough.

Butter a baking tin and add dough. Bake at 160°C/320°F for 45 minutes.

—SUGAR SYRUP
YIELDS 1.9 KG

1 kg water
1 kg sugar

Place both ingredients in a stockpot and bring to a boil. Leave to cool and reserve.

—SWEATED ONION
YIELDS 1.2 KG

4 kg julienned onion
50 g extra virgin olive oil

Heat the oil in a casserole and add the onion, cooking for 24 hours over low heat. Cool and reserve.

—TOMATO WATER
YIELDS 2.5 KG

8 kg tomatoes

Wash the tomatoes and blend, transfer the liquid into a container and refrigerate for 12 hours to decant. Remove any foam that may have floated to the surface and keep the liquid. Reserve refrigerated.

—BEEF GRAVY
YIELDS 200 G

1 kg beef bones and trimmings
160 g mirepoix (basic recipes, p.427)
1.5 kg water
Extra virgin olive oil
Salt

Set the bones and trimmings on a baking tray and brown at 200°C/392°F. When brown, remove excess fat and transfer into a stockpot together with the mirepoix. Deglaze with water any browned bits from the bottom of the baking tray and add this juice to the stockpot. Cover with cold water and cook for 2 hours over low heat. Next, strain and reduce to 200 g. Adjust salt and reserve.

BRINE

The technique of seasoning meat and
fish in light brine has been reclaimed.
It entails submerging the product in a
solution of water and salt— 8 to 10% in
proportion to the amount of water— for
a certain amount of time depending,
mainly, on the size and consistency of
the ingredient (fish takes a few minutes
while meat takes a few hours).

This immersion gives several positive
results:

– The product is salted evenly and
  regularly, not depending on the hand
  of the cook who salts the product.
– The result is a juicier product after
  cooking, as the interaction of the salt
  and the proteins results in a greater
  ability to retain water within the
  muscle fibres, which absorb the brine.
– The salt softens the muscle structure
  and the fibres, which results in tender
  meat and fish.

—BRINE FOR FISH
YIELDS 1 KG

1 kg water
100 g salt

Bring water to a boil in a casserole,
then remove from heat. Add salt.
Leave to cool and reserve in a covered
container until using.

—BRINE FOR MEAT
YIELDS 1 KG

1 kg water
80 g salt

Bring water to a boil in a casserole, then
remove from heat. Add salt. Leave to
cool and reserve in a covered container
until using.

OUR SILICON BAKING MOULDS

Liquid silicon
Catalysing agent

Line up on an aluminium tray any
ingredients from which you wish to
make a mould. Fix the lower part of the
ingredients with drawing pins, and coat
them with a mixture of liquid silicon
and catalysing agent. Shake the tray
carefully to set the silicon and leave to
stand for 12 hours.

Next, turn the tray over to detach the
whole silicon block and remove the
drawing pins. Then, also remove the
product so that only its concave shape
remains on the silicon block.

2.
GLOSSARY

A

Agar-agar: gelling agent obtained from the red algae *Gelidium* and *Gracilaria*. It is sold in powder form, mixed with liquid and boiled to activate its gelling attributes. The gel can hold up to 80°C/176°F.

Aiguillette: long and narrow cut obtained from both sides of the breast of poultry. By extension, any narrow cut of meat is also referred to as aiguillette.

Albumin powder: protein normally obtained from egg whites used as an emulsifier.

Alginate: additive extracted from brown algae used as a gelling agent, thickener and stabiliser. It's one of the components used to make spherifications.

Amaretto: Italian distilled alcoholic beverage with a bitter almond taste, made from apricot or almond stones.

Apricot sprite hyssop: plant belonging to the *Lamiaceae* family. Its orange-coloured flower has several culinary uses.

B

Baking powder: chemical yeast often used in pastry making.

Beurre noisette: butter heated until its colour is golden-brown and aroma reminiscent of hazelnut.

Blanch, to: to immerse raw food in boiling water for a brief period of time in order to clean, consolidate, or facilitate the peeling of products, among other purposes.

Blanquette: cooking white meat, although occasionally also fish or vegetables, in white stock with aromatic ingredients.

Blast chill: lowering the temperature of food quickly.

Bristol Cream: commercial brand of sherry made from a mixture of oxidative aging generous wines (mainly Olorosos) and a substantial amount of neutral sweet wine or concentrated and rectified Mosto grape.

Brunoise: finely cutting vegetables into small dice of one to two millimetres.

C

Calamondin: *Citrofortunella microcarpa.* Citrus fruit of about three to four centimetres in diameter, characterised by its thin rind and minute, pulpy, and aromatic segments of a very acid taste.

Calcium lactate gluconate: a mixture of two calcium salts (calcium gluconate and calcium lactate) from lactates or mineral products, used with some gelling agents (alginate) in spherification.

Carrageenan: additive obtained from red algae from the *Rhodophyceae* family. It is used as a gelling agent, thickener, emulsifier and stabiliser. The most common are kappa and iota.

Chartreuse: traditional French liqueur named after the Grande Chartreuse monastery it comes from. Its recipe is still a secret, although it is known to contain plants such as lemon balm, hyssop, saffron and cinnamon. Not too long ago it was produced in Tarragona, where it had great recognition.

Citrus caviar: pulp of the finger lime.

Clarify: to remove any impurities from a stock or liquid in order to obtain a clear and pure result. In the case of butter, it consists of melting it and eliminating the whitish butterfat that forms, together with other milk solids that float to the surface; with this process, pure butter is obtained.

Comté: French cow's cheese made from a cooked and pressed paste. It comes in circular discs forty to seventy centimetres in diameter.

D

Dextrose: sugar obtained from the transformation of corn. It diminishes the activity of water, enhances aromas and is highly antibacterial. It is normally sold in powder form.

Duxelle: sauce made from shallots and mushrooms finely chopped and normally fried lightly in butter. An essential element in classic French cuisine.

E

Enoki golden mushroom: *Flammulina velutipes.* The only difference to the enoki mushroom is its yellow or orange colour and shorter stalk.

Enoki mushroom: *Flammulina velutipes.* Mushroom used commonly in Asian cuisine. It grows on tree trunks known also as enoki, and is found in bunches. It has a whitish colour and long stalk, as well as a very small cap. It can grow in the wild or cultivated, although the second is the most common.

F

Finger lime: also known as Australian finger lime, is a citrus fruit native of the Australian undergrowth. The fruit is shaped as a long cylinder and its peel is thin. Its inside contains tiny spheres filled with sour juice reminiscent of lemon, with an aroma of Asian spices like pepper. In Asian cuisine, it is used to combine with raw molluscs and bivalves (oysters, clams), and with raw fish. At the restaurant we get it from our nearby producer, Baches.

Foyot sauce: Béarnaise sauce enriched with meat glaze.

G

Gastrovac: pot and equipment to cook food sous-vide while preventing them from losing their properties. Water boiling takes place at 35°C/96°F without pressure. It was developed jointly by the Polytechnic University of Valencia and chefs Javier Andrés and Sergio Torres.

Gelée: a type of gelatine obtained when a liquid preparation is solidified thanks to the thickening elements that incorporate in it.

Gellan gum: gelling agent obtained from the fermentation of the bacteria *Sphingomonas elodea.* It must be heated to 85°C/185°F with a liquid to produce the gelling effect.

Glucose powder: dehydrated glucose syrup with a high level of anti-crystallisation and a stabiliser used often to make ice creams and sorbets.

Glycerine: product of vegetable origin used to emulsify or as an ice-cream stabiliser. It prevents freezing better than sucrose, therefore it is used to reduce the sweetness of ice-cream without diminishing its ability to prevent freezing.

Gold leaf: fine edible gold sheet.

Greaseproof paper: baking paper used both to store and to cook products while preventing them from sticking to the container.

I

Indian cress: *Tropaeolum majus.* Large, red flower from South America which, due to its pleasant flavour, is widely used as a seasoning in cuisine, raw as well as marinated in vinegar.

Inverted sugar syrup: mixture of sugars 1.25 times sweeter than sucrose.

Iota: gelling agent derivate from a variety of red algae that produces a soft and elastic gel. It tolerates temperature, which facilitates making hot gelatines.

Isomalt: artificial product from sucrose used as a sweetener due to its high stability in very humid environments and very high temperatures.

J

Jerusalem artichoke: *Helianthus tuberosus.* Tuber similar to potatoes but with knots; it can be eaten raw or cooked.

K

Kappa: gelling additive obtained from red algae that forms hard and strong gels and is thermoreversible. It gels quickly when the temperature is lowered, which is why it is often used to coat foods.

Kumato: tomato variety characterised by its dark green, nearly black colour, sweet and intense flavour and rounded shape. It ripens from the inside, so its flesh is always crisp.

Kuzu: starch obtained from the root of *Pueraria lobata*, a plant of Chinese and Japanese origin of the Fabaceae family. Of a neutral taste, it thickens liquids making them translucent after cooking. It is dissolved in cold and, depending on the cooking time different softer or harder textures can be obtained. At El Celler de Can Roca we make a thickening agent from this starch.

M

Maltodextrine: carbohydrate obtained from processed tapioca starches. It adds volume and texture to food and in gastronomy is used mainly with fats.

Mandolin slicer: device used to cut food into very fine and uniform slices.

Manzanilla Pasada: Manzanilla wine further aged, of oxidative aging (called *velo de flor*, or flor yeast, which offers light oxidation notes as the yeast layer is exhausted in the casks after years of aging) and with a slightly higher alcohol content.

Maple syrup: syrup made from maple sap.

Marshmallow: sugar or corn syrup sweet with beaten egg white, gelling agents and flavourings.

Microplane: commercial name for a type of graters that are very fine and precise, adapted for citrus peels, nuts or cheese.

Mirepoix: mixture of vegetables (onion, carrot, leek, garlic...) chopped and used to scent stocks, roasts and other preparations. Any vegetable cut into dice of approximately 1.5 centimetres is also referred to as mirepoix.

Mousseline: mayonnaise sauce whipped for an airier texture.

O

Oblaat: fine transparent sheet made with oil, soy lecithin and potato starch, originally from Japan. It has no taste or smell, which is why the flavour of whatever is put inside it remains intact. It is difficult to handle in humid conditions.

Oloroso: sherry wine of the Palomino grape variety, topped with 17% of alcohol volume to suppress the formation of flor yeast. It is aged in casks with a slow oxidation, through the traditional system of Criadera and Solera. It is dark in colour and of an intense nutty aroma; it has a robust structure and full body. It can be either dry or slightly sweet.

Orly batter: coating batter.

Oxalis: plant genus with over six hundred species characterised by their high oxalic acid, which provides the leaves with an aciculous taste and aroma.

Oyster sauce: concentrated sauce of a brownish colour made from oyster water reduced and cooked on low heat with soy sauce. Used widely in Asian cuisine.

P

Pacojet: powerful crusher able to process and emulsify frozen foods and produce mousses, ice creams and sorbets.

Pak choi: a type of Chinese cabbage of a mild, very characteristic taste. Both stalk and leaves can be eaten, cooked or raw.

Parfait: creamy preparation with a high fat content, which gives it a characteristic oiliness and consistency.

Parmentier: potato purée enriched mainly with cream, egg and cheese.

Patchouli: aromatic plant similar to musk used in the perfume industry.

Pearly razorfish: *Xyrichtys novacula.* Also called raor razorfish. Fish from the Labridae family that feeds on crustaceans, molluscs and fish. It is found near the coast in the Mediterranean sea and the Atlantic ocean.

Pectin: product obtained from apple or the peel of lemon or other citrus fruits. It is used as a gelling additive. An acid medium is required for its use, as well as a high proportion of sugars. It is widely used in pastry making to make pâte de fruits, jellies and marmalades.

Phytoplankton: edible paste obtained from the production of algae in conditions similar to the open sea—light and salty water—in a laboratory.

Pineberry: *Fragaria chiloensis.* A fruit similar to strawberries but white and with a taste reminiscent of pineapple. Originally from America. At the restaurant we get it from our local producer in Sant Miquel de Campmajor, Mas Bertrà.

Pistillata algae: *Gigartina pistillata.* Red algae of earthy smell, slightly nutty flavour and crisp texture.

Pith: the white tissue lining the peel of citrus fruits.

Quindim: Brazilian sweet made with sugar, egg yolk and grated coconut.

Rocoto pepper: very spicy and pulpy variety of chilli.

Roner: (see 'The beginning of sous-vide at El Celler de Can Roca,' page 313)

Rotaval: (see 'The Rotaval: sauce making technology,' page 154)

Royale: (see 'The Royales,' page 101)

Salad burnet: aromatic herb from the Rosaceae family, whose leaves have a flavour reminiscent of cucumber.

Salamander: grill.

Salmis: game stew practised especially on woodcock, mallard, pheasant and partridge.

Shiso: *Perilla frutescens*. Plant from the mint family grown in India and Eastern Asia. Its oils produce a very strong taste, comparable in intensity with mint or fennel.

Silica gel: silicon dioxide in granules made synthetically from sodium silicate. It absorbs water and therefore used to keep products, whether they are food or otherwise, free of moisture. It is sold in small bags.

Softened butter: intermediate state between liquid and solid butter obtained by leaving butter at room temperature so that its texture turns creamy.

Sucroester: product deravative from sucrose used as an emulsifier and stabiliser.

Sugar pump: rubber pump used to blow sugar.

Tear pea: a variety of pea characterised by its small, fresh and soft seeds.

Tomato concassé: brunoise made with peeled and seeded tomatoes.

Tonka bean: seed from the *Dipteryx odorata* tree originating in tropical America. France was the first country to import these seeds, highly used in pastry making.

Velouté: smooth and velvety cream obtained by binding a liquid with egg yolks, cream and butter.

Vinic alcohol: ethyl alcohol produced by the distillation of wine.

Xanthan gum: thickener obtained from the fermentation of cornstarch with a bacteria present in cabbage. A very small amount of gum is required, so the organoleptic features of the liquid thickened are not disturbed. It works cold or hot.

Yuzu: *Citrus ichangesis x Citrus reticulata var. Austera*. Citrus fruit from Eastern Asia, originally from China and later introduced in Japan and Korea. It can look like a grapefruit, orange or tangerine with the size of the latter. Its peel is yellow-green, depending on its ripeness. It is very sweet and aromatic. At El Celler we get it from our local producer in Sant Miquel de Campmajor, Mas Bertrà.

3.
ANALYTICAL CATALOGUE

1986

Sea bass filled with shellfish

Hake with garlic
and rosemary vinaigrette

Aubergine cake with goat cheese sauce

1987

Sole à l'orange

Courgette and shellfish cake with cava

Chicken thigh with prawns

1988

Cod with samfaina

Creamy cheeks

Lobster parmentier
with black chanterelles

1989

Pig trotter carpaccio

Squab with red berries

Sirloin steak with herb
and spice butter

Prawn suquet

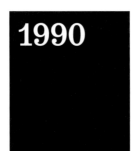

Scampi bouillabaise,
crisp bread and rouille

Chestnut and truffle capuccino

Cod esqueixada

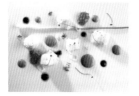

Banana and chocolate millefeuille

Rossini tournedos

Squab rice

Black botifarra blinis

Snails with spider crab and fennel

Glazed wildberries with sabayon

Fresh cheese cake with peach

Pumpkin preserve with pink pepper

Veal head ravigote style with turnips
and pickled vegetables

Rabbit shoulder confit with cinnamon

Oysters with Foyot

Pig trotters with sea cucumbers
and artichoke chips

1993

Chocolate custard with mint

Pig jowl with samfaina

Leek pressé with prawns and truffle

Sea cucumber suquet with potato,
lard and saffron terrine

Scallop with marrow
and passion fruit

1994

Salad with artichokes
filled with foie and orange

Cod brandada millefeuille

Red mullets with orange
and sweet potato

1995

White and green asparagus
with cardamom oil

Apple within an apple
within an apple

Penny bun and bone marrow tartlet

1996

Black botifarra and sea urchin rice

Bacon with octopus
and pickled vegetables

Oxtail filled with bone marrow

Egg at low temperature with truffles

Mango and goat cheese ravioli

Woodcock roast

Apple timbale and foie gras
with vanilla oil

1997

Cod with spinach, raisins
and pine kernels

Clams with red grapefruit
and Campari

Coconut and watermelon

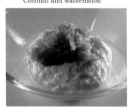

Berry infusion
and mascarpone ice cream

Sea bass with green apple
and vanilla oil

Skate with sweet potatoes and calçots

1998

Rice with partridge and cuttlefish

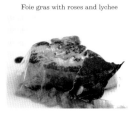

Foie gras with roses and lychee

Sardines with anchovy ice cream

Sardine and piquillo pepper terrine

Chocolate, mint and strawberries

1999

Iced bonbons

Orange blossom cream

Cod escudella

Hare à la Royale

Charcoal-grilled sole with Riesling
and white truffle sauce

Mussels with marrow and orange

Steak tartare

Tuna marinated with berries
and black olives

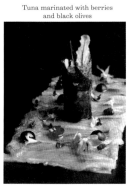

Caviar omelette

2000

Pheasant and truffle cannelloni

Scampi in tempura, fresh almonds, apple compote, penny buns and curry

Suckling pig with quince and garlic

Honey slush with vanilla cream

Mussels with lemon

Squid parmentier

Egg yolk with sea urchins

Pear tatin

2001

Anchovies, truffle and merlot

Cod brandada

Sea bass with peas

Cesar's mushrooms, parmesan and yeast

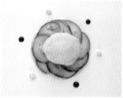

Monkfish with romesco bread

Soufflé coulant

Crustacean velouté

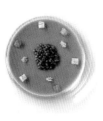

Clams with sweet potato
and bergamot

Squab with juniper ice cream

Crustacean with spice smoke

Monkfish liver with beans

Foie bourbon

Mediterranean garden

Miracle by Lancôme

Red grapefruit and Campari
rose with clams

Sardines marinated
with sangria granita

Fresh herb soup with verjuice,
snails and scotch bonnets

Cherry soup with prawns
and ice cream made from the stone

Duck terrine with pears

Hot aspic with artichokes,
orange and truffle

Trésor by Lancôme

Suckling lamb with sheep milk

2003

Chicken wings with scampi
and seaweeds

Verdejo salad

Anchovies with texturised olive oil

Cherry with smoked eel

Scampi with green tea
and the juice from its head

Sea cucumber with sea water

Monkfish liver with Talisker
and seaweed stock

Sirloin steak with Lagavulin

Distilled foie, strawberries and pepper

Eucalyptus ice cream,
vanilla compote and green herbs

Lobster with vanilla and corn

Lightly smoked sea bass with kefir

Hake with hazelnut hollandaise

Squab parfait

Poularde breast with mango
and black olives

Turbot with salicornia,
fennel and lemon

Fennel velouté

Scallop with orange and green tea

Scallops with truffle

2004

Winter salad

Cock's comb with scampi
and comté rice

Cod cheeks smoked with rosemary

Squab with roses and strawberries

Orange chromatism

Envy by Gucci

Scampi smoked with curry

Foie, apricot and amaretto

Prawns with fideuà without noodles

Saffron-smoked lobster with lettuce

Macaroni filled with foie
and parmesan

Loin with roasted pepper juice

Razor clams with tomato,
Parmesan and pistachio with basil

Loquat filled with foie with Viognier

Poularde with St. George's mushrooms

Sardines, bread and grape

Cherry soup with cockles,
wasabi and ginger

Trout, yellow gentian and almonds

2005

Eel with Olivares sweet wine

Foie gras bonbon

Lamb brain carpaccio
with yogurt and mint

Squab with anchovies

Brazil cup

Endives with foie

Fig with foie and saffron

Lamb loin with morchellas
filled with their stalks

Miracle for Ever by Lancôme

Oyster with Champagne

Parmesan powder, prawn,
traditional balsamic vinegar
of Modena and lemon preserve

Egg yolk with morchellas and Oloroso

Apple soup with anchovies
and tomato granita

Charcoal-grilled penny bun soufflé

Mackerel loin with
roasted pepper distillate

Vegetables with Riesling

Lamb with herb curry
and yogurt emulsion

2006

Cod with bread soup

Cod cooked on low heat and fried
with green apple mayonnaise

Charcoal-grilled snails
with alfalfa distillate

Carolina by Carolina Herrera

DKNY by Donna Karan

Ferragamo by Salvatore Ferragamo

Kin din

The plant

Veal sweetbreads with San Simón, coffee, truffle and lemon

Strawberries with texturised pink cava

Coche-Dury oyster

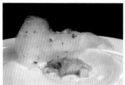

Baby octopuses with shallots and cocoa

Red mullet with citrus fruits

Truffle, foie and artichoke Royale

Sardines with liqueur and grapes steam

Cucumber peel soup with clams

Fall 2006

Turbot in its juice and lard

Venerable

Kid loin

2007

Artichoke and Parmesan salad
with Cynar slush

Coffee and rocket rice

Bloody Mary 2007

Botritis

Asparagus with Viognier

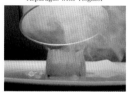

Foie with Palo Cortado and seaweeds

Prawn with Amontillado

Bulgari mussels

Peas with eucalyptus distillate

Poularde ball with truffle
and its parfait

Artichoke Royale with
sunflower seeds and orange

Fall 2007

Pickled vegetable flowerpot

Turbot fin with dry powder made
with its mojama and citrus fruits

Green salad

2008

Red chocolate box

Avocado cannelloni filled
with pine kernels

Kid head

Cherries 2008

Charcoal-grilled beef chop
and padrón pepper seeds

King prawn and Albariza soil

Rock mussels

Charcoal-grilled oyster with
citrus fruits and sea water pearls

Sardines marinated
with roasted aubergines

Cherry sorbet with Campari

Veal terrine with truffle
and pickled vegetables

Crustacean velouté with glasswort,
sea urchins and peach

Lamb with aubergine

Sea urchin filled aubergine
with black tea powder

Scampi and cocoa bonbon

2009

Spider crab with pig trotters

Petit-fours box

Neck of lamb with peach

St. George's mushroom consommé
with pine kernel ice cream
and avocado

Sorrel millefeuille with oyster
and caviar sorbet

Monkfish filled with its liver
and peppers from around the world

Broccoli toffee, sea urchins
and citrus caviar

Oyster carpaccio

Tuna neck consommé with
padrón pepper seeds

Soft bean consommé with
sea urchins and peppers

The world 2010

Wild boar sirloin with pink pepper
and persimmon, clove and cinnamon,
and Balinese long pepper ravioli

Veal sweetbreads, foie, yuzu,
salsify and black chanterelles

Lamb bone marrow with peas

Oyster with chickpea consommé

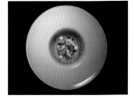

Iced watermelon with coconut
and tarragon

Tendons with olives

Artichoke omelette

Crustacean velouté

2011

Duck with eel

Woodcock, charcoal-grilled apple
and pomegranate vinegar

Moka

Mollusc platter

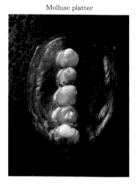

Morels with sheep milk skin

Oyster with black pearl

White truffle

Mackerel loin with pickled vegetables

2012

Sea bream with chicory

Carpano bonbon

The pine tree

Truffle foam and incense smoke

Fig with cloth-wrapped cheese

Milk chocolate stew granita with butter ice cream and yuzu compote

Hare à la Royale Narcís Comadira, Volnay sauce

Fresh walnuts

Oyster with game

Freeze-dried oyster

Wild quail tartlet

Pear with maple syrup and black beer

Hare à la Royale royale

Fall 2012

The whole red mullet

The whole prawn 2012

Prawn omelette

Lamb with liquorice smoke

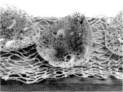

4.
RECIPE
INDEX

5.
INDEX

RECIPES EXPLAINED IN THE BOOK
Other dishes mentioned in the book
Culinary preparations (and book titles)

I

The previous evening

We had arranged to meet tomorrow, but I drop by El Celler today. I have spent many days and many evenings here and at the first restaurant, next to the one belonging to their parents. Also, at the usual place where Josep and Montserrat still—after nearly fifty years—prepare popular meals.

That may be the reason why I think in this notebook it will be difficult to draw a distinction between the product of immediacy—what I will experience tomorrow—and what will come out of the machinery of induced memory that impels me to the miniscule evocations that are starting to arrive now, all of a sudden. I talk to Josep about way back when a group of friends and I used to go to Can Roca to watch the highlights of the football match on Sunday evenings. I remember having kidneys and fried squid. And a small TV set where we watched the repeats. Josep replies that, back then, by the time we were having dinner he was already in bed. But now, I think I may able to attest that he hardly ever sleeps. The same goes for his brothers.

It is early morning and he and Joan are still talking, good-naturedly, to a few customer-friends about the benefits of certain duck livers and Josep's experience visiting a vineyard that same afternoon. Early the next morning they will be up and ready by the entrance, with its light tiles and water grooves and grass tanks, with ivies that welcome you as you arrive to El Celler. Illuminated now is the first of the courtyards, across from the elegant, sober and powerful facade. They greet the last table of people who dined in the private room and lingered around for a drink at the front room. They both talk to me about an idea I will not be able to shake off my mind. "People gift us their time." It's an extraordinarily interesting concept. It is, in fact, the essence—if we must find one—of El Celler.

II

The wee hours of the morning, with the three brothers

Jordi arrives next. I seize the opportunity of having the three of them around to discuss my theory. It all takes place in a friendly atmosphere. The dining room is empty and dark. That evocative combination of light pouring onto the table and the darkness around it has been dissolved. Those who come here, come not to eat, but to have an experience. It reminds me, I say, of the words of Steiner: about the cadence of living in Europe. A slow pace that helps the traveller notice the street signs and attend a history class. Or how Baudelaire described being a *flâneur*, wandering around on the street, walking, observing and thinking. This "gift of time" is in fact the origin of modern age. It is about the need to fill up and face the "terrible weight" (going back to the start: *Le Spleen de Paris*) of the passage of time. And what is the poet's solution? "You have to be always drunk [...]. On wine, poetry or virtue [...]. So as not to be martyred slaves of time, be drunk." By this time we have moved from the sofas and end our conversation standing outside. "Drunk? Sure?" asks Josep. "Living in a different reality," I say, "you know what I mean."

The customers of El Celler do not, in fact, gift that time, but instead wish to fill it up. To experience that intoxication. Artistic, of course. Vital.

Here, at any given moment—now, throughout the night, or tomorrow when I return—there is always a sense of tranquillity, the perception of another rhythm, indifferent to speed.

I jot down all these feelings in a hurry in a black notebook with an elastic strap I purchased exclusively to write what I know or what I will discover about El Celler. I show it to the brothers, the three of them. I already have a few entries. They laugh. "Let's not get carried away," they say. Their modesty is not feigned, but the result of having spent their lives behind a counter or around a cooker, having the aroma of stew about their bodies. Of people from a humble background who do not want to go beyond what is in plain sight. To eat is to eat, I agree, but I try to persuade them that everything I say is also true. It is also to become rich with experiences and confront death. The entries in my notebook read: 'Generosity, affection, wild passion.' They agree. And once again, I remember those fried squids from the past. In fact, I believe we are at the same point, an identical place. It may be time to go to bed. They look tired and I am getting carried away.

III
A day at El Celler with a black notebook

The following day, at 07:30

I'm up early. I will spend the day at El Celler and yesterday I already went to bed very late and harbouring too many theories. I need a shower to regain strength. There are two sides to being dazzled by El Celler. One visit invites (and demands) a contemplation that transcends gastronomy. But there's also fun, simple fun, magic, performance. A fixation with evanescence. The moment. The dishes that will stay in our memory in the years to come. My first suggestion was to pose as a cook or a waiter in order to experience each hour more closely. They laughed again. They must have thought their guide ratings would plummet once they realised a klutz like me was figuring in the kitchen or dining room. And I won't do it. Instead I will be a stowaway. That is, I will be around hoping not to be noticed.

08:30 at the front door

Joan is there already. Later, Josep arrives. They ask me what I want them to do. And I ask them what they want me to do. We get on well immediately. What I mean is that they do not need to do anything and I will do the same. Observe. Spend the day together. Have some coffee. It's early in the morning and the dining room tables are still bare. They are only tables, neutral circles, pieces of wood that now sit there somewhat lethargically. Exhausted. I am reminded of a poem by Josep Carner, the one about the girl who, upon her return from the dance, feels both tormented ("the rustling of abandoned silk") and delighted ("the jewelled flickering of the mirror"). What was (the euphoric tables of the previous evening) and is no longer there, and the promise and delight of a new, renewed existence (the pieces of wood that will be, with an incipient vigour, tables again). They have not yet been re-clothed. They are not yet wearing the tablecloths that will become the exact flat surface where the culinary dance will take place.

09:10, thinking about stones

Boulders from the nearby forests, shapely pebbles, rolling stones carried by
the streams, broken rocks whose shape has been rounded off by a slow, caressing
process, in a road to perfection, now stored, smooth and moist to the touch, in
a box before making it back to the dining room, day after day, like a discreet
reminder of the trio. At this moment, they have not yet been set on each of the
tables.

The stones were not there when El Celler first opened, perhaps because Jordi came
into the picture a bit later. I remember at the beginning the first restaurant
had a neon sign that read: 'El Celler de Can Roca' in clear, stylish letters,
but I don't remember the symbolism being so manifest. Now it is. Stone is the
link not only to their name but also to their origins and nature, and a central
figure. It is both subtle and primitive. A detail that demands no explanation—not
a metaphor, but proof—and will always sit silently on each of the tables that
have yet to be set up.

The idea is to take pictures with my mobile phone. For personal use. Like the
doodles I draw in my notebook. In order to have an image close at hand to remind
me of that particular dish, a glance or a gesture of the cooks. It reminds me
that some time ago I did the same while dining at El Celler with a friend. I
didn't understand why people took pictures of what they were about to eat,
but I'm sure it has to do with the time we feel the need to replenish, with
the accumulation of experiences that exhaust our ability to make assessments.
Then you go back there with your photographs, perhaps to re-live the slow pace
you had experienced. So, the fact is that I photographed the table. Now that
table returns to me with a certain mystical air, the same kind of mysticism
that Kubrick gave to his spaceship. There is a black background, nothingness.
Also a part of a white sphere that is actually a tablecloth. In the centre,
a plate with a wine cork. At the edge of the circle that could be the limits
of the planet, three stones of different sizes. Three rocks, or Rocas. They
lean inanimately against each other and form a unit that instils a spirit of
soundness and wellbeing at the table, in the world. This is a true metaphor. The
rocks, the three of them and nothing else, without *arêtes*, give life to this
space; they make it possible to define a before and after. They create brightness
and darkness; they begin a new story every time their still and yet (what a
wonder) active and beneficent presence is illuminated.

Nothing is ready yet.

09:35, Joan strolls around the triangle

Would it be too daring to attempt to describe each of the three brothers in
one word? Now I see Joan strolling, alone, along the triangular perimeter of
the dining room, with its minimalist garden in the middle. The first garden is
welcoming. But this one, the second, encircled by the clothed tables and the
discrete warmth of the dining room, records time. It gathers the interchange of

perceptions offered by El Celler. The third garden in the back, with its aromatic plants, is where nature manifests itself in the somewhat absent, wild, but also pensive style of British gardens. Josep is the first garden: beneficent warmth. The second is Joan: a reflexion of the form that hides the meaning. The third is the controlled madness of Jordi. But now that I think about it, it could be the other way around. Or perhaps the three of them are all three things. For sure. That must be it.

Listing the conjunctions, links, harmonies, and differences of the three brothers could fill this whole notebook. It is a curious, unheard-of, but most of all, productive occurrence. Brotherhood isn't an exercise in kindness as a result of familiar conventions. It is the oil that turns the gears, the grease that keeps the machinery running, ready to produce. I jot down 'life project, personal growth' and also 'three worlds coming together'. I believe they have mentioned this to me. And at the same time, the fact that they come from the same place and have set foot on the same land and used the same pans and feel heirs to the same lineage, has an added value that may be impossible to find anywhere else. Creative brotherhood.

Meanwhile, Joan strolls around, alone. The cooks and dining room wait staff arrive. A woman does the cleaning.

VI
A day at El Celler with a black notebook

10:10, before a meeting

I ask Josep to accompany me to the wine cellar, a sanctuary made up of boxes and the box where more boxes echo, where sound reverberates in moisture and wine becomes music. When I say sanctuary I see how it might seem exaggerated, but I'm saved by the dictionary. I don't refer to it as a place of worship, but as a place to "pay respect to the intimate nature of something in particular." That is exactly what this place is. I have been here before and will never forget the first time I came in. Mozart (a divertimento, a minuet), Casals, Massenet, Poveda. And silk, alabaster, slate, coarse soil, metal spheres, aged wood. And above all, Josep's conversation. Now that everything is still silent (not entirely, of course: an insistent murmur is starting to be heard—phones ringing, a TV crew is coming to film), I want him to transport me back to that first speech. I don't like that name for it. Lecture? Story? Journey? Journey, perhaps. Josep wanted to describe the topography of his passion, but he also transformed the known geography into a familiar territory of which he's the tireless guide. Did he establish a canon? Yes, of course. The mythical Burgundy; the unhurried effervescence of Champagne; the disconcerting clarity of Sherry; the tension the soil and the centuries brought together in the Priorat; the luxury of living in the diurnal and sunny Riesling. His canon doesn't undermine the rest—as sometimes critics do—but comes from a clear and simple idea: the need to make his name. Today, Josep shows me the wine cellar again. The two of us.

Later I will return with other people, but undercover. This is the journey of the wine lover who knows all about wine, but whose aim was to build here not a thesis but a domesticated dwelling, a place to inhabit under the protection of the Lares. He is the type of actor, I ponder, who plays his role with the same conviction in every performance; what he says is not a memorised script, but an incursion into a soul that opens up to be seen and teaches. They are words spoken to be understood once again, every time. As Catalan writer Gabriel Ferrater said: like our homeland.

We must finish up. Joan is requesting our presence. They must devise a strategy for a presentation for a gastronomic conference.

10:40, at the meeting

The term meeting may sound too serious. I would like to think that in fact there are times in which the three brothers shut themselves up in a room (perhaps at the old Celler, where now they do photo shoots and welcome interviewers) and sit down to plan their future. But the truth is that I always see them standing around, like when they eat at their parents' house. They stand because that's what they've done their whole life; they stand because that's how they normally exist and behave in this trade. So they stand around when they get together in their office, where there is a coffee machine, just like they create and discuss and propose and invent by the blackboard in the kitchen. They catch the idea while describing its vague, almost imperceptible flight. It is not a matter of letting it fade even more. It's like cooking. Shaping immediacy. Letting the ephemeral stand on top of a heap of well rooted grass.

Today they are preparing a speech for Jordi. He will talk about his lactic dessert, about that subtle combination of flavours and textures centred around the colour white and pure. Also about ice cream. Then, Jordi picks up speed and goes on talking about the innovations of the cart that will go around the dining room for the final explosion of the meal—in a sense going back to the essential, original promises. And also about the extravagant adventure that is Rocambolesc, its design and the reconstruction of a playful and naïve space.

Jordi is a bit like that: a sort of naivety that regards no feat as impossible. And the truth is that, because in the end he makes things a reality, he proves he was right. He is a free spirit working with precision.

But I leave them and ask if I can go into the kitchen. They say yes, no need to knock.

VII
A day at El Celler with a black notebook

Almost 11:00, I walk into the kitchen

I want to see the scene before it all begins. The deliveries come in through a side door facing the aromatic herb garden. Outside, the tables are set. Tablecloths have been placed gently on top; their descent soft like gauze. Followed by plates, silverware, the three smooth, rounded rocks.

I want to see the kitchen. It's already crowded. I stroll around every area. I see meat being cut with precision, the preparation of sweets such as the truffle that will hide inside an exploding rock. Also the machines, the vacuum sealer, the perfume-cooking machine —Joan's inventions. Slow cooking, a ritual in which low temperatures are the necessary magic to produce a marvel. This time the stills are not working, but I've seen things you couldn't even imagine; that you wouldn't believe. I've seen moist soil being liquefied and transformed into perfume. I've seen how this machine could synthesise the memory of generations, centuries upon centuries of the slow movement of rock and moss. And all those moments are not lost like tears in the rain, but become the rain. Drop by drop, the scent remains in the still.

I'm slipping back into science fiction. I'd better get hold of myself. But the truth is that, when seeing the refinement of the technique, it's hard not to be carried away by the idea that we're not in a kitchen, but a laboratory. The difference is that the aim here is not to excel in the discovery and consider everything done once the experiment has been successfully completed. No. The highest expression of the invention is the incredibly brief quintessence of wet soil that will be tenderness on the plate and will be offered as a sacrifice, in order for the dish to be a beautiful and effective construction.

11:30, still in the kitchen

The *mise en place* is underway, the necessary arrangement of time and space, staples and preparations and sauces to make everything work. It operates like a watchmaker's shop, where the artisan tries to fit the mechanism to perfection so that when the time comes to tell the time there are no mistakes.

What I see at the entrance holds me back. Messi's signed jersey, a montage of the Sistine Chapel, in which God infuses life into a man who looks like coach Pep Guardiola, sheets of paper held by magnets, menus, schedules, news and, above all, the blackboard.

A wall, with two sockets near to the ground, where the Roca brothers write. The main feature of a waxed surface is that anything written or drawn on it with chalk can be erased. Everything can disappear. Here, when I look at the blackboard of the Roca brothers, I get the sense that the silhouettes of the words that are part of their ideology will never vanish. Are indelible. So yes, there are signs of words that have disappeared, but also the certainty of continuity. The 'pentimenti' might have been mistakes or strolls that were a detour, roads not trodden. To achieve harmony we must have heard dissonance. Those old writings are still there; they haven't been completely erased. This blackboard is a slab that contains the history of an exemplary gastronomic style. It's like a cave where the traces of its first inhabitants and their first attempts still remain. Where each new inscription, however durable, is also aware of its transience.

I read: "Poetry, grace, courage, nerve, breaking with fear and rigidity, stopping to think, inexpensive but rich, sense of humour, magic, mistakes, challenge, emotions, opposites." An encyclopaedia entry could be written about each one of these ideas, a compendium of everything that El Celler represents. They are there, linked to a specific dish, like a constant reminder that leaves room for variations around the same melody.

VIII
A day at El Celler with a black notebook

Around 12:00, about to eat

At this hour the sunlight in the dining room is pure. Serenity. An intense calmness, a respite before the commotion. White trees make the stage, this minimalist, irregular, clean space, expands upwards.

Jordi tells me we're about to eat. At Can Roca. That old image of fried squid comes to mind. We all go there together and it looks like a procession. We walk a little road from El Celler up to the Taialà hill, where their father, Josep, used to stop in his GE-3929 coach. I do the maths while we walk in line, everybody dressed in their work clothes. Cooks wear their apron, waiters wear their jacket. Three plus nine plus two plus nine is twenty-three: 23. Two: Josep

Roca and Montserrat Fontané, and three: their three sons. That old coach is an apparition. Although it seems to be parked in front of the restaurant, it's been there for about fifty years. And Can Roca is also still there, as when the couple decided to start the business.

Today they have macaroni, lentils and charcoal-grilled ribs. They also have squid. I also see myself, many years ago, sitting at a Formica table. The brothers, all three of them, standing, as always, next to their mother. They are trying to find out what else she's cooking. No escudella today, instead a roast. They taste it. We have some fruit and go back.

Everyday life at El Celler is a collection of rituals, and eating at their parents' establishment may be the most important one. It reminds one of a promise, like taking ancient routes to evoke a miracle that is centuries-old in order to rekindle tradition. Theirs is a secular, youthful and gastronomic procession. The original restaurant welcomes its children and anyone who works at El Celler, before they start their workday, and they march as if about to get a daily blessing from history, a safe-conduct to embark, day after day, on a new road.

IX
A day at El Celler with a black notebook

12:48, in the hallway

I sit on a chair in the hallway that leads from the main entrance to the wine cellar. I take a picture. An unexpected play of mirrors is the result. A sort of multiplication of the three brothers, spreading around with the staff, ready to welcome the first customers who will give them their time. It isn't only about brotherhood, in the best sense of the word, nor about a life project, which is how they speak of themselves, but about the alignment of the stars in a dance performed by all the workers of El Celler—in the kitchen, the reception area, the dining room, with precision, relaxed and expectant.

I go out onto the patio. There are people arriving, going up the ramp, observing the house, waiting for someone; some walk up to the door of the restaurant. They look at me as if asking for permission. We are back from lunch and everything is set.

In the garden, I sit on a sofa and remember an autumn evening in 2009, when El Celler got its third star. A group of friends got the news over the phone and gathered to celebrate the accomplishment. But that may be an imprecise term. What is more of an accomplishment, the slow and continued ceremony of each daily meal, or the medal that brings you up to the next rung on the ladder? So the idea was to carry out a strictly private ceremony. No great fuss, no waving flags. Just an ovation. Long and spontaneous applause that resounded around the entrance to the new Celler. Someone spoke—Josep, I believe—and also present were their parents, excited, as well as the whole staff, to share the joy. It was a cold evening in Girona and that simple tribute still reverberates; a tribute with a modesty proper of someone who has no desire for fireworks, but perseverance and rigour.

That night, as I recall, one of the dialogues between Marco Polo and Kublai Khan in Calvino's *Invisible Cities* came to mind. In it, Marco Polo describes a bridge, stone by stone, and the monarch asks which stone is capital and supports

the whole bridge. The traveller indicates that supporting the bridge is not
the job of a single stone. The secret lies in the arch formed by the stones.
Khan reflects and adds: "Why do you speak to me of the stones? It is only the
arch that matters to me!" And Polo replies: "Without stones there is no arch."
Stones, rocks. I thought that evening in 2009.

I think of it again today.

X
A day at El Celler with a black notebook

13:15, back in the wine cellar

Josep leads some customers and I to the wine cellar. He's tireless. Probably
because he knows, as Joan and Jordi do, that part of the magic of the restaurant
consists of transforming every single visit into a unique moment that does not
begin or end at the table, awaiting whatever comes next, but that contains—an
instant that stretches out in time—a crucial aspect that includes touch, smell,
aroma, observation, letting go, entering a universe in which, for instance, the
soundtrack, the music that complements the wine or is present within the calm
discipline of the kitchen also matters. I study the faces of those who enter
the wine cellar or those who, led by Joan or Jordi, come into the kitchen while
they're working. They watch respectfully, careful not to slow down the process,
with a certain adoration. They sense they're dealing with a living organism,
moving before their astonished eyes. Pictures are taken. Later, they will sit
down and watch the show. They will be part of it. But now it feels like being
backstage, not to see the actors put on their make up, but to appreciate a
truth: the blossoming of the song depends on the warming up of the voice. They
sniff, pause, and look. Then, at the table, they will remember those original
moments.

It is as moving to experience it alone as it is to secretly watch how others
are initiated. In fact, it is even more so. I write 'Descartes', and next to it:
'wonder is the first of all the passions'. Paying attention to how wonder prevails
is, conceivably, even more pleasant. Because you see your own reflection, as if it
was you enjoying the discovery all over again. Like the first time.

XI
A day at El Celler with a black notebook

13:35, in the kitchen

It might be the one thing I most look forward to. Going into the kitchen.
Sharing a meal. I had even considered disguising myself as a cook, an assistant.
Washing my hands and helping out, for example, to place a piece of truffle on
top of a soft and fluffy roll. I discard the idea immediately. It's not so easy.
It would, in fact, be like wanting to work in a goldsmith's workshop with the
ability of a lumberjack. Or like playing the piano with snow gloves. What I mean
is that an apparently simple task can be the key for the whole structure to
function. If that miniscule part was not delicately placed, if it was not the

most important detail in the world, everything would fall apart. Everything? What to call that everything? Machine? Orchestra? Team? Any comparison is fitting, and they all somewhat resemble reality. And Joan? The engine, the director, the coach? Always, in any instance or any situation, a calm man. This is a kitchen where everything is controlled, where activity is not calculated by speed but by concentration; where there are no screams, but metronomes. When service begins the appearance of normality, of an unhurried workshop where the a jewel is set with the precision of a surgeon turns wild, but this wilderness has a measured rhythm. If this movement was seen from above, the image would resemble the determined, orderly lines drawn by ants. Here, however, ants have a conscience. I mentioned a roll, but I could say the same of the cover that traps the smoke in a quick turn, of the chocolate that turns into a rock, coated with cocoa butter and black chanterelles. Or that edible sand beach where the charcoal-grilled shrimp lies and its head and legs become pleasant, an optical illusion that conceals nature and conceals in nature.

XII
A day at El Celler with a black notebook

14:10, still in the kitchen

Now I am what you could call a privileged observer. I sit on a stool, behind the counter at the entrance. I eat and take notes under an overhead light. I watch the blackboard again as well as other scattered details, like a picture of the dish that eats the world. Before, I saw cooks arranging the delicious, fragile fruits of Mexico, Peru, Lebanon, Morocco and Korea; flashes, reconstructions of an essence on a wire tree like balls in a shooting game at the fair. Joan tells me about the Kilometre 0 in this journey around the world. These concepts don't clash, but understand each other. There are no dogmatisms here, but one of the concepts written on the blackboard: enchantment. I refer back to the dictionary. To enchant, to fascinate, "to fill with great delight". And to be enchanted, to be charmed by something. Fascination in front of the inexplicable that will vanish like a theatre performance evaporates. All to return the following day. Here I write: Tadeusz Kantor. Where does the thought of one of the greatest Polish directors now come from? I saw him once on the stage. He had already staged the play; he could have seen it from the stalls. But he was on the stage, stomping on the floor with the walking stick he carried in his hand, keeping time, stating the rhythm he considered suitable for the performance.

Joan does the same today. No stomping on the ground. Only with his mere presence.

16:20, drinking cognac

The last customers are still having their coffee and drinking spirits in the entrance hall. I'm with them and just finished reviewing my notes and the pictures I've taken. Now, from a distance, the world looks like a Cézanne painting.

I will ask the Roca brothers about their pictorial references, their collaborations with artists. The time when Joan was inspired by Proust; or the hare they dedicated to the poet Comadira. Josep's devotion to words and his need to explain, to understand, to sit down and reflect. To be able to formulate a culinary language not only from recipes or procedures, but from poetry. To be aware of what they are trying to convey and, on the other hand, prevent the thought from being noticeable in the final product. The menu must flow like prose that is both well-sculpted—constant—and free. An undulation. The way rolling stones glide along when carried by the wind.

Now they have a meeting with the staff. I leave them. They will discuss some tests that were first written on the blackboard, later prepared in full, and now are waiting for a final verdict, a confirmation to expand the body of dishes that are part of the history of the Roca brothers.

The dining room turns again into a space of naked tables. It will be illuminated again in the evening, this time by a light that makes me think of Majorcan poet Bartomeu Rosselló-Porcel: "All my life is bound to you, like flames at night to the darkness."

One day some friends said to me that dining at El Celler was dining in a place where brightness and darkness merged, a space suited for tasting the diaphanous presence of food while becoming engrossed in confidentiality. In a few hours, the trees of the minimalist garden will become outlined, proud and bare, like spears of fire in the dark.

19:20, briefly before returning to El Celler

I will come back for dinner and will finish my notes for the day.

This time I think about the times I've spent there, with friends, or family. On one occasion we went to celebrate a birthday at the old Celler with my parents. My father was an English professor at the Culinary Arts School and he adored them. My father had the natural elegance that I now see in the Roca brothers. It lacks excesses. It possesses a very fine twist of humour, almost imperceptible in its subtleness, like the veil of milk of their *meunière*. I think back to the day in which a laureate of the Nobel Prize for literature ate a book made of caramel, as if it were made of crystal, at El Celler. Deconstructed, as it ought to be with literature, "the strange dignity of the useless," as (I come back to him) Steiner would put it. To break down. To refuse to accept harmony and perfection without the awareness of the threat (the possibility, almost the need) of failure or extinction. This is how a work of art is created: at the limit, either piercing through it or crashing with it. The Roca brothers, I write, are conscious of that fragility. I have said it before. To lock the ephemeral in a cage is to admit we face a job of Homeric proportions, perhaps impossible. Are they tempted by the ineffable, as Ferrater would write? Perhaps they are. That is the drive to create. But there is also the calmness of the goldsmith who knows that everything, even achieving the sublime, depends not on the flowery arabesque, but on absolute patience.

XIV
A day at El Celler with a black notebook

21:00, dinner

I continue writing, but now a friend of mine is keeping me company. It may be necessary to share the experience of eating in a place like this with someone else. I'm sure of it. You need to be able to comment on the loftier of ideas or the most nostalgic evocation. The wonder you observe and taste is multiplied when shared, because you know it will remain forever. Like a bond. "We went together to El Celler." When you remember an episode of this nature, when the sudden memory of a dish, a combination, a sauce, or a taste returns to live in the present moment, then you will think about whoever was with you that evening.

She's wearing a navy blue dress, short with zippered pockets. I have come to think I would be unable to eat here alone. And if I was to be noticed, if the customers saw me, they might think I'm an inspector for some restaurant guide. So I dine with her and remember past dinners, dishes I cannot forget like that apple timbale, the cigar ice cream, the lobster parmentier. And so many others. All the people with whom I've dined at El Celler arrive. They sit at our table. And so does grandma Angeleta and my parents. My friend does not know there are so many more with us at the table.

And nonetheless it is only her and I, alone, also ready to carry out a task that is both pleasant and complicit: to transform this time into a solid space, to build moments of such intensity but never stuffy. This is a good place for that. I see that the Roca brothers are still busy. We have some coffee. "Still carrying that notebook around?"

EL CELLER DE CAN ROCA

This English language edition published in 2016 by
Grub Street
4 Rainham Close
London SW11 6SS

Email: food@grubstreet.co.uk
Twitter: @grub_street
Facebook: Grub Street Publishing
Web: www.grubstreet.co.uk

Copyright this English language edition © Grub Street 2016

First published in Spanish by Librooks Barcelona S.L. under the title
   El Celler de Can Roca. El libro
© Joan Roca, Josep Roca, Jordi Roca, 2013
License granted by Jorofon S.L. (Roca Llibres) and Librooks Barcelona S.L., holder of the
exploitation rights.
© Written material: the respective author
© Photographs: the respective photographer
   Gastronomic photographs: Francesc Guillamet and Quim Turón
   Atmospheric photographs: David Ruano and Paco Amate

A CIP record for this title is available from the British Library
ISBN: 978-1-910690-29-1

Printed and bound by Finidr, Czech Republic

Note about the recipes
The measurements of all the dishes included in this
book have been calculated for tasting menu servings,
except when indicated as snack.